TANK
TRACKS

9TH BATTALION ROYAL TANK REGIMENT AT WAR 1940-45

To all who served in 9th Battalion Royal Tank Regiment:
'May God send us to war in such company together again, when need is'
Lord Howard of Effingham on the sailors of the English fleet that fought the Armada, 1588

TANK TRACKS

9TH BATTALION ROYAL TANK REGIMENT AT WAR 1940-45

PETER BEALE

SUTTON PUBLISHING LIMITED

First published in the United Kingdom in 1995 by
Alan Sutton Publishing Ltd, an imprint of Sutton Publishing Limited
Phoenix Mill · Far Thrupp · Stroud · Gloucestershire

Paperback edition first published 1997

British Library Cataloguing in Publication Data

Beale, Peter
Tank Tracks: 9th Battalion Royal Tank Regiment at War, 1940–45
I. Title
940.541241

ISBN 0-7509-1519-6

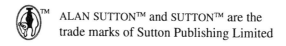

ALAN SUTTON™ and SUTTON™ are the
trade marks of Sutton Publishing Limited

Typeset in 10/12pt Times.
Typesetting and origination by
Sutton Publishing Limited.
Printed in Great Britain by
Butler & Tanner, Frome, Somerset.

Contents

Acknowledgements

Many ex-members of the 9th made contributions to this history in the form of photographs, maps, taped and written recollections and other items such as drivers' log-books, instruction manuals and so on. These contributors are most warmly thanked, and are here listed:

Bob Anderson, Bill Andrews, Les Arnold, Peter Boden, Peter Bracewell, Geoff Brewer, Laurie Brown, Crombie Cordiner, Fred Critchley MC, Doug David, Ginger Gadd, Fred Glasspool, Ray Gordon, Dickie Hall, Jack Hilton, Stan Hinsley, John Hodges, Ronnie Holden DSO MC, Gordon Horsewood, Harry Hurt, Jim Hutton, Ossie Joyce, Ernie Leatham, Taffy Leyshon, Mrs Ingrid Link (Sidney Link's widow), Brian Marchant, Paul Nutkins, John Oakley, Brian Powell, John Powell, Jim Proctor, George Rathke, Cyril Rees MM, Jack Richardson, Cyril Smith, Bob Taylor, Viv Taylor, Bill Thompson, Charlie Thomson, Tom Tomney MM, Berry Veale DSO MC, Tommy Wolf and Jack Woods.

Other people contributed in various ways, and their help is most gratefully acknowledged: David Fletcher, Head of the Tank Museum Library, and his staff for the prompt and generous response to requests for information, and for permission to reproduce photographs; Jess and Barry Greenwood, widow and son of Trevor Greenwood (ex-C Squadron) for permission to quote from the diary Trevor kept during the NW Europe campaign 'One day at a time'; John Roberts (head) and Peter Johnson of the Cartographic Section, School of Geography, Sydney University, who produced the maps; Jonathan Falconer of Alan Sutton Publishing for his encouragement, help, and prompt action; Les Arnold for making several visits to the Imperial War Museum and the Public Records Office to obtain information; John Powell for visits to Normandy to take photographs; My secretary Colleen Jones for her excellent and speedy conversion of several manuscripts into clear and accurate typescript; George Forty for a copy of the address made by the Mayor of Beaunay to C Squadron in September 1994; Henk Bredevolt of the Military Museum of Roosendaal (probably our favourite town in Holland) for photographs and maps; Ray Gordon for his dedicated and impeccable administration of the whole project (I told him several times that he should have been at least a Brigade Major); and my wife Shirley, who helped and encouraged me in every possible way during the many months that went into the compiling of this labour of love.

PETER BEALE

Death at Maltot, 10 July 1944

Major Douglas Ballantine also died of wounds on this day. I heard his last message over the wireless saying, quite cheerfully, that his tank had been hit three times and that he was trying to get through the hedge into the orchard. He then dismounted to talk to his Reconnaissance Officer, Ronnie Kirby, and the CO of the 7th Hampshires. While they were talking there was a very heavy bout of mortaring and Douglas was wounded in the head and chest, and both his legs were broken. At this stage tanks were on fire all around and the counter-attack started to come in. Douglas was in a ditch with two of his crew, Paddy Murphy and Bill Quinn. Bill says that he was gradually getting weaker and weaker but kept on trying to help his tanks to get back out of it. All this time the place was being swept by machine-gun and mortar fire. Bill went to find the Infantry Medical Officer but he had been killed. Bill managed to get blankets and a ground sheet to make Douglas as comfortable as possible but it was obvious that he could not last long unless help arrived very quickly.

After about an hour of this Douglas sent Bill and Paddy away saying there was nothing they could do for him and that they must save themselves. At this time the counter-attack was almost on top of them. He was hardly conscious at this stage. Bill made several attempts to move him but it was too painful for him and their position was pretty hopeless. Bill and Paddy managed to get away and joined up with several more de-horsed crews and crawled back towards the start line through the corn.

At this stage about three-quarters of A Squadron had lost their tanks and were trying to get back one way or another. The Padre and our own ambulances made repeated attempts to get forward to the Squadron and succeeded in picking up about twelve men, but the position was impossible. Later in the day when C Squadron attacked there must have been a good number of our men still about the area who would have come under our own artillery barrage. For days we tried to reach the place to recover the tanks and see what was left but it was not until 8 August that we were finally able to do so. Then we recovered and buried nineteen bodies from the burnt out tanks and buried them together with Douglas at Eterville.

Extract from the diary of Captain John Hodges, 9th Battalion Adjutant

---

The worst day for A Squadron was at Maltot on 10 July. We were moving across a field of yellow rape and through my periscope I could see tank after tank stop and catch fire although there were no signs of German tanks firing. One began to feel uneasy and the constant sound of small arms fire against the turret made us realize that things were going to be tough. Ted Spight from one of the brewed up tanks appeared just in front of us looking very dazed so we opened up a pannier door and laid him on the tool box behind the driver. Soon afterwards we were hit and *Iceni* rocked to a standstill. The interior of the turret suddenly became intensely hot, a dry scalding heat. I kept my eyes shut shielding my face with my hands. The left hand was not wearing the leather gauntlet glove with which we were issued, the right hand had a glove on. After seemingly minutes, but it can only have been a very short period, I stood up and pushed open my turret hatches. We were yelling and I tried to release the clip which held the bag for holding the empty shell cartridges, but it jammed and could not be budged. I tried to do this in order that both Jock and Dickie could move over to my side of the turret in order to get out

Crew of troop sergeant's tank Iceni, 2 Troop, A Squadron, Farnborough, 19 May 1944. Back row: Ray Gordon, Jack 'Hutch' Hutchinson. Front row: Bill Morris, Sgt. Jock Smith, Dickie Knight. Hutch, Bill, Jock and Dickie were burnt to death in their tank on 10 July 1944; Ray escaped with burns, but had to spend the next four years in and out of hospital.

because Jock could not open his cupola flaps as shortly before we were hit something had struck the top of the turret and jammed it shut. I pulled myself out of the turret and fell over the side hitting the tracks and toppled on to the ground. As I laid there I could see a large hole slightly forward of the turret (I believe it was an '88 shot) and flames started coming out of the turret together with the sound of exploding ammunition. The dreadful cries of my crew trapped in *Iceni*, even now nearly fifty years later, occasionally return to remind me of the horror of 10 July 1944. To my everlasting sorrow I was unable to help even one of those young men with whom I had lived in intimate contact that was part of a tankman's life when in action.

My face became swollen and very tight making it difficult to see and the skin of my left hand hung down in black strips from an arm which was bloodless and white. Lt. Shep Douglas, my troop leader, crawled along the field. 'Who are you' he said, not recognizing one of his own troop to whom he had given orders earlier that morning. I followed him across the field of rape, crouched low because we could hear gunfire, to a gap in the hedgerow where infantry were in position. The look of horror on their faces which changed to looks of pity when they saw me will remain for ever in my mind. It is a look which I would never want to inflict on another human being. I was helped to a medical truck, given an injection and that was the end of 10 July for me.

Recollections of Ray Gordon, wireless operator in Sgt. Jock Smith's tank, 2 Troop,
A Squadron

What were the paths that led the 9 RTR to Maltot? and what happened after Maltot? This history describes the birth of 9 RTR in the First World War and its rebirth in the Second World War, and then describes where it went to and what it did until it was disbanded in December 1945. The story starts in 1916.

Honour at Moreuil

T he 9th Battalion of the Heavy Branch Machine Gun Corps was formed in December 1916, and was designated 'I' Battalion. The battalion went over to France as part of the 3 Tank Brigade in time to take part in the third Battle of Ypres that started in July 1917. This battle dragged on for nearly three months in mainly waterlogged country which gave little opportunity for the tanks to prove their value.

The Battle of Cambrai, on the other hand, took place over well-drained undulating country where the tanks had a proper chance to show what they could do. Advancing at 6.20 a.m. on 20 November 1917 the attack, with the 'I' Battalion forming part of the leading wave of tanks supporting III Corps of the Third (British) Army, achieved complete surprise. The initial success was so striking that on the next day the bells of London were rung in joyous acclaim of

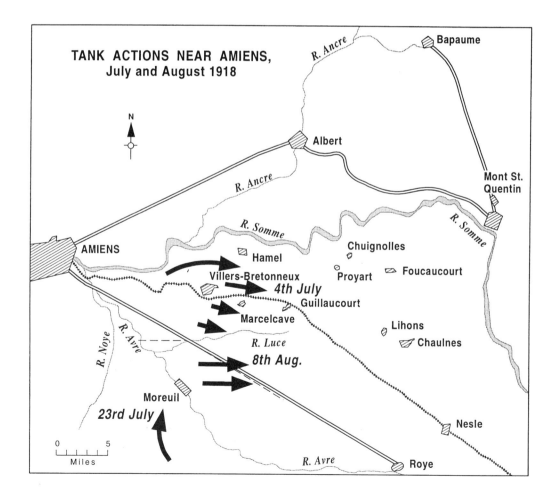

the 'victory'. Lack of reserve formations meant that the territorial gains were retaken by the Germans within two weeks, but the experience had provided a key to a longer-lasting victory.

In the spring of 1918 the Germans, relieved of the pressure on their eastern front by the aftermath of the Russian revolution, launched a series of attacks on the western front. In March they advanced west towards Amiens, in April north-west towards Hazebrouck, and in May and June south towards Chateau-Thierry. Although they had made great gains, they were held. And with the failure of their attacks the naturally cautious General Pétain was able to say in mid-June 1918: 'If we can hold until the end of June, our situation will be excellent. In July we can resume the offensive; after that victory will be ours.'

They did hold until the end of June, and in July the offensive was resumed. On 4 July six Australian infantry battalions, working in close co-operation with sixty tanks of the 5 British Tank Brigade, attacked to the east of Amiens. With consummate ease and only small losses they captured the ridge running from Villers Bretonneux north to the Somme at Hamel, this action being generally known as the Battle of Hamel.

A major attack was now planned for 8 August, an attack that was to be given the name of the Battle of Amiens, and the day itself was later said by Ludendorff to be: 'the black day of the German Army in the history of the war'.

But before that day a further 'curtain raiser' was arranged to test the resistance of the Germans and to improve the position of General Debeney's First (French) Army in the Moreuil sector of the line. Impressed by the outcome at Hamel, the French asked the British for the loan of the 'Cambrai Key', their own tanks being engaged on the Marne.

The tank troops to be loaned consisted of the headquarters of the 5 Tank Brigade (Brigadier-General Courage) and the 'I' Battalion Tank Corps (Lt.-Col. H.K. Woods). The attack they were to make in support of the French 3rd Division (General Bourgon) became known as the Battle of Sauvillers, or alternatively the Battle of Moreuil. It had as its final objectives the capture of the Bois de St. Ribert in order to outflank Mailly-Raineval from the south, to abolish certain highly objectionable German batteries which lay near the Bois de St. Ribert, and to advance the French field guns eastward so that they could bear on the high ridges dominating the right bank of the River Avre.

The attack was ordered on 17 July to take place on 23 July, and much preparation, besides three stages of movement, had to be done. However, 'the tanks felt that they would be eternally disgraced if they were obliged so much as to hint that they would like even a day's postponement of this, their first battle with the French'. Moving by nightly stages the 9th reached the scene of the attack twenty-four hours before the attack was due to go in, although reconnaissances and mutual discussion of the plan had begun on 18 July. To help improve communication, one English-speaking Frenchman was provided for each tank.

The attack began at 5.30 a.m. on 23 July. All troops were stimulated by visits from Brigadier Courage, of whom it was said: 'From the nature of his suggestions and advice, a very ordinary thinker could easily come to the conclusion that he did not care for the Germans!' The first-wave tanks advanced through a fairly heavy enemy barrage to clear the Bois des Arrachis, destroying a number of machine-guns, and then advanced to capture the first intermediate objective – Sauvillers village, Adelpare farm, and Les Trois Boqueleaux. They arrived fifteen minutes before the infantry, and had two tanks knocked out by shells.

In the second phase the tanks of B and C companies moved forward in support of their infantry on either side of the Bois de Sauvillers. In so doing they outstripped and lost touch with the French infantry, and while trying to regain contact six tanks were put out of action by a German battery south of the Bois de St. Ribert.

To the west of this action a battalion commander of the 51st Regiment of French Infantry

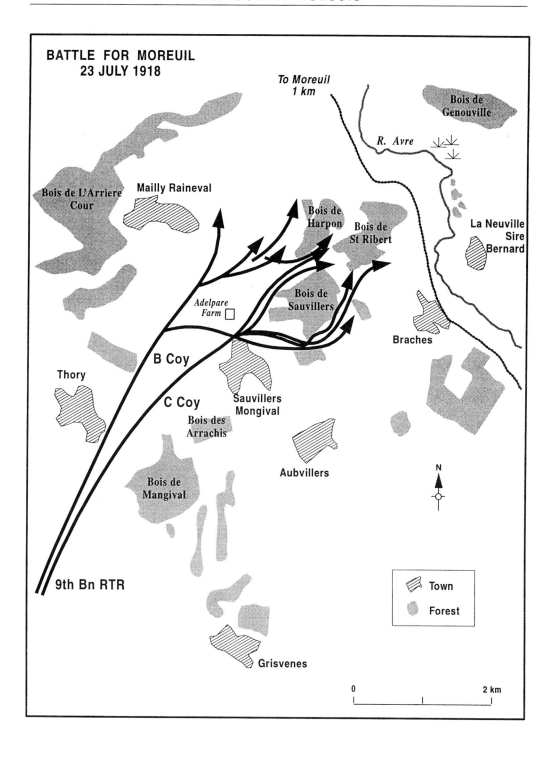

**BATTLE FOR MOREUIL
23 JULY 1918**

To Moreuil
1 km

Bois de
Genouville

R. Avre

Bois de L'Arriere
Cour

Mailly Raineval

Bois de
Harpon

Bois de
St Ribert

La Neuville
Sire
Bernard

Adelpare
Farm

Bois de
Sauvillers

Braches

B Coy

Thory

C Coy

Sauvillers
Mongival

Bois des
Arrachis

Aubvillers

N

Bois de
Mangival

9th Bn RTR

Town

Forest

Grisvenes

0   2 km

requested help from OC B Company 9th Tanks to capture the Bois de Harpon. An improvised attack was quickly planned, and seven tanks and the infantry captured the wood and a hostile battery, only two tanks being damaged.

By the evening all objectives had been taken, and the French were very well satisfied with the action, as were the tanks. The French had more than seven hundred casualties, but the tank-led 3rd Division lost little more than the other two French divisions engaged, even though it had the main role and twice as large a frontage. Tank corps casualties were 54, and of 36 tanks engaged, 15 were knocked out, 11 irretrievably. On the other side of the account the Germans lost 1,858 prisoners and unknown numbers killed and wounded, and also lost 5 field guns, 45 trench mortars and 275 machine-guns.

This action was a prelude to the black day of the German Army, when the Cambrai Key was again used with great effect. For the 9th Battalion 23 July had two additional honours. Before they went back to the British sector they had the privilege of being inspected by General Debeney. He expressed extreme pleasure at the way in which the tanks had fought, and in his special order of the day gave the battalion praise of which they will ever be proud.

'Finally, I owe a special tribute of thanks to the battalion of British tanks whose powerful and devoted assistance has aided and assured our success. Commanded by an experienced and skilful leader the tanks have again added to that rich harvest of laurels which this new arm has not ceased to gather since its first appearance in September 1916. They have given to the division the finest example of bravery, of energy, of comradeship in action and of training for war carried to the highest degree of perfection. Their assistance has enabled the infantry to gain a brilliant victory in which they themselves share largely.'

The battalion was awarded the Croix de Guerre avec Palmes as a regimental decoration, worn by all ranks as a lanyard in the colours of the Croix de Guerre. This honour the 9th shares with only three other units of the British Army, all of them infantry: 2nd Battalion, Devonshire Regiment; 4th Battalion, Kings Shropshire Light Infantry; 8th Battalion, West Yorkshire Regiment.

But the 9th also has a special distinction which almost certainly will remain ever unique to them. General Bourgon, commander of the French 3rd Division, awarded the 9th the honour of wearing the badge of his division. A replica of this badge is worn on the upper left sleeve of everyone serving in the 9th Battalion, proudly showing its motto '*Qui s'y frotte, s'y brule*' ('Touch me, and you burn').

CHAPTER I

UK: Rebirth and Adolescence

REBIRTH AT GATESHEAD, 1940

On 24 May 1940 George Rathke, along with five others, was posted to the 3rd Battalion RTR. George had been in the army for three months, and in that time had qualified as a motor mechanic class 2. The 3rd were in France, fighting with the Rifle Brigade to form a defensive ring round Calais.

George and the other reinforcements reached Folkestone where they were stopped, and told that the 3rd were being evacuated from Calais. Only about eighty actually returned. The survivors and the intended reinforcements were sent to Bottisham near Newmarket, where they were eventually brought up to strength and equipped with Crusader tanks. They entered into training in preparation for joining Wavell's army in North Africa, and in due course were issued with tropical kit and given ten days embarkation leave.

When George returned from leave and reported to the guard room he was told to read battalion orders. There he found himself on a list of about forty who were told to hand in their tropical kit and become 'the detachment to the 3rd Battalion'. Doug David, who was on the same list, describes the detachment as a 'Home details unit'. The detachment, under the command of Major Bill Andrews, moved in September 1940 to Thornaugh Hall, half way between Peterborough and Stamford. Doug remembers it as being about seventy to eighty strong, and a strange mix of regulars, reservists and conscripts. Both Doug and George were made provisional unpaid lance-corporals, a rank well-known and heartily disliked for its onerous responsibilities, no extra pay, and less rather than more respect from everyone. It becomes clear, however, that both Doug and George, along with others such as Monty Mount, Jack Sutton, Frank Summers and Bill Root, had been selected as potential leaders and trainers.

In October Bill Andrews went to Gateshead with Ian Sanderson to select suitable billets for some 600 new recruits who were to form a new tank battalion. Shortly after the billets had been secured the detachment travelled in a few 3-tonners and 15-cwt trucks from Thornaugh to Gateshead and were housed in Rose Street School. George Rathke remembers the journey vividly: 'I was acting as a despatch rider on a motor cycle and the rain poured down the whole way. I had no kit other than my greatcoat and beret, so I was literally soaked to the skin.'

Planning to create a new tank unit from people conscripted directly from civilian life meant that many tasks had to be done, but in particular that there was an effective command structure; that there were instructors for basic military training and for the technical training required by tank crews.

In October 1940 Lt.-Col. Paddy Whitsitt arrived as Commanding Officer elect, and Major James Dewhurst as second-in-command. Other officers who arrived around this time, as recollected by Bill Andrews, included Bob Crisp, Paul Quick, James Snook and Bob Warren.

Basic military training consists of foot drill and rifle drill (generally known as square-bashing) and the ability to look after yourself and your equipment. The necessary instructors for basic training were obtained by holding what George remembered as 'a very strict cadre session under RSM Nobby Noble. We each had to take turns in commanding a squad in square-bashing etc., and finally eight of us were made sergeants. I only had one stripe then (provisional unpaid)

Tommy Wolf outside Rose Street School, Gateshead, 1993. Fifty-three years earlier Tommy and nearly 400 others arrived at this chilly home at the rebirth of 9 RTR in the Second World War.

so going up to sergeant was a very big jump'. Doug David also records: 'I was promoted to sergeant with only eight months total service and was, I admit, somewhat amazed.'

The billets selected by Bill Andrews consisted of the Rose Street School and the Prior Street School. Both schools had playgrounds which were ideal for square-bashing. These may not have been the thoughts of the 350 or so embryo soldiers who arrived in late November 1940 straight from civilian life. This intake coincided with the formal rebirth of the 9th Battalion RTR on 27 November 1940, when the battalion colours and honours were handed back by the 3rd Battalion RTR. An important link with the 9th of the First World War was maintained by the appointment of Staff Sergeant Chew as Provost Sergeant. Sgt. Chew had fought with the 9th in 1918, and had also experienced fighting in France in the early summer of 1940.

The civilian soldiers who arrived at this strange and almost certainly chilly home were mainly born between 1905 and 1910, and were thus in the thirty to thirty-five age group. Many of them came from the north of England, and those joining the 9th later were impressed both with the north country accent and the leavening of maturity in almost every part of the battalion.

Doug David remembers that basic training was given in units of thirty by the regular and reservist sergeants and those that had been through RSM Nobby Noble's cadre. The new recruits were progressively allocated to squadrons and troops, and in C Squadron as an example the Squadron Sergeant Major was Tommy Barnett and the Sergeants were Doug David, Monty Mount, Jack Sutton, Frank Summers and Bill Root. George Rathke was allocated to B Squadron as Troop Sergeant of 9 Troop.

On completion of basic training tank soldiers have to learn the technical skills required to be part of a tank crew. There are three main groups of skill: driving and maintenance, gunnery, and operation of the wireless.

Driving and maintenance comprises the ability to drive various sorts of vehicle and to carry out basic maintenance; the precise duties in relation to basic maintenance are clearly defined for each type of vehicle. It is also very useful to have an understanding of how the principal systems of a petrol or diesel-engined vehicle work, for example the engine itself, transmission, braking, suspension, steering.

Gunnery involved a knowledge of how to use and maintain the different types of armament carried either by an individual or on a vehicle. All members of an armoured unit have weapons to protect themselves and their vehicles. In some cases these weapons can be moved or carried by an individual (pistols, rifles, machine-guns) and in other cases they are mounted on a vehicle in such a way that they are not normally moved (tank main armament and machine-guns). The main things that a soldier should know – and therefore must be taught – about any weapon that he may have to use include adjustment, loading, firing, and cleaning; cleaning includes stripping, cleaning the component parts, and re-assembling.

To operate a wireless set effectively a tank soldier must be able to tune the wireless set to a given frequency; to understand and use the procedure for speaking correctly; and to carry out basic maintenance on the wireless set.

Later in the war most civilians who joined a tank unit went first to a training regiment where they learnt the basic military skills and the technical tank skills. The teaching of the technical skills was greatly helped by appropriate equipment and training aids, but life in late 1940 was

Doug 'Dave' David, one of the very early members of 9 RTR in 1940. He was promoted to sergeant after only eight months' service, and subsequently became SQMS of C Squadron, SSM of A Squadron, and RQMS.

more urgent, and 9 RTR had to do all this training itself. Doug David records that after the basic training, technical wings were formed to teach the three basic tank skills. He became a driving and maintenance (D & M) instructor along with Frank Summers, and Captain Dennis Studdard was officer in charge of the D & M wing.

Basic and technical training went on at Gateshead for six months and then in May 1941 the unit moved to an area more suitable for training with tanks. Doug recalls moving 'with reluctance from Gateshead, where the civilians lined the streets to wave us goodbye. Gateshead had been good to us.'

OTLEY AND THE FIRST CHURCHILL TANKS

In May 1941 the 9th left Gateshead and moved to Farnley Park, Otley, Yorkshire. Otley is some 10 miles north-west of the centre of Leeds, and 6 miles east of the better known Ilkley. It was undoubtedly the nearby moors that made Otley so attractive to the War Office, either with a beret or without. By this time all ranks had had their basic and technical training, and had been grouped into squadrons, troops, and supporting echelons. They were now ready to train on the tanks in which they would fight.

Tommy Wolfe remembers the move to Otley, and what the 9th found when they got there.

In May 1941 we made another move to a place called Otley in Yorkshire, and we were surprised to find that this time it was to be under canvas. The tents were already up when we arrived and we were sorted out about six to each tent; the ablutions were just two rows of sinks with water taps running the whole length above, about twelve taps on either side and these were out in the open too with cold water.

The 9th had been allocated the role of a heavy tank unit, and would therefore be armed with heavy, or infantry, tanks. The British Army's policy in the late 1930s was to have three broad categories of tank, namely light, lightly armed and armoured, to serve as scouts; cruiser, with high velocity 2-pounder guns, that could use their speed and range to carry out long-distance strikes; and the infantry tank, slow, heavily armoured, working alongside the infantry and having a tough hide to absorb punishment.

In September 1939 the General Staff requested the engineering firm Harland and Wolff in Belfast to design an extra large infantry tank based on the First World War principles; this was designated the A20. The first prototypes were delivered in June 1940, at a time when the British Army was desperately short of every type of fighting vehicle. To speed up production the A20 was scaled down to a design designated A22, which was given the name 'Churchill'. The redesign was done by the director of tank design, Dr H.E. Merritt, and a team of engineers from Vauxhall Motors. Vauxhall Motors were then instructed to have the tank in production by June 1941, a time schedule so tight that it allowed no time for user or development trials.

Vauxhall succeeded in making the schedule, but were so conscious of the vehicle's deficiencies that they included in the user's handbook a disclaimer, which is here partly quoted and partly paraphrased:

All those things which we know are not as they should be will be put right. In nearly every case the cure has already been found, and it will be introduced as soon as the new materials or parts become available. We are aware of defects, but basically the Churchill is a good

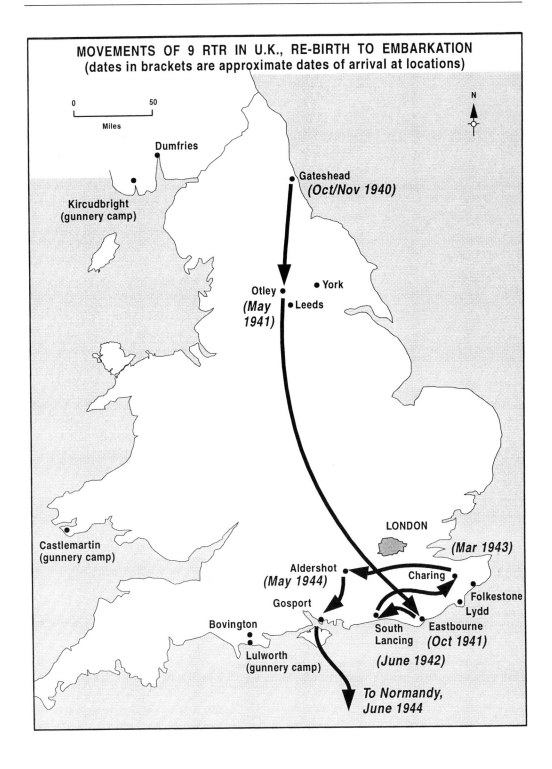

MOVEMENTS OF 9 RTR IN U.K., RE-BIRTH TO EMBARKATION
(dates in brackets are approximate dates of arrival at locations)

tank. In these abnormal times it is thought better to produce the tank as it is, and to carry out the modifications we know to be necessary in the field units.

The 9th had the dubious pleasure of being one of the first units to be equipped with Churchill tanks, and special efforts were made to familiarize them with their new vehicles. Doug David remembers: 'Sergeant Jock Renton and myself had special training (and civilian billets) at Vauxhall's where the tank was assembled.' George Rathke appears to have had it slightly better: 'Sergeant Steer and I were sent on a six weeks' course to Vauxhall's in Luton where we saw for the very first time the Churchill tank which was under construction. We worked alongside Vauxhall's work force. We had civvy billets and very good they were too, and we were also given extra pay by the management which was much appreciated.'

Back at Otley shortly afterwards the unit's first Churchill arrived at Otley station to be met by Captain Stan Tresize, the battalion Technical Adjutant, along with George and Sergeant Steer. Eventually the full quota of tanks arrived, and intensive training in both driving and troop manoeuvres began on the Yorkshire moors.

Doug David, Jock Renton, George Rathke and several others had training at Vauxhall's in driving the Churchill; it was not particularly easy to drive 'especially in the handling of the gearbox, which was quite difficult'. Doug and the others were appointed D & M instructors, and spent many chilly hours on the moors. It could get worse, too. George recalls 'going out on one scheme with eighteen tanks and returning with only four. The rest were scattered all over the moors until the fitters managed to get them moving again and back to harbour. I was lucky, my tank *Immune* kept going. But my troop leader Teddy Mott in *Inspire* and troop corporal Ronnie Beard in *Impulse* were stranded all that night on the moors'. Tommy Wolf describes some of the hassles and frustrations in learning to drive:

It was here that the first Churchill tank was delivered and we were told that the little peashooter sticking out of the turret was called a '2-Pounder'. What we could not understand was why was there such a small gun attached to a huge tank like that. Then one day the Churchill was taken on to the moors, with a few spare crew to learn how to drive etc. Then catastrophe struck for the tank started to sink into the ground and no way could we get it out. We tried digging but to no avail. Eventually a Scammell was brought in and even that could not shift it; then an LAD vehicle came up and even the pair of them could not move it, for they had to use a long tow-rope in case they became bogged down. While all this was going on some of us were digging beneath the tracks of the bogged Churchill and stuffed all the gorse bushes we could find, plus planks of wood from the LAD wagon under the tracks. Eventually with the help of the Churchill's own engine it was pulled out on to firmer ground. It was late in the evening when all this finished and we spare men never got to drive that day.

As both George Rathke and Tommy Wolf have described, the Churchills met the expectations of Vauxhall Motors in proving very unreliable. From mid-1941 to the end of 1942 various changes were made to improve both mechanical and fighting performance. These changes resulted in Churchills designated Marks I, II, III and IV. The Marks III and IV had a 6-pounder gun as the main armament, and a Besa 7.92 mm machine-gun was mounted alongside (co-axially) with the 6-pounder. Another Besa machine was mounted in the driving compartment and was operated by the co-driver.

The first time Churchills saw action was at Dieppe on 19 August 1942, where they were used by the Calgary Regiment of the Canadian Army. This unsatisfactory and costly operation, 'Jubilee', did have at least two positive aspects: it showed that the Churchill could take a lot of punishment, and it also sparked the development of specialized armoured fighting vehicles that played such an important part in the Normandy landing.

Production of Churchills went on during the second half of 1942, and modifications were made continuously. In October and November six Churchills, sent to North Africa for experimental purposes, were commanded by Major Norris King in actions at Kidney Ridge and Tel el Aqqaqir. A technical report on these actions stated: 'these tanks were used on both occasions a considerable distance in advance of the Sherman tanks which formed the main attack. They came under very heavy fire and stood up remarkably well.' In fact the six tanks absorbed 106 hits from AP and HE projectiles, and only one was knocked out.

An important and immediate consequence of the actions of 'Kingforce' was that 25 Army Tank Brigade and 21 Army Tank Brigade, both equipped with Churchills, were put on notice for despatch to Tunisia to support the First Army. Where they went, proving once again that they could take a lot of punishment and move over very difficult country; one German commander reported that he had been attacked by 'a mad tank battalion which had scaled impossible heights and made me withdraw'.

This action took place on 26 February 1943, and was followed by other equally successful and demanding actions. Also in early 1943 came several other announcements: production of an additional 500 Churchills was authorized, of which 300 were to be armed with a 95 mm howitzer in place of the 6-pounder main armament; tanks equipped with the 95 mm were designated Churchill Mark V, and they acted as close support artillery, able to engage targets such as infantry strong points, anti-tank guns, and mortar batteries much more effectively than the 6-pounder.

On 20 April 1943 the War Cabinet announced that a new 75 mm gun would be mounted in a Churchill to be designated Mark VI, and that production of Churchills would continue throughout 1944 at least, bringing the total produced to 5,000. In May it was announced further that 200 examples of a new type, the A22F, were to be built. These were to have frontal armour increased from 102 mm to 152 mm in thickness, and the construction generally was to be welded rather than riveted. The 75 mm version of this design was the Churchill Mark VII, and the 95 mm version the Mark VIII.

Various other modifications were made as these progressive Marks appeared, but the Churchill remained instantly familiar throughout its entire life. The engine, gearbox, transmission, and steering were very little changed, and driving a Churchill presented the same unique peculiarities in all Marks I to VIII.

The 9th was one of the first units to be equipped with the Churchill, and with Churchills we fought and lived for the rest of the Second World War. It was very good across country, could climb steeper gradients than most other tanks, could take a lot of punishment, but was always under-gunned compared with its German opponents. For this weakness in armament many tank crews paid with their lives.

EASTBOURNE AND LANCING: EXERCISES AND GUNNERY CAMPS

In October 1941 the 9th moved from Otley to Eastbourne. As Doug David recalls, Eastbourne was then a town which could have been the target for a German invasion, and the presence of a battalion of tanks was reassuring. In addition the South Downs immediately to the west of Eastbourne were very suitable for troop, squadron and battalion training in moving tank formations across country.

Dickie Hall joined the 9th in January 1942. He had been in the army since September 1939, and towards the end of 1940 was posted to Lulworth as a Staff Sergeant gunnery instructor. By the end of 1941 the pressure for instructors at Lulworth had eased, and because Dickie was one of the junior instructors he was moved to a field unit, in his case C Squadron of the 9th. As Dickie recalls: 'C Squadron was billeted in and around Meads, about a mile from Eastbourne Station. These roads were slippery with thick snow and ice and all were lined with elm trees (Dutch elm disease had not then arrived in Britain). The Churchills had those air intakes that protruded some 9 inches from each side of the body of the tank. As we proceeded up the road to Meads all the tanks tended to slide into the gutter. By the time the whole squadron had passed that way just about every roadside tree had a gouge out of the trunk at air intake height! The scars can still be seen today.' Doug David recalls even further that 'many brick walls and street lamps were demolished by learner drivers during our stay in Eastbourne in that hard winter'.

Both Doug and Dickie remember the German hit and run raids. Doug recalls: 'The Cavendish Hotel received a direct hit from a Luftwaffe bomb while the RAF who were billeted there were having lunch in the dining room; many casualties unfortunately.' Dickie says of the same raid: 'The plane circled over the town and came directly over us. My gunner quickly had the Bren gun out and gave it a good burst. The plane came down along the coast and we liked to think that we had helped in its destruction'.

In some of the training exercises on the downs live ammunition was used. Dickie again: 'I was 13 Troop Sergeant at the time. One day we were advancing just ahead of the infantry behind a creeping barrage of 25-pounder high-explosive shells. Someone forgot to increase their range and as a result we took a direct hit on our front left hand horn. This broke the track but otherwise did little damage. We had all the hatches closed and did not realize we had been hit until we came to a sudden halt. It made a bit of excitement for the day!'

The infantry might well have been those of the 53rd (Welsh) Division, which around this time was reconstructed into a 'New Model' Division. It consisted of two infantry brigades and one tank brigade, which was the 31 Tank Brigade. This brigade consisted of the 7th Battalion RTR, 9th Battalion RTR, and the 141st Regiment of the Royal Armoured Corps (141 RAC). 141 RAC was a battalion of the East Kent Regiment (The Buffs) that had been converted to armour. The idea of the new model divisions was to develop co-operation and understanding between infantry and armoured soldiers, each becoming more aware of how they could help the other. A very important spin-off was the personal relationship that could develop, together with trust and confidence. These new model divisions were later converted back to being three brigades of infantry, and the tanks became independent tank brigades. But co-operation between infantry and tanks had to happen, and in fact the 9th, then in 34 Tank Brigade, fought very effectively with 53rd Division in the Battle of the Reichswald in February 1945.

Another exercise of a rather different type was one in which a troop of tanks simulated a seaborne landing from a tank landing craft (in more formal military parlance these were called Landing Craft, Tank, or LCTs). This exercise took place on the waters of Loch Fyne in Scotland; to which chilly venue the tanks and their crews had been moved by train. From George Rathke:

Each morning before first light one troop of fifteen men was ferried out to an LCT anchored in the middle of the Loch. The LCT held three Churchills, and the idea was that as dawn approached the three tanks would carry out a practice landing on the shores of the Loch.

On the morning that 9th Troop's turn came, we were lined up on the small pier waiting to board the ferry when who should arrive but Major Pearcy (generally known as the Mad Major). He asked us if we had our Mae Wests on. Yes, we said. OK, follow me. He turned, took two steps and vanished off the edge of the pier. We finally amidst loud laughter managed to drag a very wet and bedraggled squadron leader out of the Loch. We didn't see him again for the rest of that week!

As mentioned earlier, the tanks were taken from Eastbourne to Scotland by train. Each tank was carried on a 'rail flat'. Loading the tanks on to the flats was a time-consuming and delicate operation. First, the string of flats was shunted into a siding which had a ramp at the end of it. Then the first tank drove up the ramp at the end of the siding and then drove along the complete length of the flats; because the width of the tank was slightly greater than that of the flats, this required some very careful driving, and it was generally necessary for someone to guide the driver. When the tank reached its appointed flat, it was secured by chaining it down; the chains were attached to the flat by shackles, and to the tank by shackles, and were tightened by turnbuckles. This process went on until the complete string of flats was loaded; the loading and fastening were then checked by railway inspectors. The tricky nature of the driving can be imagined. But this was in daylight and in the summer. Think of the difficulties either at night or when the flats were icy!

Some comments that were raised include Jim Hutton, 1 troop, A Squadron: 'OK in daylight but you had to be a heavy smoker at night-time – puffing on a fag was how we guided the

A tank commander guides a Mark I Churchill on to a 'rail flat' which will transport it to a tank gunnery range 200 miles away.

Members of a tank crew secure their tank to a 'rail flat' by shackles, chains, and turnbuckles. L/Cpl. Jim Hutton, Sgt. Tony Lyall and Tpr Kit Harlow are chaining up, while George Garnsey and Tiny Booth watch.

drivers on to the flats. Many a tank commander disappeared between wagons when walking backwards'; Dickie Hall, 13 troop, C Squadron: 'I joined the regiment in January 1942 at Eastbourne as they were returning from a very cold exercise at Melksham in Wiltshire in freezing conditions. Their arrival was dramatic, everything had a coating of freezing snow. As a result driving off the rail flats was hazardous – to say the least! I think one tank slid off'; Doug David, talking of the 9th at Eastbourne: 'More and more training here including driving exercises putting our tanks on and off rail flats at Eastbourne Station. It was here that through carelessness I received two Mark IV fingers; I carry the scars and deformed fingers to this day.' Mark IV refers to the Churchill Mark IV, but all Marks – and, indeed, all tanks – could cause similar injuries; which were the result of a heavy metal object falling or closing on a person's body, generally a hand; that object was often one of the hatch doors, but there were many heavy objects that could move unexpectedly in a tank. A final comment about rail movements comes from Ronnie Holden:

Loading tanks on to flats took a whole day in the marshalling yard. The length of the loading line was such that we could load only eight tanks at a time. The eight loaded flats were shunted out to where the complete train was being assembled, and eight empty flats were shunted in. At last it was finished and the whole train of 9 RTR was on the move. But then we had to stop at Willesden Junction. Everybody had to get out, unhitch each coupling, and reverse it to the other way up. This took from 10.30 at night to 4.00 in the morning, and the reason for having to do it was that the London Midland and Scottish regulations were different to the Southern. We were not amused.

Some of the places that the tanks went to by train were gunnery camps. These were camps where the tank crews could practise firing their tank weapons (as opposed to their personal or ancillary weapons such as pistols, rifles, and Bren guns). A tank gunnery range has to be in rather a special location. An armour-piercing (AP) shot fired from a tank's main armament has a high muzzle velocity and a flat trajectory, and thus tends to skim or bounce off a surface. This was particularly vividly demonstrated to some members of 9 RTR who were transferred to 4 RTR in July 1945 and went with them to Italy in January 1946. A tank gunnery range had been established north of Pordenone in the foothills of the Tyrolean Alps. The AP shot was fired into the foothills, which there rose fairly steeply to a 3,500 ft high ridge. But on a few occasions the shot bounced off the surface, soared over the ridge, and landed some 5 miles the other side of the ridge. The villagers of Barcis soon made their feelings known!

One of the ways of dealing with this problem in the United Kingdom was to have ranges so placed that the tanks fired out to sea. Obviously shipping lanes had to be avoided, and the locations for tank ranges were thus remote, and in some cases desolate – for example Castlemartin in the far south-western extremity of Wales, and Kirkcudbright on the northern shore of Solway Firth.

Gunnery camps had two main purposes. The first was to give the gunners the opportunity to test and adjust (T & A) their sights and then check that they had done it correctly by actually firing. Sighting the gun was done by bringing the cross-wires on the telescope on to the target, making corrections for distance by elevation or depression. The fundamental requirement was that the telescope and the gun barrel were precisely aligned with each other, and this was the process of testing and adjusting.

The second purpose was to give the complete crew the experience of fighting the tank. The commander and the driver moved the tank across the ground as smoothly as possible. The commander, the turret gunner, and the hull gunner engaged targets that presented themselves, and the wireless operator loaded the main gun and supplied belts of ammunition for the turret machine-gun. All in all, everyone was busy. The targets to be engaged were visual simulations of men, tanks, anti-tank guns and other targets that would be met in battle. The simulations were often plywood cut-outs mounted on light timber frames, and they could be raised or lowered to represent appearance or disappearance. They could also be checked to see whether the particular tank firing had made any hits, and then the targets were repaired or replaced for the next tank.

The unfortunate people who had to manipulate the targets were called the butt-parties. It was a job that was lengthy, boring, and occasionally highly dangerous. There was a system of signalling which indicated when a tank could fire and when it absolutely could not. When the signals indicated 'no firing' then the butt-parties could emerge from their bunkers and go to the targets, check hits, and make repairs. Sometimes, however, signals were difficult to see, crews were careless or over-enthusiastic, commanders were flustered or distracted. As mentioned earlier, some of the simulated targets were cut-outs of men. One tank commander ordered his gunner: 'Man, 800 yards, fire.' But the gunner had glimpsed something out of the corner of his eye, and quickly traversed the turret and started to fire at the target. 'No, no, no,' screamed the commander, 'those aren't men.' 'Yes they are,' replied the gunner sturdily, 'they're running.'

A Churchill Mark III moves across the tank gunnery range at Lulworth, Dorset. The crew were expected to engage targets representing tanks, anti-tank guns, vehicles and men, all of which would be randomly presented.

A Churchill Mark III fires; the gunnery instructor crouches behind the turret at the moment of firing.

Jock Cordiner tells a similar story that happened when he was in training:

The 'powers' having concluded what I was able to do least badly sent me to train as a driver operator. I drove as well as most and was quite exceptional at morse (for what that was worth in the tank business). Very early I was banned from using guns as I had taken out a Pennines shepherd's hut with a 6-pounder without (a) permission to do so, (b) checking that he was far away, and (c) without aiming at it. I thought the 'powers' were a wee bit unfair to me as drivers regularly dismantled bits of Richmond's houses without much fuss. Maybe the shepherd wasn't insured?

Move to Lancing, Summer 1942

Dickie Hall remembers: 'Just about at the end of our time at Eastbourne we were inspected by Winston Churchill. We all stood at crews front while he walked along and inspected us. Then he said he wanted us all to do three circuits of the area of the downs in front of him. I think nearly all the tanks made it, although there may have been one or two failures. We never heard if he was satisfied, but eventually we went to Normandy so I suppose he was.'

The stay at Eastbourne ended with an exercise which took the 9th to a new location, a large wooded area at Castle Goring near Worthing. Everyone was billeted at South Lancing, which was some distance from the tanks at Castle Goring. As a result the Squadrons A, B and C took turns at camping at the tank park for three days at a time. Doug David recalls that 'many pints were downed at the local pub called The Fox'.

15 Troop, C Squadron on manoeuvres on the South Downs, 1943. In front of Ilkley are: Ron Bradley, Sgt. Dickie Hall, Ted Pestell and Dave 'Pop' Sherman.

While at Castle Goring/Lancing Lt.-Col. Paddy Whitsitt, Commanding Officer from the rebirth in 1940, left and Lt.-Col. Sir Nugent Everard, Bt. (also known as Paddy) took over. He was a very keen horseman and almost always wore riding breeches. As a result he was given the nickname 'Harry Wragg' by the irreverent – Harry Wragg being one of the leading jockeys of that time. On one occasion Bob Warren, then commanding B Squadron, decided he would check the general knowledge of some of the more recently joined soldiers. 'What's the name of the Colonel, Dobb?' Without hesitation the answer flashed back, 'Sir Harry Wragg, sir!'

CHAPTER 2

Prelude to Manhood

CHARING: GEARING UP FOR WAR

C haring was heaven. Maybe it always has been. Even today it is pretty heavenly.' So Jock Cordiner remembers Charing, and indeed it is heavenly, besides having some special connections with heaven. Pilgrims on the road from Winchester to Canterbury found Charing a natural halt on their long slow road, a halt where they could enjoy the hospitality of the village huddled round the old Archbishop's Palace and the Church of SS Peter and Paul. The 9th also found Charing a hospitable halt on their long road from Gateshead to Germany, and it was here that they matured into a well-knit fighting unit.

Dickie Hall recalls the move:

In spring 1943 we took part in a huge movement control exercise (probably the one called 'Tiger') which meant packing up ready to arrive at a new location at the end of the exercise. This turned out to be Charing, and HQ was at Pett Place. Initially A Squadron was at Stalisfield, B Squadron at Longbeéch, and C Squadron at Halls Place, which was a large

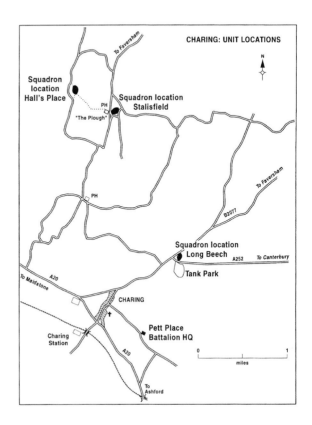

13 Troop, C Squadron in the tank park at the top of Charing Hill, 1943. Back row: Jock Pearson, Sgt. Tom Tomney, Cyril Handley, Bernie Kirkpatrick, Don Foster. Centre row: Bill Pinkney, Frank Risbridger, Cpl. Alf Beale, Norman Hopkins, Doug Ashworth. Front row: Ginger Kirk, Lt. Laurie Le Brun, Cpl. Harold 'Tosh' Brook, Cyril Rees, Vic Crowe.

grassy area with one house in the middle. Our huts were built round the edge. Later B and C changed over and C had the benefit of gravel paths and the nearness of the tank park. This was on the other side of the Charing to Canterbury road at Longbeech and consisted of a long concrete track winding through the woods with bays off it for each individual tank.

The roads between the squadrons, especially those from the tank park at Longbeech out to Stalisfield and Halls Place, were narrow Kentish country lanes with sharp corners, high banks and hedges, and some steep gradients near Halls Place. With the Churchills moving to the squadron locations from time to time the roads suffered, especially at the corners, and in some places existing roads were replaced with concrete sections. These are a lasting, and certainly useful, memorial to the sojourn of the 9th.

The remotest of these locations was Halls Place. Cyril Rees remembers this as 'a large irregular-shaped field about the area of two football pitches on gently rising ground. On the eastern side of the track running through the camp were the Nissen huts containing the guardroom, cookhouse, dining room, officers' mess, sergeants' mess, orderly room, stores and a NAAFI of sorts. On the western side were the troops' huts, latrines, ablutions, and some other miscellaneous huts.'

The backs of these huts were close to the perimeter fence and dense woodland, with some mature trees overhanging the huts. 'It didn't take this rookie very long to learn that nobody braved the elements to stagger up to the latrines in the small hours of a winter's night. You simply opened the back door and with a couple of steps you could piss through the wire fence into the wood beyond without too much shrinkage or dying of exposure. I can't remember that anyone was charged with "urinating in the squadron area" under that all-embracing misdemeanour "conduct prejudicial to good order and military discipline".'

While the use of the latrines could sometimes be circumvented, the use of the ablutions could not. Cyril again:

Then there were the ablutions, and they were primitive in the extreme – a structure of corrugated iron on a bed of concrete; and with no concessions to draught-proofing, the wind fairly whistled through. There were two showers in the same building, but of course no privacy. You stood on a duckboard laid on the concrete and the shower head appeared to be a rose from a gardening watering can screwed on to the end of some half-inch galvanized pipe. It alternately sprayed scalding and then icy water on the unfortunate bather – not too bad in summer, but a daunting experience in the colder months. There was no escape, because you had to sign the bath book to prove attendance.

Stalisfield and Longbeech had some advantages over the remote Halls Place. Stalisfield camp was at Stalisfield Green, which above all things had The Plough public house. There was also a hut which could be used as a dance hall, well remembered for the throbbing rhythms of

B Squadron dance band at Pett Place, Charing, 1943. Back row: L/Cpl. Frank Whitehead, vocalist; Cpl. Mattie Grey, bass; Cpl. Bill Holyoake, drums; L/Cpl. Tommy Thompson, piano. Front row: George Rawe, accordion; name unknown, clarinet; Bobbie Stewart, violin; Cpl. Harry Wall, guitar.

B Squadron band heard dimly through a haze of alcohol. There was a path through the fields from Stalisfield to Halls Place, a path that late on Saturday night might well be strewn with bodies of the fallen.

Longbeech camp was at the top of Charing Hill on the main road from Charing to Canterbury, and thus had more immediate access to the good roads leading in particular to Maidstone and Ashford. It was also very close to the tank park and as Cyril says 'just a couple of minutes was enough to reach the tank standings at our usual tank park stroll'. But it was a rather small and cramped site, and nearer to Battalion HQ than the other two squadrons. This could mean an occasional nocturnal visit from the RSM to check on the alertness of the guard, not an always guaranteed commodity.

Battalion Headquarters itself was half a mile outside Charing village at the lovely old Jacobean house Pett Place. Sections of HQ Squadron were housed in Pett Place and its various outbuildings, and other sections occupied buildings in Charing. Les Arnold, for example: 'On arrival at Charing some of us joined Recce Troop on Honeys and were billeted at the Swan Annex.' The Swan was the pub at the junction of the London–Folkestone A20 and the Charing–Canterbury A252, and the Recce Troop therefore were conveniently placed for a drink.

At Charing the composition of the unit was gradually changed to include some younger soldiers. Many of the original Gateshead intake were now between thirty-five and forty. Some had been promoted and posted away from the 9th having acquired specialist skills or experience, and some were not fit enough for the rigours of life in action. Thus for various reasons a considerable number of people joined the 9th in 1943 and early 1944. What were their impressions?

Brian Marchant was posted to the 9th from the 58th Training Regiment at Bovington:

I had requested a Churchill battalion of the RTR; Churchills, because I thought it had more escape routes than any other tank; and the RTR because it promised to be less of a blanco and brasses outfit than, say the 11th Hussars or the 17th/21st Lancers. Of the same mind were Johnny Oakley, Des Page, and Jack Woods. We might have been mistaken about the chances of a quick exit, but we were heartily reassured about the 'bull' aspect only minutes after arriving at the 9th, our first field unit. We had travelled all day by train from Dorset, the first leg being that to Waterloo and the final haul by the old steam train from London to Charing.

We were picked up by a truck at Charing station and whisked into the black wilderness of Kent, eventually arriving at C Squadron, then in a large field at Halls Place. In the blackout, especially, the place was unprepossessing, to say the least, and a far cry from the immaculate 'spider' huts and roadways of Bovington. After the usual formalities, we were ushered into our respective huts. I can't remember who accompanied me on this introduction, but it was not a happy experience!

The door was opened and shut rapidly, and there we were. The scene that met my eyes was hideous. The air was blue with tobacco smoke, reinforced by the fumes from the stove, throbbing with heat, in the centre of the hut. On this stove was a 4-gallon petrol can, cut in half, being prepared for general ablutions, no hot water being available elsewhere. The hut seemed to be filled with double-tier bunks, every one of them draped with stained denims, sundry items of webbing, Woodbine tins, pieces of half-eaten cake, various small-arms and a variety of towels. In the depths of these bunks lurked the actual personnel, mostly in various stages of undress. Somebody was shaving with a mug of water from the petrol can 'cauldron' boiling on the stove. It was like a gypsy encampment.

They all looked up at the two intruders who had been propelled into their sanctuary without so much as a by-your-leave. They looked, and looked again in utter disbelief. We stood there, in Field Service Marching Order (FSMO), blanco immaculately applied, brasses gleaming, boots boned to perfection, trousers with razor edged creases. 'We're the new boys from 58th Training Regiment', I said, not without some apprehension. There was a stunned silence. Only the hiss of the Tilley lamp was audible. 'Oh, My God', somebody moaned. 'I don't believe it', said another. 'They look like toy soldiers', said a third. Finally, a voice from the gloom said loudly, 'In the morning you'd better rough up that blanco, hide those boots and put on the oldest denims you can find, otherwise they'll have us blanco-ing and polishing every bloody night for evermore.'

But from that moment on we were accepted as members of the gang, and there began for us a period of very happy associations. It was the first time I had served with men of such varied ages and backgrounds. In the 58th, we were all 'Young Soldiers'. Here, we had a smattering of older men among us, like Jock Usher (I remember him as being much older than me, but possibly there was not such a great difference), Trevor Greenwood, for whom I had a great respect, and several others from whom I learned much. I remember that there was a lot of humour, and, above all, a lot of good comradeship, the like of which I was never to experience again to the same degree. It was quite remarkable.

Jock Cordiner came from Scotland, from the back of Bennachie. After joining the 9th 'for the first time I began to feel that I belonged to something and experienced pride in being a soldier, albeit in a foreign land with a weird assortment of odd bods whose tongues were equally foreign; my cockney mate, for example, with his 'won't be round termorrer, lie-dy, the donkey's pissed on the straaawberries'.

The transition from the spit and polish of the training units to the relaxed purposefulness of the field units was also observed by Cyril Rees, Jack Woods, Ray Gordon, Bill Thompson and many others. For young officers joining the 9th at Charing there was a similar transition, from the formality and almost peacetime pomp of Sandhurst to the reality of a field unit. Thus, Peter Boden: 'On arrival I was told that I was to be in C Squadron, but that they were all in Eastwell Park on field training. So off to the tanks to meet the Squadron Leader Monty Grant. He welcomed me and told me that I'd got 14 Troop, but for the moment to ride around on one of the tanks and pick up what I could. The best thing I picked up was in fact 14 troop and was fortunate enough to remain their troop leader throughout the campaign, one of the three troop leaders who lasted the whole distance.' The other two were Gerry Wells from A Squadron and John Stone from B – quite fortuitously, one from each squadron.

Exercises

The function of a field unit is to operate efficiently as a unit in the field, able to arrive at the right place at the right time and to have its supply column actually supplying. This sounds easy enough, but many things can and do go wrong. The only way to gain facility and expertise at moving from one place to another is by practice, and this was the function of an 'exercise'.

Ronnie Holden records the time he joined the 9th and

soon there was to be another of those national exercises, this time called 'Spartan' for one month in the depth of winter; apart from the military manoeuvres, some few hundred miles on tracks, sometimes on transporters. The main purpose, however, according to my reckoning, was to test out the human ability for survival on clothing, cooking, only short spells of sleep under open air or tentage conditions. Under no circumstances was it allowed to supplement rations. Towards the end of one day we crossed the Thames by Bailey Bridge and thence proceeded via some half dozen largish houses, gardens, fences, garden walls, chicken runs, orchards, until we reached the road. This all took place in the dark, no lights were allowed except for one very small rear light to each tank. With approximately 100 tanks, those poor gardens, those poor people who owned and no doubt loved them! Thence across country to some larger estate where every tank had to enter between two very large brick-built gate columns without touching them – 'a strict order'. It was nearly the last tank to get through that hit one column, bringing it down and demolishing it.

Other exercises were designed to test the unit's ability to face up to manoeuvring in a rigorous climate, such as a spell at Shakers Wood near Thetford in the depths of winter. The wind from the North Sea howled across the flat lands of Norfolk and made it, said John Powell, 'so bitingly cold that we appreciated the warmth of those dreadful issue long johns. Still, we had a chance to sample the fleshpots of Bury St. Edmunds.'
John also remembers

A training period based in Hove, with exercises around the Devil's Dyke on the South Downs. This was spent in pleasant weather, and was spoiled only by an enforced 'fast' designed to prepare us for possible shortage of food on active service. Being housed in the leafy seaside suburbs with the tanks parked outside like so many suburban cars was a novel experience for us. The availability of easy train jaunts to London, with or without official pass, was an added bonus – most ticket collectors turned a blind eye to our 'Preston Park Return' tickets as we alighted from the last non-stop London train of the night! [Preston Park was less than 2 miles from Brighton Station, while London was more like 50 miles.]

The South Downs provided good firm going for the tanks and plenty of space; their two disadvantages were a shortage of woods (to simulate the countryside of North West Europe) and some very steep slopes. The Churchill had a fairly tricky gearbox, and the driver's handbook contained a stern warning to drivers to 'never change down on a downhill gradient'. It also contained a warning related to the brakes, which was to 'never allow the vehicle to gain so much momentum on a slope that maximum braking effort is required to control it. Such misuse causes excessive wear, and in extreme cases may burn the linings and so render them ineffective.'
Johnnie Walker, troop corporal of 8 Troop, B Squadron, was taking his tank down one of the slopes when the driver, Jack Wakeford, sensed that the slope was becoming steeper and he needed to change down. Although a very experienced driver, he missed the change. Jack's instinctive but mistaken reaction as the tank rapidly gathered momentum on the close-cropped grass was to jam on the footbrake. To the astonishment of the other tanks nearby two large clouds of white smoke suddenly arose from the gearbox compartment of Jack's tank. It then proceeded to gather speed relentlessly, until at the bottom of the slope it had probably achieved a greater speed than any other Churchill ever. Up the slope on the opposite side it went, quickly losing momentum and slowing down, until Jack was able to whack it neatly into third gear and drive on up the slope as if nothing had happened; the applause could almost be heard above the noise of the tanks. All the fitters had to do was to replace all the brake linings.
In early 1944 Dickie Hall wrote: 'About this time we took part in another movement control exercise called Canute. All vehicles were labelled with their dimensions and weight to assist in loading at our port of embarkation. We then made a timed journey to Hythe where we headed for a newly built "hard" in front of the old lifeboat station. After being checked in we turned round and drove the tanks back to barracks.' These barracks, as John Powell recalls, were those at Shorncliffe. 'We garaged our Churchills in stables originally designed for cavalry horses.'

8 Troop, B Squadron at Stalisfield, April 1944. Back row: Roy Barber, Jimmy Aldcroft, Jack Wakeford, Dennis Fitzgerald, Reg Terrington, Sammy Dangerfield, Clem O'Connor. Front row: Norman Fraser, Ronnie Larner, Cpl. John Humphreys, Lt. Peter Beale, Cpl. Johnnie Walker, Charlie Mansell, Percy O'Bourn.

The War Establishment of the 9th included eighty-five first reinforcements or spare crews of all ranks, sixty-five of these being troopers. In action they would unfortunately be required to replace battle casualties. But what could they do on an exercise, merely the simulation of a battle? Jack Woods explains:

Spare crews on an exercise spent the entire time in the back of a 3-tonner relaxing on camouflage nets being transported from goodness knows where for goodness knows what reason. Once I had to drive a broken down tank back to camp at the end of the convoy. Its intercom wasn't working and somebody had to perch on the front to guide me by flapping his hand to the right or left in front of the driver's visor. All went well until we came across a convoy of 5.5 prime movers parked in column by the side of the road facing towards us. One of them was projecting into the road rather more than it should have been and I showed my disapproval of that by hitting it with my offside air louvre and taking the side out. Oh, dear! Up on Squadron Leader's Orders and remanded for the CO. In telling my side of it I explained that I had only about a fortnight's experience on A vehicles. He raised his eyes heavenwards and sighed: 'I have to give you something, the artillery bods have brought the charges. Do you accept my award?' I replied yes; I have never met anyone who answered no to that question. His award: to pay 7*s* 6*d* towards the cost of damages at 6*d* per week; my pay at the time was 17*s* 6*d* per week, so I thought he was pretty fair. [In a civilian estimate the damage would probably have been several hundred pounds.]

Because there were more than one hundred wireless sets operating on the same frequency, it was highly necessary to have tight radio discipline. This was particularly so because when one set was transmitting it denied transmission to all other sets on the net. In action the most important links were between the CO and his Squadron Leaders, and between the Squadron Leaders and their Troop Leaders. On an exercise the messages were not always so important. Jim Hutton was in 1 Troop, A Squadron. He has recorded a tape of his memories, and with regard to exercises he has this to say:

> While we were on one scheme up in Norfolk, over the radio came the message that the CO wanted his batman who was in B Echelon; the CO called up that he wanted his latrine to be prepared for him when we got to the end of the days scheme and the batman came up and said, 'Would you say again, over', and the CO called out, 'Would you have my latrine prepared for me when we arrive at the laager, where you are at B Echelon'; the batman came up again and said, 'Will you say again over', and so some bright spark on the radio called out, 'Will you have the CO's shithouse ready when he gets to the other end? Out.' Somebody called out, 'Will you get off the bloody air!'

The result of all this training was probably evaluated optimistically or pessimistically by the higher levels of military management. But John Powell at the coal face had this to say: 'Generally a very amiable and variable fourteen months of simulated battle training which honed our skills and general competence and made our troops, squadrons, and the battalion as a whole into reasonably effective units. We didn't learn much about being 'under fire' but we became passably good at managing our vehicles, navigating and communicating. And most of the gunners felt confident about hitting a half-way decently presented target.'

FOOD, FITNESS AND FOLLY

Food was a major pre-occupation with young men living a largely outdoor and vigorous life. Army food was generally very good, but it did depend greatly on the skill of the cooks. When a unit was static, meals were cooked and served centrally for each squadron, and the cooks were members of the ACC (Army Catering Corps). Two members of the ACC are particularly well remembered. Sgt. Kenneth ('Busty') Nuttall was the squadron cook for B Squadron. He was a regular soldier, and after the war he was chosen as the cook for an army advertising poster. An ACC officer said: 'he has such a cook's face!' And a cook's body, too. But he and his team turned out good meals.

C Squadron had its catering identity also. Cyril Rees remembers: 'The mention of Jack Loake's stew will no doubt bring a tear to the eyes of many of those who sampled it – good old Jack!' Possibly an exceptionally pungent vindaloo. Jack was also remembered with honour for his speciality for the sweet course, 'browpad'. This was named in memory of the padding against which a gunner's brow was pressed when looking through his telescope. The browpad, also used as forehead protection in other parts of the tank, was a plastic foam centre covered with leather. Browpad with custard was undoubtedly an acquired taste!

On exercises or in action crews had to cook for themselves. It was generally assumed that the tank commanders, particularly the troop commander, had neither the time or the aptitude to cook for his crew – almost invariably a correct assumption. But as time went by some really good cooks showed out. In one of the newsletters published in 1945 10 Troop of B Squadron reports: 'On the recommendation of the whole troop we understand that Doug Bignell and Titch

Caldwell will shortly be transferred to the ACC or the cookhouse where they will give Sgt. Nuttall instruction in cooking.'

Fitness is a prerequisite for any soldier. In Montgomery's words:

Total war demanded total fitness from the highest to the lowest. I remember the case of a stout old colonel who went to the doctor and said that if he were to do the 7-mile run I had made mandatory it would kill him. The doctor brought him to me. I asked him if he truly thought he would die if he did the run; he said yes, and I saw a hopeful look in his eye. I then said that if he was thinking of dying it would be better to do it now, because he could be replaced easily and smoothly. It is always a nuisance if officers die when the battle starts and things are inclined to be hectic.

Evidently the colonel did run and did not die. But Monty's point is that soldiers have to be physically and mentally attuned to long periods of stress and to remain functioning effectively. This applies to tank units as much as any others, even though they are vehicle-borne for much of the time. The squadrons had PT classes on a reasonably regular basis. Laurie Le Brun, generally known as Bruno, was the troop leader of 13 Troop in C Squadron. To his consternation he was sent to a three-week PT course for officers at the Army School of PT at Aldershot. Emerging shattered but fitter, he was immediately appointed Squadron PT officer and told to take the PT classes at 6.15 in the morning. He used to say that even if he generally felt rather bad, he could see a lot of people who were feeling much worse.

At Halls Place Bob Warren, B Squadron Leader, decided to take a different approach to fitness; the squadron would go on an 18-mile route march. To ensure that everyone kept marching in the column Bob decreed that three officers should march at the back and do their best to encourage people to continue marching. Recognizing, however, that some of the squadron were nearing forty and did not normally take much strenuous exercise, it was arranged that a 3-tonner would act as a long stop some half mile behind the column. Every 3 miles there was a ten-minute halt. After the second halt a few people began to complain that they could go no further, and after close questioning as to their reasons for falling out they were allowed to wait for the truck. John Stone was one of the troop leaders marching at the back, and he always said that the excuse he liked best came from George Horsfield. George was quite a short man, and his job in the squadron was to drive that exotic chariot, the slave battery carrier. He fell to the back of the column with the obvious intention of falling out. 'What's the matter with you, Horsfield,' said John, 'why can't you keep going?' And the classic reply: 'It's me crutch, sir; it's too low.'

'Folly' includes all those after-hours pursuits undertaken by all ranks. Many of them were not folly, of course, but the activities most conducive to subsequent remorse were generally connected with drink or women.

Caring military custom allowed the use of 3-ton trucks to take people to the local centres where entertainment of various sorts might be available. Charing village contained several pubs, and there were other small pubs in the country between Charing and the outlying squadrons. These were all right for weeknights, but the weekends demanded wider opportunities. These might be had at Faversham, Ashford or Maidstone, and it was to these towns that the 3-tonners went in their R and R role of 'passion wagons'. Sometimes people were even lucky with the passion part of it. Freddie Smart recounted his meeting with Trixie, one of the ladies who frequented the Maidstone dance hall. As he was taking her home she confided that she had recently been to her doctor and he had told her that what she needed was a man. I'm just what the doctor ordered, said Fred, and proceeded to give her the doctor's medicine standing up in a shop doorway.

Slave battery carrier. This vehicle was used to recharge batteries, and the crew (a driver mechanic and an electrician) serviced electrical equipment and dealt with electrical faults on all vehicles.

Bedford 3-ton, 4-wheel-drive truck. This came in several forms: General Service (GS); fitted as a kitchen, as an office, or as a store for technical spares. In GS form it carried petrol, ammunition, rations, personal equipment etc., and served the vital role of a 'passion wagon'.

5 Troop, A Squadron at Farnborough, May 1944, in front of troop corporal's tank India. *Back row: Bob Taylor, Wilf Wagstaffe, Ginger Elliott, Ben Willoughby. Centre row: Nobby Clarke, Sid Haddricks, Victor Mills, Johnnie Walker, Roy Hughes, Harry 'Lofty' Hurt. Front row: Cpl. Jim Armstrong, Sgt. Tony Griffiths, Lt. Gerry Wells, Cpl. Albert Johnson, Bob Gadd.*

A passion wagon trip was not always plain sailing. Harry Hurt recalls: 'Another A Squadron character was the 3-ton truck driver 'Crackers' Cracknell; his driving explains his nickname. Crackers was driving a passion wagon back from Faversham; sitting beside him was Gaffer (Lt. Gerry Wells, troop leader of 5 Troop), and in the back were thirty or so others. Crackers took a bend too wide and too fast and turned us over on to our side in a ploughed field. By pure coincidence a police car came along a couple of minutes later and took the injured – two people with broken limbs – off to hospital. I went round to the front to see if Crackers and Gaffer were OK. Crackers had climbed up through the driver's window, now on top, and Gaffer then climbed out. Are you all right, I asked Gaffer. Yes, thank you, he said, and promptly passed out!'

Postscript

Another memory of Harry Hurt's illustrates something of the spirit that had developed in the 9th by this time:

We had in our hut at Stalisfield a young soldier who always spent evenings in bed. He was a very nice quiet lad, but used to get the mickey taken about this habit. Other lads would come back from the canteen at 9 o'clock at night, wake him up and tell him that it was nearly time for parade. He would hop out of bed, go to the ablutions hut, return to our hut and then be

25

told that it was 9 o'clock at night. Unbeknown to us all he suffered from tuberculosis and died from this while we were still there. At a subsequent parade our squadron leader, Duggie Ballantine, proposed that we should send £50 from squadron funds to his mother who was a widow. An unknown voice from the ranks shouted: send her the lot. This call was immediately echoed from everybody and Duggie agreed that this should be done. The sum that was sent to the lad's mother was £300 – quite a lot for 1944.

EMBARK: PREPARATION AND REALITY

By April 1944 the 9th were, as John Powell recorded, ready to fight even if they had no experience of being fired at. They were thus ready to take part in the invasion of Europe. The invasion was planned to take place over a string of open beaches, and the link up behind those beaches would create the initial bridgehead. Landing over those beaches was achieved by using various forms of landing craft. These were ships of very shallow draught which were able to sail close to the beach, let down a ramp, and allow the cargo to exit on to the beach via the ramp. The types of landing craft included Landing Craft Infantry (LCI), Landing Craft Tank (LCT), and Landing Ship Tank (LST).

There was no guarantee that any of the landing craft would be able to drive right up on to the beach, and methods were developed for waterproofing vehicles so that they could land in several feet of water. Waterproofing required some special equipment, such as vertical extensions to the air louvres, sealants (notably the ever popular Bostik), and training in the correct methods of doing it.

6 Troop, B Squadron at Stalisfield, April 1944. Back row: Cpl. Reg Southern, Tom Bollard, John Powell, Stan Hinsley, Tosh Morris, Smudger Smith, Sammy Joule, Cpl. Bill Minton. Front row: unknown, Bert Walkling, Sgt. Gordon Dobinson, 2nd Lt. Freddie Smart, Cpl. James, Charlie Horner, Bob Ungless.

Bob Anderson, John Purdy and Tom Tomney were sergeants with the 156 RAC (Highland Light Infantry). 156 RAC was disbanded in 1943 and Bob, John and Tom were posted to the 9th, Bob to 12 Troop, John to 11 Troop and Tom to 13 Troop. Bob recalls: 'Later in 1943, after I had joined the 9th, I was sent on a tank sealing course to Bovington. As luck would have it the course was delayed for a week so we were given an extra seven days' leave. On completion of the course I did not rejoin the 9th but was detailed to supervise sealing tanks and other vehicles at Crawley where I stayed for the remainder of the year. I finally got back to the 9th in January 1944.'

Bob must have been a marvellous source of knowledge to C Squadron generally and to 12 Troop in particular when it came to sealing the tanks and other vehicles. To carry out this task the 9th moved from Charing – with much regret – to the area of Aldershot and Farnborough. We were all housed in peacetime barracks, and in some ways the traditions of peace time lingered on. This was particularly so in relation to food, which was both good and plentiful. There was a strong suspicion of being fattened up for the kill.

The process of sealing was in some cases accompanied by changing the main armament, as Dickie Hall remembers:

We took out the 6-pounder gun and put a 75 mm in its place. This meant that all turret and hull ammunition racks had to be taken out and replaced, plus the tricky job of hauling the old gun out and fitting the larger calibre in its place. That having been done we set about sealing up the tank so that if need be we could land off an LCT into six feet of water (in the event we landed into six inches!). We fixed metal box sections on to the air intakes and extensions to the exhaust pipes. These were supported by rods and connected to a central release, operated by a Bowden cable. All periscopes, air vents, gun mantlet and gun barrels were covered in fabric and sealed with Bostik. Under each piece of fabric was a coil of explosive cable and all were connected to a central switch. At the touch of a button all the fabric would be blown off, and when the Bowden cable was pulled the two air intakes would fall off. After all this work we took the vehicles through a deep-water dip to see if we were watertight. This brought several small jets of water to light which had to be sealed again.

Bostik made a strong impression on many people, as for example Jock Cordiner: 'I never, ever want to see, smell or touch Bostik again. Underwater practice in that lake was fun, though.' And John Powell: 'We learned how to waterproof our vehicles, and also how difficult Bostik is to remove from hands and clothes.' Les Arnold remembers the testing: 'We tested the effectiveness of the sealing of our Churchill (one of the tanks forming part of BHQ) at Frensham Pond between Farnham and Hindhead.' Cyril Rees saw at least two tanks test how good their sealing was:

13 Troop tested their sealing a few miles away at Cove. An artificial lake with a gently sloping concrete base enabled the tanks to move into the water, usually in first gear, until the water level was high enough to cover every area that had been sealed up to the driver's visor level which hadn't been sealed at this time. For safety's sake we weren't able to drive on public roads totally closed down. Having reversed out of the lake on to dry land there seemed to be no water sloshing about round my feet so our sealing had worked.

I watched one of our other tanks also testing; when about 30 yards out into the lake with water level half-way to the bottom of the air louvres, sprays of water started to eject from the back of the gearbox. The tank stopped, and with screaming revs began to reverse out of the lake. From this time until the tank reached dry land the amount of water coming out of the

Officers of 9 RTR at Pett Place, Charing, April 1944. Back row: Lts. Alan Chapman, John Stone, John Brecknell, unknown, Seymour Francis, Geoff Brewer, Shep Douglas, unknown, Dusty Miller, Bertie Cross, unknown. Second row: Lt. Arthur Moore, Capt. Peter Myatt, Lt. Neville Lord, Lt. & QM Pat Patrick, Lts. Mac Lister, Peter Boden, George Erskine, Les Wintle, Laurie Reynolds. Third row: Capt. Ronnie Kirby, unknown, Lts. Alan Morgan, Frank Drew, Peter Beale, Gerry McMahon, Teddie Mott, Jimmy Cargill, Capt. Ken Kidd, Lt. Jim Pickin. Seated: Capt. Sidney Link, Major Ronnie Holden, Major Duggie Ballantine, Major Berry Veale, MC (2 i/c), Lt.-Col. Sir Nugent Everard, Bart (CO), Capt. John Hodges (Adjutant), Major Bob Warren, Capt. George Eaton, Capt. Bert Mockford, Capt. Roger Long, Capt. Roger Brooke. On ground: Capt. Paddy Knox RAMC, Lt. Frank Haydon, Lt. Dickie Wolskel, Capt. Laurie Branson REME.

top of the gearbox compartment resembled a minor waterfall in reverse. Clearly, a major breakdown in some area of the sealing. The Sirocco fan, which was a close-working fit between the engine and gearbox compartment, drew air through the air louvres and radiators and blasted out a warm vertical jet of air from the rear of the gearbox. Under normal circumstances this was a place to dry wet clothes or get warm.

The amount of water shooting into the air on this occasion suggested a desperate bid to reach dry land before the water drowned the electrics; luckily they made it, and kept their feet dry.

Other preparations were being made; as Dickie Hall explains: 'We were now fully laden with all sorts of ammunition which we were to need in the near future. We were all issued with a small plastic box with a set of concentrated foods, water-purifying tablets, sweets and loo-paper; this box was to see us over the first 24 hrs or so after we landed.'

To Gosport

The 9th were still at Aldershot/Farnborough on 6 June 1944. Trevor Greenwood was troop corporal of 15 Troop, and on this day he started to keep a diary almost without interruption until April 1945. The first entry: '6 June 1944. It has happened at last. Heard first rumours at 8 a.m. Much evidenced restrained excitement. We are not affected . . . yet! Apart from numerous Lightnings saw little evidence of second front all day. This evening saw amazing procession of aerial tugs and gliders, all heading south. Heard radio 9.0 p.m. . . . King's speech. News later confirmed success of landings; fighting 10 miles inland at Caen.'

Sgt. Richard Trevor Greenwood (always known as Trevor) 15 Troop, C Squadron. Trevor kept a very comprehensive diary during the campaign and recorded very vividly the actions and movements in which he took part. His diary has been painstakingly and lovingly transcribed by his son Barry.

Clearly it would not be long before the 9th sailed, and the vehicles were taken through the penultimate stages of sealing. The War Diary records: 'On 11 June the advance party left Aldershot for France and the following day the battalion moved by train and road to the marshalling area near Gosport.' The composition of the advance party is not certain, but there was one definite inclusion, the battalion office. Jack Hilton remembers: 'I was a corporal and the Chief Clerk was Vic Masten from the Newcastle area. I was a clerk as I wore spectacles and had poor eyesight. We were posted to Aldershot in preparation for the invasion. On 6 June, a beautiful morning, we had been advised that the RAF in great force would be bombing the Normandy coast. We were ready for moving and our HQ and office would be a soft top 3-tonner. A tarpaulin cover was slung inside which held all our equipment, typewriters and personal gear to make sure it would be dry when we landed. Our personal weapon was a bazooka.'

The technical name for a bazooka was a projectile infantry anti-tank or Piat. What it says is what it was, a projectile that could be used by a soldier on foot to destroy a tank at short range; an essential ingredient was that the soldier should have strong suicidal tendencies.

The main body of the 9th arrived at Lee-on-Solent on 12 and 13 June. Dickie Hall: 'We offloaded from the rail flats at Eastleigh, a fair distance from the port area, and I remember travelling slowly in convoy through the area of market gardens with the locals very busy picking strawberries. We had been issued with french francs printed on pale blue notepaper marked "Allied Forces", but we still had English money so we bought some of the strawberries.'

The 9th was billeted in whatever accommodation was available, mainly warehouses and tents. By now there was not much to do except wait, occupying the time in whatever pursuits could be found. The War Diary: 'An odd assortment of kit was distributed which included a pamphlet on France and a number of French phrases "not to be shown in public" (what on earth could those have been?!). The marshalling area provided less excitement but more entertainment. The final stage of sealing was completed within a few hours of arrival, and departure was delayed by the heavy seas in the Channel. During the period of waiting every available penny was raked together, but owing to the tax on beer it was soon again in the hands of the Government.'

Jock Cordiner had a more positive experience during this time: 'That Sunday morning in the outskirts of Gosport the outlook was very unfriendly. Then I spied a house called Bennachie. There's only one Bennachie, a prominent hill near Aberdeen. Scruffy me knocked at the door. No hope here, I thought, until in answer to my "I come from the back of Bennachie" came the answer from Madame "Bring the gentleman in, Lottie". Breakfast was served for me and a few mates, breakfast as we had never known it. The lady, it transpired, had been born and raised at the back of Bennachie.'

Dickie Hall managed to meet somebody much closer: 'We were to spend one night here at Lee-on-Solent, where one of my sisters in the WRNS was stationed. As luck would have it we were more or less right outside the Wrennery. I slipped away and surprised her, and she got round their cook to bake us a fruit cake to take with us; it certainly helped to cheer up the contents of the plastic box.'

Most people, however, were without kinsfolk or relatives, and had to find what pleasures they could. Shep Douglas and Peter Beale found a pub that said 'Open 7 p.m. for one hour only'. On storming in at 7 p.m. they found it full of locals who had used the back door. Realizing their limited time, they decided to see what they could drink in one hour. The final tally was eight pints each.

Embarkation and Crossing the Channel

The weather in the Channel during June 1944 was not good. Montgomery writes in his memoirs: '5 June. We met at 4 a.m. A heavy storm was blowing in the Channel and it was clear that if we had persisted with the original D-Day of 5 June we might have had a disaster. But the met. reports indicated a slackening of the storm and a period of reasonable weather on 6 June. Indeed, the experts predicted reasonable weather for some days after the 6 June before the next period of unsettled weather arrived. On that Eisenhower decided to go.'

The weather varied between 6 and 19 June, but was not sufficiently bad to prevent a steady allied build-up and the construction of the Mulberry harbours. However, the morning of 20 June was brilliant with sunshine, too coldly brilliant, perhaps. The weather changed, and for three days the breakers roared ceaselessly on the beaches. 'No such June storm had been known in the Channel for over forty years', wrote the British official historian; and a very large part of the 9th sailed to Normandy through this storm.

The War Diary:

By 19 June the weather was considered sufficiently settled to allow further embarkation, and Battalion HQ, A Squadron and part of B Squadron were loaded on LCTs. There were not, however, sufficient of these craft for the whole battalion, due to the number smashed on the Normandy coast by the rough seas, and the remainder of the battalion were allotted LSTs, one of which was American – those who were lucky enough to cross on this ship not only had a pleasant journey across, lasting four days, but also enjoyed the pleasant experience of American food. The Channel, however, had not calmed to the extent presumed by the embarkation authorities and neither craft nor ship was able to land until 21 June, except for the echelons which got ashore on 19 June. Each craft had a different experience to tell; anchors and kedges had been lost; tanks had broken from their chains and bulged the sides of craft, causing certain alarm; balloons had broken loose and torn away rigging; and a high percentage of the battalion experienced the agony of being seasick.

There are many personal accounts of this journey. Jock Cordiner: 'The big dipper ride to Normandy was unforgettable. The Yankee crew were prepared to feed us like lords, but the pitching of that flat-bottomed bucket, plus galley smells mingled with those from the engine room, was too much for us all. We lay a'deck, nauseated, drenched, and ready to die – no, not for King and country – just die!'

John Powell: 'It was almost a relief to set sail – if that is the right term for the slow, wallowing, stinking progress of those shallow-draught flat-bottomed tank landing craft. The sea journey was both awesome and dreadful: awesome for the long lines of craft marking the passage between England and Normandy; dreadful for the storm-whipped turbulence of the Channel and the motion of the ungainly craft. The matelots were helpful in offering us use of their mess-room and mugs of rum-laced cocoa, but I among others was so seasick that I took to the turret of the tank and sat through most of the long passage nursing a sickbag. Landing against the full might of the German Army would be almost a relief after the miseries of seasickness!'

Les Arnold: 'We had an atrocious crossing; most of us were sick and our LCT lost its anchor and barrage balloon and broke its back. The scuppers were full of water to the extent that you had to jump for the toilet basin and try not to land in the water. But at least one good thing happened to us. For some reason the CO had boarded our HQ Churchill *Invincible* for the crossing. He must have felt sorry for us because apart from being sick we had to man the

Vickers machine-gun in case of possible air attack. He opened a bottle of brandy for us all to have a tot. I am not sure whether it was to help us with seasickness or to give us Dutch courage for the landing, but either way it was much appreciated.'

Jack Woods: 'We landed in Normandy after, for me at least, a horrendous journey. The LST on which we travelled did everything but sink, and there were times on that journey I wished that it had, I wanted to die. They tell me the food was excellent, it was an American LST. I wouldn't know, they still owe me my rations.'

George Rathke: 'We finally landed in Normandy on Juno beach after a terrible crossing in appalling weather. At times the LST seemed to stand on its head, and once several of us had to go down into the hold to rechain some of the tanks. They had got loose and were sliding about, and could have punctured the hull quite easily.'

Peter Boden seemed to have a slightly more agreeable journey:

Finally on to the hard and up on to an LST with a barrage balloon fore and aft (these later became entangled and had to be cut free). The American crew did all they could to make us feel at home on their ship – food was good but the ship was dry! Quoits, games, sickbags, last minute orders and then cast off only to anchor later because of the storm. Eventually our LST took up position in the convoy and made its way to the beach at Arromanches. Our skipper had lost his anchors on a previous trip so had to edge his ship on to the beach and drop his ramp to provide an almost dry landing – after all the time we had spent waterproofing!

Not every LCT landed bows-on to the beach. Peter Beale:

It was said that LCTs and other landing craft were fair-weather boats and pretty uncontrollable in any sort of high sea. Certainly the skipper of my craft found this to be so. During the night of 20 June he told me that the LCT was no longer under control because the engine had become clogged with sand. Whereupon he hoisted a black ball and we drifted sideways-on towards the beach, the waves breaking over the craft and copious quantities of salt water pouring down the air inlets erected to allow the tank to wade ashore. The morning came and our LCT, along with many other craft, lay broached-to on the sandy beach. John Humphreys got into the driver's seat and sat down in a foot of water – we had done the waterproofing well enough to keep the water in as well as out.

CHAPTER 3

The Scottish Corridor

OPERATION 'EPSOM': FORMING UP

Strategic Situation

The great storm described in the previous chapter delayed the arrival of several follow-up formations, but did not change Montgomery's Normandy strategy. This strategy's main points were:

1. to hold the left shoulder of the bridgehead in the area of Caen;
2. to be continually aggressive on this front, and thus draw German reinforcements, especially tank formations, on to the British Army;
3. by doing so to weaken the German opposition against the Americans in the west of the bridgehead, and thus make it easier for the Americans to rupture the bridgehead and break out south, east and west;
4. to expand the left shoulder of the bridgehead, with the particular objective of encircling Caen.

Montgomery's first attempt to encircle Caen was by a pincer attack which took place between 9 and 18 June. The left hook of this attack was made by 51st Highland Division and 4 Armoured Brigade. They were to start from the airborne bridgehead on the far east of the line, and their objective was Cagny. The more powerful right hook was to be delivered by XXX Corps with 7th Armoured Division leading. This attack was to start at Bayeux and end at Villers Bocage and Evrecy. The ring was to be sealed by dropping British 1st Airborne Division between Cagny and Evrecy. Between the left and right hooks the Canadians were to advance in the centre.

As the allies advanced, however, reinforcements continued to arrive to help the Germans already stoutly defending their positions. One particularly potent reinforcement was the 101st SS Heavy Tank Battalion, one Tiger I tank of which, commanded by Obersturmführer Michel Wittmann, was reported to have accounted for twenty-five British armoured vehicles of the 7th Armoured Division at the outskirts of Villers Bocage on 13 June. The allied front on the eastern side of the bridgehead had been advanced, but there was still a long way to go and much fighting before Caen was to be encircled.

On 18 June twenty allied divisions were ashore facing eighteen mainly understrength German divisions. Montgomery believed that he could crack the enemy line and this time successfully encircle Caen, using the troops of VIII Corps who were just beginning to land on the beaches. The attack, this time with the right hook rather nearer to Caen, was to begin on 22 June. The storm of 18 to 22 June postponed the attack, in fact by three days, but the battle plan remained the same.

Three corps were to take part: on the British right the 49th West Riding Division of XXX Corps was to seize the vital ridges of Fontenay and Rauray on 25 June; in the centre VIII Corps was to thrust for crossings of the Odon and the Orne on 26 June; further to the left the Canadians of I Corps were to move up to Carpiquet airfield, and 51st Highland Division was to break out of the airborne bridgehead to approach Caen from the other side.

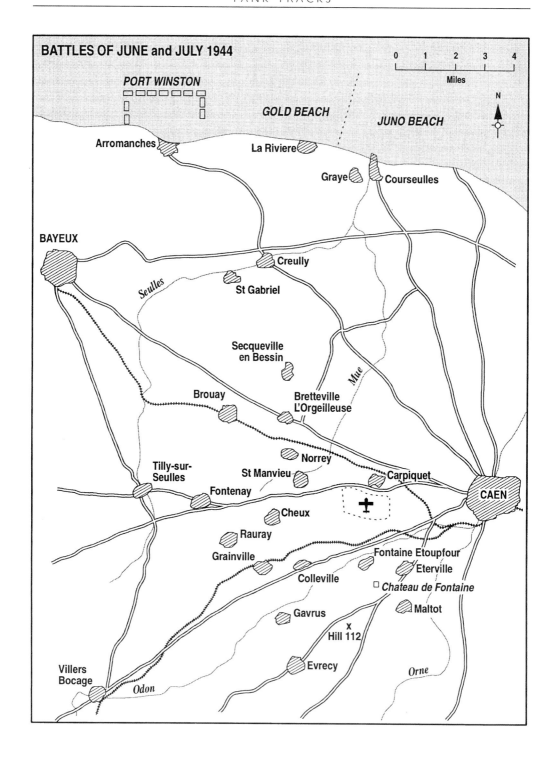

BATTLES OF JUNE and JULY 1944

0 1 2 3 4

Miles

N

PORT WINSTON

GOLD BEACH

JUNO BEACH

Arromanches

La Riviere

Graye

Courseulles

BAYEUX

Creully

Seulles

St Gabriel

Secqueville
en Bessin

Mue

Brouay

Bretteville
L'Orgeilleuse

Norrey

Tilly-sur-
Seulles

St Manvieu

Carpiquet

CAEN

Fontenay

Cheux

Rauray

Grainville

Fontaine Etoupfour

Eterville

Colleville

Chateau de Fontaine

Gavrus

Maltot

X
Hill 112

Villers
Bocage

Evrecy

Orne

Odon

The plan for VIII Corps was for 15th Scottish Division to lead, supported by 31 Tank Brigade (including 9 RTR) and 4 Armoured Brigade; mopping up behind them was to be the task of 43rd Wessex Division, and 11th Armoured Division was to advance also, ready to break out from the Odon bridgehead and quickly wheel left round the southern outskirts of Caen.

Role and command of a heavy tank battalion

Before commencing our first action it is useful to understand what we were supposed to be doing. Heavy tank battalions such as 9 RTR were grouped into army tank brigades, generally consisting of three battalions. The 9th were in 31 Tank Brigade from early 1941 until the end of August 1944, and in 34 Tank Brigade for the remainder of the war. On 2 February 1945 tank brigades were redesignated armoured brigades, so the 9th was in 34 Armoured Brigade from 2 February 1945 to 1 July 1945.

The role of tank or armoured brigades was close support of infantry in attack or defence. The tank formations were assigned to one of the army corps, which in the British and Canadian sector in Normandy were II Canadian and I, VIII, XII and XXX British (army corps were generally identified by roman numbers).

The Corps Commander, as Berry Veale explains shortly, could allocate the tank brigade or its constituent battalions to infantry formations in the corps. During the campaign in North West Europe the 9th supported the following infantry divisions; the list also shows the abbreviation for each division:

15th (Scottish) Division	15 (S)
43rd (Wessex) Division	43 (W)
49th (West Riding) Division, also known as the Butcher Bears	49 (WR)
51st (Highland) Division	51 (H)
52nd (Lowland) Division	52 (L)
53rd (Welsh) Division	53 (W)
59th (Staffordshire) Division	59 (S)
3rd Canadian Infantry Division	3 CAN

To most people in the tanks or echelons, supporting these different divisions meant merely that there was a different set of signs to follow and a different set of infantry to work with. But what did it mean at Battalion HQ? Lt.-Col. Peter Norman (Berry) Veale had been CO of the 9th since mid-July. He was a very experienced tank soldier, having fought with 8 RTR in North Africa where he won the MC. He describes the things that had to be done every time the tank brigade or the 9th was ordered to support a different infantry formation:

So what does the CO do anyway?

The wars and battles that we are all familiar with as far back as recorded history; two opposing armed groups met in battle. One would defend and the other attack. The stronger or better equipped or better trained would prevail and win the battle grabbing all the loot, women and land and they would kill or enslave the losers.

Up until the First World War it was still like that but on a bigger scale; and then at the end of 1916 the tank was introduced into the equation and the concept changed. The defenders dug themselves into trenches or pill-boxes and the attackers developed mobile pill-boxes or tanks. Then the defenders added tanks or mobile pill-boxes with machine-guns and big guns and once again the more skilful or better equipped side won the day. That's how it was in the Second World War and the 9 RTR was formed and trained to work closely with the infantry.

They were one of the many subsidiary units added to the army to assist the infantry in achieving their objective and making sure they did not get pushed off.

So how do we get down to the CO 9 RTR?

Let us assume plan is made and segments of that plan dished out to the various elements of the attacking force. Our army corps, for example, is allocated a specific task with an objective and timing so as to coordinate its operation with that of other formations. An army corps divides its objective into parts and deals out these parts to infantry divisions under its command. Corps may judge that one of its divisions could use some tank assistance so it calls an infantry tank brigade, one of its 'special' units under command, and orders it to send one of its I Tank Regiments over to that infantry division and place it under command of that Divisional General.

Now we are getting somewhere: Brigadier Tank Brigade calls up Infantry Division General to tell him that 9 RTR will be under his command for this battle and CO 9 RTR will be reporting to his HQ shortly for orders. Brigadier Tank Brigade orders CO 9 RTR to report to the General of the infantry division under whose command he will be for this battle. CO 9 RTR calls in his 2 i/c and Adjutant and tells them of the orders he has received and for them to set the wheels in motion. Previous training will guide the Adjutant to set in motion all kinds of Administrative and Quartermaster (A & Q) tasks. The 2 i/c will alert Squadron Commanders and get the Intelligence Officer to obtain maps and all relevant information for use in passing on any orders and likely moves which might result.

At this first meeting between Infantry General and CO the main point is basically an introduction, allowing the General to know who he has had added to his command and how best to use him. His Chief of Staff would also want information on who his tank contact is going to be (Adjutant), where the tanks are located and how to get its A & Q requirements integrated.

The General will outline his orders from corps and make some preliminary plans. The CO will ask Chief of Staff for all information available regarding maps and intelligence as well as own and enemy troops. These are all preliminary moves culminating in a closely knit group of men and machines carrying out an attack with an objective in view.

The CO's job is to advise, encourage and assist in the preparations and to stand by for passing on all incoming information of the battle during its progress. If he has control of any tank unit in reserve, he may order its engagement to reinforce or otherwise maintain the impetus of the operation. The operation may be complete on attainment of the objective or the passing through of exploiting formations. The attachment of the tanks in support of the infantry is not released until the Division Command orders it. He may then return 9 RTR to command of the tank brigade. Brigadier Tank Brigade will issue orders to CO 9 RTR to rendezvous at some map reference which could be from whence they started. At this time the CO will be concerned with collecting reports of the action from Squadron Commanders and Intelligence Officer, recording casualties of men and tanks, requisitioning replacements, checking on recovery of breakdowns etc. These tasks are among those that a well-trained unit will carry out as routine but it must be urged on with all due diligence. Training of replacement crews and checking out of new tanks and equipment is put in hand with all due haste so that the CO can report the 9 RTR as back up to strength and ready for further orders. Nothing to it really!

The War Diary

Any battalion on active service or in action was supposed to keep a record of where it went, what it did, what casualties were suffered, and what changes there were in positions of responsibility. The person maintaining the war diary was the battalion Intelligence Officer (IO).

On active service, such as in training, on exercises, and so forth, it was reasonably easy to write the war diary. In action, however, the IO was in one of the Battalion HQ tanks, and was subjected to the hazards of battle and the jolting rides of cross-country movement. It was thus much more difficult to keep a detailed record at the time when the significant history of the battalion was happening.

The war diary contained as much as possible of the following information: transfers from one formation to another, and the physical movement needed for those transfers; plans for action, showing other units taking part; records of what happened in action, including taking or failing to take objectives, enemy opposition, casualties to men and tanks; changes in command at significant levels; occasional observations of a personal, humorous, or anecdotal nature.

The IO for the first few months of the campaign was Lt. Frank Haydon. He was promoted to Captain and command of the Recce Troop in September 1944 and Lt. Laurie Le Brun, previously 13 Troop Leader, was appointed IO.

9 RTR's part in the initial plan: extract from the War Diary

On the night of 24 June the battalion did a road march to the area Secqueville en Bessin, and there spent the day resting and preparing for battle. The following night the battalion left for the FUP (Forming-up point), which was the line of the railway just south of Bretteville l'Orgueilleuse. The battalion arrived there at 0200 hrs.

Using the Caen–Bayeux railway as a start line, the intention was to attack with two infantry brigades up supported by a tank brigade. When a hole had been made in the enemy defences elements of an armoured division would pass through to establish a break-out from the original bridgehead.

9 RTR were under command 15th Scottish Division:

The general plan was as follows:

Phase 1: Right: 7 RTR (less one squadron) in support of 46 Infantry Brigade to cut the Tilly–Caen road and secure the high ground Haut du Bosq;
Left: 9 RTR (less C Squadron) to attack St. Manvieu and La Gaule.

Phase 2: With the left flank secured by 15th Reconnaissance Regiment:
* C Squadron supporting 1st Battalion the Gordon Highlanders (Gordons) to capture Colleville and Mondrainville, and if possible secure a bridgehead over the River Odon south of Mondrainville;
* One squadron 7 RTR with one battalion 227 Brigade to capture Grainville-sur-Odon;
* Elements of 11th Armoured Division to pass through, seize bridges over the River Odon, and then occupy high ground point 112 and point 113. RAF support and artillery barrage of about 600 field and heavy guns were to precede the attack.

Moving up to the start line

The battalion moved from the beaches, wherever they landed, and concentrated in the area of St. Gabriel. One of the first to land and move inland was Jack Hilton in the battalion office truck. 'We landed and took out our gear. We as part of HQ had to follow a certain coloured tape which landed us in an assembly field. There were other coloured tapes for other parts of the unit. We were soon reminded it was war and we were in it. In this field a German had been buried – his rifle stuck in the ground and his helmet on top; but they had left one of his arms

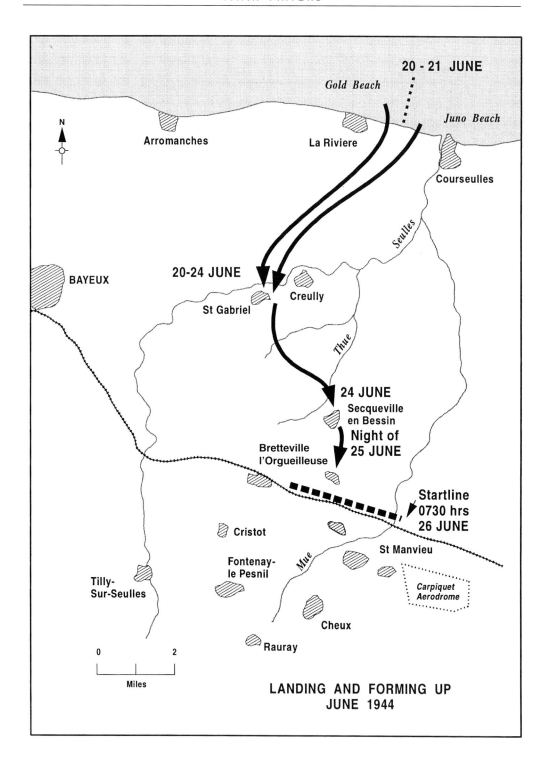

LANDING AND FORMING UP
JUNE 1944

sticking out vertically and his fingers were peeling back like banana skins. This was my first experience of death – there were many more. Our colonel and many of the Churchills were unable to land for about a week because of the wild gale blowing.'

Jock Cordiner's experience with the route from the beach was rather more of a confrontation: 'Coming ashore in our Humber scout car, Brad and I had the dubious honour of leading a column along the road going inland. Our instructions were very clear – to turn right at the first crossroads and after a certain distance go into a tree-lined field on the left. Approaching the crossroads a sergeant military policeman waved us straight on. I indicated right (Brad was driving). As we drew alongside there was a furious argument between the MP and me, but we stuck to our plans. We were later told that the MP was a German, though I can't vouch for the truth of that.'

George Hendrie was the troop leader of 1 Troop in A Squadron, and Jim Hutton was his driver. Jim recalls 'We came off the beach, we blew our waterproof sealing and off we went and I think we laagered up at a place called St. Gabriel.' But evidently not everyone blew off the sealing: Dickie Hall:

After all our hard work sealing up the tanks we went off into six inches of water, and set off inland along newly bulldozed roads, or rather 'tracks', through the countryside. It was hot and dusty and we longed to be able to stop and brew up. We stopped and unshipped all the ironwork, which had proved unnecessary. We were not allowed to explode the charges to blow off the fabric covers, which was understandable, because the whole squadron doing this would create a panic in those who had had quite enough for their nerves already.

I do not remember doing much in that field in the day or two we spent there. We consumed the contents of our plastic boxes and my sister's cake. Round about our area were many vehicles, ours and theirs, which had been knocked out and were burnt. Some of the Sherman tanks had nasty holes in the turrets and hulls, and we wondered how our Churchills would stand up to '88s. We would not have long to wait.

Tom Tomney was the troop sergeant of 13 Troop, commanded by Bruno Le Brun. Tom's driver was Cyril Rees, who remembers the journey to the forming up point as being

fairly uneventful. We followed tracks already made through fields and standing crops, the many vehicles churning up the dry earth, for the weather was quite sunny. We had lost our front mudguard, and with my visor open it was necessary to wear goggles to cope with the minor dust storm we created. I think if I had had my pulse checked, it would probably have read a bit higher than normal at this time. I did not feel scared, just a bit apprehensive, wondering what was ahead. (After all, the countryside was much like you could have found in Sussex and Kent with fields, hedges, and similar crops, and the noble but ragged elms here and there. The one noticeable difference was the occasional wrecked or burnt vehicle, and the sad spectacle of dead and dying cattle).

When we arrived at the forming up area there were already many vehicles of various sorts, trucks and carriers of the infantry, the artillery and their guns and limbers and of course some Churchills. I picked my way to our allotted position guided by Tom Tomney, then halted when ordered. Then started the last minute check. Hoppy was already checking the net and other radio tasks and Ginger was checking all the armament. I topped up with about 20 gallons of petrol. A quick oil check revealed all in order.

I was glad to find no trace of a leak round the union to the hydraulic receiver; in the past many of us found that vibration caused the joint to weep and consequently making throttle controls unresponsive when you pressed the pedal, due to air getting in the system, so there was no need to bleed the hydraulics, thank goodness. I decided to put another shim in the offside track so we all mucked in and tightened it a bit. After we had done all this we had a chance to look around, to see what was happening and to chat to the other crews. From the viewpoint standing on the engine hatches I saw an AEC Matador explode in spectacular fashion, flames leaping high into the air. This happened about 300 yards to our front, the whole thing burned furiously for about twenty minutes and was totally destroyed. A petrol wagon perhaps, but no idea of the real cause.

A high-pitched shriek of a tank in low gear and struggling hard gradually got nearer, and eventually a Sherman came into view. It took a few more minutes before the source of all this noise became apparent. What this gasping Sherman had towed into view was enough to make me feel very uneasy indeed. When the whole works stopped about 30 feet away I, and most of us in the troop, had a close-up view of our first Tiger.

It was to me an awesome sight. The great gun sticking out from the massive turret, the interlocked road wheels, and the wide tracks. To compare our puny 6-pounder with this giant's '88 was a salutary experience. How the hell, I thought, can we possibly compete with these monsters? They seemed to be superior in all the most important departments. But before having time to ponder these matters we were ordered to mount.

Les Arnold was the gunner in one of the two tanks at BHQ that were designated observation post (OP) tanks. In action they would be attached to a sabre squadron and commanded by a Royal Artillery officer acting as a Forward Observation Officer (FOO). Les recalls that the CO of 9 RTR, Sir Nugent (Paddy) Everard acted as his tank commander during the crossing from Gosport to Juno beach.

Eventually we came ashore at La Vallette which was a Canadian landing area on D-Day. The CO was still acting as our tank commander and we proceeded inland following the 31 Brigade green diabolo sign.

Ultimately we laagered in a meadow close to some orchards between Banville and Reviers. We were allowed some free time in the evenings and Jock Caldwell who had joined the regiment came to look me up and we went to the local inn to sample some calvados. We stayed at Banville for some days and then on the afternoon of 25 June we were briefed on the next day's action. Infantry from 15th Scottish Division were moving up accompanied by their pipers; they could be heard for miles and cheered us up considerably. During the evening we moved down towards the start line nose to tail with very little light; I remember we passed close to a railway line and just missed diving into an anti-tank ditch. Ultimately we laagered with the rest of B Squadron near Bretteville L'Orgueilleuse. My tank now had on board a Major and wireless operator controlling a battery of 25-pounders under the direction of B Squadron Leader Bob Warren. Our Churchill had two 19 sets, one for communication with the squadron and the other for communication with the artillery battery.

Trevor Greenwood was in 15 Troop of C Squadron. He came across the Channel in an American LST and landed on 22 June.

Landed about 5.30 p.m. And what a sight! The beach looked like a ships' graveyard, although most of the beached vessels were not really wrecks; they were merely high and dry awaiting the next tide. But there certainly was some evidence of the last fortnight's fighting. One landing craft completely overturned . . . one steam tug holed and lying on her side . . .

etc. etc. Looking back on the bay, there was an amazing mass of shipping; and the sky was full of balloons – local ones, and on more distant beaches.

We landed dry – what a waste of waterproofing! Halted by the beach and removed most of the sealing; then drove inland to the assembly area. Much evidence of the war en route; fields still marked with Jerry skull and crossbones and 'Minen!' Our lanes clearly marked and taped. Country lanes already being widened and improved. Mass of wrecked vehicles by beach. Simple graves by roadside bearing wooden crosses, steel helmets, etc. Terribly depressing sight. Army vehicles everywhere; and all troops look terribly dirty, but brown and cheerful. This entire region is just a huge army camp. God knows what all the vehicles are for; some weird looking monsters. Later drove on to concentration area; first of C to arrive. A echelon been here since Monday! Worked on tank until dark, then dug long and wide shallow trench to sleep in. Ran tank over afterwards for roof against shrapnel and anti-personnel bombs.

Three days later from Trevor's diary (25 June): 'Moved to new location late last night; only about 3 miles nearer front, but we spent four hours en route. Awkward route, probably for security. Conferences all day; all troop leaders doing little but study maps. Our first action is now imminent and everyone is more serious. A and B doing one attack . . . C another, and later in day.'

Jim Hutton was left in St. Gabriel. His journey up to the start line was full of pitfalls:

Anyway we moved off, having had a meal and got ourselves sorted out we moved off and in the night they said they would put a barrage up so the enemy wouldn't hear the tanks moving. Off we went and all we went by was the convoy lights down at the bottom of the tank in front. I was driving along and the next thing I knew the light just disappeared and I carried on and didn't know whether to halt or stop. I didn't get any commands I just carried on and the next thing I knew it was going down at an angle of 45 degrees, straight down. And all of a sudden, bang, and stop. What had happened was the tank in front of me had gone down one of either the Rodney or the Renown's shell holes, which I suppose was about 30 foot deep. He went down this shell hole and flattened in the bottom and I went down at right angles on top of him. So there we were, I was at 45 degree angles on his engine covers and that's how we stopped all night cause we couldn't get out, there was no way I could reverse out, it just wouldn't have it. So we stayed like that all night and more or less slept in an upright position, standing up. Next morning the Scammels and a couple of tanks came along and pulled us out but that was a massive hole and I shall never forget that, it was quite a funny experience, but not funny at the time, like.

John Stone remembers his journey to the start line as a very long night:

We were just leaving Secqueville when we had a minor mechanical breakdown on my tank. Two choices: get on Fred Hackett's tank and let him bring mine up when it was fixed; or let Fred go in the squadron column and me bring up the tank. I decided that I would be more certain to get my tank to the start line – no disrespect to Fred. It took the fitters nearly two hours, and by that time the lingering twilight had nearly gone. We clanked along slowly and lonely, following the 'route up' signs. This ground had been taken and held by Canadians. Suddenly from a ditch on the side of the road a Canadian voice 'Pick'. Obviously a challenging password; what to answer? 'Shovel' I said. 'Axe, you stupid bastard', was the tender reply. We clanked on and eventually reached the squadron laager two hours before stand-to on 26 June 1944.

Officers of C Squadron at Pett Place, Charing, April 1944. Standing: Lts. Peter Boden, Frank Drew, Seymour Francis, Alan Chapman, Laurie Le Brun. Seated: Capt. Sidney Link, Major Ronnie Holden, Capt. Ken Kidd.

Ronnie Holden, commanding C Squadron, recalls the move to the start line: 'After landing, time was spent studying photomosaics, maps, and defence overprints; just enough to whet our imaginations and make sure all guns and tanks were in perfect order. We reached our forming up position which was in dead ground behind the start line. I left no one person in doubt as to our task ahead.'

'EPSOM': DAY ONE, 26 JUNE 1944

9 RTR War Diary

Attacking with A and B Squadrons up, the battalion crossed the start line at 0730 hrs following closely behind the artillery barrage. By 0815 hrs the River Mue had been crossed. No strong opposition had yet been met, but the infantry found it difficult to clear the enemy from the high crops which provided cover for snipers; there were also snipers in the trees. At 0940 hrs house clearing on the objectives (St. Manvieu and La Gaule) had begun. Armour had been reported in the area south of Cheux, but by 1125 hrs objectives were clear except for one strongpoint in St. Manvieu which was finally destroyed by Crocodiles. The infantry dug in and the tanks remained in support to assist in beating off counter-attacks which were made on a small scale south of La Gaule and east of St. Manvieu. No heavy anti-tank guns had been encountered, but one tank commander (Corporal Nobby Killick, 2 Troop, A Squadron) had been killed during the barrage and three tanks damaged. It was estimated that at least two companies of enemy infantry had been killed.

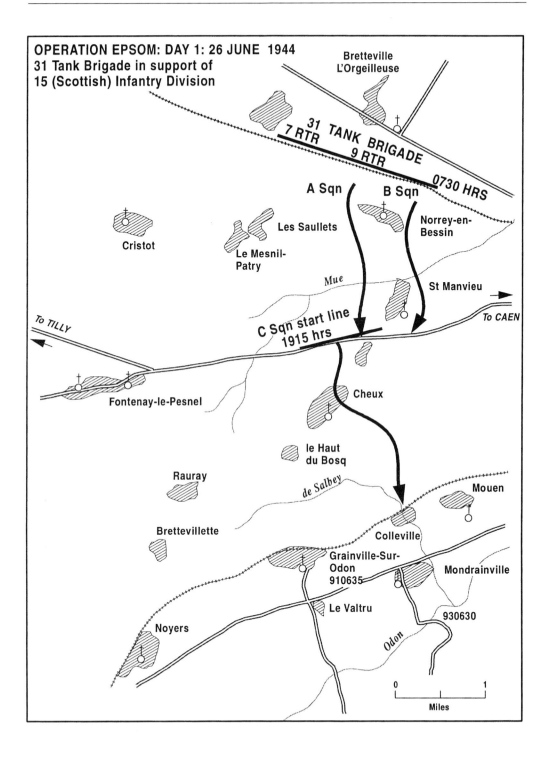

OPERATION EPSOM: DAY 1: 26 JUNE 1944
31 Tank Brigade in support of
15 (Scottish) Infantry Division

Bretteville
L'Orgeilleuse

31 TANK BRIGADE
7 RTR
9 RTR
0730 HRS

A Sqn   B Sqn

Les Saullets

Cristot

Le Mesnil-
Patry

Norrey-en-
Bessin

Mue

St Manvieu

To TILLY

C Sqn start line
1915 hrs

To CAEN

Fontenay-le-Pesnel

Cheux

le Haut
du Bosq

Rauray

de Salbey

Mouen

Brettevillette

Colleville

Grainville-Sur-
Odon
910635

Mondrainville

Le Valtru

930630

Noyers

Odon

0   1

Miles

43

At 1515 hrs a regiment of 11th Armoured Division with reconnaissance elements passed through and established themselves on the high ground north of Cheux. The threat of an armoured counter-attack had not yet developed.

At 1915 hrs, without artillery support and the expected air attack on Grainville and Colleville, C Squadron began their advance in heavy rain. They pushed across the Tilly–Caen road and had great difficulty in getting through the sunken narrow roads of Cheux. They eventually got on to the 100 metre ring contour south of Cheux and moved forward down the slope to support the infantry (1st Battalion The Gordon Highlanders) into Colleville through the high corn. Heavy anti-tank fire, which included self-propelled 88 mms and Panthers, was encountered on the left flank (supposed to be held by 15th Reconnaissance Regiment) and to the front.

Continuous rain made it difficult to locate the targets and gradually one tank after another became a casualty. By splitting the squadron so that half engaged the enemy tanks and self-propelled guns, while the remainder pushed on to help the Gordons, there were further casualties. The Gordons were in trouble with mortars and snipers at the approaches to Colleville, but eventually they got there. However, they were not in sufficient strength to hold it and were forced to withdraw under persistent mortar fire.

By last light only six tanks of C Squadron were still engaged, and under cover of darkness they moved forward in an effort to collect the remainder of the infantry still pinned to the ground; not more than a company was found. In the darkness the tanks moved back into Cheux and spent the remaining few hours of the night in the farmyard.

For his determination to achieve his objective despite heavy opposition Major R.E. (Ronnie) Holden, Squadron Leader of C Squadron, was later awarded the MC.

St. Manvieu, taken by John Powell (B Squadron) in 1993. The mud and the high banks were just the same in 1944.

Neither A or B Squadrons were relieved until dark and they laagered on their respective objectives. The casualties of C Squadron's action were not as heavy as anticipated. The Churchill proved that it could take a lot of punishment and that it was slow to burn. Complete write-offs in tanks later proved to be five. Three tank crewmen in C Squadron were killed, Corporal Jim Chapman, Trooper David Gotobed, and Trooper Roy Painter. At first light C Squadron moved to the battalion area north of Cheux.

Personal recollections, 26 June

For most people in battle there is great uncertainty as to what is happening, and there are hours of hanging around waiting, interspersed by moments of urgency, action and terror. Normandy was a curious place for understanding and moving over the terrain. There were some large open fields covered with ripening corn standing four to five feet high. Good to advance through in some ways, but good also for snipers. Then there was the bocage, anathema to the tank in attack. The dictionary defines bocage as 'the wooded countryside characteristic of northern France, with small irregular-shaped fields and many hedges and copses'. Many of the boundaries between the small fields consisted of banks with hedges on top of the banks. These were hostile to tank movement for two reasons: in starting to cross the bank the tank's thin underbelly became exposed, and it had to be a slow exposure; then in going down the other side of the bank the driver had to tip the tank gently over the top so that the landing on the other side was not too bone-jarring. While the crew might appreciate being quickly into the next field, a heavy landing shook everything in the tank and gave rise to comments on the driver's parentage, skill, and probable future sexual experiences.

One person who was able to see the picture in spite of the confusion was Ronnie Holden. The War Diary has described the intelligence, cool-headedness and gallantry with which he commanded C Squadron. His own account is very modest:

The infantry we were supporting was the 1st Battalion The Gordon Highlanders commanded by Lt.-Col. Sinclair (later General). H Hour arrived, and I gave the order to advance. At this point all hell was let loose, enemy artillery, nebelwerfers, anti-tank guns, tanks, the lot. Now immediately to our left flank after our start line was a 100 ring contour of high ground; according to our original information this was to have been held by 15th Recce for the protection of the Gordons and ourselves. In fact it was held by German panzers Marks III and IV. This caused heavy casualties on the Gordons and five of our tanks were put out of action. The original advance came to a temporary halt while a running battle was fought out between the squadron's left flank troops and these panzers. At the same time our right flank troops were dealing with heavier German tanks to our front. I fired off smoke to off-centre right in order to reform, and we were able to re-establish the front to our advantage; we were also able to pick up the wounded from the Gordons and our own tanks.

Daylight was fading fast and fuel and ammunition were getting low. The Gordons were dug in, and we found a taped path running through a minefield which allowed us to retire to laager. There we prepared a little food and had two or three hours sleep. There remained only nine operational tanks of the squadron, with many wounded crews. This was the end of our first day of battle.

Ronnie's attack took place in the late afternoon of 26 June. The morning attacks were made by A Squadron on La Gaule and B Squadron on St. Manvieu. Ray Gordon was with 2 Troop of A Squadron. 'I recall a long day with hatches closed most of the time with some shots fired but

Normandy, 26 June 1944. Tanks of A Squadron advance south from the battered church and village of Norrey-en-Bessin on the way to the start line of their first battle, Operation 'Epsom'. (Imperial War Museum, B6054)

no recollection of seeing enemy tanks. On return to laager in the evening we were told that our troop corporal, Nobby Killick, had been killed. What a shock for all of us to realize that the false feeling of our first action being rather like a scheme in England was a myth – now completely burst. This first contact with the enemy was for real, and we now knew that death, injury, or mutilation might well lie ahead for each one of us. Sleep did not come easily that night.'

Jim Hutton also remembered Nobby Killick's death – and a few other incidents of 26 June:

Anyway, we then started to move into a bit of action and I remember Corporal Killick was our first casualty, a mortar, a German (Nebelwerfer) one of these moaning minnie mortars hit him in the turret, he was in the turret and the mortar hit him smack on the top and he was our first casualty, Corporal Killick. And we went into an action near Cheux with the 15th Scottish and we had a shot in our front idler which put us out. We were still able to move but we had to come out and the ARV came out and took the old front idler out and we were replacing the new idler. It was being lowered into position as the Gerries stonked us with the moaning minnies and nearly finished us off. But we all managed to dive for cover and get out the way and we got this idler back in in double-quick time, mended the track and drove back and joined the rest of the squadron.

When we were moving back up towards Cheux we heard a large bang and quite a bit of concussion inside and we were all shook up like but we didn't think much more of it until we got to our destination which was to line up on a hedgerow. When we got there we had a look around outside and on the engine cover at the back was one of these German panzerfausts, with the wooden stem and the flexible fins. What had happened was this Hitler Youth merchant was up the tree and he fired this panzerfaust when we had passed his tree. He hit our back bin and it peppered it just like a bloody pepperpot and all it did was stop the panzerfaust from hitting the main armour, it just hit the bin and blew everything to bits, didn't it. But in this bin was my best BD, my best suit and it was rolled up with me trousers and me jacket and the battledress blouse, and the fragments had penetrated it in about two or three different places. When I unrolled it it was peppered like one of these Japanese, what do you call it, origami, this paper when they tear the papers up; that was my battledress up the creek.

On this first day B Squadron had only minor casualties, one of them being the troop sergeant of 6 Troop, Jackie Gallagher. John Powell recalls how it happened:

After a couple of days or so to adjust we were thrown into our first action at first light on 26 June, by which time we had become accustomed to the routine of life on active service and to the sounds of warfare, including the incredible noise of heavy shells passing overhead from our warships to batter the enemy lines. The start line for our troop ran through a Norman orchard. We were agreeably surprised to find that a rum ration was issued to us before action, no doubt compensation for moving-off at first light!

My first introduction to battle was almost a farce: as our tank commander, Sgt. Jackie Gallagher, guided the driver through the orchard we ran over a mine and lost a track. The sergeant was shocked but seemed unhurt except for a few marks around the face and soon organized the repairs.

It took a while to replace the damaged track section. It was heartening to see the imposing streams of infantry and armour that passed us as the battle moved on. In our haste to rejoin the squadron our navigation went awry and we went seriously astray, into or near enemy lines as I recollect. We eventually found our way back to join the others, after I had to use morse code for my first and only time ever (we were beyond radio speech contact with HQ), and settled down to the routine of the night-time laager.

Guns had to be cleaned, wireless 'net' checked, minor repairs effected and refuelling and re-arming with fresh ammo had to be carried out. The arrival of the cooks' 3-tonner with the hot food was a welcome diversion although stew and tinned peaches served in the same mess tin made for a novel cuisine.

George Rathke remembers the mine blowing a track off Jackie Gallagher's tank: 'Back in England I had been on a course on anti-tank mines. Somebody remembered, and I was instructed to go forward on foot to see if there were further mines in the area we were going to pass through. I discovered, lifted, and made safe some fifteen mines in the area; they were made safe by inserting split pins in the detonators. All the mines were British.'

Les Arnold also remembers Jackie Gallagher's track being blown off and much else besides:

On 26 June we stood-to at about 4.30 a.m. and could hear the intense bombardment being put down by our artillery. We moved out of laager about 7.30 and immediately two B Squadron Churchills ran on to landmines – we believed they were Canadian. We left them behind, crossed the Caen–Bayeux road and moved through early morning mist and cornfields towards St. Manvieu. We were accompanied by some infantry of the 15th Scottish and apart from some small arms fire we encountered little opposition. We did fire HE and Besa to deal with Spandau fire from a small copse. The infantry captured some Hitler Youth soldiers who came swaggering into our lines; this attitude annoyed us particularly because we had heard that some of their units had shot Canadian prisoners. We proceeded round St. Manvieu towards Cheux with two B Squadron troops and diverted through a sunken lane. It was getting busy now and we were nose to tail with bren carriers and artillery; we were also under mortar fire. We left the lane and took to the fields and continued towards Cheux. As we approached the village we received small arms fire from a barn and replied with HE. Just after midday we received orders to retire back towards St. Manvieu. As we withdrew we saw a couple of Shermans on fire a few fields away, probably part of the 11th Armoured Division. We had a brew and then later in the afternoon we moved out to support some infantry who were trying to take a strong point south of Cheux.

We did this with caution because two Churchills and a Cromwell were on fire just there, one of the Churchills with its turret blown off. We pulled back close to St. Manvieu for the night, during which an ammunition quad was hit by '88 fire and exploded. Later in the evening some 141 RAC Crocodiles set fire to woods and buildings close by which held snipers and other enemy troops. These burnt most of the night and the enemy concentrated artillery and mortar fire on them; so we stayed in the tanks or dug in under them.

Freddie Smart remembers the mines at B Squadron's start line as well: 'We were just making a final brew, and the water was coming to the boil on the pressure stove. Suddenly there was a loud explosion in the squadron area. "Mortars!" someone shouted. There was an immediate rush to get everything and everybody into the tanks. The water was spilt, the pressure stove put out, the whole thing tumbled into the tank. But no more mortars? It's not a mortar, some stupid prat ran over a mine. So we set out for the start line, even more edgy because of the mine explosion, and still thirsty!'

Reg Terrington was wireless-op to Peter Beale, commanding 8 Troop. He recalls: 'We crossed the start line and after a short while we were in the middle of a substantial barrage of shells. We couldn't tell whether they were ours or theirs but either way it was most unpleasant. Peter told me afterwards I looked a bit green but I was still smiling. He looked the same!' A and B Squadrons reached their objectives without too much difficulty and with relatively few casualties. But as the War Diary has told, C Squadron had a much tougher and a much longer day. This is reflected in the memories of some of the crews.

Bob Anderson, troop sergeant of 12 Troop: 'Early on 26 June my troop commander, Frank Drew, was called to Squadron HQ to take over as Squadron 2 i/c. So I took his position as troop commander. We went into action for the first time at Cheux. My troop came under heavy fire from German '88s and all three tanks were knocked out by hits right through the front.

My driver, Dave Gotobed, was badly wounded. We managed to lift him free of the tank and were attending to him when the ambulance jeep arrived and took over. That was the last time we saw Dave. He died before he reached a hospital. In the confusion after we were hit my wireless operator disappeared; I don't know whether he was taken prisoner or not but we never saw him again. My corporal's tank was also knocked out but no casualties. My third tank was hit exactly the same as mine and the driver Roy Painter was severely injured and died the next day. The remainder of my crew, Vernon Lovell, John Thompson and myself spent the night in a knocked out 15-cwt truck, and we rejoined the squadron next day. I was issued with a new tank, a new driver, Roy, and a new wireless-op Ronnie.'

Fred Glasspool was wireless-op to Corporal Bill Starkey, troop corporal of 15 Troop. Their tank was called *Irlam*. 'Our first knowledge of the real thing was at Cheux. As green troops *Irlam* came out on to high ground and before we had fired a shot in anger our track was smashed and the turret wouldn't traverse. We bailed out into a cornfield and found our way back to the infantry through a hedgerow. The Recce Officer's scout car was there and we were pointed in the right direction by his driver Jack Woods. We all had a lot of admiration for the Recce Officer and his group.'

The Recce Officer of C Squadron was Captain Ken Kidd, and Jack Woods explains how he came to be Ken's driver on 26 June:

The battalion having been warned for action with the 15th Scottish Division in the forthcoming battle for the Odon River code-named Epsom we moved forward into the division's 25 pdr. area where we received a rollicking from the Echelon Commander for not digging in. Digging in! Who did he think we were, Infantry? The echelon was later to realize the wisdom of his words, but the MT bods had dug a hole big enough to lose a vehicle in and they had a good card school going on, nothing was happening, they were comfortable and what the hell! Briefed on the coming battle by the Squadron Leader we learned that the battalion was to advance through Cheux, C Squadron executing a right hook to support the Gordon Highlanders through Colleville, didn't mean much to me at the time. However, I was summoned to report with my kit to the Reconnaissance Officer, Captain Ken Kidd, who needed a driver for his scout car, his driver L/Cpl. Farmer having managed to do a hatch job on his fingers and therefore couldn't drive. Captain Kidd gave me permission to drive around a bit in the car to get used to it and the next morning together with the RO and Tpr. Egan, his operator, I went into battle for the first time in my life. It was a lousy day, pouring with rain. We passed some of the 7 Bn RTR Churchills being loaded back with ominous holes in their turrets just to cheer us up and spent a very wet and uncomfortable day as part of the Gordons' CO's convoy, finally getting up to the tanks later in the day and witnessing a scene which was to remain with me for the rest of my life, C Squadron Churchills on the skyline blazing merrily and pouring out dense clouds of black smoke with their ammunition going off like a firework display. Their de-horsed crews (those who were still alive) were coming back through the corn, their faces registering the shock of what had just happened to them. The infantry, having been unable to reach their objective, were returning also and were regrouping on the road prior to digging in defensively. Captain Kidd asked the infantry if we could be of any use to them, but his offer was politely declined. We then rejoined the squadron to learn the story of the battle and the losses. What shook us all was the fact that we had been encouraged to believe that our Churchill tanks were practically invincible and the truth was very sobering indeed.

Irlam was the troop corporal's tank of 15 Troop, and the troop sergeant's tank *Ilkley* was commanded by Dickie Hall. His account starts on the evening of 25 June:

We were all told that the following day would be our first action. That evening the Padre came round and we had a few prayers; I think we all felt better for it. Next morning the whole squadron set off in line ahead and had many pauses which lasted into the afternoon. We heard on the radio that A and B Squadrons were in action – snippets of talk on the intercom and the A set; quite a few German prisoners were marched past looking very glum. Our time came late in the afternoon. We were to advance through the village of Cheux and up on to the ridge where there would be little opposition. Then we were to move on to the next ridge and try to secure a crossing of the River Odon. It started to rain and as we were approaching the ridge on the right flank we saw some tanks had been hit and set on fire. I saw green tracer coming towards us, one to the left and one to the right. The third was a direct hit on the turret.

We fired back along the ridge at what was either a Tiger or a Panther, and reversed to be able to come up again in a different position. This we did and ended up three-quarters on to him. We came under fire straight away and received several more hits, mostly on the hull. Because we were at an angle to the enemy none of the shots penetrated the armour, but when we tried to reverse prior to coming up on to the ridge again my driver Bill Cruickshanks told me he had lost his hydraulics. As we were still under fire it was only a matter of time before we would lose the crew as well as poor old *Ilkley*.

I gave the order to get out, and we all met up in a large shell-hole nearby. We came under mortar and sniper fire, but due to the very wet cornfield no one was hit, although many mortars landed very close. We all walked back through Cheux and reported to the B echelon vehicles. I have a blank as to what followed. I remember sleeping that night in a tent, and later we were kitted out and given a new tank.

Taffy Leyshon was with 11 Troop: 'Our first action was at Cheux, our first casualty was Corporal Sid Chapman. Our tank was hit twice and we lost a bogie and the exhaust pipes. We lost the squadron, but three of the lost tanks picked up about twelve wounded soldiers from 15th Division and took them to their regimental aid post. After the war I met one of them and he told me how relieved he was to be picked up.'

Tom Tomney was troop sergeant of 13 Troop, and his driver was Cyril Rees. Cyril had just seen the awesome bulk of a captured Tiger, but before having too much time to ponder on it they were ordered to mount:

Our forming up point was a large fairly flat field growing a crop of flax. It was criss-crossed by tracks of various vehicles which had reduced this crop to a series of rectangles, squares, triangles or other geometric forms of various sizes, all spoilt. I started the engine and closed the top hatches, leaving the visor open. The oil pressure and the ammeter readings were satisfactory. We had topped up with petrol so both gauges showed full. There was no need to look at the water temperature because we had only just started up. 'Driver advance' came Tom's instruction over my headset. I engaged first gear, let in the clutch, and we were off. Tom had already told me the approximate part of the crest I was to make for so I was able to choose my route. We passed the burned-out skeleton of the Matador and shortly began to climb. We were approaching a tree-lined road which crossed from right to left. I selected a convenient gap between two trees; the road was higher at this point so there was a small bank, about 3 feet high but not too steep. I started to climb in 2nd gear, then with a stall change to 1st dropped gently on to the road. With a minor steering change we passed between two more trees on the other side of the road, changing direction to bring us at roughly right angles to the crest ahead. We climbed steadily and stopped short in a hull down position. It had by now started to rain heavily and this was drifting through the top hatches. Shortly, Tom ordered 'driver advance' and we were over the crest in a few minutes. Now I could feel the adrenalin pumping! I changed up and as we got near the start line Tom ordered me to close my visor. This created a dreadful dilemma because the periscopes which were my sole vision of the terrain ahead were covered with mud thrown up by our mudguard-less tracks.

I was now driving blind, and was relying on the occasional short sharp direction from Tom, but he had his own problems. Should I open the visor, or should I stop and clean the periscopes? Both options were tactically impossible. I drove on in second gear trying to get as near as I could to the eyepiece to see where I was going. A few minutes later the front of the tank dropped sharply and the front idlers buried themselves in the far side of an anti-tank ditch. I tried first gear to try and pull us out, but to no avail. I tried reverse gear with the same result.

So what happens now? Where were we? The tank was at a fairly steep angle, I guessed about 45 degrees. The rain, pouring in through all the hatches, ran through to the front compartment, and we could splash our feet about in the small pools that were forming. And what was happening to the rest of the squadron?

We could hear scraps of messages floating about on the headphones but the atmospherics made deciphering difficult. It did seem, though, that the squadron had lost tanks and suffered casualties. I deemed it safe to run the engine now and then (in spite of the steep angle) in order to top up the batteries.

We could hear noises of battle close at hand, explosions and machine-gun fire. Don Foster decided to open his hatch a little to see where we were. I opened mine a couple of inches to look around as much as possible. Countryside on my right but to the left was a farm, and beyond that what must be the tower of Cheux Church, together with a number of stone-built houses. I decided to push the hatch further open to get a better view. At that moment, something struck the cast steel cover over the ventilating fan outlet and whistled off – seemingly to the right. Maybe we were targeted? Was there a sniper in the church tower? It would have been ideal if Tom could have checked with his binoculars, but clearly he couldn't risk putting his head out of the hatch. I raised my hatch again slightly to see if I could spot any movement but it was too gloomy. We wondered if we could put an HE through the louvres near the top of the tower, but the angle we were at made traversing the turret to line up on this target difficult. It was now drizzling and it was getting darker. A Sherman approached slowly from our left front, with the commander and operator both with their heads out above the hatches and clearly making for the rear area. I used this opportunity to leap out of our tank, and, keeping low, ran across to stop the Sherman to ask the crew to try and pull us out. They declined forcibly and told us to get our own recovery tank to do the job. (On reflection, the Sherman would not have been man enough for this job.) By this time it was getting dark, some infantry were straggling back looking pretty tired plus the occasional carrier and tank. It was a great relief when our Armoured Recovery Vehicle turned up and made short work of towing us out of the ditch. We followed the ARV for about twenty minutes until we found an area with lots of tanks parked and infantry putting up bivouacs. We rigged our tarpaulin up on to the tank in the usual manner, put another one on the ground, unrolled our bedding rolls, and wet, cold, tired, and dirty, we were asleep in double-quick time. In the morning it had stopped raining, but a depressing sight met our eyes. A pile of casualties was laid along a hedge about 30 feet from where we had spent the night.

A quick wash and a brew-up renewed our spirits and Tom had now got a map reference of the present squadron laager which was about a mile away. It wasn't long before we once more rejoined the fold. We parked alongside a hedge with the rest of our troop who thought we had bought it. The rest of the squadron were dispersed round the field and were camouflaged. It was fairly early in the morning and very soon we were all ordered to parade immediately. We hadn't forgotten how to parade properly, even under these conditions. Then the SSM, Phil Edwards, called the roll. Dave Gotobed, Roy Painter, Sid Chapman and Ted Keeble were missing.

A quiet and subdued squadron left the parade. We had served our apprenticeship and had become soldiers in 24 hours. Most of us had stories to relate as we went about making ourselves a meal and getting cleaned up. Most of us had got away with it – this time. I counted my blessings as we got stuck into some maintenance and tried not to dwell too much on the future.

Trevor Greenwood's record of 26 June was made on 27 June:

Yesterday, I had grave doubts as to whether this page would ever be written. I felt as though I had been condemned to death. But it is obvious that I have survived. We left harbour at 7 a.m. for the front line, only about 3 miles away. Held up for an hour en route . . . slap in the middle of a concentration of our artillery. And they had just started a barrage. What pandemonium! The earth itself shook noticeably. Jerry must have had a hell of a time. Village of Cheux had only been taken by our troops that morning, and there was much evidence of the battle. The stench of dead cows in adjoining fields was awful. Several human corpses along route . . . one, recognizable as a Jerry by torn bits of uniform, had been run over on the verge, and tanks had subsequently passed over his body. It was just a pulpy mass of bloody flesh and bones. No one appeared to be bothered by it. Our own troops were too busy 'digging in' against possible counter-attack to worry about dead bodies. The village itself was a shambles . . . just a mass of gaunt-looking walls and chimney-pots, with a few remaining houses full of shell-holes. Snipers were still busy in some of these houses. Kept my head down! Beyond village, everything was bustle and chaos. Enormous numbers of men and vehicles moving forward.

We took up our start position in a large field below the crest of a hill: 5.00 p.m. Our infantry were in position too . . . some hundreds of them. Had seen them on the way down. A sturdy looking crowd . . . mostly Scotties . . . all smiling and cheerful. I think they were really glad to have our support. They asked us to swipe hell out of Jerry!

Had previously received our orders and were thoroughly conversant with plan of attack and ultimate objective. We also had a pretty good idea of where enemy's main anti-tank guns were, from previous reconnaissance. Close to our zero hour, word came through that sixty Panthers had appeared within a few hundred yards of our line of advance. Hells bells! Poor little C Squadron!

But very soon, and before we started, the Panthers advanced on our position and were engaged by some fairly heavy stuff . . . 17- pounders, I think. After about an hour, Jerry must have retired: he certainly didn't get through! . . . and we commenced our delayed start at 6.15 pm. Infantry ahead and rifles at the ready over the crest . . . towards the woods where we knew there would be trouble. By 7.00 p.m. the battle was on. Anti-tank guns were firing like hell . . . and so were we. Very soon, I saw one crew bale out, tank on fire. They crawled away in the long corn, avoiding Jerry snipers and machine-guns. Advance proceeded: infantry kept 'going to ground' because of Jerry's machine-guns. We sprayed those woods with Besa, tons of it . . . and HE and AP . . . and smoke. Impossible to see anti-tank guns in woods. Could only fire at their 'flash'. Advance proceeded slowly: two or three Jerry tanks appeared and were engaged: they disappeared. More of ours were hit: some burning . . . crews bailing out.

Found myself behaving rationally and quite calm. Was really terrified just prior to 'going in'. Eventually we retired and waited . . . it seemed hours to me. We were on the battlefield all the time. We should have left, but stayed in case infantry required more assistance. Good job we did. We had to advance a second time later on to help them out. Awful business. Major Holden was grand. Picked up many men and some wounded – one stretcher case, and removed them to rear. Were in action until it was too dark to see . . . must have been 10.30 p.m. Our loss eight vehicles, all blazing away when we finally departed about 1.00 a.m. Next had difficulty in returning to our lines. Front very fluid and we might have been shot up as an enemy counter-attack if not careful. Recce Officer Ken Kidd went ahead to contact our forward troops.

Eventually crawled into Cheux about 2.00 a.m. Lay quietly in Cheux: guard on each vehicle. Snipers still in ruined building, firing constantly. Left Cheux 4.30 a.m . . . only just in time: heard later that enemy counter-attacked Cheux soon after we left, using Tigers etc. But our troops retained the village. Eventually harboured couple of miles behind front line, and learned we were scheduled for another attack immediately! Thanks to Major's strong protest we remained in harbour for rest etc. Had no sleep for two nights and no food for many hours. Even water was a godsend during the action. Vehicles also need attention . . . those that remained! Disappointing result to our hard fight; no advance made at all. Infantry badly beaten up. Opposition was far greater than anticipated. Where were our aircraft as promised? May have been weather. There was a terrible deluge during the height of action. Periscopes almost useless; much water in vehicle; clothes soaked to saturation; infantry must have been half drowned. They had a bad time; survivors we picked up were thankful for our re-appearance. Pity we couldn't have saved more of them: a grand lot of lads.

'EPSOM': CONSOLIDATION AND CLOSE DOWN

The broad picture, 27 June–2 July 1944

One of the aims of Montgomery's bridgehead strategy was to draw German armour on to the British sector of the front. This is exactly what the first day of Epsom did. The six German armoured divisions already in Normandy grouped to make a counter-attack on the 'Scottish Corridor'. The II SS Panzer Corps, summoned from Russia on 12 June, arrived in Normandy between 25 and 27 June, and was thrown piecemeal into the counter-attack. The German armoured divisions were armed with Panzer Mark IVs and Panzer Mark Vs (Panthers). The Churchill had a reasonable chance against the Mark IV, but the Panther was very difficult to knock out. And there were three heavy tank battalions of the Mark VI, or Tiger, that were even more formidable.

The remaining days of Epsom consisted of attempts by the British to lengthen the corridor, counter-attacks by the Germans, and finally withdrawal and consolidation by the British, leaving a bridgehead over the River Odon. An evaluation of Epsom after the event summed up the positives and negatives in this way. In terms of ground, it had been no more than half a success. In terms of lives it had been extremely costly, roughly a quarter of the infantry having been killed or wounded. But in terms of strategy it was a three-fold triumph: German armour was pinned down to the British sector, giving the Americans a better chance to break out of the western end of the bridgehead; by creating threat after threat Montgomery forced the Germans to react to him, and denied them the opportunity to mount a massive offensive of their own to split the bridgehead in two; the move of the formidable II SS Panzer Corps from Russia made it easier for the Russians to crack the Germans on the eastern front shortly afterwards

As far as the 15th Scottish Division, 31 Tank Brigade and 9 RTR were concerned it meant that these few days were spent in a number of efforts to push forward to the River Odon and beyond, forming up to meet counter-attacks, and being subjected to fairly constant shelling and mortaring, as well as the odd visit from a German plane.

The War Diary

27 June: A and B Squadrons carried out mopping up operations south of Cheux in the area Grainville-sur-Odon and Colleville. Here again the fighting was fierce with Panthers infiltrating from a flank after an area had been cleared. Some German armour remained well camouflaged

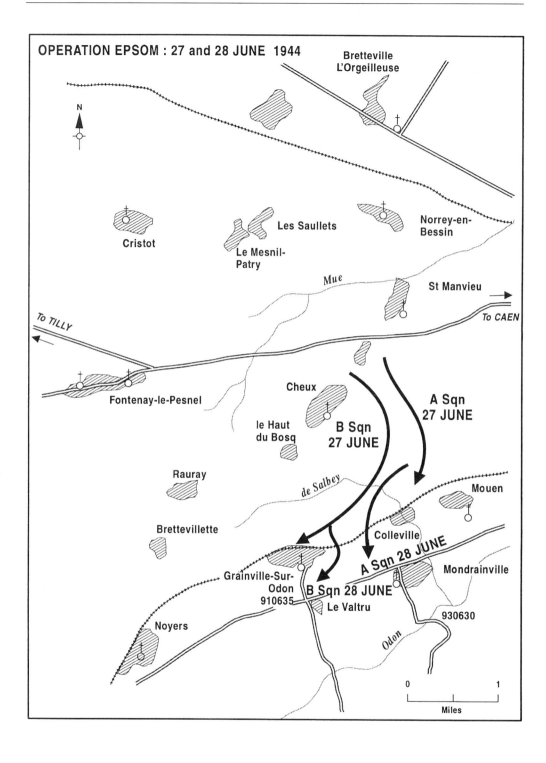

OPERATION EPSOM : 27 and 28 JUNE 1944

Bretteville
L'Orgeilleuse

N

Cristot

Les Saullets

Le Mesnil-
Patry

Norrey-en-
Bessin

Mue

St Manvieu

To TILLY

To CAEN

Fontenay-le-Pesnel

Cheux

le Haut
du Bosq

B Sqn
27 JUNE

A Sqn
27 JUNE

Rauray

de Salbey

Mouen

Brettevillette

Colleville

A Sqn 28 JUNE

Mondrainville

Grainville-Sur-
Odon
910635

B Sqn 28 JUNE

Le Valtru

930630

Noyers

Odon

0   1
Miles

in an orchard behind a hedgerow and opened up only at point-blank range. Ten Panthers were located in this area and two of our tanks were lost. Lt. Mott (9 Troop, B Squadron) was severely wounded, having his legs amputated below the knee. By dusk infantry had been supported into Grainville and Colleville and were firmly established. The tanks laagered north of the Caen–Noyers railway line.

28 June: By 0950 hrs A and B Squadrons had put the 9th Cameronians on the crossroads between Grainville and Le Valtru. The opposition was strong with enemy tanks resisting and counter-attacks being frequently made from the direction of Noyers and Haut des Forges north-east towards Grainville and Le Valtru. Three Panthers had been destroyed, however, during the day.

29 June: At first light C Squadron relieved A and B Squadrons and took up a position south of the railway crossing at Colleville. Elements of 11th Armoured Division had now crossed the River Odon at and were in position on Hill 112. C Squadron were shelled and mortared during the day, standing at immediate notice to support the infantry should further counter-attacks develop on Grainville. At 1800 hrs a strong infantry and tank counter-attack developed. Two Panthers had infiltrated into Grainville and German infantry were attacking Le Valtru. C Squadron deployed north-west of crossroads and gave all support possible, and it was estimated that 600 enemy dead were left on the ground as a result. C Squadron Reconnaissance Officer, Capt. K.A. Kidd, worked magnificently during the action to maintain co-operation between the tanks and the infantry, and was later awarded the MC. Following this abortive attack an armoured counter-attack was made south of Haut du Bosq, but this was also later repulsed. C Squadron remained in position till dark. The only casualties were due to mortaring, which had also damaged two tanks.

30 June: 11th Armoured Division withdrew during the night and C Squadron stood by at 0430 hrs under the threat of another counter-attack. Nothing developed until the afternoon when sixty tanks of 9th SS Panzer Division attempted to cut off all troops south of Cheux by again attacking Haut du Bosq; this was beaten off. C Squadron were relieved by 7 RTR and joined the battalion north of Cheux in time to watch RAF bombing enemy tank concentrations in the Villers Bocage area. This was the first time that the RAF had been seen in action and morale rose considerably.

1–2 July: The battalion stood by to repulse further counter-attacks in conjunction with 43rd Division. The plans were never put into effect and it appeared that the Germans had decided not to reinforce failure.

Personal recollections, 27–30 June

As the War Diary records, A and B Squadrons were in action on 27 June, pushing south and south-west towards the Odon, but subjected from time to time to German counter-attacks. Les Arnold was in one of the BHQ OP tanks, and had been joined by his Royal Artillery Major some days before. The Major commanded the tank and had his own wireless operator to communicate with his gun batteries. This meant that Les acted as the tank gunner but also had to operate the wireless set on the regimental net. 'The whole set-up gave Dicky Carr (the driver) and me nightmares. The artillery people had no idea of tank crew procedures such as driver start up and gun traverse details so we had to do our own thing up to a point. I was given gun control which is as you know very difficult because visibility through the telescope is so limited. I am convinced to this day that on the odd occasion when I looked out of the turret that we were erroneously some distance ahead of the rest of the Second Army.' Specifically on 27 June Les and Dicky got up early:

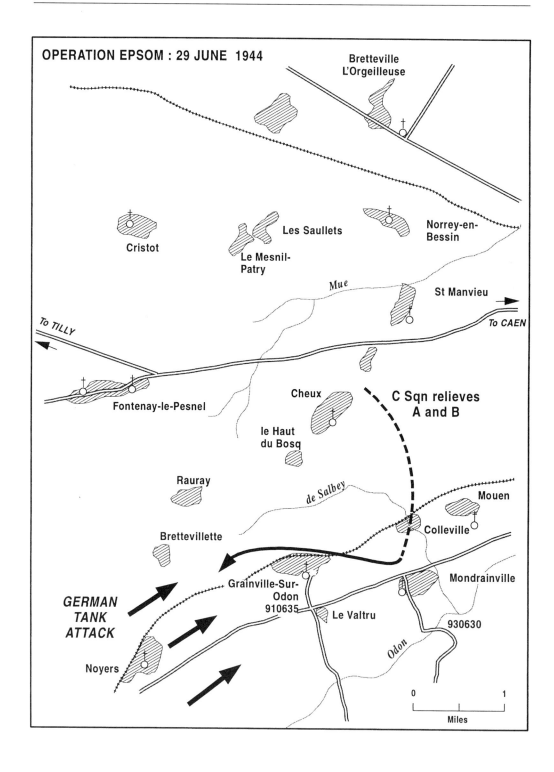

OPERATION EPSOM : 29 JUNE 1944

Bretteville
L'Orgeilleuse

Les Saullets

Norrey-en-
Bessin

Cristot

Le Mesnil-
Patry

Mue

St Manvieu

To TILLY

To CAEN

Fontenay-le-Pesnel

Cheux

C Sqn relieves
A and B

le Haut
du Bosq

Rauray

de Salbey

Mouen

Brettevillette

Colleville

Mondrainville

GERMAN
TANK
ATTACK

Grainville-Sur-
Odon
910635

Le Valtru

930630

Odon

Noyers

0   1

Miles

We stood to at 4.30 a.m. and our artillery Major went off to a briefing with Bob Warren. Just before midday we moved out picking up some infantry from the 43rd Wessex. They climbed on to the tank and we proceeded towards Colleville; we were getting some rain and the smell of dead cattle and horses was quite sickening. We passed through some mortar fire and then some wounded being transported on jeeps. We went along a narrow lane where the banks and the overhanging branches restricted turret traverse. We moved off the lane into a field where we were fired at by what we believed to be Panthers. Some Shermans were on fire so we moved carefully. Our artillery Major decided to call down a barrage of 25-pdrs to move the German tanks holding up infantry of the Rifle Brigade. This seemed to work because the infantry moved out of their dug-in positions and attacked over the ridge with Piats.

We then moved towards Grainville which we heard had been cleared by 11th Armoured Division. Things quietened down then and we were able to have a quick brew up. Late in the afternoon we pulled on to a high point near Grainville from where we could see the houses of Grainville and Colleville. I immediately noticed through the gunner's telescope some armour and half-tracks crossing into a wood below and asked the artillery Major for firing instructions. He said he thought they were ours, but to me they were almost certainly Mark IVs or Panthers. And about half an hour later two of our Churchills down near the village were hit by enemy fire. We drew back from the edge of the hill and the Major called for 25-pounder fire on the point where the armour had entered the wood. After the gunners had put down a couple of salvoes an infantry officer hurried across to us and asked us to stop firing as it was dropping on his troops who were attempting to get into the wood. We then had a troubled night with Very lights falling in the valley below and we stood to all night keeping a turret watch.

The tanks that Les saw being hit were a part of a group comprising 8 Troop (Peter Beale), 9 Troop (Teddy Mott) and 10 Troop (Geoff Brewer) from B Squadron. They had advanced down from the high ground south of Cheux in the direction of Colleville and then had wheeled right with the outskirts of Grainville as their objective. The situation was fluid, and counter-attacks could be expected at any time. Geoff Brewer advanced first and reached Grainville, but on the way his sergeant's tank, commanded by Harry Simmons, was hit. Harry and Johnnie Jebb were wounded, and Mike Crawley and Ted Mycroft were killed. Ken Virgo commanded 10 Baker, and when halted on the outskirts of Grainville had an altercation with a persistent young German who wanted to drop a hand grenade or some other unpleasantry into Ken's tank. The result was an early grave for the German and a Military Medal for Ken. 8 Troop followed behind 10. Peter had only two tanks at that moment, because Corporal Johnnie Walker's 8 Baker was temporarily off the road with a mechanical problem. Moving across the fields from Colleville towards Grainville Sgt. Reg Evans was on the left. His tank was fired on by enemy in the woods to the south. The projectile did not penetrate the side of the hull, but the concussion set off the smoke discharger at the back of the tank. 'Bail out', shouted Reg to the crew, and acted on his own command and took off rapidly north-east through the corn. The rest of the crew dismounted less rapidly, but Ronnie Larner, the driver, stayed in the tank and continued to drive it steadily towards Grainville. Jimmy Aldcroft, Charlie Mansell and Roy Barber walked on the lee side of the tank as it drove forward, but after a short while they thought 'stuff this for a game of soldiers' and got back into the tank. Jimmy commanded the tank for the rest of the day and in recognition of his initiative and good sense was awarded a mention in despatches and promoted to lance-corporal. On being asked later what it felt like when the enemy AP shot hit the hull close to where he was sitting, gunner Charlie Mansell replied: 'It certainly warmed up my arse.'

Shortly after 8 and 10 had reached Grainville Teddy Mott's 9 Troop was sent round to the south of the village to clear its southern flank. But in a hedgerow a German tank waited unseen until Teddy was 100 yards or so away and then opened fire. Teddy's driver and gunner, Wally Anderson and Bob Myring, were both killed. Jimmy Deem and Jock Robertson were both wounded and burned, and both of Teddy's legs were smashed below the knee. He managed to get out of the tank himself, but left one leg on the track guard and had the other amputated after he had crawled back through the fields and been taken by ambulance jeep to the medical services.

George Rathke was Teddy's troop sergeant, and remembers Grainville very well.

On 27 June B Squadron was given the job of taking Grainville-sur-Odon, a small village completely surrounded by orchards. 10 Troop went in and came under anti-tank fire. Sgt. 'Cushy' Simmons' tank was hit and Simmons wounded, and the other two tanks were pinned down and unable to move.

9 Troop under Teddy Mott was then sent to try an out-flanking movement round the southern side of the village. We moved off, myself as troop sergeant in *Immune* on the right, Teddy in *Inspire* in the centre, and Cpl. Jakeman in *Impulse* on the left.

We came to a gap in the trees and being on the right I was the first to turn into the opening. I found myself facing the village church some 150 yards away, and in front of the church a Honey recce tank burning fiercely – I never did find out who it belonged to. I halted and Teddy came alongside on my left and proceeded a few yards further forward and then halted.

I had just started to talk to Teddy when there was a big flash and *Inspire* was hit, flames belching out of the turret. I saw the wireless-op Jimmy Deem throw himself out of the turret and then heard a shell, presumably aimed at my tank, whistle overhead. I had by then told my wireless-op Bert Watson to send out smoke from the 2-inch mortar; I also directed my gunner George Rawe on to the spot where I thought the shots were coming from, and we fired two AP rounds and began to reverse having concealed ourselves in smoke.

Having reversed about 100 yards I halted and looked around for any survivors from *Inspire*. I spotted Jimmy Deem running toward some other tanks of the squadron among the orchards. Suddenly several German machine-guns opened up on him and he fell to the ground. We engaged the machine-guns with Besa and also fired a couple of HE shells into the hedgerows concealing the German machine-guns. All this happened in a matter of minutes – which seemed like hours.

I reported the incident to the Squadron Leader, Major Bob Warren, and was instructed to return to the squadron. Having got back and dismounted from *Immune* I heard a shout, and moving to the edge of the trees I saw Jimmy Deem, limping badly, coming towards us. Several of us ran forward and helped him back, and he was soon on his way to hospital.

The following morning I was sent in *Immune* down the main street of Grainville to do a recce. I was full of apprehension, but fortunately found that the Germans had evacuated the village during the night. Was I relieved!

After their immense efforts on 26 June and the very strong representations of Squadron Leader Ronnie Holden, most of C Squadron had 27 and 28 June to rest and refit. But not all, as Jack Woods remembers (Jack was at that time driving the squadron's Humber scout car):

The squadron had been given two days off to 'lick its wounds' as the Squadron Leader put it, the replacement tanks were coming up and the fitters were busy welding track plates as a sort of 'applique armour' but for us it was away first thing to report to Infantry Brigade HQ where we found an armoured counter-attack coming in. Their Brigadier was standing in the middle of the road with his arms outstretched, exhorting the bewildered Jocks who were streaming up the road to go back to their positions, and there were rumours of a breakthrough by Tiger tanks. After a short stay we left to visit the infantry positions, passing through Colleville where we were nicely stonked and where I saw my first dead enemy, a small group led by a sergeant and freshly killed, the Jocks who had done the job crouching under a nearby hedgerow. Along a nearby road, where on a crossroads a half track was burning merrily its infantry component hanging over the side all killed. Then into the infantry positions via the hedgerow which was too steep for the car which duly bellied and had to be extracted by a Bren carrier while a Spandau stitched a line of bullets up our backs. Mission accomplished and away by an easier exit and back along that road – it transpired afterwards that at the time the road was the front line – and into enemy territory where the Recce Officer left us to recce on foot with instructions to come and get him if he was longer than ten minutes. How green we were, standing in the road with not a personal weapon in sight and the Bren stowed. He returned, we did a smart about turn and hared off at the double the way we came, straight over the crossroads and into friendly infantry positions, where as there were enemy tanks coming up the road behind us it was decided to abandon the car and bail out. What I remember of the rest of the day is of a PzKw MK IV being knocked out by an infantry 6-pdr and the Recce Officer capturing the commander's cap and then disappearing in the general direction of the mêlée, and of Tpr. Egan crouched by the side of the car at the open escape door trying to raise the squadron: 'Hello Sugar Niner, Hello Sugar Niner, report my signals', time and time again and finally getting through after using as many aerial extensions as he could find and the squadron suddenly appearing over the horizon like a cavalry charge.

In the period 27 to 30 June the three sabre squadrons were all in action for much of the time, but it so happened that on the 27th most of the casualties were in B Squadron, as has been described, on the 28th most of the casualties were in A and on the 29th in C.

Ray Gordon, 2 Troop, A Squadron: 'On 28 June A Squadron were in action in the Colleville/Grainville/Cheux area. I remember seeing a wounded infantry soldier with his arm hanging off who we directed to a medical unit; the memory of many dead cattle with stiff legs pointing to the sky, bloated like balloons and an overwhelming stench. A German tank appeared at an angle between trees in a small wood. Jock ordered Dickie to fire and it was hit broadside (it couldn't traverse its turret thank goodness), the crew jumped out and our Besas started speaking. Later that day I saw flame-throwing Churchills attack a stone farmhouse – the horrifying hiss as the flames hit and stuck on the building.

On this day A and B Squadrons helped the 9th Cameronians on to the crossroads between Grainville and Le Valtru, and then received several counter-attacks from the south and west. In A Squadron there were casualties in 1, 2 and 3 Troops. Jim Hutton, driver to George Hendrie commanding 1 Troop, tells on tape some of what happened:

I also heard Ted Costin and his crew – Corporal Jackson – heard them being engaged by a Tiger tank as they came through the hedgerow at Colleville when three of their crew members were killed. That was the last I heard of Ted. He was buried near Cheux, in the evening after the action in a shallow grave and I went to the service there, very moving. Never forget poor old Ted. The other two were Jock Pettigrew and John Samuels.

Anyway, in the action at Cheux, my troop was engaged in taking on two German armoured vehicles, I believe one was a Panther and other was a Mark IV. We were told that they had been knocked out, that smoke was coming from the Mark IV and we went up to this

Crew of troop corporal's tank Impetuous, *3 Troop, A Squadron, Farnborough, May 1944. Back row: Ted Costin (driver), Cpl. Jim Hudson (tank commander), John Samuels (co-driver). Front row: Jock Pettigrew (wireless-op), Tpr Woods (gunner). Ted, John and Jock were killed in an engagement with a German tank at Colleville on 28 June 1944.*

hedgerow, and as you know the driver on a hedgerow is just looking at the hedge and turret is in a hull down position and just the turret poking over the top. Tony Lyall nipped off in between the tracks and the hedge and he was doing his business. And while this was going on this German tank gunner climbed back into what we thought was a knocked out Panther and opened up. He fired a shot and it hit the top of the turret next to Trooper Butterfield who was sitting on the top and it splashed him with fragments and I remember his face getting smothered in blood. But it just nicked a little vein on his forehead and of course the blood spurted out cause it was a red hot fragment that hit him. The next thing we got one smack in the turret which penetrated the triangle dead centre on the front of the turret and the shot penetrated the 2-inch phosphorus grenades and set them off. Kit Harlow, our gunner, was sprayed with all the phosphorus. He came out screaming his head off and bailed out and Jimmy Bennell took the full force of the shot through his stomach and that killed him instantly. I was knocked unconscious with the impact and when I came around the pannier door was open and my co-driver was gone and I happened to shake myself and get me head together and doing so I got a perforated eardrum and me ear was terrible, terrible pain I got from me left ear. And I got out and we managed to get hold of Kit Harlow and we got together the crew and we made our way around the back of the tanks to where the infantry were. German snipers and the Germans and the British were all firing at us because they didn't know who we were, they thought we were Germans and the others thought we were British and it was all over the place. Anyway we got back to where we thought the British were and they happened to be the 53rd Welsh Division who we were with at Charing. This

Welsh chap called out 'Hande hoch, stick yer hands up' and I said to him 'You get stuffed you Welsh git, I'm English' and they said 'Oh alright boyo' and we made our way back. Anyway we got back and we went back to forward recovery and we managed to get a new tank and replenished and we spent the night at the back and came forward again to the regiment.

On 29 June C Squadron came back into action. As the War Diary recalls they took a lot of shelling and mortaring in the morning, and then did some sterling work near Le Valtru in the afternoon. In fact their casualties during the day were only three people wounded, and two of them recount how it happened:

Sergeant Bob Anderson, 12 Troop:

On 29 June we went back into action. This time we came under heavy mortar fire. A mortar shell landed on top of my turret and as my head was out at the time I took the blast in the face. I think it landed so close that most of the blast went over my head. However, I was blown backwards, my head and neck hit the back of the cupola and I was blinded. I said 'I cannot see; bail out'. Now as the gunner sits in front of and below the commander he cannot bail out until the commander has. My gunner, Johnny Thompson 'assisted?' me by grasping me by the legs and throwing me out. As I went out the top my snatch plug caught on the cupola handlebars. The cord wrapped round my neck, my head again hit the turret, and my back hit the tracks. Johnny quickly loosened my headphones and I dropped to the ground. That was the last thing I remember until I rejoined the battalion on 10 August. [Not surprising!]

Sergeant Dickie Hall of 15 Troop was one of the other casualties:

With the new tanks a day or so later (29 June) we went into action again beyond Cheux. Once again there was much stopping and starting as we moved forwards through the many orchards, most of them bounded by earth banks topped with hedges (a little like Cornwall). We had been firing both guns and then two disasters happened. First Eddie Wild went to change the type of 75 mm shell, and when the breech was opened only the shell-case came out; all the cordite propellent was everywhere, and the shell was still in the barrel. The Besa co-ax stopped firing, and in clearing the stoppage we had a blowback into my right hand. As we could not fire at all we withdrew. I was making a lot of mess in the turret due to the cut in the artery in my hand! Back at the trucks I told the crew to clear the guns while I went to get my hand fixed. What happened next I don't know, but I found I was lying on a stretcher with a pair of forceps sticking out of my hand and being bound for Blighty. I felt bad at leaving the squadron under these conditions. We were put on an empty Tank Landing Craft, the whole deck area was taken up with stretchers.

CHAPTER 4

Hill 112

'JUPITER', 10 JULY 1944

The broad picture, 3–9 July

Pressure was kept up on the Germans at all points on the perimeter of the bridgehead, particularly at Carpiquet aerodrome and Caen. On 4 July the 3rd Canadian Infantry Division, supported by the tanks of the Fort Garry Horse and Crocodiles of the 79th Armoured, attacked the village of Carpiquet and the aerodrome. These were defended by 12th SS Panzer Division (Hitler Youth) under the command of Kurt Meyer. Though very few in numbers, the teenagers of the Hitler Youth were aided by a few tanks and '88s, very effective artillery and mortar fire, and the fact that Meyer was able to tap into the Canadians' radio transmissions. The Germans were forced out of Carpiquet, but not out of the aerodrome.

The next step for the Canadians and the British was a direct attack on Caen. At 2150 hrs on 7 July 2,500 tons of bombs were dropped on the northern outskirts of Caen. At 0420 hrs on 8 July I Corps launched the ground attack of Operation 'Charnwood', the capture of Caen. The 3rd British Infantry Division was on the left of the British advance, the 59th in the centre, and the 3rd Canadian Infantry were on the right, starting from where they were at Carpiquet. The attack had limited success, in that I Corps reached the line of the River Orne running through the centre of Caen, while the Germans pulled back into the industrial suburbs of Colombelles and Faubourg de Vaucelles.

The battle for Caen died down, but Montgomery needed to maintain pressure on the British front. The Americans had been attacking for a week and had made little progress. The 2nd SS Panzer Division, Das Reich, had been moved to the American sector, and Panzer Lehr was on its way.

Operation 'Jupiter', the plans for which had been drawn up some days before, had the strategic objective of bringing armour back to the British front, and the tactical objective of reaching the River Orne south of Caen. The specific objectives were: on the right flank of the advance Hill 112; on the left flank of the advance Chateau de Fontaine, Eterville, Maltot; and exploitation to the Orne at Feuguerolles. The British troops taking part in 'Jupiter' were: 43rd (Wessex) Infantry Division, plus 46 (Highland) Brigade and a brigade of the 3rd Canadian Infantry Division; tank support consisted of 31 Tank Brigade (7 RTR and 9 RTR), and 4 Armoured Brigade; artillery support was provided by the divisional artillery of 43rd Wessex, 15th Scottish, 53rd Welsh and 11th Armoured, as well as the heavier guns of two Army Groups Royal Artillery (AGRAs).

9 RTR in Operation 'Jupiter': before and during

Extracts from the War Diary

2–7 July: The battalion was concentrated north of Cheux and a recce was ordered in conjunction with 130 Brigade (43rd Div) of the area Verson – Eterville – Maltot. The recce had two purposes:
1. to find a suitable route across country, including a crossing of the River Odon, so that tanks could reach the area Fontaine–Etoupefour.

2.   to discover suitable forming up points (FUPs) for all squadrons prior to an attack south-east from Fontaine–Etoupefour.

No natural route was available, but with the Royal Engineers blasting trees, bulldozing hedgerows, and fording the river, a route was made and marked. All troop leaders went forward to know the location and nature of their respective FUPs, and then crawled forward to get a glimpse of the ground over which they might be attacking. During these recces it was possible to see the battle of Carpiquet aerodrome which the Canadians were still trying to capture. With the recce complete the battalion, less B Squadron, was ordered to rest and moved to south of Bronay. B Squadron moved to just north-east of Colleville with objects of counter-attacking any enemy advance from east or north-east and of blocking the Caen–Villers Bocage road.

7 July: B Squadron rejoined the battalion and during the evening a heavy raid by 450 bombers on the area north of Caen was watched with a certain amount of excitement.

9 July: Reports showed that I Corps was breaking into Caen from the north and east. By 1800 hrs all Caen north of the River Orne had been captured; Carpiquet aerodrome and the road Verson–Caen were also reported clear. Operation 'Jupiter' was now possible.

Plan: 31 Tank Brigade in support 43rd Division
        Right: 7 RTR, less B Squadron, with 129 Brigade to attack and capture Hill 112;
        Left: 9 RTR with 130 Brigade to capture Chateau de Fontaine, Eterville and Maltot.
Phase 1 (9 RTR): B Squadron with 5th Dorsets to Chateau de Fontaine at H-hour (0500 hrs).
Phase 2:   C Squadron with 4th Dorsets to Eterville at H + 75 minutes.
Phase 3:   A Squadron with 7th Hampshires to Maltot at H + 180 minutes.
Exploitation: 4 Armoured Brigade to move to St. Martin 9760 and Feuguerolles.
                 46 Brigade with B Squadron 7 RTR to advance north-east towards Caen.

At 2000 hrs 9 July the battalion moved to Forward Assembly Area (FAA) north-east of Colleville.

10 July: At 0300 hrs the battalion moved to FUP area Fontaine–Etoupefour. The move was covered by artillery and no difficulties were encountered. Battalion HQ was established at Bas de Mouen, just north of the River Odon.

Phase 1: At 0500 hrs B Squadron advanced with 5th Dorsets and in fifteen minutes Les Daims had been taken and only machine-gun fire had been encountered. It was known that elements of 10th SS Panzer Division threatened the left flank and twelve Panthers were reported roaming in the area of Eterville. A troop of 17-pounder self-propelled anti-tank guns (SPs) took up positions to guard against this threat while B Squadron pushed on to the Chateau. Resistance was still confined to machine-gun fire and snipers, and soon 6, 7 and 8 Troops were working round the Chateau. By 0552 hrs the 5th Dorsets had captured their objective; one tank had been lost on the left flank due to anti-tank fire later discovered to have been a 75/55 mm. At 0614 the objective was reported secure with the infantry firmly established on the line of the road from Fontaine–Etoupefour to Maltot. About thirty prisoners had been taken, a number killed, and at least six machine-gun positions destroyed.

Phase 2: By 0635 hrs C Squadron were advancing to Eterville with 4th Dorsets. As their Besa fire tore through the corn the Germans came forward with their hands up. Prisoners were identified as belonging to 1st and 2nd Battalions of the 22nd Panzer Grenadier Regiment. As 4th Dorsets neared Eterville B Squadron moved up and gave added support from the right flank, destroying two anti-tank guns. The threat from the left remained, but a further troop of

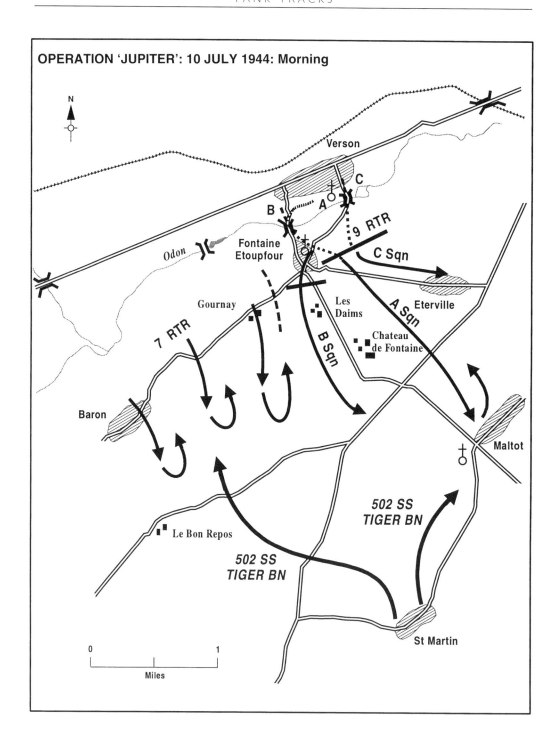

OPERATION 'JUPITER': 10 JULY 1944: Morning

N

Verson

C

B A

9 RTR

Odon

Fontaine
Etoupfour

C Sqn

A Sqn

Eterville

Gournay

Les
Daims

Chateau
de Fontaine

7 RTR

B Sqn

Baron

Maltot

Le Bon Repos

502 SS
TIGER BN

502 SS
TIGER BN

St Martin

0   1

Miles

17-pounder SPs and 11 Troop of C Squadron were in good positions waiting for the first sign of enemy tanks. By 0735 hrs Eterville had been taken and B Squadron rallied north of Les Daims. Heavy enemy mortar fire was concentrated on Eterville.

Phase 3: At 0815 hrs A Squadron advanced between B and C Squadrons supporting 7th Hampshires in their attack on Maltot. B Squadron was in position to provide support from the right flank of A's attack. Up to now the whole attack had gone perfectly, but at 0835 hrs A Squadron was severely worried by anti-tank fire from four German SPs in the area of the orchards just north of Maltot. As soon as an artillery concentration was brought down in this area 8 Troop of B Squadron reported anti-tank fire from the reverse slopes of Hill 112 and that two tanks had been knocked out.

On the right of 9 RTR, 7 RTR were attacking Hill 112 in support of 129 Brigade. They had made substantial progress, but at 0933 hrs a strong enemy counter-attack was made on Hill 112. 7 RTR suffered a number of casualties including their CO, Lt.-Col. Gaisford, who lost an eye, and the 2 i/c Major Bob Fleming who was killed. The right flank of 9 RTR's advance was thus enfiladed, and anti-tank fire was also reported from the high ground dominating Maltot to the west of the River Orne. The impetus of the attack was failing – two Tigers were in Maltot making the advance of the infantry extremely difficult and A Squadron's movement was hampered by a troop of Tigers on the southern slope of Hill 112, firing north-east.

At 1156 hrs A Squadron were still struggling to support the infantry in Maltot who were now confronted with another Tiger. The German infantry were now counter-attacking and only nine tanks of A Squadron were left. Major Douglas Ballantine, OC A Squadron, dismounted in an attempt to make contact with the CO of the 7th Hampshires (Lt.-Col. D.W.G. Ray), but was severely wounded by mortar fire and subsequently died.

By 1200 hrs 2 i/c A Squadron (Capt. Bert Mockford) reported that he had only four tanks capable of fighting, and further reports stated that counter-attacks were being made with tanks and infantry from north-east and south-west of Maltot.

The battalion was disposed as follows:

B Squadron and elements of A in hull down positions on spur south of Chateau de Fontaine with infantry and anti-tank guns dug in.

C Squadron had joined Battalion HQ in forward rally after release by 4th Dorsets. BHQ had been mortared and shelled periodically causing severe casualties among the wounded that had been brought in.

From 1300 to 1600 hrs there was a stalemate, the enemy making no attempts to push their counter-attack any further. A new plan was devised whereby A Squadron 7 RTR (Major Dick Joscelyne) were to put the 5th Battalion Duke of Cornwall's Light Infantry (5 DCLI) on Hill 112 and C Squadron 9 RTR to put 4th Dorsets into Maltot. B Squadron were to give support from the right in the opening phase. 4 Armoured Brigade were waiting to go through.

The advance began at 1640 hrs and despite anti-tank fire from south-west of Maltot C Squadron had put the infantry into the village by 1700 hrs. But ten minutes later C Squadron were being shot at from the rear, for once again enemy tanks had infiltrated under cover of the spur north-east of Hill 112. Eight Tigers were also moving in on the left flank, and the infantry were pulling out of Maltot under pressure.

At 1935 hrs C Squadron was also forced to withdraw under the cover of supporting fire from B Squadron. Mortaring and shelling was almost continuous and at 2030 hrs all tanks rallied at the FUP; later they moved to join A Echelon north-east of Mouen to replenish and collect reinforcements.

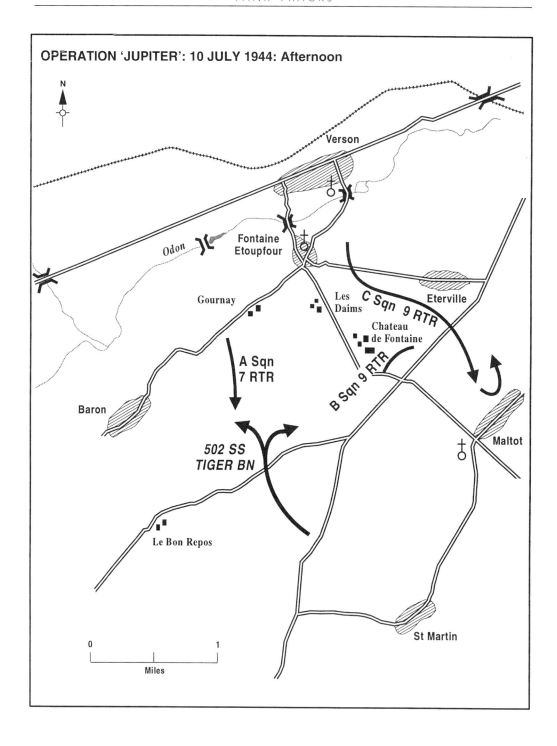

OPERATION 'JUPITER': 10 JULY 1944: Afternoon

N

Verson

Odon

Fontaine
Etoupfour

Gournay

Les
Daims

C Sqn 9 RTR

Eterville

Chateau
de Fontaine

A Sqn
7 RTR

B Sqn 9 RTR

Baron

Maltot

502 SS
TIGER BN

Le Bon Repos

0   1

Miles

St Martin

During this day the battalion suffered sixty-five casualties (more than a quarter suffered in the entire North West Europe campaign), of whom twenty-two were killed, thirty-four wounded, and nine taken prisoner. Sixteen tanks had been knocked out, of which six were recoverable.

Personal recollections, 10 July

This day was the worst day for the 9th in the whole campaign, and we incurred more than a quarter of all the casualties we sustained in North West Europe on that one day. And the severity, at 34 per cent killed, was well above the normal ratio of killed to total casualties. How did the day seem to the individual? Not good, as the following accounts testify.

Capt. A.E.W. (John) Hodges, Adjutant:

Attack on Maltot area and pt 112. In the morning B Squadron attacked Chateau de Fontaine from just south of Verson. Attack was successful and was exploited to the high ground 500 yards beyond. C Squadron then attacked Eterville and all went well. About 1100 hrs A Squadron formed up with 7th Hampshires to pass through these positions and capture Maltot. The tanks reached the orchards surrounding the village and the infantry entered. At this stage everything seemed to go wrong. The tanks were caught in a murderous cross-fire from beyond the river on their right and from woods and the reverse slope of 112, the latter being the objective of 7 RTR who failed to take it. Very heavy mortar fire came down and the inevitable counter-attack with tanks came in. The Hampshires were reduced to company strength and at this stage only four tanks out of eighteen were left to fight. These joined up with B Squadron who succeeded in holding the general line chateau and Eterville. About 6 p.m. C Squadron attacked Maltot with a fresh set of infantry – as before the outskirts of the village were reached – but no further progress could be made.

This was a disastrous day for A Squadron. Young George Hendrie was killed early on. An 88 mm shell struck the commander flap and decapitated him. The crew managed to bring the tank back to the start line and he was buried by the Padre together with an infantry soldier under an elm tree near Verson. He was a very popular young officer and his death was a great shock to us all. Major Ballantine also died of wounds on this day. I heard his last message over the wireless saying, quite cheerfully, that his tank had been hit three times and that he was trying to get through the hedge into the orchard. [The story of Duggie Ballantine's death, as recounted by John, was given in the Overture to this history.]

The 9th's total casualties on 10 July were 65; of these 41 were in A, 14 in B, 8 in C, and 2 in HQ. And of the 41 casualties in A, 16 were killed. Among those killed were the squadron leader Duggie Ballantine, troop leader of 1 Troop, George Hendrie, and troop sergeant of 2 Troop, Jock Smith. Among the wounded were Capt. Ronnie Kirby, Lt. Shep Douglas, Squadron Sergeant-Major Monty Bradley, and Sergeants Frank Quinn, Gray, and Nobbie Norman. It was a grievous blow. Ray Gordon's account of the deaths of Jock Smith, Bill Morris, Dickie Knight, and Jack Hutchinson, and his own wounding was also given in the Overture to this history. Another A Squadron memory was that of Jim Hutton, driver to George Hendrie, troop leader of 1 Troop:

Anyway, getting away from there we moved on then to Maltot and I remember Sergeant Norman and his crew coming up on the A set and he called out that he was in trouble, that the Germans had surrounded him and he came on the air and said 'What shall I do. I am surrounded by Germans', and somebody – some bright spark over the air called out 'Stick your bloody hands up!' (chuckle). Anyway he was taken prisoner there and if you look in a book called *Hill 112* you will see that Sergeant Norman and his crew were taken prisoner by the German SS and there's quite a good picture of them being interrogated. The other thing was a bit hair-raising; somebody came up on the air and called out, 'To my left there are fifty Sherman tanks approaching, to my left.' 'Say again, over.' 'Fifty Sherman tanks.' 'Did you say Sherman or German?' and he said 'Sherman'. 'Oh', he said, 'thank goodness for that.'

The second part of Jim's recollections of that day are not nearly so cheerful:

Now at Hill 112 I never forget on the Sunday Lieutenant Hendrie had his birthday. He was twenty-one on the Sunday and we all got drunk on Calvados, had a good knees up and a good singsong and all that. Anyhow, Monday morning first light, we were briefed to go into Maltot towards our objective which was between C Squadron and B Squadron; A Squadron was to come through the middle and take a feature but we got hit so badly, I think out of eighteen tanks there wasn't many, I think only five of us managed to make it. But we got hit on the turret and it hit dead centre of the turret ring and the main armament couldn't traverse and water in the canteen splashed all over the place because that's the side it came in. I felt this cold water over the back of my neck and I couldn't make out what it was but then the tank commander Lieutenant Hendrie called out 'We'll carry on with the front machine-gun' cause the main armament couldn't be traversed. So we carried on firing the front machine-gun and the next shot hit the cupola and took Lieutenant Hendrie's head – decapitated him and his

Crew of troop sergeant's tank Illusive, *4 Troop, A Squadron, Farnborough, May 1944. Back row: Sandy Sanderson, L/Cpl. Bill Dawkins. Front row: Bert Munns, Sgt. Nobby Norman, Dave MacIntosh. This crew was captured on the outskirts of Maltot on 10 July 1944. On page 125 of* Hill 112 *by J.J. How there is a picture of this crew being interrogated by SS Oberführer Harmel, Commander of 10th SS Panzer Division.*

body fell down into the turret. I felt warm liquid on the back of my neck, which I knew was blood and on turning around I spotted his body with no head and I didn't know whether the rest of the crew were alive or dead in the back. By this time I decided to swing left and swing right cause I knew they had got a beeline on us and they were out to destroy us so I swung hard left and then stopped; swung hard right and moved forward, swung left, right and done a complete swing around. We had a hit on the side, on the right-hand pannier door, my side, and it hit there and ricocheted off scooping about half the metal out and we swung around and we had another hit on the back which was on the louvres, on the metal chocolate bar on the louvre, nearly penetrated the petrol tanks but it managed to bounce off. Finally I did a complete turn, which I thought was a complete turn and we had one hit the back which hit the top of the gearbox and ripped the top of the selectors off, the cover for the selectors. We managed to keep going and we drove for about a mile, a mile and a half and we stopped and we hadn't a clue where we were and 'Busty' Cliff, that was my co-driver – Corporal Cliff – he said 'Which way do we go now?' So I looked at a compass, I said 'Well if we go that way we are going north towards England so that's the way we want to go' and just as we were about to move we saw a column of tanks coming along a hedge with the rally flags flying and the guns traversed rear which was C Squadron returning from an action, the same action, and we managed to join in with them. We saw the OC and he said tag on the back and we'll take you back to your squadron. When we returned to the forward echelon Sergeant-Major Bradley and a Padre came over and asked us if we had any casualties and we said 'Yes, I think there's three in the turret'; but on looking they found there was only one, Lieutenant Hendrie was dead and the other two were more or less dumbfounded, more or less just struck dumb and they managed to come out and we were all OK eventually. Sergeant-Major Bradley said 'Get yourselves some tea and get some sleep and try and get over it' which we did and that was quite an experience there. We found out that the squadron had taken a hell of a bashing. And I never forgot Sergeant-Major Bradley, he was a marvellous man. They got the webbing slings in the turret and managed to take Lieutenant Hendrie's body out and they buried him. That was quite an experience.

SSM Monty Bradley was remembered as a marvellous man by many people including Jim. Harry Hurt of 5 Troop recalls: 'Nobby Clark of 5 Troop told me that Monty was wounded at Fontaine–Etoupefour on 10 July. Some wounded tank crew, of whom Nobby was one, were waiting at the FUP to be evacuated. A stonk came down, Monty threw himself on top of a tank crew member to protect him from further wounding, and was himself wounded as a result.'

Bob Taylor was gunner to Cpl. Fred Armstrong, troop corporal of 5 Troop commanded by Lt. Gerry Wells. His tank started from the orchards around the Chateau de Fontaine.

We left the orchard and proceeded across fields looking for enemy positions when we saw our Troop Sergeant Tony Griffith and his crew taking shelter at the rear of their tank, which had been knocked out by enemy fire. He signalled to us to give us some idea where the enemy were firing from. Vic Mills, our operator and loader shouted 'Traverse Left'. As I did I saw a flash from I presume a German 88 mm and I fired at the flash. But we had been hit in the turret where the 2-inch smoke rounds were stored and in the next instant we were on fire, flames were coming up from the turret floor and I shouted to the crew to bail out.

The driver and co-driver got out OK, and Cpl. Fred Armstrong, the Tank Commander, got out suffering with burns to his face and hands. I proceeded to bail out, but my pistol lanyard got caught on the arm rest of the 6-pounder gun and in the process of getting my lanyard free the flames burnt my hands and face. Eventually I got out of the tank and joined the rest of the

Crew of troop leader's tank Impudent, *1 Troop, A Squadron, Farnborough, May 1944. Back row: Jimmy Bennell (wireless-op.), Kit Harlow (gunner). Front row: L/Cpl. Jim Hutton (driver), 2nd Lt. George Hendrie (tank commander), Cpl. Busty Cliff (co-driver). Jimmy and George were killed and Kit and Jim wounded at various times during the Normandy campaign.*

crew at the rear of the tank, as we were being machine-gunned by the enemy. It was then I was told that Vic Mills, our operator, had been killed as the '88 shot had entered his side of the turret. The tank was well alight by now and there was nothing we could do as the ammo started to explode.

We waited for a while then we started to make our way back to the orchard, which meant that we had to cross a field of tall wheat or corn. We had to keep bobbing up and down to find our direction to the orchard, and to keep out of sight from the German infantry, as they were in the same field.

As we got near the road we came upon a wounded German soldier sitting against the hedge. When he saw us he lifted his rifle and pointed it at us so we pointed our pistols at him and he slung his rifle to one side and raised his hands in surrender.

But we were more concerned with getting treatment for our burns. We got back to the orchard and were given first aid, then Fred Armstrong and myself were taken to Bayeux and shipped to England for hospital treatment.

B Squadron

B Squadron moved off at 0500 hrs. Their first objective was Les Daims and the final one the ridge just beyond the Chateau de Fontaine. John Powell was the wireless-op in the troop sergeant's tank of 7 Troop; his account starts after the end of the 'Epsom' battles:

The lull in operations lasted just a few days until we were told to prepare for the next action. Details are hazy but I remember moving up to the start line ready to support the Hampshires and Dorsets in their advance on Chateau de Fontaine and Maltot. As always we moved off at first light and fairly rapidly achieved our first objective, whatever that may have been.

All seemed quiet and we were awaiting our next move, feeling confident and probably slightly complacent at our initial success when the tank was hit in the engine compartment. The impact was unmistakable but not as horrifying or noisy as had previously been imagined. During the second or two that we were adjusting to this situation another round penetrated the left side of the turret, presumably igniting the ammo as the tank started to 'brew-up' immediately. An intercom. and visual check quickly revealed that tragically our greatly liked and respected young gunner, L/Cpl. Johnny Foden, had taken the full force of the projectile and was beyond help. He must have perished mercifully quickly. The tank was now burning furiously and the rest of us needed to abandon ship smartly. Machine-gun rounds were striking the side of the turret so we waited for a lull, hoping that the machine-gunner would need to change belts. The remaining four of us jumped out. Our troop-leader's tank was nearby and, being pointed in the right direction towards our own lines, we started to trudge back. Tankies without their vehicles are a bit like shell-less tortoises on the battlefield and we felt strangely vulnerable.

The noise of battle sounded increasingly distant as we crossed the open Normandy fields. On our way we came across a young German infantryman, SS as I remember, who had a leg wound. On being offered a cigarette he showed what he thought of it all by spitting at us! A stretcher was found from somewhere by someone and we took turns at carrying the unhappy young man back with us.

Like I said, we were unused to being on a battlefield without inches of armour plate around us. Some mortar rounds or shells started whistling around and we dropped. Too late. When I returned to consciousness the others were getting up but I couldn't move. I tried to shout but only a whisper came out. The others noticed my plight and our sergeant examined me, turned me over and put a field dressing on my back. I couldn't feel my legs but was assured that they were still there. Someone went to get help while I was given a cigarette to keep me occupied. My very brief war was certainly over.

John records what happened after that: 'Flown back in a very bumpy Dakota for further attention to my spinal injuries, I spent months and months in hospital recovering some use of my legs. Eventually I was invalided out.'

Peter Beale was commanding 8 Troop with Taffy Jones as his troop sergeant and Johnnie Walker as his troop corporal. They reached the objective beyond the Chateau de Fontaine without any difficulty, and waited there while C Squadron successfully attacked Eterville. When A Squadron began to experience difficulties in Maltot, B Squadron moved a little further south over the ridge, with 8 Troop on the right flank. At this stage no one realized that 7 RTR's attack on Hill 112 had been repulsed by the Tigers of 502nd SS Battalion, and that these same Tigers were prowling round up there looking for new targets.

Ronnie Larner was Taffy Jones' driver. 'What's going on, Sarge?' asked Ronnie. 'Nothing at all, Ronnie,' says Taff, 'we're safe as houses here.' Five minutes later, Peter was standing in his tank.

I was looking ahead through my binoculars in the direction of Maltot, trying to see what was happening down there. Suddenly I caught a flicker of movement to my right. Good God! Both Taffy's and Johnnie's tanks are on fire. Shot must be coming from the right, Hill 112. Haven't the 7th got that? Whatever, John, hard right, face up the ridge, Norman, smoke; message to Bob, two have gone, putting down smoke, backing off ridge; Reg, take the tank back off the ridge, I'll go and see if I can help the others.

Hill 112 in 1993 with the 43rd Division memorial to the right. The German Tiger tanks up here had a field of fire that enabled them to destroy many of the Churchills of 7 RTR and 9 RTR on 10 July 1944.

So I got out of the turret and down on to the ground and walked towards the blazing tanks. The Tigers on the reverse slope of 112 were still firing in our direction, and their shots were low enough that I could see them snickering through the corn. Going as they were at slightly over 800 metres per second, they looked most unhealthy.

The only person I could find was Roy Barber, who had suffered burns. I helped him back towards the Chateau and the RAP. As we were level with the Chateau we heard an incoming moaning minnie stonk. In the ditch, I said. And from the ditch I saw a mortar land 60 metres away, then another 30 metres away, the two making a straight line aiming directly at us. Not good odds, I thought. But the next two were some way behind us, and before too long Roy had got back to good hands at the RAP.

C Squadron

C Squadron had two major actions during the day, as the War Diary has related. Trevor Greenwood was the troop sergeant of 15 Troop, which was commanded by Seymour Francis. As they were moving off on the night of 9 July Seymour's tank suffered a broken bell crank in the gearbox. Seymour changed to Trevor's tank. There was no spare in the fitter's truck, so the Battalion Technical Officer (BTO) had to return to base to get one. Trevor's narrative starts very early on the morning of 10 July.

Probably one of the worst days I will ever know . . . BTO returned about 1.00 a.m. . . . having had to return to St. Gabriel for new part. Something of a feat to make return journey in darkness . . . no lights, no roads etc. Job finished about 2.30 a.m. . . . and we moved off to find the squadron: only a hazy idea of their location, but we found them eventually . . . about 3.30 a.m. Just in time to form up for march to Verson and FUP. It was a horrible journey. Cold – hunger – fear: terrible fear . . . these were only a part of the nightmare. I suppose the journey was about 3 miles, but it seemed longer. The territory was only newly occupied . . . and there were the usual obvious signs . . . visible even in the dark. Dead cattle . . . almost always lying with legs pointing upwards . . . usually one or more legs blown off by blast or shrapnel; a horrible sight. Vehicles, both ours and German, dumped in ditches along roadside; villages . . . completely ruined and desolate; silent but for our noise. Sentries and guards standing at road junctions etc. . . . very much on the alert . . . waiting . . . listening . . . peering . . . snipers everywhere.

Our FUP was just south of Verson – from where we were scheduled to launch an attack on Eterville with 4th Dorsets: zero hour for us was 6.15 a.m. As we neared Verson, the noise became worse . . . terrifying. An enormous barrage was being laid down close by for 'B' . . . who were going further west at 5.00 a.m.

At Verson, ruins as usual and we did more damage to walls and houses . . . unavoidable in the narrow lanes and darkness. Enemy only just cleared out of the place.

We were in Verson about 5.30 a.m.: our FUP a field immediately south of village, just below hill crest. We were now able to see fairly well, but it was not fully daylight. As we manoeuvred into position, I noticed a tremendous barrage falling on our left flank . . . about a quarter mile away. This was a grand sight: it was the smoke screen promised: without it, our left flank would have been completely exposed. Right flank was OK . . . B had already gone in there.

But the barrage was not the only activity. Jerry was sending over tons of mortar. It was falling around us, literally plastering the cornfield. There was so much machine-gun fire . . . both coming and going: . . . Jerry machine-guns were still only a few yards ahead of us. Kept my head down as much as possible!

At 6.00 a.m., our infantry were in position, to our rear: the mortar fire must have been terrible for them, but they seemed unconcerned. I cannot describe my own reactions about this time. I am always too much afraid for cohesive thought just prior to action: . . . mentally paralysed with fear, I suppose. But my physical behaviour was quite normal. Up to now, I haven't even experienced any trembling! Queer, that!

At 6.15, the major's order came over the air 'advance'. We commenced to move up the gentle slope . . . into what? Eterville lay half a mile beyond the crest, in a shallow valley.

The air was very busy: B had been fighting for an hour on our right, and seemed to have reached their objective: that was some consolation. And on the left flank, we had our white wall of smoke: I felt very secure from that quarter . . . and I knew that this smoke would continue for four hours: I felt very grateful for the artillery. By now, I had become quite normal: deadly calm and unworried: it is not natural. Every fibre of my being was concentrated upon the one thing . . . enemy gun flashes: . . . miss them, and . . . there may not be a second chance. Most of my observation was done thro' the periscopes: too much machine-gunning over the top. Closed down occasionally when mortar became too concentrated around us.

We reached the crest . . . and there were the enemy running for cover . . . towards Eterville and the trees ahead. Our Besa opened up . . . every bush and shrub: every tree: every haystack: anything and everything that could hide a body . . . was raked with machine-gun fire.

Our infantry were now among and ahead of us . . . and soon, prisoners started to come in: odd couples of Jerrys popping up from the corn, hands raised . . . scared to death.

At least three haystacks were now on fire from our incendiary machine-gun fire. The smoke from them was a bit of a nuisance, blowing across our front. Ahead, lay the trees immediately in front of Eterville: they were my worry. Jerry has a habit of concealing Tigers and Panthers in the woods. They usually open fire when we are too close to take evasive action . . . and one hit from an '88 at 400 yards . . . !

Very soon, we opened up with HE on the village . . . there were as yet no signs of any '88s. The infantry kept steadily on . . . walking warily through the deep corn, but always going forward . . . forward. Our Besa fire passed over them, but it must have been uncomfortably close. Grand fellows those infantry lads: so brave and calm.

I felt terribly grateful towards them when I saw them among the trees: they would report any hidden AT guns and tanks. My vehicle was behaving well . . . and putting down smoke fire: crew worked splendidly: damned hard work too. And how we smoked cigarettes! Pedder solved the match problem by getting his lighter to work with gun buffer oil! And in the midst of an action! Mortars were still troublesome: as good as any air force to Jerry!

Time has no meaning during action: some time during the fight, Very lights were seen from the village, and we knew the infantry were 'in': they had done a grand job and occupied the place with remarkable speed. We just remained on the high ground . . . keeping on the alert from any armour . . . and a possible counter-attack.

Meanwhile, the smoke was still literally pouring down on the left: B had done their job on the right, and now our front seemed reasonably safe: The tension was less acute . . . but always there was the mortar and snipers and the necessary vigil for lurking Tigers and Panthers.

Later, when the village had quietened down, we withdrew to original start point . . . and replenished our depleted ammo racks . . . the SSM was there waiting for us.

Mortar was now quite regular and all around us: we hadn't lost one in the action! Thank goodness it was over: we seemed to have been fighting for many hours . . . but it was only 10.00 a.m.

And now we had time for a brew and a few biscuits and a little rest, in spite of continual mortaring. We were very exposed, in the middle of a large cornfield, but we couldn't withdraw further in case we were needed to repel a counter-attack. The hours passed . . . maybe two or three . . . and we were all hoping for the order to withdraw. My crew, in particular were dreadfully tired, having had no sleep the previous night owing to the breakdown. And the awful tension of the action had had its effect. And then . . . the Colonel's voice over the air to the Major: another 'party' was being arranged for us: stand by for further action!! God! What dreadful depression!

Shortly, we learned about the 'party'.

A had passed through C and B to carry out a further attack to the south on Maltot . . . and things weren't going so well. It appeared that A had been hammered pretty badly. We were scheduled to launch a further attack on Maltot with fresh infantry. And we had been complimenting ourselves upon our neat little action in taking Eterville so quickly and without loss to ourselves. But now!?

Once again that terrible fear . . . Well . . . we went in . . . via scenes of recent action . . . dreadful scenes. As with Eterville, we plastered the woods around Maltot with machine-gun fire and plenty of HE. My gunner asked permission to have a go at the church spire, just visible above the hill crest: he was given permission, and got two lovely hits with HE – the steeple toppled. It might have harboured an enemy observer.

Once again, we were assisted by the artillery laying a grand smoke screen on our left flank. The infantry seemed to have little difficulty in entering the woods . . . and so down to the village. We did not follow: remaining on the high ground on the alert for enemy armour. We knew there were at least three Panthers in the village . . . or in the vicinity.

Occasional burst of machine-gun fire from enemy dug outs, and a few snipers, but we dealt with them. We must have passed an hour or two on that crest . . . and then came the Major's voice over the air appealing to the Colonel for further assistance in the village for the infantry. Things seemed to happen rapidly: 3 SPs were promised . . . but it seemed a poor response.

And then I noticed one of our tanks on fire. What on earth was happening? There were no signs of enemy on the hill, and our infantry were in the woods and village. It seemed like a counter-attack in force, judging by Major Holden's further appeal. He had somehow contacted the infantry commander.

Suddenly I heard some heavy gunfire . . . and the swish of shells. Hells Bells! *My* tank was being fired at. Two misses! Darned if I could see any gun flashes or tanks. I peered frantically through the periscope . . . there seemed to be at least one more tank in difficulties and several smaller vehicles on fire.

And then the Major's voice . . . *he* wanted help . . . smoke. He got smoke . . . all of us poured it out as fast as we could. In a matter of seconds, our former peaceful hill crest was pretty well littered with burning vehicles – and smoke . . . a dense fog. I noticed one or two nearby vehicles moving away, but where to? Soon I couldn't see a thing but smoke, but gave the driver orders to advance: better to go anywhere than stay and be shot up. Eventually found my way back to lower ground away from the danger zone . . . but I was still hazy about the situation. All the same, I felt convinced that something pretty bad had happened.

Very soon, infantry appeared running towards us . . . and away from Maltot. Were we withdrawing? Some sort of retreat seemed apparent. We were too far ahead to regroup and deploy for further action, so we withdrew to our laager north of Eterville . . . the latter being now well consolidated by the infantry.

And there we waited . . . being fiercely mortared meanwhile. Ultimately, and without warning, we turned about and withdrew . . . accompanied by terrific mortar fire: it seemed certain that we were under observation, so accurate was the mortaring.

Through Verson . . . and fields and orchards and lanes to a point about 2 miles north-west of Verson. A rather hectic journey and rather bewildering. Arrived after dark – in a field – our final halt for the day.

My crew had been in the tank almost continuously for about 28 hrs! And no meal in the period: but we had biscuits, and one 'brew up'. Heard alarming rumours about casualties etc. but things were too obscure to worry about. Bed was imperative. Rolled myself in a couple of blankets, and slept beneath the tank.

AFTER 'JUPITER', 11–25 JULY 1944

The 43rd Wessex Division remained on Hill 112 and the ridge with furious counter-attacks from Germans and British alternately. The Churchills of 31 Tank Brigade were in place further north of the ridge to repel German advances over the ridge. Montgomery continued to hammer at different parts of the German front, and the next major effort was towards the ridge to the west of 112. The 15th Scottish plus a brigade of Royal Welsh Fusiliers (53 Div) with 34 Tank Brigade in support executed Operation Greenline. This had as its objectives the villages of Esquay, Evrecy, Gavrus and Bougy. The latter two were taken, the former two not; but the Germans were kept busy and engaged from 15 to 18 July. During this time preparations were being made for Operation 'Goodwood', a thrust to the south on the eastern side of Caen. This was made by all three armoured divisions at that time in Normandy, 7th, 11th, and Guards; it started on 18 July.

The attack was preceded by a massive air bombardment. But the Germans had very effective anti-tank forces in depth, and the British tanks ground to a blazing halt on 20 July.

On that day, far away to the east, a bomb exploded at 1242 hrs. Adolf Hitler did not die, but the repercussions of the explosion caused uncertainties and hesitations to run down the chain of the German higher command. In a short time this showed benefits to the allied forces, but not to the Canadians who assaulted the Verrieres ridge in Operation 'Spring' on 25 July. Sixty men of the Royal Hamilton Light Infantry reached the summit, fifteen came back, and 342 lay dead or wounded on the ridge's forward slopes. It was much the same for the other Canadian units.

But on this same day the allied strategy triumphed. 'Goodwood' might have been a tactical failure, but strategically it succeeded. The Germans, expecting a further assault, brought in fresh troops from east of the Seine and shifted a panzer division east from the Caumont sector. There were now seven panzer and seven infantry divisions facing fourteen British divisions, while twenty-one American divisions faced two panzer, one panzer grenadier, and six infantry divisions. Operation 'Cobra' was launched at Saint-Lô on 25 July. During the period 11–25 July 9 RTR as part of 31 Tank Brigade remained in a counter-attack role, mainly just north of the Hill 112 – Chateau de Fontaine ridge.

The War Diary

11/12 July: Battalion remained in the same location north-east of Mouen, obtaining reinforcements and replacements which included ten Mark VII Churchills, at the same time standing by to assist 7 RTR who were still in the area Hill 112 in a counter-attack role. Major P.N. (Berry) Veale, MC, was promoted and transferred to be CO of 7 RTR, who had lost both their CO and 2 i/c on 10 July.

13–16 July: Battalion moved to Les Saullets just north of Cheux to rest, and on the night of 16 July moved to relieve 7 RTR in counter-attack role at Chateau de Fontaine and Hill 112. 129 Brigade (43 Div) were the infantry in that area. Battalion moved into position in the area of Gournay at last light, and all crews began digging deep holes in which to sleep.
Just after 2300 hrs, following mortar and shell fire, the harbour area was machine-gunned and bombed by six Junkers 88s. The CO, Lt.-Col. Paddy Everard, was wounded in the head and back, Trooper Stan Agar was killed, and Troopers Bell, Edmunds, Sharpe and Wright were wounded, as well as L/Cpl. Cunningham and Cpl. Cove. Major Bob Warren took over command.
Shelling and mortaring continued throughout the night.

17 July: At first light HQ, B and C Squadrons moved out to an area about one mile due north of Hill 112, squadrons deployed with two troops up. Mortaring continued throughout the day, and in retaliation a shoot was carried out by all 75 and 95 mm guns, resulting in the silencing of a machine-gun that had been worrying the infantry.
An SP was forced to disclose its position and infantry reported a Panther set on fire, but no confirmation was available. At 1930 hrs a further shoot was made on the centre of St. Martin which drew heavy retaliation from enemy mortars resulting in three minor casualties.

18/19 July: Very similar to 17 July – intervals of mortar and shell fire. Recces and plans were made for counter-attack roles. Shoot carried out on a wood on Hill 112 reported to harbour three Tigers. Lt.-Col. P.N. Veale was transferred back from 7 RTR and assumed command of the battalion.

21 July: At 1430 hrs an enemy counter-attack threatened and B Squadron moved up to the crest to give moral support to the infantry. Heavy mortaring resulted in Major Bob Warren being wounded in the right hand and side, his wireless operator Sgt. Mick Tito having his right hand blown off, and Cpl. Reg Southern and Bert Wilcox also being wounded.

No counter-attack developed, but a party towed away a number of dead cows whose stench did more to lower morale than persistent mortaring and shelling.

7 RTR were brought up into the area to attack Maltot corresponding with a Canadian attack on Etavaux. Following the attack and corresponding with a Canadian attack on St. Andre sur Orne 9 RTR were ordered to be prepared to attack Feuguerolles sur Orne and St. Martin.

22 July: 1815 hrs. Support given to 7 RTR attack on Maltot with 75 and 95 mm fire aimed at Nebelwerfers in area 70 ring contour just north of St. Martin. First shoot drew heavy mortaring but there was no reply to the second shoot. During this time Major Holden got mixed up with his slidex and reported 'dead'. Persisting in this report, he was advised to call skeleton O groups.

[Note: Slidex was a system for coding map references and other information to keep them secure from the enemy].

23/25 July: The intensity of mortaring and shelling decreased and a further shoot was carried out on an 88 located on Hill 112, but no further orders were received concerning attack on Feuguerolles and St. Martin. On 25 July, after watching rocket-firing Typhoons brassing up enemy position south of Caen, the battalion received orders to move to Fontenay Le Pesnil.

After nine days of air attack at night and shelling and mortaring at all times during the day and night, no one was sorry to leave.

The attack on Feuguerolles and St. Martin which was to have been done down a valley dominated on both sides by enemy positions had not promised to be the best of adventures either.

Personal recollections, 11–25 July

The War Diary records the continuous bombardment of the area just north and east of Hill 112. This was a constant theme in all the accounts of these few days. John Hodges:

16 July: We moved up at dusk to take over a counter-attack role from 7 RTR at Gournay just north of pt 112. Here we remained until 26 July, losing each day three or four men from mortar fire. During the whole of this period the place was mortared and shelled all day long and we lived in holes beneath the tanks. At night there was always a visit from German bombers and heavy shelling, so one way or another there was little sleep. On the first night we had hardly stopped the engines before the bombers were over dropping flares and bombs. One landed between the CO's tank and mine. He was underneath his with two of the crew. One was killed and the CO badly spattered with shrapnel and was evacuated. Geoff Brewer, who was standing on top of the CO's tank, was blown off but suffered little more than a severe shaking!

Altogether it was a most unpleasant night and our casualties were four killed and a score injured. I joined forces with Bob Warren who took over command. On 19 July Berry Veale came back to us as CO from 7 RTR.

B Squadron had to go forward as a counter-attack was reported. A mortar bomb fell on Bob Warren's operator's flaps making a pretty good mess of Sergeant Tito. Bob wasn't too bad but will probably lose a couple of fingers. Mike Reynell took over B Squadron.

C Squadron, led by the second-in-command's tank Ich Dien, *moves towards the front line in the area of Hill 112 on 16 July 1944. (IWM B7584)*

During the shoots carried out by the battalion between 22 and 24 July the Recce Officers of the squadrons acted as forward observation officers. Taffy Leyshon explains how it was with C Squadron:

> Hill 112 all the tanks were lined up as if ready for attack, no camouflage, shelling and mortaring morning, noon and night. C Squadron HQ Troop had Major Holden's and Capt. Link's 95 mm howitzers. Capt. Kidd who was my officer had a scout car and a tank. Once I drove the scout car with Trooper Patchett towards the German lines and hid behind a knocked out tank. Capt. Kidd then crawled out with field glasses and intercom and sent messages to Patchett; Major Holden's tank would fire a shot, two adjustments then Capt. Kidd crawled back. Get out quick he said.
>
> We used the gun next day to support an infantry patrol. A Spandau machine-gun opened up on them, Major Holden was in communication with the officer, and three shots put the Spandau out.

Jock Cordiner was upset and embarrassed by mortars:

> Mortar bombs gave me the creeps. On Hill 112 I had gone some 200 yards to the loo, that delightful hole in the middle of nowhere topped with a wooden seat and surrounded by a canvas screen. No sooner was I comfortable than a moaning minnie attack started. I dashed for cover, my pants around my legs and my shirt tail flapping in the breeze, jeered and

cheered by half the squadron. Just before that, while still with HQ, Brad and I had dug holes and were asleep behind the lines. It was raining hard and our holes were sodden, but safe. We were awakened by the Duty Officer and ordered to drive to Hill 112 with something very urgent. We were groping our way along the black lanes when a severe air attack started. We both dived out of the Humber into a ditch on top of a few startled infantrymen. When the raid moved on we did also. As we came uphill towards the tanks a bomb or shell caught an ammunition dump just off the road and almost simultaneously another hit a fuel dump on the other side of the road. We were silhouetted, roasted, and in severe danger of being blown apart. I never knew a Humber could be driven so fast.

In the confusion of this sort of action, and because of casualties and transfers, it happened sometimes that people were left very much to their own devices. Almost invariably they did their very best to get back to where they could be useful. Jack Woods:

My next taste of action was during the Maltot battle. After a lengthy journey seemingly all over the bridgehead the echelon decided to laager in a field strewn with enemy slit trenches, guess what? surprise, surprise, we were heavily stonked, suffering casualties including some fatalities so off we went again on another joyride finally catching up with the tanks where

An international half-track in a Normandy village, July 1944. The half-track was lightly armoured, and had a good cross-country performance. It was used by tank repair crews, for the evacuation of the wounded, bringing up relief crews, and for bringing up supplies where there was likely to be enemy fire.

they had laagered for the night and servicing them in the dark. The next day, I was off again, this time to Brigade Workshops with a tank requiring an engine change and where I was instructed to stay with it until it was repaired. Needless to say nobody else had heard of that order and once the ARV had dumped me in a field near the workshops, I was forgotten about for a day or two, eating and sleeping with the fitters and nobody the least bit concerned about who I was and what I was doing there and where for all anybody cared I could have nicely sat out the rest of the war. I soon got cheesed off with that however, there was nowhere to go as everything was mined so I reported in for further orders much to the surprise of the REME bods who quickly shipped me off to the Forward Delivery Squadron.

Sitting on the reverse slope of Hill 112 was not a totally painful recollection for everyone. John Stone remembered two items connected with food:

At one place round there we were in a potato field. All we had to do to get fresh spuds was to do a neutral turn in the field, and hey presto, a bucketful. Somehow we seemed to have plenty of time to experiment with food. The compo packs (a box containing tinned and similar food for fifteen men for one day) were really quite good. There was a problem with the tea, however. A tin contained pre-mixed powdered tea, powdered milk and powdered sugar. The question was, how to brew it? The tea needed infusing and the milk simmering, and a proper compromise seemed unattainable. We tried all sorts of ways, but our favourite was to brew it for thirty minutes, and then add three spoonfuls of sugar per cup. The <u>original</u> Sergeant-Major's tea!

Trevor Greenwood describes some of the food his crew obtained, and then the problem of disposing of the end product.

July 1944. B Squadron tanks move forward in the area of Hill 112. Dead cattle were everywhere, and the smell of decaying flesh was all-pervasive. (IWM B7435)

Boiled chicken for lunch: didn't have any myself. Have no stomach for local poultry or livestock. Everything seems diseased and lifeless, but this must be my imagination. My four colleagues really enjoyed the chicken . . . with boiled potatoes, grown locally. Most of the crews now seem to have a dead chicken hanging on their tanks. There are many more running wild in nearby village, also many tame rabbits. Know of at least one crew, in B, who have shot a young calf . . . and had veal!

Believe we are moving 'in' again this evening: to relieve 7th who are standing by on Hill 112. Troop officers out on reccy this morning. Have done a reccy myself, with Bill Geary. Neither of us are partial to 'rears' in full view of everyone. And our present lav. is about the worst we have had so far. We explored the ruined village . . . but too many troops about. Went as far as a wood half a mile away . . . but everywhere there are troops, hoards of them. Eventually, we had to swallow our pride . . . and perform very publicly. I was amused by the easy going manner in which my crew solved the urinary problem on Monday during the action. We were several hours at a stretch inside the vehicle . . . .and even back in the forward rally, it was really dangerous to leave the vehicle owing to mortar and snipers. The problem was solved by using a small empty oil tin . . . this being passed up to me for emptying through the hatch, at intervals.

At one of those forward rallys, I had a more urgent need, and simply had to leave the tank. I crawled beneath the rear with a spade and dug a hole . . . I felt fairly safe from mortar . . . but just as I was hitching up my pants, there came the ominous 'whining', followed by crashes dangerously near. I simply dived head first further beneath the tank . . . and stayed there, literally with my pants down!

CHAPTER 5

Break-Out

BREAK-OUT FROM THE BRIDGEHEAD

The broad picture

On 25 July the Americans launched Operation Cobra at Saint Lô. The attack was preceded by a bombardment of the German positions by 3,000 aircraft, and was itself on a 6,000-yard front with an assault force of three infantry, one motorized, and two armoured divisions.

The first day's advance was slow, but by nightfall US VII Corps Commander, General 'Lightning Joe' Collins, guessed that his corps was practically through the German defences. Early next morning he launched his exploiting force, and here began a campaign of rapid movement. By 30 July VII Corps had reached Avranches, nearly 40 miles from Saint Lô, and through this gap poured General George Patton's Third US Army, fanning out west, south, and east. By 6 August Patton was approaching Le Mans.

To attempt to stem this flood the Germans transferred forces from the eastern or British sector of the bridgehead, and to keep the pressure on the Germans Montgomery attacked south from the area of Caumont in the direction of Vire on 30 July. Another prong of this attack by the 43rd Wessex was directed south-east, and on 6 August the commanding height of Mont Pinçon was taken. Further to the east again the 59th British Infantry (Staffordshire) Division was directed to establish a bridgehead across the River Orne in the area of Goupillieres, north of Thury-Harcourt. This they did on the evening of 6 August.

The War Diary

26 July: After a night march the battalion concentrated at Fontenay le Pesnil and here came under command 59 Div. The battalion had the task of supporting 176 Infantry Brigade in counter-attack roles on four positions: Haut de Bosq, Rauray, Point 126 and Brettevillette.
The country in this area had been heavily mined by the enemy and, consisting of small fields bounded by thick hedgerows and ditches, was undoubtedly the most difficult tank country that the battalion had yet encountered. The field of vision was generally less than 100 yards and in any deployed movement there could not be any visual contact between troops. Large tree stumps, torn and gashed by shell fire, together with the deep ditches provided natural tank obstacles.
It was essential that each area was very carefully reconnoitred so that should an emergency arise each Tank Commander would know beforehand the exact line of advance of each tank. These areas were under constant shell and mortar fire, which added to the difficulties, and at 1800 hrs B Squadron suffered a most unfortunate disaster.
The troop leaders of this squadron went forward for a rendezvous with Major Reynell, who was then making his plan just north of Brettevillette. Dismounting from the half-track an S-mine was exploded, resulting in the deaths of Lt. Smart, Lt. Wolskel, and Sgt. Nicholls. Lt. Beale and Lt. Cargill were wounded and the latter died in hospital a few days later.

31 July: The reconnaissance and forming of plans for these counter-attack roles lasted four days and on 31 July a demonstration was given by two troops of C Squadron with a company of 7 Norfolks of the method that had been adopted in clearing this type of country.

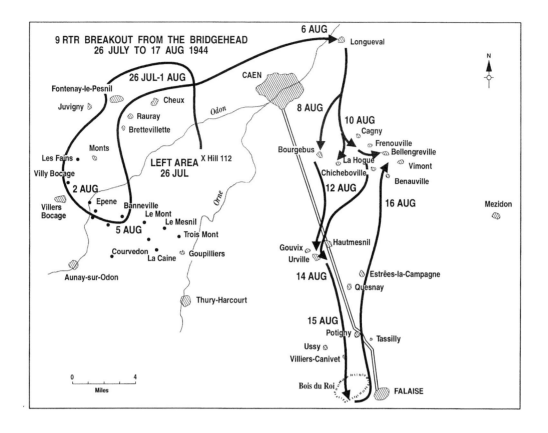

9 RTR BREAKOUT FROM THE BRIDGEHEAD
26 JULY TO 17 AUG 1944

Since 29 July 197 Brigade (59 Div) had been patrolling in strength, sometimes assisted by tanks of 7 RTR. The general impression gained from prisoners-of-war was that the enemy were withdrawing under the pressure of concentrated artillery fire, together with lack of food, sleep and at times ammunition.

1–5 August: 9 RTR as part of 31 Tank Brigade supporting 59 Div moved forward across the River Odon and towards the River Orne. No contact was made with the enemy but there were large quantities of anti-tank and anti-personnel mines.

At 2230 hrs 4 August information was received that 31 Tank Brigade was to come under command I Corps as from 0600 5 August. I Corps was under command First Canadian Army on the eastern edge of the bridgehead.

Personal recollections, 26 July–6 August

Trevor Greenwood's diary describes the farewell to Hill 112:

Jerry gave us a parting farewell last evening. First of all, we were mortared . . . followed by a bombing raid. We were partly under cover, by a hedgerow, when the bombers came over just before midnight: we remained very still and quiet . . . and nervous! Several bombs whistled down ominously . . . but not too close to us. Maybe their targets were the nearby artillery. It must have been a fairly extended raid because AA fire was visible all along the front . . . followed by dull red glowing on the clouds as fires broke out.

83

Our journey commenced midnight: pitch dark. Nearing the Odon more mortars came over. Crossed the river at a 'ford': and then were allowed to use convoy lights . . . a tiny rear glimmer which helped a lot.

The northern hillside of the Odon valley was an amazing sight. Several miles of it were visible to us as we left the river: visible because of the searchlights, and the long lines of artillery constantly blazing away. Shells screamed over our heads . . . audible above the roar of our own vehicles. The entire hillside seemed to be alive, constantly spitting forth great long tongues of vivid white flame as each gun fired. The whole scene carried a background of leaping and waving searchlights, and red tracer AA, literally pouring upwards at the bombers. Personal precautions are impossible under such conditions. No question of keeping one's head down in the turret . . . a commander simply *has* to observe the ground to help the driver in the darkness.

Half an hour later, we had left the valley, and headed west for our destination – Fontenay-le-Pesnil . . . via Marcelet. We travelled flat out . . . away from the guns and bombers. A ridiculous speed, but fortunately the road was perfectly straight and fairly free from obstructions . . . very few low-hanging telephone wires etc.

Reached harbour 1.30 a.m. . . . in a field: I expected we would have been at least two hours later. Most of the crews settled down for an hour or two's sleep inside the tanks. Few of us remained on guard. We are still fairly close to Jerry here . . . about 2½ miles. At 4.30 a.m., our forward MG units opened up with heavy fire . . . about a mile south. And then Jerry replied with HE shells. Had to take cover.

Had an hour's sleep on gearbox hatch 6–7 a.m. Breakfast . . . and then maintenance on vehicles and guns. They needed it. Infantry here are North and South Staffs: seem a decent lot of fellows. We are already indebted to them for potatoes, ciggys and tea. Have been out here a month – on Tilly sector and Caen area.

John Hodges recalls the move from Hill 112 to Fontenay-Le-Pesnil:

26 July: We moved to Fontenay-Le-Pesnil for a couple of days rest. An immediate recce was ordered with infantry of 59th Division as we were in a counter-attack role. During this recce at Brettevillette B Squadron troop leaders received a severe set-back. They were in a sunken road when some mortars fell in the next field. Freddie Smart and Sergeant Nicholls were instantly killed. Peter Beale and Jimmy Cargill badly injured. Later Cargill died in hospital. We buried them all in a wood near Fontenay-Le-Pesnil [The cause of these casualties was in fact an S-mine].

Peter Beale remembers the occasion very vividly:

We went on this recce in the fitters' half-track and Nicky (Fitter Sergeant Bill Nicholls) was driving. We hadn't been in the area before, and didn't see the 'mines in verges' sign at the beginning of the lane. We got out at a point from where we could go forward to meet Mike, and some of us got on the bank to look over into the field. Suddenly, bang! I felt as though I had been hit in the back with a sledge hammer, and fell to the ground. I found I could get up, and moved over to Freddie. Help me, he said. I took out the morphia syringe we all had to deal with pain and injected it into his forearm. But both his legs were smashed to pieces from the thighs down and he died in five minutes. Poor dear Fred, such a good friend.

Mines were most unpleasant things, and the S-mine was very nasty for the individual. It was the shape and size of a tin of baked beans, and was activated by its detonator prongs. The prongs were depressed by a foot treading on them, and the detonator was activated. The prongs were released when the person's foot moved off them, and two explosions took place one after the other. The first one blew the can 3 feet in the air, and the second one exploded the can and its contents of metal pellets. One description of the effects of an S-mine suggests that both legs would be amputated and the man <u>might</u> survive; but if he was not a father already, he had lost his chance.

Jack Woods found himself at the Forward Delivery Squadron in late July, and it was not a place entirely to his liking:

The Forward Delivery Squadron, there's a prospect to cheer a body, it lived up to its reputation, the days I spent there were days too many and I was relieved to be sent back to the battalion in a replacement tank commanded by Sergeant Dickie Hall. We joined the battalion convoy as they were moving through Villers Bocage towards the River Orne taking on board infantry of the 7th Royal Norfolks, 59 Div, en route, finally deploying before the river in what Captain Sidney Link, 2 i/c C Squadron described as an arrow in the next day's *Daily Mirror*. We thought that we were destined to cross the river the next day, but no, we were pulled out and despatched to the other end of the bridgehead to support 49 Div and the Canadians in the battles to close the Falaise gap. En route I was transferred to B Squadron where I joined the crew of a troop leader's tank *Inspire IV* where I remained for the rest of my service with the 9th. Lt. David Scott became troop leader roughly the same time and the

Crew of 9 troop leader's tank Inspire V *at Lichtenvoorde, Holland, April 1945. Jack Woods, Cyril Smith, Bob Hay, Lt. David Scott, L/Cpl. Len Lennard.*

rest of the crew were, Troopers Bob Hay, a gritty Brummie, Cyril 'Smudger' Smith and Len Lennard a German Jew with a penchant for disappearing for the night whenever we laagered and magicking himself a woman out of nowhere. The War Diaries will record what further actions 9 Troop took part in in Normandy, the bowels of a Churchill tank are no place to acquire an intimate knowledge of the terrain covered, that had to be left to those who knew. It was mostly 1,000-yard jobs from Point A to Point B, remaining on the objective all day and pulling back at dusk to service the tank and get a hot meal if possible.

WITH THE CANADIANS TO FALAISE

As the Americans poured through the western end of the bridgehead, Hitler saw on studying the maps that all supplies and reinforcements for the American advance had to squeeze through a corridor only 12 miles wide, with its main road junction at Avranches. He forced his reluctant commanders and troops to gather all the armour they could muster for a push westward from Mortain to close the corridor. They pushed on 6 August, but the Americans defended stoutly and the allied airforces had clear skies. The result was that the German position became completely out of balance, and they lost tanks desperately needed to give them a chance of a fighting withdrawal to the east.

On 7 August the First Canadian Army, formed on 1 August and commanded by General Harry Crerar, attacked from their positions south of Caen in the direction of Falaise. This was called Operation Totalize. The first stage was an advance at night with tanks and armoured personnel carriers (APCs). APCs were used to ferry infantry forward with substantial protection against shelling, mortaring, and small arms fire. They were largely the idea of Lt.-Gen. Guy Simonds, commander of II Canadian Corps. They were created by taking the armament out of 105 mm self-propelled field guns. The code-name for these vehicles was 'Priest', and the APCs were intially called Unfrocked Priests or Holy Rollers; later they were called Kangaroos. The first stage was completely successful. The second stage, a daylight attack by the 4th Canadian Armoured Division and the Polish Armoured Division (both in action for the first time), was not nearly so successful, and ground to a halt 8 miles short of Falaise.

The Canadians next operation was 'Tractable', starting on 14 August. This was to take Falaise, and did. The Americans were coming north towards Chambois, the Canadians and Poles south-east to Trun and St. Lambert-sur-Dives, where they met on 19 August. The Falaise pocket was tenuously closed, although determined bodies of Germans fought their way back to the east. By this time the allies were themselves advancing to the east, the Canadians along the Channel coast, the Americans towards Paris, and the British to the River Seine.

31 Tank Brigade fought with 59 Div at the beginning of the break-out, and First Canadian Army at the end. This change meant a long and slow switch from one part of the front to another.

The War Diary

6 August: Now under command First Canadian Army the battalion arrived after a long and dusty march in I Corps area, and when darkness had fallen at 2230 hrs moved to the Forward Assembly Area to support 70 Brigade of 49 Div in a counter-attack role.
Note: First Canadian Army consisted at this time of II Canadian Corps and I British Corps. One of the divisions in I Corps was the 49th (West Riding) British Infantry Division.

7 August: These defensive areas were reconnoitred by squadron leaders, each to be a strong point supported by a battalion of infantry. The areas were La Prieure, Cagny, and Lepoirier –

Frenouville. These defensive areas were linked with Operation 'Totalize' which had as its objective the capture of Falaise. They were designed to give protection to the lines of communication of II Canadian Corps from left flank attack as well as to form a strong defensive base should Op 'Totalize' not go according to plan.

1800 hrs: A warning order was received that 31 Tank Brigade with 146 Infantry Brigade (49 Div) may be required for further flank protection roles during Totalize.

8 August: 1130: 9 RTR ordered to close gap on left flank from Frenouville to Bellengreville to allow 153 Brigade of 51st (Highland) Division to attack wooded area north-west of Secqueville la Campagne. C Squadron now moved to area Four and A Squadron to area Bourgebus. B Squadron was in reserve with BHQ.

There was spasmodic shelling and mortaring during the day, some of our medium 5.5 inch shells falling in B Squadron's area, but there were no casualties.

1915: Battalion moved to rear rally area Grentheville and at a conference with the Commander of 146 Brigade Operation Egg was outlined.

9 August: Orders received as follows:

31 Tank Brigade supporting 49 Div to secure left flank area Bellengreville – Vimont – Chicheboville;

7 RTR to support 147 Brigade from Frenouville south-east to Vimont;

9 RTR to support 146 Brigade from wooded area near La Hogue to Vimont.

At the time this plan was made the situation was very fluid and obscure; the enemy were fighting local actions, but there was a general belief that they were withdrawing.

Operation Egg was never given a definite H-hour, and was to be put into operation only if a definite defence centre round Vimont was encountered. Consequently various phases of Operation Egg were completed by troops other than those given the task and there appeared to be no coordination at all.

1700 hrs: reports issued as follows:

1st Leics (147 Brigade) in Star Wood

147 Brigade to send patrols to Vimont and 4th Lincs were to take over from 1st Leics.

1905 hrs: Battalion moved from Grentheville to area of crossroads north of La Hogue and almost immediately two troops of C Squadron were asked to support the Hallams who were making for Chicheboville. The support was given and no serious enemy opposition was encountered; the Hallams dug in on the outskirts of Chicheboville and the two troops of C Squadron rejoined the battalion, having destroyed snipers and mortar positions.

10 August: At first light A Squadron moved to area Star Wood with the intention of linking up with the 1st/4th Kings Own Yorkshire Light Infantry (1/4 KOYLI) and supporting them to Bellengreville. They remained in that area all day, however, as the infantry walked into their objective and decided to go no further. C Squadron first supported the Hallams with two troops in consolidating Chicheboville and later, as resistance stiffened, with the whole squadron in an attempt to clear wood to the east of Chicheboville. At 1040 hrs this wood was clear but heavy mortaring forced the Hallams to draw back to Chicheboville at midday.

49 Recce met no serious opposition during its patrols that required the support of tanks, so B Squadron remained with BHQ where shelling caused several casualties (see below).

C Squadron stayed with Hallams till 2000 hrs and then joined the battalion, claiming the destruction of three Spandaus and several mortar positions. Shelling was persistent in the battalion area and more casualties were incurred. On this day Sergeants Frank Holding (A), Bill Turner (HQ) and Tom Phillips (C) were killed, as was Trooper Tom Park; Sergeant Bill

Basham, Lance Corporals Brown and Telford, and Troopers Bowen, Gunn and Reynolds were wounded.

12 August: A plan to capture Benauville (Operation Tempest) was made, but the attack did not develop. The battalion left the area to join II Canadian Corps for Operation Tractable.

13 August: At 1700 hrs the CO was called to Brigade HQ and Commander 31 Tank Brigade outlined the plan for Tractable. The brigade was made corps reserve, and 9 RTR were to take up a position at Estrées la Campagne to prevent any attempt to cut II Can Corps lines of communication during their attack on Falaise.
1900 hrs: Battalion left harbour area and at 2105 hrs concentrated in the area of Urville 0750; there was no shelling or mortaring in this new area, which was a welcome change.

14 August: CO and squadron leaders were informed of the defence areas which had been allocated to them.
1200 hrs: the squadrons had moved to their areas and were also on the edge of the safety line for the heavy bombing that was to be administered by the RAF at 1400 hrs. For the first hour the bombing seemed to be very accurate, and the wood that the battalion was watching was ripped and battered on its northern edges. But heavy explosions and huge columns of smoke to the rear proved that one wave of bombers had lost their target and were dropping bombs on the area of Hautmesnil where it was known that the field artillery and the Polish Armoured Division were concentrated.
This exhibition lasted for about half an hour, and the morale of the battalion and its opinion of the RAF dropped considerably. The last half hour of bombing was fortunately directed on to the correct targets.
As the last bomber flew away A Squadron reported suspected enemy tanks firing in their direction; one tank was hit, but the shot did not penetrate.
1640 hrs: Two Shermans belonging to a Canadian Armoured Brigade HQ came into the battalion area with casualties. The CO of a Royal Artillery formation said that these two vehicles were the only survivors of the Brigade HQ, and that the other wounded were unattended. Capt. the Revd Patrick McMahon and the RA Colonel took out a half-track ambulance but within ten minutes it was seen to be in flames, hit by an unlocated anti-tank gun. A party sent out later on foot returned with the news that the Revd McMahon had been killed and almost unrecognizably burnt.

15 August: Recce Troop, patrolling south, captured a prisoner of the 1054 Grenadier Regiment, 85th Division. All POW confirmed that their forces were withdrawing, and that 85 Div had been rushed into the line after a three-day forced march with vague orders to defend Falaise.
The original plan of II Can Corps was now changed and the battalion was ordered to support 4 Can Infantry Brigade (2 Can Inf. Div) in a thrust on Falaise with the main road as the centre-line. The first order was that the battalion was to give support in establishing a firm base in the area Potigny, Ussy, Bons-Tassily.
1400 hrs: Battalion leaves present area. Reports indicate that the Germans were withdrawing as quickly as possible and orders were no more than 'Keep bashing on (KBO)' to Falaise.
To comply with this terse and elegant order B Squadron was to support the Essex Scottish to form a vanguard. A Squadron was allotted to the Royal Hamilton Light Infantry (RHLI) and C Squadron to the Royal Regiment of Canada (RRC) should these battalions require tank support.
2000 hrs: B Squadron start with Essex Scottish at Torps with the first objective of Villers Canivet. One mile south of Torps light infantry opposition and machine-gun fire was met but quickly cleared. A series of short sharp actions were fought, one resulting in the capture of an

88 mm anti-tank gun. Heavier opposition was met in the area Bois du Roi, but this was effectively dealt with. Failing light resulted in the infantry taking the lead with two companies up.

2330 hrs: The high ground north-west of Falaise had been reached and B Squadron spent the night in close laager, enduring heavy shelling and mortaring but suffering no casualties. The squadron had advanced 3½ miles and captured 100 prisoners. Commander 4 Can Inf. Brigade gave orders that the battalion was to remain in its present location for the night, but was to join B Squadron at first light.

16 August: 0830 hrs: Battalion was deployed right A Squadron left C Squadron in support of B Squadron. No further orders had been received, and no further information was available. The Bois du Roi to the rear was being shelled by our own artillery as well as being mortared by the enemy, and now and again it produced machine-gun fire.

Following a request for information, each of the three infantry brigades had no clear idea as to the intention of the other, or for that matter of their respective dispositions. Orders were finally received that 6 Cdn Brigade would clear Falaise and that 9 RTR should form a firm base with 4 Cdn Brigade in their present location.

1400 hrs: Orders were received for the battalion to move across country to harbour in the area of Chicheboville. C Squadron moved first and the shelling and mortaring increased. Later one B Squadron tank was hit and set on fire by 88 mm, but there were no casualties.

Everyone regretted not being able to enter Falaise, but appreciated the rest the following day having covered more than 40 miles in 30 hrs.

Personal recollections, 6–16 August

In these few days the British and Canadians experienced for the first time rapid movement against the enemy. The battle became very fluid, and at times it was very difficult to say where the allied troops were and where the Germans were. This was quite different to how it had been in the bridgehead, where positions of both sides were clearly known and advances were painfully slow. It took a while to get used to the changed circumstances, and the combination of all factors led to one overwhelming impression of this period of the campaign – confusion. Also in people's memories stand out the assaults by mosquitoes, the terrible destruction of the areas east and south of Caen, the mortaring and shelling, and the bombing that dropped in the wrong place. John Hodges writes on 8 August:

> The past week has been employed in moving right around Caen to the east of the bridgehead for an attack with the Canadians due south to Falaise. The bombing was a wonderful sight at night and we saw one bomber completely disintegrate in the air. We were about 1,000 yards from the nearest bomb and the blast was something tremendous. The whole of this area is infested with mosquitoes, making it impossible to get any sleep. Everyone is covered with a mass of bites. The weather is very hot and the countryside very, very dusty. Dead animals everywhere and movement involving any quantity of dust brings down shells.

Trevor Greenwood and his troop leader Seymour Francis had been left out of battle (LOB), and were back with the support vehicles in B Echelon (the tanks constituted the fighting or F Echelon). Tank crews were left out of battle periodically, both to allow them to rest and recuperate from the strain of fighting, and also to ensure that there was always a reserve of experienced tank crews. Trevor and Seymour were LOB just before the move round to First Canadian Army, but as Trevor records it didn't do them much good:

6.8.44: with B Echelon at Cristot.

Went to bed 10.30 last night . . . having spent some time organizing a comfortable spot of earth: had a bad time night before with lumpy ground. Was dozing off about 11.00 when I heard my name mentioned close by. Soon learned the horrible truth. Mr Francis and I had to return to F Echelon immediately: transport would pick us up in fifteen minutes! I felt slightly amazed! So did Mr Francis. Mr Boden and Sgt. Debenham had turned up to take our places on B Echelon. Damned cheek. We hadn't even been LOB – no battle had been fought! Crawled out of bed: Debenham seemed to take a delight in re-laying *his* bed in my warm spot.

About an hour elapsed before we found all kit etc. in the darkness. Departed in a jeep . . . 'F' were harboured beyond Villers Bocage and the surrounding country was lousy with mines and booby traps: two of our B vehicles were shattered day before by touching grass verges: one driver killed. About 5 miles south we entered newly won territory. It felt weird and unnatural . . . very quiet – very still – very smelly – very deserted.

Roads were quite narrow . . . and we knew all grass verges were still heavily mined . . . the engineers having had no time to attend to them. Passing oncoming traffic . . . especially large lorries – was a nightmare. *Their* drivers knew about the mines and so did we . . . but ours was only a jeep! We always had to veer over to the verge . . . and I just hung on and waited for the bang! Fortunately, it was a moonlight night, and we managed to survive . . . but I don't recommend such journeys . . . especially for nervous cases.

Reached the tanks 1.30 a.m.: all crews asleep. Spread my own bedding on ground . . . and dozed off. Awakened 4.30 a.m.: felt lousy: We managed some breakfast . . . tea and tinned bacon and departed 6.00 a.m. for area E of Caen . . . about 30-mile run: A new sector for us. Most of journey over field tracks: dust appalling. Went via Cheux, Marcelet . . . and skirted Caen to N. Reached assembly area 1.00 p.m. seven hours for 34 miles. Tank in shocking state . . . dust about an inch deep everywhere: guns hopeless. Spent about three hours tidying up.

Jock Cordiner remembers the mosquitoes: 'Mosquitoes in parts of Normandy more than bothered me. Was it by the River Orne or the Odon? We were stopped on the bank while another formation passed through. Most of us sat on the river bed all night, water up to our chins, to avoid the mossies.'

Trevor evidently wasn't quite so close to the river on the night of 7 August, but still had a rotten night:

Reveille 5.15 a.m. 'Stand to' 5.30 – 6.00 a.m. No cooking of any sort until after 6.30 a.m. Spent about four hours in 'bed' last night . . . and what a night! We discovered a new secret weapon . . . mosquitoes! The bloody things almost ate us alive. Half the squadron have blistered faces this morning. Very few seem to have had much sleep. The Major is in a bad way. No sleep at all last night, in spite of three almost sleepless nights previously. Believe the MO is trying to do something for us. Wasps and flies not so bad here . . . yet! But prefer them to mosquitoes. Feel sure many nights like last will drive us all mad. Maybe the Orne (about 2 miles away) accounts for the mosquitoes.

On 10 August the 9th made one of their many moves around this time, as John Hodges records:

Moved to La Hogue and Secqueville which were bombed yesterday. Complete and utter devastation everywhere and a horrible smell of burning and rubble. Lots of mines about and plenty of odd shells fall. While harboured up on a hill were heavily shelled. Two men in A

Squadron killed by shell which fell just behind the half-track and four wounded. About 6 p.m. Headquarters must have been spotted for the shells began to land a few feet away. The half-track was hit in the radiator and the aerials blown away. Decided it was getting more than a joke and moved Headquarters about half a mile away. Found out later had been riding my bike over a minefield most of the morning.

Although the village of La Hogue had been very heavily bombed, there was still life, as Cyril Smith remembers:

We moved back round Caen and entered La Hogue after it had been erased by a heavy bomber raid. At that time I was the wireless-op in *Impulse*, the troop sergeant's tank in 9 Troop B Squadron. Out of the rubble came a distressed tiny black and white kitten. We took it on board, to be attended to later. After bivouacking down for the night we examined it and found it to be a tom. He was too young to take any solid food, and had to be given liquid through a rubber tube. Consequently he was named Titti La Hogue, and signed on as spare crew.

This little cat became a great inspiration to us in the art of survival. He would never leave the vicinity of the tank. He may have lost his hearing, because noise never bothered him. Titti went through many escapades with us. His place was sitting on the tool box behind the driver or in the co-driver's pannier bin. Only once did he get too near the clutch pedal, but fortunately squawked a warning in time.

Cyril Smith, 9 Troop, B Squadron, a member of troop leader David Scott's tank Inspire. *From the rubble of La Hogue Cyril rescued a kitten that became a faithful crew member of* Inspire *for some months.*

91

One morning in a flax field in Belgium Titti was missing. We decided he had been taken prisoner by either friend or foe. We found him later, but didn't put him on a charge. Instead he had a double ration of sardines and machonochy's soup with a good rollicking.

Unfortunately some weeks later it became Titti's turn to enter the green fields. His eyes became badly affected with some type of liquid, possibly acid, giving him great pain. We had to administer an overdose of chloroform, and buried him at the side of a canal in Holland. It gave us great sadness, knowing that we had lost a faithful crew member. His ninth life ended as a tankie.

The second stage of the Canadian attack on Falaise was Operation 'Tractable'. This began on 14 August with a preliminary bombardment by the RAF and four AGRAs (Army Groups Royal Artillery). As the War Diary described, the first and last parts of the RAF bombardment were on target, but the middle part was not. It felt to many people as though they were being bracketed by the bombs, and it would be only a matter of time before the 9th was bombed as well. John Hodges writes on 14 August:

Moved to Gouvix and to Estrées-La-Campagne in preparation for the big Canadian break through towards Falaise. Something went wrong with the RAF bombing attack. We were about 1,000 yards from the nearest positions that were to be bombed. The first wave dropped their bombs plumb on the target but the succeeding waves dropped them well behind us – among the Canadians and the Poles. It was most unpleasant and one felt pretty hopeless. Gradually the bombs crept closer to where we were and we threw out yellow smoke and waved. Fortunately none landed among us but it was a terrifying two hours. Later Headquarters Canadian Armoured Division was shot up in front of us and the Revd McMahon went forward in an ambulance to try and pick up survivors. An 88 mm shell went straight through the ambulance killing the Padre and a stretcher-bearer (the latter had been one of my clerks). The driver got back with scratches and severe burns. McMahon was a great little man and it was a great blow to us all.

Cyril Smith remembers the death of the Revd Patrick McMahon, the RAF bombing, and a particularly close call with an anti-tank gun:

After joining the Canadians we were in the area of Quesnay in a hull down position watching the wood. Two Shermans were knocked out, to our front. Smoke was belching from one of them.

A half-track with a Red Cross flag flying came through from the rear, obviously with the task of dealing with survivors. Bang! No respect for the Red Cross sign. It was knocked out. We were informed that the RC Padre Capt. McMahon was on board. He was found later in the corn, where he had died of his wounds.

Later on there was a huge bombing raid to our front by the RAF. We had to use yellow smoke as the bombs were creeping closer and closer. At least they destroyed the area where the '88 fire was coming from.

We then moved out to a point on the Caen–Falaise road during late afternoon. It was then 'Tank Commanders Wireless Ops to OC's tank for briefing'. The outcome was a night op to close the Falaise gap, supporting the Canadian infantry. B Squadron were leading with 9 Troop up.

God, this meant me in the leading tank (if blood's brown I'm wounded), because I was troop officer's wireless-op. This is how it turned out. We set off during the evening, with infantry up front. When it became dusk we heard a bang bang on the side of the tank. It was an infantry man with his rifle butt. 'Advance very slowly', he said. 'We believe there is an '88 anti-tank gun somewhere up front.'

Five minutes later, 'Flash bang' as I was looking through my periscope. I swear to this day that the projectile travelled between the gun barrel and the driver's hatch. 'Smoke, driver reverse' shouted my troop officer, David Scott. I squeezed the 2-inch mortar trigger. I always had 'one up the spout' set on minimum range, which was only a few feet in front of the tank. I fired two more bombs as *Inspire* rolled backwards. We could only reverse a short distance, because of our troop sergeant's tank.

'Flash bang' the second shot was about 20 feet in front. He was firing blind as it was almost dark, and we were on a sunken road. He was in a field 90 degrees to our right. We were now stationary, covered by our own smoke, and unable to do anything except cringe in dreaded anticipation. 'Will it be now?' 'Where is the third shot?' 'Will he miss again?' 'Has our luck finally run out?'

The third shot never arrived. After what seemed like eternity, an infantry officer jumped on board with 'OK boys, '88 silenced'. After that we could never be grateful enough for the infantry.

We saw the gun later. It was a 'dual purpose' 88 mm on a high mounting, and its barrel was splayed out like a small palm tree. They had silenced it all right.

Trevor Greenwood knew that the bombing attack was due to take place:

Left harbour 12 noon: moved 2 or 3 miles E to defensive position. Our 'briefing' included details of bombing programme for today. Three or four woods immediately S and E of our position were to be blasted from 2 p.m. until 4 p.m.

Reached our area at 2.00 p.m., just as RAF four-engined bombers commenced bombing wood 2,000 yds to our front. What a sight! Horrible: terrifying . . . and yet fascinating. The whole earth trembled: trees rocketed sky-high . . . enormous fountains of earth shot upwards: smoke – fire – death. God help the Germans in that wood! Hundreds of bombs rained down in the first few minutes. We were thrilled by the RAF. This was direct support for us with a vengeance. Every one of us felt more cheerful. Knowing too that our very heavy attack had commenced at 12.00 noon and that the end of this campaign may not be far off.

It was about 2.30 p.m. Many waves of bombers had unloaded their bombs where we wanted them . . . but suddenly, a stick of bombs fell on a point about a mile to our *rear*. Was it Jerry? No! There were two or three dozen Lancasters over the spot: one of them must have dropped his bombs accidentally over our own lines . . . the damned fool! Hard luck on our lads, but an accident can't be helped.

More waves of bombers appeared, and most of these too dropped their bombs over our lines. The awful truth dawned: They were bombing the smoke laden area indicated by that first stick . . . even though it was 2 miles N of their most northerly target.

Why couldn't they be stopped? We endured hell, even though we were fairly safe from the bombs. What a contrast with our former jubilation! Half an hour later, more bombers dropped their loads over another area . . . slightly west, in our lines. The destruction behind us was now becoming greater than ahead. And so it went on . . . with our own bombs murdering our own men . . . and dropping nearer to us as the afternoon wore on. We put out yellow smoke flares in a frantic effort to save ourselves. I saw bomb doors opening as the planes approached . . . and expected to be blown to hell any moment. They were quite low . . . about 3 or 4 thousand feet. I saw Very lights being fired from the ground as signals to stop the bombing. I heard machine-gunning in the air . . . and was afterwards told that Spitfires had been trying to divert the bombers. I heard later too that a little Auster went up to try and stop this ghastly blunder. But it went on. I didn't know then that there was no liaison between our ground forces and the bombers. I could only wonder, at the time, and my heart wept. So much depended upon today's action: the war even may be shortened by its success. It had been planned carefully and secretly . . . We had almost looked forward to it. And now . . . this thing.

This 'little Auster' was piloted by Lt. Eversley Belfield, who was then Air Observation Post Pilot with the Canadian Army. His prime purpose was to observe from his Auster the fall of shots from the AGRAs so that they could make corrections as necessary. He saw from the ground the first wave of bombs fall perfectly on Quesnay Wood. The second wave's bombs, however, fell well to the north in areas occupied by allied troops. He rushed to his plane, started it up and climbed at full throttle firing Very cartridges as he went. Just below a large formation he twisted and turned to attract their attention, and felt confident that all further bombardments fell on their intended targets.

The day after the bombing débâcle was the day of KBO to Falaise. Ronnie Holden recounts how it seemed to him:

We then moved off on to the main road and went down to a number of small villages where the German Army were taking breakfast and had not realized that enemy tanks were among them. Just before we got to Falaise we had the order to form a regimental laager which we did in a very large circle next to the Brettvillette wood where we could hear German Nebelwerfers being fired off back to positions we had been in. Our laager was a massive one with guns pointing in all directions of the compass and under cover, we sent out raiding parties to try and stop the Nebelwerfers from firing back, but as they were all mounted in vehicles we were never in time to get them in their firing positions. The result of our laager was to stop all traffic, particularly the enemy tanks and other vehicles moving back into Falaise, for at the time Falaise was being attacked by British forces supported by RAF fighter-bombers and were being hit very hard indeed. We remained in the laager for the whole day and nothing of course could get past us although from the west the enemy tanks were taking pot shots at us but without effect.

THE BATTLES OF THE BRIDGES, 17–26 AUGUST 1944

The Battle of the Falaise Pocket was not really complete until the end of two bloody actions fought by the Canadians at St. Lambert-sur-Dives and the Poles at Point 262. But while these final actions took place, the allies were beginning to sweep to the east.

On 20 August Montgomery's orders were for the complete destruction of the enemy forces in north-west France, and then to advance north and east to destroy all enemy forces in north-east France. This demanded that 21st Army Group, once all Germans in the pocket had been eliminated, should advance to the Seine with all speed. The Second British Army were to cross between Mantes and Louviers, and the First Canadian Army in the neighbourhood of Rouen. Once across the Seine the Second Army would drive north to the Somme between Amiens and the sea. From Rouen the Canadian Army was to wheel left and quickly seize the whole of the Le Havre peninsula.

Meanwhile Bradley's 12th Army Group was to assemble to the west and south-west of Paris,

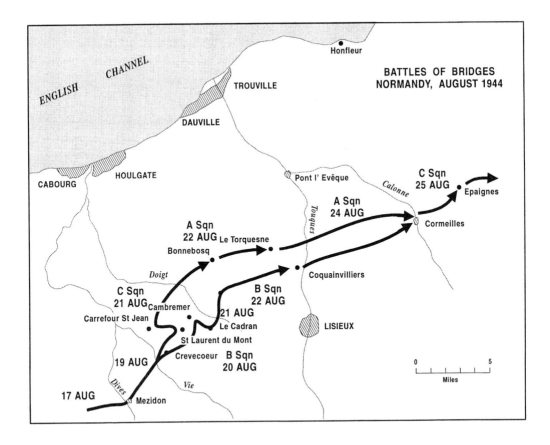

BATTLES OF BRIDGES
NORMANDY, AUGUST 1944

ready to advance on the line Orleans–Amiens. From there Bradley would be poised to move north-east towards Aachen and Brussels or east to the Saar.

The Canadian advance to the Seine on the left flank of 21st Army Group involved crossing the rivers Dives, Vie, Doigt, Touques, Calonne, and Risle. Consequently, the battles of the bridges were undertaken.

The War Diary

17 August: 1600: Orders were received that 9 R Tks were again under comd 49 Div and that Bn should move to just west of Mezidon and take over from 7 R Tks by 0600 hrs on 18 August.
It was known that the 10 DLI had a small bridgehead over the R. Dives at Mezidon, and that enemy were holding pt 66 in some strength – all other bridges had been blown. The task given to the Regt was to support 49 Div in widening and strengthening the bridgehead when RE's had built bridges over the River Dives.

18 August: 1115: At a conference held at 49 Div HQ, the Div Comd stated that the opposition on east of R. Dives was not sufficient to justify the use of tanks in support of infantry, and to ease traffic problems across bridge at Mezidon – the only one complete – no tanks should move across that bridge. 9 R Tks should carry out a recce to see whether it was possible to use the 'Jumbo' Churchill at possible crossings of the River Vie so that it could be crossed quickly when it became necessary. RHQ, B & C Sqns were allotted to support 146 Bde and A Sqn to support 70 Bde.

1400: Maj Holden and Capt. Kidd (C Sqn) carrying out recce for bridge crossing over the River Vie had their scout car destroyed by 50 mm A/Tk fire. They brought back information that a Jumbo bridge would not span river at this point.

19 August: 0708: At 0630 hrs Bn passed through Mezidon and concentrated short of the River Vie. Capt. Brewer, reconnoitring another possible bridge site over the River Vie was badly wounded in the stomach by Spandau fire, but brought back information that tanks could not be used at that point either.

0740: 49 Div issued orders that as no effective infantry crossing had been made across R. Vie tanks would not yet be required. During the day information was received that the first bridge over the River Vie available for 49 Div forward elements would probably be that built by 51 Highland Division and that 9 RTR should be prepared to cross there with A Sqn supporting 49 Div Recce, B Sqn supporting 147 Bde and C Sqn 146 Bde.

20 August: 0830: A Sqn move forward to be on call to support 49 Div Recce forward in bounds.

1130: B Sqn cross bridge and assemble in area of Crevecoeur to support 147 Bde.

1325: C Sqn leave harbour area in order to contact Hallams (146 Bde) north of Crevecoeur to support them to high ground near St. Laurent du Mont.

1430: B Sqn prepare to attack supporting RSF and thence to the line of the River Doigt. B Sqn pushed on in front, clearing the way for infantry and had reached their first objective by 1515 hrs. At 1600 hrs, RSF began taking over and at 1725 B Sqn pushed on again. No serious resistance was encountered; light A/Tk gun fire and MG fire was met but quickly dealt with so that by 1912 hrs they dominated the area of the bridge, and the infantry arrived half an hour later to begin securing the position covered by the tanks.

C Sqn met with many delays in their effort to contact the Hallams. In avoiding mines and keeping clear of the main roads, an occasional tank became temporarily ditched, and the leading troop hit mines in a defile which caused further difficulties. But by 1710 hrs contact with the Hallams had been made and a plan was made to attack St. Pair du Mont, the attack to start at 1830 hrs. Civilians reported that main enemy forces had already retreated north to high ground.

C Sqn attack started at 1630 hrs but the advance was slow due to difficult going which included the pushing down of houses to get through. At 1915 hrs the tanks began climbing the high ground which had an incline of about 1 in 4 with a field of view at times limited to less than 50 yds, due to foliage. Nevertheless, the tanks were on their objective at 1940, ahead of the infantry, and had destroyed 1/75 mm A/Tk gun and 1/50 mm Fd gun.

One tank had been knocked out resulting in the death of Trooper Taffy Bridgeman and the wounding of Lt. Arthur 'Dinty' Moore. Tpr. Fred Barker, Tpr. Johnny 'Tiger' Boland, Cpl. Bill Geary and Tpr. Tommy Latham were also wounded by mortar fire and three tanks were ditched. B Sqn suffered no casualties at all.

A Sqn was never required to support 49 Div Recce but Capt. P.M. Myatt was accidentally shot in the leg.

21 August: The tasks for the day were as follows:

C Sqn to support KOYLI in an attack on St. Laurent du Mont and then to secure the road through Carrefour St. Jean;

B Sqn were to move to Crevecoeur-en-Auge and then NE to Cambremer;

The nature of the ground, hilly and wooded, made it quite impossible for the tanks to attack in a deployed formation. So it was decided, as enemy opposition was expected to be light, that the infantry would attack in an orthodox manner, but that the tanks would move behind along roads when possible and either take over the ground from the infantry or be brought up to destroy any strong point encountered;

The KOYLI had little difficulty in securing their objectives and by 1200 hrs C Sqn had assembled in area Carrefour St. Jean. B Sqn were at Crevecoeur with the DWR exploiting to Cambremer. By 1350 hrs it was realized that this type of attack against a retreating enemy was no good at all and far too slow, so it was decided to advance on two-thrust lines so that contact is maintained with the enemy and allowed no respite.

C Squadron in support of 146 Brigade were to advance through Carrefour St. Jean, Bonnebosq and Le Torquesne to the River Touques. B Squadron in support of 147 Brigade were to advance on a more southerly axis through Le Cadran and La Roque-Baignard to the River Touques.

1830: C Sqn were approaching Bonnebosq which was offering resistance and it was apparent that an attack would have to be put in to clear it. The Sqn deployed to cover the village and sealed the exits while KOYLI attacked.

2015: Bonnebosq clear and infantry established themselves for the night. By 2100 hrs B Squadron had reached La Roque-Baignard. They had been held up by poor roads, mines and A/Tk fire. One 75 mm A/Tk gun had been captured. During the afternoon the Recce Troop had been patrolling bridges and roads and at 2230 hrs killed thirty German infantry in woods to the west of the River Touques.

22 August: The advance on thrust lines continued but A Sqn replaced C Sqn and joined up with 4th Lincs, while B Sqn continued on their route with RSF.

Little opposition was met. A Sqn reached the River Touques at 1400 and B Sqn reached the river an hour and a half later. Both bridges had been blown, but RSF found a footbridge which they crossed, supported by tanks. Heavy mortaring resulted in Tpr. Wilf Woodfine being killed and twelve people being wounded.

Capt. Frank Drew of A Sqn was also wounded in the head as a result of mortaring.

As the tanks had no field of fire in the low ground by the river and no alternative positions were possible, B Sqn joined HQ. C Sqn joined HQ at 2030 hrs.

24 August: It was not till about 0900 hrs that class 40 bridges had been made across R. Touques but two-thrust lines had been planned to converge on Cormeilles.

Owing to the short time available for maintenance and the little rest that the tank crews were getting, 144 RAC came under command 49 Div and were allotted the southern route. A Sqn supporting 56 Bde were to advance on the northern route. Steady progress was made throughout the day and at 2115 hrs A Sqn was supporting 2nd Essex into Cormeilles. Only pockets of machine-gun fire and small number of tank obstacles and mines had been encountered.

Bn HQ established itself during the day to the west of Cormeilles where it was joined by C Sqn at 2015 hrs. B Sqn remained at its old location.

25 August: The advance was delayed awaiting completion of class 40 bridge at Cormeilles but at 0830 C Sqn crossed R. Calonne supporting 2 Glos as the leading formation of the brigade group. The axis of advance was to be through Epaignes and thence north-east to the River Risle in the area of Pont Audemer.

Enemy defences were soon found to be centred round Epaignes, La Houssaye and La Heberdiere. C Sqn quickly surrounded Epaignes but the infantry insisted on putting in a number of small attacks which were all abortive.

Later, however, it dawned upon the infantry commander that a coordinated attack had to be made in some strength. This was put in at 2100 hrs and Epaignes fell within an hour.

C Sqn during the day had destroyed 2/75 mm A/Tk guns; killed about 100 inf and captured Adjt of Bn Schleue (346 Div). One tank had been hit by a Faustapatrone which penetrated the turret and killed Trooper Ken Button of 14 Troop. It seemed that Epaignes had been the centre of resistance guarding Pont Audemer and if the infantry had not delayed so long it might have been possible to have got to Pont Audemer before dark, which would no doubt have resulted in the capture of a considerable amount of equipment and personnel.

A Sqn had remained in reserve at Cormeilles. Much to the delight of the inhabitants, Major Mockford took the salute in the Square during a march past of the Free French forces and placed a wreath on the cenotaph. Later, there was a celebration with champagne in the Town Hall and the whole Sqn had been promised sheets and beds in the village.

But at about 1800 hrs Cormeilles was heavily shelled and one tank was put out of action by a 150 mm shell. This put an end to the celebrations and A Sqn joined BHQ. There were, however, no casualties as a result of the shelling.

The Brigadier, 56 Bde, expected a further advance to Pont Audemer to be strongly opposed and decided that a thrust should be made on two lines with an infantry battalion and a tank squadron on each.

On the northern thrust line the 2nd South Wales Borderers were supported by B Squadron from Epaignes to point 128 north-west of St. Symphorien; on the southern thrust line the 2nd Essex were supported by A Squadron from Epaignes to St. Symphorien.

26 August: 0815: A & B Sqns crossed the start line at Epaignes and by 0950 the objectives had been reached – no opposition had been encountered at all.

1130: Bridges across R. Risle at Pont Audemer were blown and the unit again became static, moving across the river the following day when the whole area south of the Seine except for the Fôret de Bretonne had been cleared. 56 Bde were finally given the job of clearing the forest but did not require tank support.

The Bn remained concentrated at Fourmetot having covered 60 miles in the last nine days. Flowers, cheers, handclapping and waves from civilians were a pleasant change, after the grim days of breaking-out of bridgehead, even if whenever the impetus to advance had been gained it had been already cheated by yet another blown bridge.

Personal recollections, 17–26 August

We last heard of Sgt. Dickie Hall when he was injured near Grainville during Operation Epsom, and was about to be shipped back to England on an empty Tank Landing Craft, its deck covered with stretchers. He records what happened to him until he rejoined C Squadron just at the beginning of the battles of the bridges:

At Southampton we were put on a hospital train and taken to Ascot, where among other things we were able to dictate a telegram to our people. (I never asked my mother what were her thoughts when the telegraph boy delivered it at home.)

After a day we went again by hospital train to Preston, Lancs, where part of the local Psychiatric Hospital had been taken over by the army. My bed was in a 'padded cell'.

My wound healed well and I was given a few days leave. My parents had known a General Woods for many years before the war, and while I was at home for those few days General Woods came to see my father, and it was a great surprise for me to discover that he was CO of the 9 RTR in the 1914 war, when the regiment was decorated by the French Fusiliers – with whom they had fought – with the Croix-de-Guerre. The General was decorated with the Legion of Honour, and it is the Fusiliers cap badge that we all wore with pride on our left sleeve.

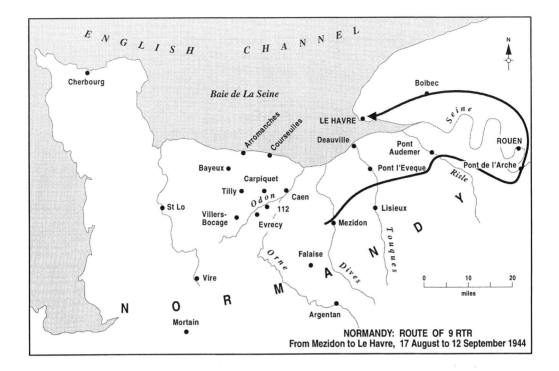

NORMANDY: ROUTE OF 9 RTR
From Mezidon to Le Havre, 17 August to 12 September 1944

I had to report to Catterick Camp (Yorkshire) where we were given new equipment, and again, after a few days, went south and crossed over to Normandy in an old troopship called *Neuralia*, and landed at Mulberry Harbour. From there we marched to a unit for sending replacement crews and tanks forward. I had a scratch crew and we had an uneventful journey, until I was glad to find that the 9th was nearby and C Squadron was in a nearby orchard. I found all the crew well, plus the relief sergeant who was willing for me to take over again, and Squadron HQ gave permission.

The changed atmosphere from the grimness of the early battles might have accounted for some carelessness in the advance between the Dives and the Seine, as Jack Woods suggests:

My next recollections were of the advance to the River Seine, crawling along in the column and receiving the hospitality of the local population (especially the women), the wine and the flowers, so much so that when held up by a blown bridge we pulled off the road into a field where we duly brewed up. We weren't long before we were receiving the attentions of the rearguard that the enemy had left on the other side of the river, we casually watched ourselves being bracketed and were caught in the open when a salvo landed among us. The result, the inevitable casualties including one fatality Trooper Wilf Woodfine who was buried there and whose grave the locals vowed to look after forever (I wonder if it is still there).

The B Squadron casualties referred to by Jack Woods were incurred at Coquanvilliers. The river, from the other side of which they were shelled, was the Touques. The other major group of casualties in the battles of the bridges was suffered in the area of St. Laurent-du-Mont, as Cyril Rees and Trevor Greenwood both remember. Cyril first:

Dennis 'Fitz' Fitzgerald, 9 Troop, B Squadron, wounded at Coquanvilliers, 22 August 1944.

St. Laurent-du-Mont: A small skirmish, scarcely worth recording in a battalion history, let alone a regimental history, I hear you say. But all skirmishes involve people, sometimes fatally. This minor event does just that.

The chateau was the highest point on the densely wooded estate, with parkland below. It was believed to be an observation and information centre for the German forces in the area. 13 Troop was part of a force which was to isolate the chateau and cut off escape routes. We were working with part of an infantry company.

Experienced though I was in many actions as a tank crew member, I felt quite isolated and on my own, just Don Foster and I moving slowly forward at tick-over speed in first gear. Not an infantry man to be seen, just the back of the troop leader's tank about 10 yards ahead.

The road we were on was narrow – about 15 feet wide, steep banks dropping to a ditch on either side. A very high hedge separated this road from the park. On the right was also a high hedge plus additional thick shrubbery. Just ahead the road curved to the right. The leading tank started to drive round this bend, hugging the right-hand verge. I watched the rear plate as it began to move out of my view, then come back into view as we also moved into the bend. A great pall of smoke and a loud bang ahead and the troop leader's tank stopped with a jerk. Some of the crew began to bale out.

On this narrow road there was no possibility of us being able to move forward so I began to reverse slowly, trying to gauge how much I needed to apply the steering levers to retrace our forward movement. When I felt the right rear begin to drop away I stopped at once and drove forward to straighten up on the road, but too late to prevent some of the LH track begin to ride up on to the points of the front sprocket. Tom Tomney had been busy on the A set, and wasn't able to stop this happening. However, it was all hands to the pump, and getting out the tools we had the track back in position in a very short time. It was a great help to have Ginger Kirk, one of the squadron strong men, on our crew.

Just as we were finished, there was a loud clatter as a rifle was thrown on to the road. A dishevelled figure, with his hands up, appeared suddenly from the shrubbery on the right. He said he was a Russian, conscripted into the German Army. Tom ordered Don Foster to cover him with his pistol and hand him over to the infantry, 100 yards behind us.

Meanwhile, out of our sight, in the park to our left, Alf Beale and his crew had moved up through the park and had straddled the road up to the chateau. It would seem that they had all dismounted and were for some reason or other about to do a recce on foot. Just then, a German staff car came down the hill at great speed, saw Alf's tank across the road, quickly turned round, and returned like the clappers up the hill. By the time Alf's crew had hurled themselves back on board and organized all systems as go, it was too late.

In the event the objectives were achieved. The subsequent comments and explanations between Ronnie Holden and Alf Beale have as far as I know never been put on record.

Postscript
The troop leader's tank had been hit by an 88 mm field gun at short range. Moving round the bend, the hull gun and mounting came first into the '88's sights and here, sadly, Taffy Bridgeman lost out.

Trevor recorded his experiences in this action the day after it took place:

D + 76 Monday 21.8.44
I have yesterday's story to finish. Our move commenced about 2.00 p.m. roughly to the east after the retreating enemy. Over La Vie river, across RE bridge. This bridge had caused the infantry much trouble the previous day. From the bridge we went N making for St. Pair du Mont . . . still in enemy hands. At a stop en route, several civilians paid their respects, shaking hands with all and sundry. The usual greeting 'bonjour, mes amis'. Drinks were provided . . . and we parted with a fair amount of tinned food.

This halt occurred a mile or two from St. Pair du Mont. Suddenly we received orders to move . . . with all guns prepared for action. The enemy had been reported leaving the village, but in fair strength on a fairly high hill just N of the village: heavily wooded on top. We had to clear the wood and help the infantry occupy it.

Our start point an orchard: the darned place was a mass of small orchards . . . and immediately ahead lay that hill . . . rising steeply for 300 or 400 feet: quite a landmark . . . and a strong defensive position: but not a suitable attack for our vehicles.

Our troubles started almost immediately after the advance commenced. Firstly, it was impossible to fire our HE from the orchards, as contact with the trees would have exploded the shells over our own men. Also, each little orchard was surrounded by a deep ditch, making progress very difficult. In the first few minutes a few tanks were having track trouble . . . mine included. I managed to 'limp' towards a hedgerow, and took what cover I could. On inspection, I found the job would take at least two or three hours . . . providing we could borrow suitable tools. That put me out of action, less than half an hour after it commenced.

While inspecting my vehicle, I noticed another about 100 yds left burning: it must have been hit! Meanwhile, the rest of the squadron were advancing painfully slowly up the hill.

Immediately in front of me, a house was blazing fiercely: we had blasted it with HE: a terrible din, and uncomfortably close to me.

We had to make some attempt to repair my vehicle, so I ordered the crew to dismount and get busy . . . hoping we were sufficiently screened by the orchard in front to make the job possible. There was some enemy MG fire to our left, but we had to take the risk.

After working ten minutes or so, an enemy HE exploded 6 yards to our right. We had no warning whatever. Immediately, we all rushed around the left of the vehicle . . . not one of us had been hit by that first shell, altho' the blast shook us. At the rear of the vehicle, two of the crew had scrambled beneath, when another shell exploded ahead of its predecessor. Again I felt the awful hot blast, and wondered why I hadn't been hit: it was only a few feet away. Beneath the tank, Geary said he had been hit . . . in the arm. He had been just in front of me, and climbing beneath the vehicle when the second explosion occurred.

He was bleeding profusely. I clambered out again to get the first-aid kit from inside the tank. Fortunately, there was no third shot. By the time I found the kit, Geary had scrambled out, and was standing beside the vehicle, blood pouring from his left forearm. Nearby, there were infantry ambulance men taking cover in a house. I took him across, ignoring our own dressings, and left the other three members of the crew beneath the vehicle.

He was bandaged up, and a tourniquet applied, but already his colour was ashen, and I felt sure he was losing too much blood. The nearest ambulance, a jeep, was a quarter of a mile away in the village. He said he could walk alright and was already speaking of rejoining the crew! An ambulance man accompanied us to the village: en route we had one 'rest' to take cover from mortar fire.

After saying goodbye to Bill (he was still conscious, but looked very sick) I had a few words with the ambulance men.

My next job was to return to my vehicle . . . and I reached it without harm . . . altho' that darned Spandau MG seemed to be uncomfortably close. To my amazement, my driver, Johnny Boland, now reported that he too had been hit by shrapnel . . . he had made the discovery in my absence with Geary! He seemed inclined to ignore the matter, as it was a very small wound on his shoulder blade . . . but I had to insist upon him having attention. And so, once again I returned to the village, via the orchards etc. We heard the crack of a rifle en route . . . and I knew a sniper was busy in the vicinity . . . A few seconds later we found Gilmore had been hit through the hand by this sniper, whose presence made things a little more unpleasant. Gilmore and Boland were both handed over to the ambulance men . . . and I haven't seen either of them since.

It was while making my second journey back from the village that I experienced what were probably my worse moments since coming over here. I had reached the first orchard . . . and a few feet to my rear was one of our vehicles apparently in trouble. Some infantrymen had appeared and I was talking to one of them when a HE shell exploded without warning a few feet away. We all dropped to the ground instinctively and I and two of the infantry fellows crawled towards a log nearby for cover. I don't know how long I lay huddled up by that log. It was probably only for one or two minutes . . . but I will never forget them. The first explosion was the prelude to a 'stonk' aimed perhaps at the tank. It was followed by twenty or thirty others . . . all within a few feet of us. Very soon, I heard a groan beside me . . . and one of the infantry lads said 'I've had it'. Soon there were more groans and the other infantry lad was hit. Meanwhile the shells came down relentlessly. I could feel the hot blast from each one: the air became thick with the acrid fumes of cordite. I knew I should have been blown to smithereens by all the laws of explosives . . . but all the time I remained conscious of being alive. At one period, I realized that all the shells were landing on my side of the log, and wondered about changing to the other side . . . but there was insufficient pause between each explosion. So I just lay huddled up as small as possible . . . and hoped . . . and hoped.

I must have become partly stupified because I remained on the ground for some time after the last round . . . until I heard some voices, in fact, and found the group of infantrymen helping their two wounded colleagues over the log. There had only been the three of us on my side of the log . . . and I alone had escaped uninjured. I cannot explain this. . . . Those on the other side of the log had been protected and were all safe. I made my way to a barn, collecting a 'Piat' dropped by the infantry on the way. There I found the two wounded lads receiving attention. They seemed in a bad way.

But I had a vehicle . . . and I had to get back. I felt afraid of returning: being more conscious of death now . . . And that Spandau was about . . . and a sniper.

I took all possible precautions traversing the orchard . . . crouching by hedges etc. . . . and eventually reached my vehicle and clambered inside. At last I felt reasonably safe. The two remaining members of my crew had wondered about my long absence . . . and had feared the worse after that 'stonk' which they had seen. The tank that appeared to have attracted the enemy fire was unhit. Its crew were inside with closed hatches. They knew I was outside in the midst of the shell fire and one of them seems to regard me as the luckiest man in the British Army. Perhaps he is right.

Well, the three of us, Pestell, Pedder and self stayed in my vehicle for some time. The repair job seemed unimportant under the circumstances. We had water and dry biscuits for our lunch/tea meal, and just waited . . . and talked. Meanwhile, the squadron were carrying out their job of scaling that crazy hill. By evening they had finished, successfully and I heard the Major over the wireless giving orders to return to a point near my own position. They appeared at dusk, and I then made contact with my troop officer and reported the wounding of two members of my crew. I needed other assistance to repair my vehicle but it could not be provided . . . so I borrowed some tools from other vehicles to attempt the job myself . . . with the Major's blessing. Mr Francis also 'loaned' me a member of his crew – Dawes – a remarkable worker. I was asked to try and make my way to harbour, about 1 mile S of the village, if I finished the job.

The squadron departed. It was almost dark: there was a burning house 70 yards in front: a burning Churchill enclosing a mutilated human body 100 yds to my right: to the left, a Spandau . . . if he hadn't been killed . . . and maybe a sniper or two. I was afraid.

We set to work in this no man's land. The silence was awful . . . punctuated by crackling from the burning house . . . and occasional 'cracks' from the burning tank: the small arms ammo. was exploding.

We worked until 11.30 p.m.: no more could be done as we needed more tools – and it was now pitch dark. I decided to spend the night in my vehicle, with my three colleagues, taking turns at guard in pairs. Too many Jerries in the neighbourhood to take risks. We informed HQ of this arrangement over the air, and settled down for our night's vigil. And now it started to rain . . . like hell. Pedder and I in the turret, observing through the open hatches, were soon wet to the skin. I seemed hungry too . . . and tired, hellishly so. In between turns we slept, somehow . . . and then came the dawn . . . to my unutterable relief. Once again we radioed HQ for further assistance and we were informed that help was already on the way: this was at 6.30 a.m.

At 7.00 a.m., no help had arrived . . . but suddenly there was a vicious 'swish' outside, followed by a heavy explosion. God! What did it mean? We had wondered whether the enemy had really been driven far back . . . and now it seemed that he was shelling us . . . the usual prelude to a counter-attack. We closed all hatches . . . and waited . . . and wondered. . . . Very soon came another heavy bang . . . and we heard shrapnel slapping the side of the vehicle. Would we be hit? or captured? Was it the end of everything? These were unspoken thoughts . . . but looks were enough.

Personally, I felt pretty secure in the vehicle . . . after my experience in the open the previous afternoon. HE does not penetrate a Churchill but a direct hit could cause severe injuries. The shelling continued for half an hour. Each shot announced itself by a momentary 'swish' . . . and then the explosion. Sometimes the vehicle shuddered . . . sometimes the shrapnel clanged on something . . . but we remained unhit. After a time, I knew that we couldn't have been under observation. It was indirect shooting, otherwise we would have been hit. But every shot seemed dangerously close and it was only a matter of time. . . . But the worst did not happen.

After half an hour, there came a pause . . . and our nerves gradually slackened off: fear-haunted eyes became more normal. . . . But what about the repair job? We couldn't carry on under such conditions. We attempted to radio HQ again – to have the promised assistance withdrawn . . . but we couldn't get a reply.

I decided to 'bail out' and try and find our way back to the unit. It seemed a more sensible plan than being shelled to death or taken prisoner. We removed breech blocks and strikers from the guns, and then hopped out . . . and bolted for the comparative shelter of a nearby orchard. Very soon I saw some figures on a roadway . . . and they were wearing khaki . . . not the grey-green of the enemy. Thank goodness for that: the village was obviously still in our hands. A little further on, we came to a roadway and there was one of our scout cars: and the driver had time to run us back to our squadron . . . what blessed relief! It was still pouring with rain, but that little journey, perched perilously on the top of that tiny vehicle, was one of the pleasantest I have ever known.

We found the rest of the unit parked in an orchard, and the men sheltering in various barns and sheds. Mr Francis and his crew were having a meal . . . and we needed no persuading to join them. How good was the taste of that hot sweet! The first I had had since breakfast the day before. We were soaked and tired . . . but there was a remarkably cheerful atmosphere as we swopped yarns and discussed the previous day . . . in that crazy little barn with its mud walls and musty smell . . . and general atmosphere of decay.

After our brief respite, news came through that the squadron had to depart immediately for another attack . . . and so our colleagues left us for their vehicles . . . and we returned to ours . . . with more tools to finish the job.

Ronnie Holden's account of this same occurrence – and he was commanding C Squadron in which both Cyril and Trevor had served – was very brief in terms of fighting, but had more information in respect of logistics:

C Squadron were on the left and involved in fighting a stronghold consisting of an old castellated building on top of the hill from which the enemy were subsequently driven off. We then descended to a place called Bonnebosq. Here we successfully covered the advance of infantry into the village of Le Torquesne. Here we found a great pile of folding bicycles which appeared to have arrived from nowhere as there was no sign whatsoever of other equipment, tracks of vehicles or anything. Therefore it was reasonable to suppose that they were there for use by anybody who came across them. From then on each tank, at least of C Sqn had one bicycle as well as a tank! They were not used very often. By this time we were getting nearer and nearer to the Seine and as we got to the river itself it was found that a German Tiger tank that we had captured some while before was too big and heavy to cross the Bailey Bridge which was provided for the weight of not more than two Churchill tanks at a time so it was abandoned on the bank.

CHAPTER 6

The Capture of Le Havre

The broad picture

The plan for the Canadian Army to capture Le Havre was described in the previous chapter. This was part of the wider plan to free the Channel ports and to overrun the V1 sites. In the early forward drive there occurred two moving events. On 1 September 2nd Canadian Division captured Dieppe; it was here, on 19 August 1942, that the same division had lost 3,000 men and, as we recounted earlier, that the Churchill tank saw action for the first time. The return was more than symbolic. Dieppe was taken almost intact, and by the end of September it became the largest useable Channel port, capable of handling nearly 7,000 tons of cargo per day. The second event was the capture on 2 September of St. Valery-en-Caux by the 51st Highland Division. It was here that most of the original division had been taken prisoner in June 1940. The Canadians' tasks now included the freeing of the rest of the Channel coast, but particularly the port of Le Havre.

Immediately before the war Le Havre was, after Marseilles, the most important port in France. Until 1516 Le Havre was only a fishing village possessing a chapel dedicated to Notre-Dame-de-Grâce, to which it owes its name Le Havre (harbour) de Grâce, given to it by Francis I when he began the construction of its harbour. Defenses and harbour works were continued by Richelieu and completed by the genius of fortification, Vauban. The English bombarded it in 1694, 1759, 1794 and 1795.

In 1939 there were fourteen basins in the harbour, the oldest of which dated back to 1669, with more than 8 miles of quays. The chief docks were the Bassin Bellot and the Bassin de L'Eure. The Tancarville canal, by which river boats unable to attempt the estuary of the Seine can make the port direct, enters the harbour by the Bassin de L'Eure.

In 1944 the approaches to Le Havre were well protected, on the western side by flooding and elsewhere by mines, anti-tank ditches and huge concrete gun emplacements primarily designed for sea defences. The garrison of over 11,000 was also strongly provided with artillery.

I British Corps, under the command of First Canadian Army, was given the task of assaulting Le Havre. This operation was given the code-name 'Astonia'. The corps consisted of 49th West Riding Division supported by 34 Armoured Brigade and 51st Highland Division supported by 33 Armoured Brigade. There had been some reorganization of the Armoured Brigades. 31 Tank Brigade was now in 79th Armoured Division, and consisted of Crocodile battalions. 34 Armoured Brigade consisted of 107 RAC, 147 RAC, 7 RTR (who came under command on 19 August), and 9 RTR (who came under command on 4 September).

The general plan was for 51 Div to attack from the north, and 49 Div to attack from the east and north-east. None of the approaches looked very cheerful on the maps with their defence overprints.

Battle of Le Havre: Operation 'Astonia', 10–12 September 1944

The official history of the Battle of Le Havre is a composite of three historical sources: the story of 34 Armoured Brigade (34 Tank Brigade until 2 February 1945); 9 RTR War Diary; and the log of radio communication between 9 RTR and 34 Tank Brigade HQ.

Between 27 August and 9 September 9 RTR moved from Pont Audemer to the outskirts of Le Havre via Pont de L'Arche, Rouen, Yvetot and Bolbec.

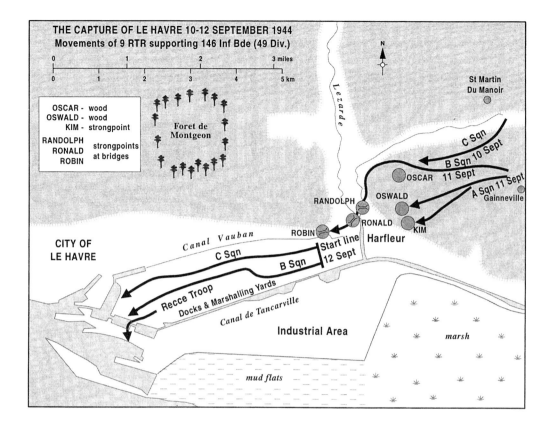

THE CAPTURE OF LE HAVRE 10-12 SEPTEMBER 1944
Movements of 9 RTR supporting 146 Inf Bde (49 Div.)

The plan of attack for 49th Division supported by 34 Tank Brigade was in three parts:

1. 56 Infantry Brigade supported by 7 RTR was to break through the German defences between the Foret de Montgeon and the River Lezarde;

2. 146 Infantry Brigade supported by 9 RTR was to clear all the enemy east of the River Lezarde up to Harfleur;

3. 147 Infantry Brigade supported by 107 RAC was to follow through the gap made by 56 Brigade and the complete division and its supporting tanks were then to advance westwards to clear the town and the dock area.

Le Havre appeared to be a very difficult place to capture. It was covered to landward by belts of minefields which proved in places to be 800 yards deep. It was fortified through several years of German occupation with innumerable concrete redoubts and deep shelters, and its Commandant, Col. Eberhard Wildemuth, had been ordered to hold out until the end of the war. There was a garrison of 11,300, plentiful ammunition for 115 guns, and sufficient food on hand for 14,000 soldiers for three months. The defences overprints were horrifying in their menacing detail.

To soften up the defences the RAF were to make a heavy bombing raid on the city's defences, including the plateau between the Foret de Montgeon and the River Lezarde.

The plan for 146 Infantry Brigade and 9 RTR was in three stages, each of which took place on the three consecutive days, 10, 11 and 12 September 1944.

Day 1 (10 Sept) To soften up and harass the defences of strong-point OSCAR and those on the western bank of the Lezarde valley;

Day 2 (11 Sept)   To clear strong-points OSCAR, OSWALD, and KIM; to force the crossing of the River Lezarde at Harfleur, including the clearing of strong-points RANDOLPH, RONALD and ROBIN.

Day 3 (12 Sept)   To advance from the bridgehead over the Lezarde to the eastern end of the docks and the city, all this area being south of the Foret de Montgeon and the plateau.

Day 1 (10 September) from 9 RTR War Diary

1815: After the RAF bombardment of plateau C Squadron deployed and engaged targets in the area of strongpoint OSWALD and on western slopes of Lezarde valley. The high explosive and machine-gun fire was accurate, heavy, and well controlled, and did much to soften and harass the defences for the attack on the following day.

Battle for Le Havre: Rear Link Wireless log

As Adjutant of 9 RTR Capt. John Hodges was responsible for communication with the formation commanding 9 RTR. This wireless communication was called the 'rear link'. The rear link log shows the sender or receiver of the message, the message itself, and the time when it occurred.

The four stations to whom or from whom messages were transmitted during the battle for Le Havre were:

34:	34 Armoured Brigade HQ
7:	7 RTR rear link
9:	9 RTR rear link
107:	107 RAC rear link

Some terms used in the rear link wireless log, for example for infantry battalions of 146 Infantry Brigade, were:

1/4 KOYLI:	1st/4th Battalion of the King's Own Yorkshire Light Infantry
4 LINCS:	4th Battalion of the Lincolnshire Regiment
HALLAMS:	The Hallamshire Battalion, this was originally the 4th Hallamshire Battalion (Territorials) of the York and Lancaster Regiment, and was redesignated in 1924. Hallamshire encompasses the area of Sheffield, Yorkshire.
OSCAR, OSWALD, KIM, RANDOLPH, RONALD and ROBIN:	Strong-points shown on the Le Havre map.
FLAILS:	Mine-sweeping tanks; those used in the British Army were the Sherman 'Crabs'.
SHELLDRAKE:	Concentrated high-explosive barrage provided by the Royal Artillery.
ANT:	German anti-tank gun.

Battle for Le Havre To/From		Rear Link Time
	11 September	
9	A Sqn's advance to OSWALD has started. Inf are being mortared – A Sqn are engaging enemy.	0537
9	C Sqn has started his supporting fire.	0545
9	KOYLI progressing towards OSWALD. They are meeting mortar fire and mines.	0559

Battle for Le Havre		Rear Link
To/From		Time

9	KOYLI are on outskirts of OSWALD and are also attacking OSCAR.	0612
9	Attack on OSCAR has advanced 600 yards but is held up by mine. No further news of OSWALD except that it is NOT yet in our hands.	
9	The attacks on OSCAR and OSWALD are held up. KOYLI say they cannot advance without our close support. This will be given as soon as the light permits.	0637
9	The support KOYLI asked for is now being directed against OSCAR and OSWALD. SHELLDRAKE is also dealing with OSWALD.	0715
9	The KOYLI who attacked OSWALD got a bloody nose. They came out and are now sitting around the outside looking at it. OSCAR will be dealt with first. When taken a new plan will be made for capture of OSWALD.	0750
9	Flails are getting to work in part of OSCAR when this is cleared the party will go on.	0811
9	Flails have made a path through the hill around OSCAR. One flail has gone on a further 100 yards and fallen into a hole. The KOYLI won't move until a path is flailed right up to OSCAR.	0835
9	The flails have made a path right up to OSCAR and the KOYLI are passing up it now.	0900
9	KOYLI in OSCAR; apparently no enemy there.	0925
9	Nothing further to report at the moment. Plot for OSWALD is still being hatched.	1003
9	A white flag was seen at OSWALD some time ago but the enemy did NOT come out. The KOYLI sent a rep into OSWALD and a conference is taking place there now.	1048
9	The conference at OSWALD has broken up. The enemy required time to bury their dead etc, but this was refused. The attack will continue shortly by all available means.	1118
34	49 Div Comd directs that all commands will press on and NOT waste time over white flags etc.	1132
9	Party is on and white flag soon appeared. However the party continued and we are putting down a lot of fire there.	1247
9	Flails have nearly completed their tasks and we should soon hear from the flamethrowers.	1300
9	Double gap completed and flamethrowers moving through now.	1307
9	KOYLI now entering OSWALD.	1309
9	KOYLI are pushing on into the woods supported by the flamethrowers and the enemy are running out of the rear of the wood with their hands up.	1318
9	OSWALD is liquidated. Attention is now being turned towards KIM.	1325
9	There are signs that the enemy are blowing up the docks. Bits of cranes etc. keep appearing above large explosions.	1344
9	Reports of a white flag at KIM. This is being investigated.	1351
9	There are about thirty Germans gathered in a large dugout at the top of KIM under a white flag. We are trying to get KOYLI to round them up before they disappear back to LE HAVRE.	1405
9	There appears to be little at KIM and what there is seems very	1445

Battle for Le Havre   Rear Link

To/From   Time

To/From		Time
	frightened. A minefield is suspected across the front and the KOYLI are going to deal with KIM by themselves.	
9	KIM is free of enemy.	1513
9	A Sqn forward rally between OSWALD and KIM.	1551
9	Viewed from OSWALD bridges appear to be intact.	1600
9	B Sqn held up not far from OSCAR where the rd is damaged. Should not be long REs are working on it.	1615
9	B Sqn on the move again now.	1620
9	B Sqn held up by mines in area OSCAR. Now moving on to join friends who are waiting for them.	1730
9	B Sqn fired at by machine-guns from block houses across the railway.	1805
9	A Sqn rear rally at position occupied last night.	1815
34	107 have a sqn on the high ground above where B Sqn are shooting. Keep good lookout.	1855
34	Give locations of pill-boxes causing trouble.	1900
9	Opposition liquidated – B Sqn instructed NOT to fire when there is opposition.	1913
9	A Coy 4 LINCS across RANDOLPH.	1945
9	RONALD has been crossed.	1946
9	B Coy at ROBIN. A Coy 200 yds short of ROBIN.	2004
9	B Sqn stopped short of ROBIN by a road block. Inf have passed ROBIN. Lincs when 1,000 yards past ROBIN met rifle fire from houses. B cannot go further road badly damaged. B have been released and are returning to location. Will meet Lincs at 0800 hrs tomorrow and continue the battle.	2115
	12 September	
9	Two Tps of C with the Hallams and two of B with the Lincs will clear area between Canal Vauban and Canal Tancarville.	0805
9	Anti-tank gun north of Canal de Tancarville, C Sqn busy dealing with it.	0906
9	B Sqn at ROBIN OC B on recce – party has NOT moved far yet.	0914
34	49 Div offers £2 for German Commander of Le Havre as prisoner. 51 Div Comdr offers £5.	0944
34	49 Div Comd now offers £6 for capture of Commandant of Le Havre.	0946
9	C Sqn still battling with ANT quite a lot of fire from houses in vicinity. No more fwd movement yet of B Sqn.	0950
9	Hospital captured by 2nd Essex.	1000
9	ANT liquidated by leading troops. HALLAMS engaged about 500 yards further back in houses. No movement yet of B Sqn.	1015
9	There is a lot of fighting going on south-east of the hospital and until this is cleared B Sqn cannot move up to the NW to join their infantry.	1110
34	Commandant of Le Havre captured by 7 RTR.	1123
9	C have prisoners from power station	
9	B Sqn reach Boulevard de Harfleur and turn right.	1142
9	C Sqn moving on and force various strong-points to surrender: telephone exchange blockhouses and brewery. All objectives achieved.	1230
9	B Sqn turn west and overrun anti-tank and machine-gun positions and take 30–40 prisoners. All objectives achieved.	1330

9 RTR War Diary, 12 September

The War Diary concludes the capture of Le Havre with the activities of the Recce Troop during the afternoon of 12 September.

1430: 9 RTR released by 146 Inf Bde, except for Recce Troop which had been doing very useful work all day in clearing and patrolling side roads. From 1600 hrs to 2100 hrs, the Recce Troop under Sgt. Findlay gave invaluable assistance to Hallams in clearing their dock area of the Bassin Bellot.

Manoeuvring up to strong-points and covering them with accurate fire they were instrumental in supplying the Hallams with about 250 PW. Released at 2130 hrs, they joined the Bn which had now concentrated near St. Martin de Manoir.

Throughout OP 'ASTONIA' the Bn suffered no battle casualties.

Personal recollections: lead-up to Le Havre and the assault

The fortnight from the end of the battles of the bridges to the beginning of the assault on Le Havre was occupied mainly by movement and marshalling prisoners. Sgt. Bob Anderson, wounded towards the end of Epsom, rejoined C Squadron just before the bridges' battles, and commented on differences in the configuration of an English and a French public convenience: 'It was then (around 17 August) that the battalion was attached to the First Canadian Army to clear the Channel ports. We crossed the River Risle at Pont Audemer. It was here that we first encountered a French public convenience. This consisted of a small building, the toilet being a 6-inch diameter hole in the floor with footprints on either side and the river underneath. On returning from the toilet my gunner Johnny was heard to remark "I am supposed to be a tank gunner, not an RAF bomb aimer."'

In the memories of those who attacked Le Havre three things stand out: that the RAF carried out some accurate bombing; that their particular tank, troop, or squadron led the advance; and loot.

Sgt. Dickie Hall, who had also recently rejoined C Squadron after being injured near Grainville, remembers the beginning of the Battle for Le Havre:

When the time came for the attack, we saw a large bomber force make a very heavy raid on the town and harbour – which we hoped would make our job that much easier. We were supposed to have infantry co-operation, but I never saw any sign of them, but we collected quite a few Maquis, who rode on the tanks and directed us to the positions of the blockhouses and other 'strong-points.' The RAF had had the desired effect because as each strong-point was approached, the troops came out and fell-in to be marched away. We investigated one or two of the strong-points and found that they were quite well stocked with tinned fruit and wine. Quite a bit of these supplies were immediately liberated! In the middle of all this, a gigantic explosion shook the harbour area, which they hoped would deny us the use of the port.

Bob Taylor was wounded at Maltot on 10 July and went back to England via a hospital at Bayeux. He recovered quickly.

After approximately seven weeks I was sent back to Normandy and posted to a tank delivery unit and by chance posted back to 5 Troop of A Squadron. Going into action on 11 September 1944 to capture Le Havre, I got a blowback from the Besa and got a fragment in my right eye, so that ended my active service with the 9th. I was taken to Dieppe to a makeshift hospital where a Major from the RAMC operated on my right eye to remove the fragment. As the operation was in progress Jerry planes came over and bombed the power station. The nurses connected an Aldis lamp to a battery to give the doctor a light to finish the operation, which was a success, so after a few days I was sent home to England again.

The Story of 34 Armoured Brigade says that 'ammunition expenditure was phenomenal, casualties negligible, and success complete'. Jock Cordiner would agree with the expenditure of ammunition: 'Le Havre, too, was memorable. My legs were cooked standing thigh deep in hot shell cases.'

Jack Woods was certain that 9 troop of B Squadron was leading the charge:

Our next action was Le Havre where we were to support 49 Div into the town from the south. B Squadron got the job of leading the battalion and 9 Troop the 'honour' to lead the squadron, well that's what David Scott said, you can imagine what we said, especially after studying the map overlays, we were not too happy. We moved off through the Crabs of the 22nd Dragoons and advanced towards Montevilliers and Harfleur, pausing to open fire on the church steeple in Harfleur to remove any possible observers. There had been no trouble from anti-tank mines but the area was strewn with anti-personnel (Schu) mines which were giving the infantry some trouble and I remember Lofty Earl of 10 Troop having to go back for something and having to tread in the tracks of tanks (a touch of the Good King Wencelaus's). We were held up by a sunken road into which we had to drop and turn right for the run to the docks area. David Scott couldn't see the drop very well so I had to get out and recce it. I found a place, *Inspire* dropped into it, pulled hard right and off came the offside track, so we were left behind, the rest of the squadron passing us by. I received a bang over my eye while I was out of the tank from something from somewhere but it was superficial and that's all we got out of it. We had to wait for the ARV to tow us out and fix the track and we rejoined the rest of the squadron in laager.

I returned to Le Havre in 1989 and went to look at the church steeple in Harfleur, I found it intact and I thought Len Lennard had missed but on enquiring I discovered that it had been rebuilt and was 6 metres short of the original.

Bob Anderson, as troop sergeant of 12 Troop, remembers the part that C Squadron had to play: 'C Squadron was allocated to run in along the main road leading to the docks. Just the job for my boys, says Ronnie Holden. The night before we were due to go in the BBC announced that Le Havre had been captured by the Canadian Army. Right lads, said Ronnie, we cannot let the BBC be liars, so we will take it tomorrow. Fortunately the Germans didn't fight very hard after the heavy bombing by the RAF.'

Ronnie himself remembers Le Havre as a successful operation:

After passing through Rouen we made our way towards Le Havre. Prior to entering Le Havre we mounted C Sqn to shoot up the lower slopes of an escarpment which appeared to have quite a number of '88s. It was here that orders were given out that the start of an attack by the 9th would be made, providing always we could get through a very heavily guarded concrete road-block leading to the road and along the side of the river to the docks, which was our objective. The start was to be made by the Sqn. Ldr. of C Sqn plus one troop who immediately ran into very heavy anti-tank fire coming from that very road leading to the docks. By the time we had got past this obstacle we then came across civilians and the

Maquis who wanted to point out various objects and targets they thought we ought to deal with, but we were in no mood and were going very fast towards our objective which was a blockhouse – very big, very strong – at the end of the road some 2 miles away. However, what happened was that the leader of the Maquis told me that until the telephone exchange was put out of order or the Germans were taken out of it, there would be lots of information passed forward into the city which would be detrimental to us. So I ordered the crews to dismount from two tanks and together we went to investigate the telephone exchange but found no Germans. We then proceeded to our original objective and our friends the Hallamshires were right up with us then, and they started to take a number of prisoners as complete chaos reigned in the town around the docks. At the same time a very large proportion of the docks, including a crane at the main gates and the dock itself, blew up with an enormous explosion and to all intents and purposes, what with blockages in the road and suchlike, our objective had been achieved.

About two months after the capture of Le Havre the 9th was static in Roosendaal. It was decided to produce a regimental newsletter, mainly to keep in touch with ex-members of the unit and others interested in what the 9th was doing. There were contributions from HQ, A, B, and C Squadrons, and the first newsletter was published in late November, shortly after a well-remembered Cambrai Day. The starting point for every contribution was Le Havre, and the word 'loot' looms large in most of them as HQ Squadron recalls:

> During the closing stages of the capture of Le Havre the squadron adopted some novel battle formations. Scout cars and even jeeps were seen to depart on mysterious missions to remote quarters of the town, whence they returned more heavily laden than when they set out. When orders were given to return to harbour the Recce Troop, owing to a technical hitch, failed to hear them and were left behind to continue the work of liberation. This was just as well, as it turned out, because a last pocket of resistance was found in the docks late in the evening. After an O Group consisting of a Brigadier, a Colonel, and the Recce Troop's very own Sgt. Gordon Findlay, a satisfactory shoot was carried out and 272 dejected POWs were extracted. A good time was had by all.

A Squadron remembered only the noise: 'We commence with Le Havre. This turned out to be just a very noisy morning for us, just sitting and lobbing HE at two comparatively small woods until the white flags appeared. Casualties, nil; ammunition expended, considerable.' B Squadron's first contribution starts after Le Havre, but C Squadron remembered several things:

> After rather a smooth piece of motoring we were finally poised without the city gates when a very definite 'to be or not be be' note was sounded. We were to be used, we were not to be used; blocks on, blocks off, start up, stand down etc., until finally we were told that we were definitely not wanted. And so to bed. From all of which you will readily understand that within a few hours we were being used after all. In retrospect Le Havre and loot have become almost synonymous terms. Certainly it was nice work and for the most part we got it. From bicycles to cameras and from lugers to liqueurs all was grist which came to our mill; the mighty blockhouses which at one time had seemed rather tough propositions were the best hunting grounds, though the FFI were pretty quick off the mark and competition was keen.
>
> The Germans caught Sydney Link swanning around outside his tank and chased him about a bit with 20 mm until finally and unbelievably he made his way back through the pannier door. It was a definite conjuring trick because when one looks at Sydney it's obviously not

Capt. Sidney Link, the well-loved and respected second-in-command of C Squadron from 1942 until the end of the campaign in May 1945.

on. Anyway the whole occasion went with a swing and all our chariots and riders returned safely.

Postscript to Le Havre

In retrospect it seemed almost inevitable that Le Havre should fall quickly. But that would not have been the view before the battle by those with a knowledge of the German strength. Although the plan of attack was excellent and its execution determined and swift, a more resolute defence would surely have lasted more than three days. The redoubtable Admiral Frisius held Dunkirk until 9 May 1945, and he was much less well equipped for defence.

Almost certainly part of the reason for the rapid capitulation was the personality and philosophy of the German Commandant, Colonel Eberhard Wildemuth. He had served in the First World War, and between the wars he had been a banker. As a reservist officer he was recalled on the outbreak of the war, and served on both the eastern and the western fronts. However, his views on fighting to the last man were more those of a banker than a soldier – and his troops, the civilian population, and the attacking allies should be grateful for it. He considered that it was futile to fight tanks without anti-tank weapons, and instructed his people that if they found themselves fighting tanks without appropriate weapons they were at liberty to surrender.

So the 33 and 34 Armoured Brigades evidently decided the issue, and it was very appropriate that Wildemuth himself should have been captured by a tank troop from B Squadron of 7 RTR. Colonel Wildemuth surrendered to Lt. Kit Bland of 7 RTR from his bed, which also contained his mistress: a nice touch of formality was added to the proceedings by the Colonel having pinned his medals to his pyjamas.

CHAPTER 7

Interlude: Rest and Travel

SURGE TO ANTWERP, FAILURE AT ARNHEM

The broad picture, 13 September 1944–7 October 1944

While the 9th were finishing the battles of the bridges and taking part in the capture of Le Havre momentous battles were being fought elsewhere. To understand why we moved or stood still we have to look at what was happening elsewhere in France and North West Europe from late August onwards.

On 25 August the 43rd Wessex Division forced the crossing of the Seine at Vernon. This allowed Brian Horrocks, commanding XXX Corps, to assemble an armoured striking force on the east bank for a massive surge north-east to Brussels and Antwerp. On 31 August this force crossed the Somme between Amiens and Villers Bretonneux, on 3 September it was at Brussels, and on 4 September entered Antwerp. It appeared that the German Army had given up, and the roads to Holland and the Ruhr were nearly clear. Unfortunately this was not so. The combination of a slow-down by the allied forces and the commitment of all German troops – particularly paratroops – to the defence of the Albert and Escaut Canals of northern Belgium blunted the allied drive. Brian Horrocks considered that the happenings during 3–7 September in effect meant that the war was going to last into 1945.

XXX Corps crossed the Escaut Canal on 10 September, and there grouped to form the land arm of Operation 'Market Garden'. This operation consisted of the dropping of airborne divisions at St. Oedenrode, Grave-Nijmegen, and Arnhem, and the linking of these divisions by the land arm. This would breach the Rhine, and allow allied forces then to swing north into Holland and south-east to the Ruhr. German forces in Holland would be isolated from Germany, the source of much of German war material would be destroyed, and the war could well end in 1944.

The airborne divisions landed during the afternoon of 17 September, and Z-hour for the Guards Armoured Division, leading XXX Corps, was 1435 hours on that day. The land forces linked up with the 101st (US) Airborne at St. Oedenrode and the 82nd US Airborne between Grave and Nijmegen, and the bridges over the Rivers Maas and Waal were captured. But the bridge at Arnhem over the Neder Rijn was 'a bridge too far', and the remnants of 1st (British) Airborne finally withdrew on 26 September.

The implications of all this for 9 RTR were two. First, after the capture of Le Havre on 12 September other units of the Canadian Army were already well up the coast. The siege of Boulogne took place between 17 and 23 September, and that of Calais between 25 September and 1 October. Both towns were captured by the 3rd Canadian Division. During much of this period 9 RTR were given time to rest and refit. When the withdrawal from Arnhem was complete the 9th, as part of 34 Armoured Brigade, were ready to move up to Holland to help stabilize and extend the allied salient leading from the Belgian border to Nijmegen and beyond.

While the 9th rests from 13–29 September 1944, it is an opportunity to look at a matter of great concern to any soldier in a front-line unit – what happened if you were wounded?

WOUNDS, SICKNESS, AND THEIR AFTERMATH

The 9th suffered 244 casualties during the course of the campaign in North West Europe and of these 68 were killed, 9 taken prisoner, and 167 wounded. A few of these wounds were caused by malfunctions of the tank armament, such as the Besa blowback resulting in Dickie Hall's injuries on 29 June. The great majority, however, were caused by enemy action. They can be grouped into five main types:

1. armour-piercing (AP) shot hitting a tank or other vehicle and causing wounds or amputations.
2. AP shot causing the tank to catch fire or 'brew', generally by igniting some or all of the ammunition stowed in the tank; this could be made worse if the petrol or hydraulic lines were fractured and caught on fire.
3. shelling or mortaring when crews of all echelons were outside their vehicles – and when they were in them sometimes, particularly in the case of soft-skinned vehicles.
4. mines, which were designed either to damage vehicles, for example teller mines, or to damage people, for example S-mines, and Schumines.
5. small arms fire, from machine-gun, machine-pistol, rifle (especially snipers') and pistol.

The systems for dealing with wounded people were in a sense similar to those for repairing tanks; the worse it was, the further back you went. There were a number of things that the wounded person or those round him could do as immediate first aid. Everybody carried a first-aid dressing, and there was a first-aid box in the tanks and many of the other vehicles. Most people also carried injectible ampoules of morphine, which could be used as some antidote to pain. Cyril Rees escaped with burns from his tank in the Battle of the Broedersbosch in February 1945: 'Someone nearby produced a tube of morphine and jabbed it into my lower arm, I think it was Frank Risbridger. It wasn't long before I began to feel drowsy.'

Many people helped their comrades to escape from damaged or burning vehicles, which at least gave them a chance to get back to more experienced medical aid. Most vehicles, certainly tanks, are not designed for quick escape. There are many projections and obstacles, and tank crews get somewhat festooned with lanyards, microphones and headsets, binoculars, map-cases, and the loops, belts and pockets of their own clothes. Ray Gordon told in the Overture to this history of the tragic consequences of not being able to free some of the obstacles to exit in his tank *Iceni* on 10 July 1944.

Once people were free of their vehicle they were exposed to shelling, mortaring, and machine-gun and rifle fire. A quick dive into a ditch was a natural and often life-saving reaction, and from that point the casualty could be moved back to the medical professionals. The general procedure for dealing with casualties is shown in Figure 1, although of course there were many variations on what could happen to a person. The RAP could be that belonging to any unit, and in many cases the medical staff (doctors, Padres and medical orderlies) went out to collect the wounded rather than wait for them to arrive at the RAP. One of the Padres in 34 Armoured Brigade was Revd Capt. Geoffrey Lampe, who won the MC for rescuing wounded under fire. Geoffrey had been a classics master at King's Canterbury before he joined the army. On one occasion in Normandy he suddenly found himself in a ditch with a one-time pupil. 'Mallorie', said Geoffrey, 'I think we last met in the Peloponnesian War.'

However it was afforded, the medical backup was generally voted anywhere from very good to superb. Les Arnold was wounded near Colleville on 28 June when he was helping to refuel his tank:

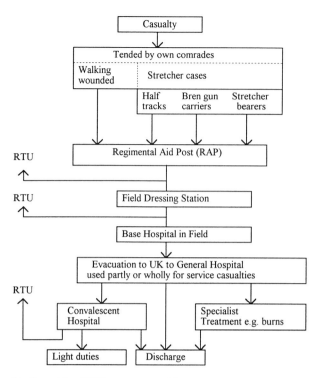

Figure 1: Dealing with Casualties (RTU: return to unit)

I got hit down the right side and my right elbow was shattered. I managed to get over the side of the tank and someone put a tourniquet on my arm. I was collected by stretcher-bearers who protected me by stopping and lying alongside me whenever mortars fell on the field we were crossing. They put me in an ambulance which took me to a Field Dressing Station, where Major Conway RAMC operated on me. I was shipped out of Normandy by a DUKW which ferried a group of wounded from the shore to the *Duke of Rotherham*. I ended up at Southampton General Hospital, and after eleven months of hospital treatment was finally discharged from the army.

John Powell was wounded by shelling after he and his crew bailed out of their tank near Chateau de Fontaine on 10 July 1944.

Like I said, we were unused to being on a battlefield without inches of armour plate around us. Some mortar rounds or shells started whistling around and we dropped. Too late. When I returned to consciousness the others were getting up but I couldn't move. I tried to shout but only a whisper came out. The others noticed my plight and our sergeant examined me, turned me over and put a field dressing on my back. I couldn't feel my legs but was assured that they were still there. Someone went to get help while I was given a cigarette to keep me occupied. My very brief war was certainly over.

The medical back-up was superb. Within thirty minutes a RAMC Bren carrier picked me up and took me to a nearby field hospital. I was placed on the operating table and dealt with immediately. The subsequent few days of nursing and medical care offered in field conditions was a revelation. I even got a visit from a representative or two from B Squadron, although how they found the time I cannot imagine. As soon as I had recovered sufficiently to be repatriated I was flown back to Oxford in a very bumpy Dakota for further attention to my spinal injuries. I spent months and months in hospital recovering some use of my legs. The remnants of my kit miraculously caught up with me later, but, alas, without my '*Qui s'y frotte*' badge.

As both Les and John have related, it could take a long time to recover from a wound, and even then the full function of the disabled part might never completely return. Burns presented a different sort of disablement. Many of the tank crew casualties were burned, and many of those had to spend months or even years attending hospitals for treatment. Ray Gordon was burned on the approaches to Maltot on 10 July 1944. Part of his story was told in the Overture to this history. What follows overlaps the last few minutes of the brewing of *Iceni*, and continues with the next four years of Ray's life; his tank had caught on fire, and he had just managed to pull himself out of the turret and fall on the ground beside the tracks.

My face became swollen and very tight making it difficult to see and the skin of my left hand hung down in black strips from an arm which was bloodless and white. Lt. Shep Douglas, my troop leader, crawled along the field. 'Who are you' he said, not recognizing one of his own troop to whom he had given orders earlier that morning. I followed him across the field of rape crouched low because we could hear gunfire to a gap in the hedgerow where infantry were in position. The look of horror on their faces which changed to looks of pity when they saw me will remain forever in my mind. It is a look which I would never want to inflict on another human being. I was helped to a medical truck, given an injection and that was the end of 10 July for me.

Memories after that are mixed – 'You are being flown home' someone said. The sound of the aircraft taking off but no memory of landing. A sudden shout by me 'I can see' (I had been blind for over a week due to my swollen face) then a transfer to the Burns and Plastic Surgery Hospital in Basingstoke which, little did I realize at the time, was to become my second home, on and off, for the next four years.

This situation for the injured soldier is the other side of the penny from the successes of winning a war. Months for recovery, many operations – some of which result in further painful periods of recovery and for some unfortunate men it means a broken body for the rest of life and that life itself severely limiting what that person can finally achieve. For myself I was indeed fortunate that while my injuries were visible they were literally only skin deep – no amputation, no limping, no internal injuries or other restricting disability. In a sense the cross that a burns victim has to bear is the reaction of the public to the vivid scarring on the face and a disfigured and unsightly hand (once described by one of my doctors as a claw to the fury of my wife). In the early days of venturing out into the world and going along a public road one is so conscious of one's disfigurement and the protective shell that you gradually build around you has not yet materialised. You feel that everyone is staring at you – some sympathetically, others with distaste and even when in a shop you hear that penetrating whisper 'Why do they let people out looking like that.' Even having plucked up courage to go into a restaurant for a meal to find that the three people sitting at the table you are directed next to get up and walk away leaving their food. You want to hide. It is as if you had inflicted the injury on yourself and were to blame for looking like that.

Gradually common sense takes over and one becomes fully aware that for the rest of your life you will always look different from a 'normal' person. Once this fact is accepted life becomes a never ending challenge. What you achieved before your injury, be it in sport, work or hobby, you try, try, and try again to accomplish – you adjust your method of approach to the problem and you solve it. You ensure that despite your physical appearance you are able to achieve in nearly every case the same result as a 'normal' person – and how satisfying that feeling is.

Looking back on my life I can now appreciate that my time in the 9 RTR made me grow up into a man. My disablement has given me a greater understanding of those less fortunate than myself and ironically being burnt (on reflection) was the best thing that happened to me in that I married Joan, the hospital physiotherapist and, as the fairy story says, lived happily ever after.

The War Diary

Following the Battle of Le Havre, the battalion was informed that a fortnight's rest was anticipated and that billets could be found in the area south of Dieppe.

On 17 September the battalion was disposed as follows: HQ, A1 and A2 Echelons – Biville La Baignard; A Sqn in Bronnetuit; B Sqn Gonneville; C Sqn in St. Genevieve.

Billets were found for all personnel, and certain comfort and rest was enhanced by the attitude of the villagers, who were kind enough to entertain by providing meals and wine – this was greatly appreciated for with petrol 'frozen' it was not possible to send 'passion' trucks to the larger towns. Being the first time that the battalion had been given a definite rest period since landing, maintenance was carried out on an extensive scale; each vehicle was given a thorough inspection and a number of engine changes were made.

In each squadron's village there were parades, dramatics, speeches, dances, and football matches, all carried out with great enthusiasm by the French villagers and the British soldiers.

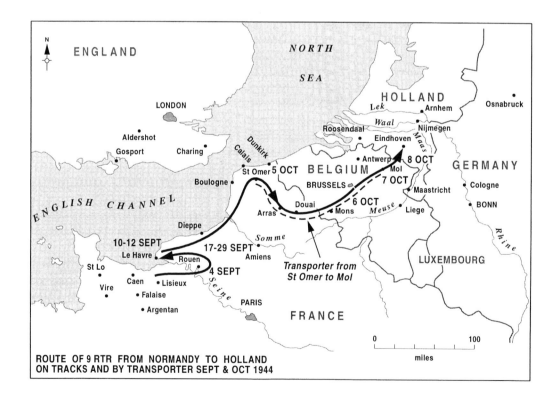

ROUTE OF 9 RTR FROM NORMANDY TO HOLLAND
ON TRACKS AND BY TRANSPORTER SEPT & OCT 1944

The battalion moved again on 29 September. The first complete rest had been thoroughly enjoyed – many had made pleasant friendships, among these were such notable personalities as the 2 i/c who bade a tender farewell to a group of fair young ladies at five o'clock in the morning, and Major Bert Mockford, who it was rumoured had acquired an affection for a certain doctor's wife.

By 1 October the battalion had reached Henneveux – a distance of 123 miles. During a short rest here, an impressive service was held in memory of those who had been killed fighting with the battalion. As the sun set behind a curtain of trees, the battalion formed up on a sloping field facing two Churchills, in front of which stood the Padre. He conducted a simple service, the message of which was that, however difficult it was to understand, no death was in vain.

The following day the battalion moved to Renescures and there awaited transporters in the final stage to join I Corps, who were now protecting the SW flank of the Arnhem salient. While loading on 5 October Lt. Les Wintle of A Sqn fell as he attempted to climb on a moving transporter and was crushed to death. An unfortunate end to an excellent troop leader who had fought so well from the very start.

By 8 October HQ, A and C Sqns had crossed into Holland and came under command 51(H) Div. B Sqn and the Recce Tp remained at Renescures awaiting further transporters. A further 100 miles had been covered on tracks, and the welcome by the Dutch was the most effusive that the battalion had encountered, even surpassing that of the Belgians, who had done everything to satisfy the general wish for comfort and wartime luxury.

Personal recollections

The first 9 RTR newsletter gives the views of the squadrons on this interlude of rest and travel. A Squadron:

> 17 September found us sitting in Brennetuit near Auffay, and for the next ten days all the tanks were in different stages of stripping, including a couple of engine changes. Quite a bit of sport was indulged in, and the squadron kept up its reputation. The rest period culminated in a squadron dance on the evening of 28 September, and we are pleased to relate that in essentials this differed in noways from any other A Squadron dance. Except that at 3 a.m. in the morning some petrol arrived, which a semi-capable squadron proceeded to pour into our chariots in preparation for a very early move. In the following three days we clocked a further 123 on our track mileage, eventually boarding transporters for the final run up to Eindhoven on 6 October. It was while loading these transporters that Les Wintle met his death falling under the wheels of a moving transporter and being killed instantly. This was a very sad end to a grand troop leader, when one considers that he had been in the thick of everything from the beginning.

B Squadron's principal recollection was a squadron concert produced by L/Cpl. George Horsfield: 'One of the highlights was a "Squadron Office" scene in which Trooper Jack Shepherd as SSM and George Horsfield as the squadron clerk gave unmistakable impersonations. Other turns included an Egyptian scene with L/Cpl. Johnnie Trotter, Cpl. Bill Holyoake and Trooper Norman Hughes accompanied by drums and dancing snakes. The star of the officers' sketch was Lt. John Stone as a French sanitary man, while in the sergeants' sketch the star was SQMS Jim Lewis as himself. Ernie Nightingale built a first rate stage and the show was greatly helped by the squadron band.'

C Squadron start after the capture of Le Havre: 'Followed a few days which were well spent in trying out the new weapons and drinks we had acquired, and in making return visits to

Some of B Squadron administrative crews in Germany, June 1945. Norman Hughes, Reg Ward, Reg Gander, Ken Ellis and 'Kipper' Kent; in the front George Horsfield.

replenish stocks – until the whole town was put out of bounds. After a smart rattle along the roads eastward we arrived at the delightful village of Beaunay where we made our home for the next ten days. On Sunday 25 September we had a ceremonial parade, during which the squadron leader placed a wreath on the village war memorial for the First World War, and we performed a march past. The salute was taken by the Mayor, Raymond Wemaere.'

Individuals had varied memories of this period. Jack Woods was, at least temporarily, extremely hopeful: 'After Le Havre the battalion settled down outside Dieppe where we heard of the liberation of Paris on the radio and lost our soft transport to support the pursuit of the beaten enemy from Normandy by the armoured divisions. We also heard rumours of a return to the UK, but got on with maintenance and changed our tracks. The tracks had been broken and the new ones nicely laid out waiting for the ARV to tow us on when we had a flap one hour's move, panic stations for a while and away we went on our own tracks both drivers spelling each other, finally loading on to transporters at Rennescure and travelling through the night (the one and only time I saw Brussels) finally arriving in Eindhoven.'

Jock Cordiner remembers the town of Bolbec and some rather summary justice:

Stopping briefly in Bolbec later there were other memorable events. First, while sunning ourselves in the square there was without warning a massive explosion nearby. The square emptied faster than Aberdeen on a Flag Day. It was reported that a huge naval gun sited on the coast had been turned round on us.

Also at Bolbec, a few of us gatecrashed an FFI trial of collaborators. We were besieged by men and women begging us to save their lives. We tried but the shooting went on in the back yard. It was a painful experience as we were convinced that not all the victims could have been guilty. No evidence or witnesses were produced. It seemed a good time for those who held power to be rid of people they disliked.

The accidental death of Lt. Les Wintle was mentioned in the War Diary and the A Squadron newsletter. It was also observed by Trevor Greenwood:

D + 121 Thursday 5.10.44
Start delayed this morning about two hours, but we eventually left harbour about 11.00 a.m. Short drive to concrete runways on local aerodrome where transporters were parked: loaded and shackled vehicles soon after. And then followed a long wait – until 3.00 p.m. when we ultimately started – crew on tank, self in transporter driving cab.

Just as we were moving off, I noticed Mr Wintle running towards his vehicle which was moving slowly into position: A few seconds later there was a commotion round about, and we pulled up. A few yards to our rear I saw a mass of torn rags dark red in colour and some pieces of a body – two feet in particular. This unrecognizable mass laying on the concrete was the remains of Mr Wintle. He had attempted to board his vehicle via the towing bar and slipped – the trailer, carrying the tank, passed over his body. The three axles, each carrying eight wheels, had completely mutilated him. A sad business this. He was very young – and had been through most of our actions without harm. How very fragile is this nebulous thread we call life!

CHAPTER 8

Access to Antwerp

AFTERMATH OF ARNHEM, RELEASE OF ANTWERP

The broad picture

The 11th Armoured Division captured the docks of Antwerp intact on 4 September 1944. On 28 November 1944 the first allied convoys reached those docks. Antwerp was then a port capable of handling 40,000 tons a day; its position, relatively close to England, close to the borders of Germany, and easily defensible by allied sea-power, made it by far the most desirable port to supply the allied armies. Why did it take so long to free the approaches to the port? And what did this mean to the 9th?

The advantage and the disadvantage of Antwerp as a port is that it is some 45 miles from the North Sea. This location makes it a very accessible point for collection and distribution. But it also means in time of war that the banks of the River Scheldt, on which it stands, must be clear of enemy occupation all the way to the sea. In early September the Fifteenth German Army occupied this part of the north European coast. Its Commander, General von Zangen, took two principal actions after the defeat of the German Army in Normandy. The first was to send some 82,000 first line troops and 530 guns to the east, where they could threaten the left flank of the north-eastern push of 21st Army Group. The second was to leave two divisions, one on each side of the mouth of the Scheldt estuary. That on the southern side was the 64th Infantry Division. It was a 'leave' division, made up of veterans of the Russian, Italian or Norwegian theatres who were home on leave in July 1944 and was thus composed of experienced soldiers. Their Commander, Lt.-Gen. Eberding, was also an experienced and determined officer.

The German force on the island of Walcheren, the northern shoulder of the Scheldt estuary, was not quite so formidable or well-led. It was the 70th Infantry Division, generally known as the 'White Bread Division'. This was because all its members suffered from some sort of stomach disorder, and it was felt easier administratively to group all into one unit where their special dietary needs could be supplied. They would have no real excuse for going sick, as they would in any other unit.

The promptness of General von Zangen was not matched with the same promptness and perception by Lt.-Gen. Brian Horrocks commanding the XXX British Corps. Horrocks writes in his book *Corps Commander*:

> It never entered my head that the Scheldt would be heavily mined, so that Antwerp could not be used as our forward base for some time; or, worse still, that the Germans would ferry away more than 80,000 troops of their Fifteenth Army plus 530 guns. If I had ordered Roberts (Major General Pip Roberts, commanding 11th Armoured Division) to bypass Antwerp and advance for only 15 miles north-west to cut off the Beveland Isthmus the whole of this force – which played such a prominent part in the subsequent fighting – might have been destroyed or forced to surrender. My eyes were fixed on the Rhine, and I knew that XII Corps were coming up on my left, and the Canadian Army on their left again.

Horrocks is very fair in admitting that he made a strategic error. His superiors were General Miles Dempsey, commanding the Second British Army, and Monty, commanding 21st Army

Group. We do not know what Dempsey's thoughts on this matter were, but Monty was not quite so fair, as his *Memoirs* (p. 285) attest: 'Some have argued that I ignored Eisenhower's orders to give priority to opening up the port of Antwerp, and that I should not have attempted the Arnhem operation until this had been done. This is not true. There were no such orders about Antwerp and Eisenhower had agreed about Arnhem.'

The correct strategy is very easy in hindsight, particularly fifty years later. But as a result of strategic and tactical decisions upheld on both sides Arnhem was not taken in September 1944 and the port of Antwerp was not accessible for nearly three months after it had been taken. The needs immediately after the failure at Arnhem (26 September) were to protect and enlarge the flanks of the Nijmegen salient; to free the approaches to the port of Antwerp; and to move up to the south bank of the River Maas as a firm northern flank for the allied forces if the campaign should be prolonged into 1945.

The 9th helped with the first task as soon as it arrived in Holland. Its task in relation to the second is well described by Eversley Belfield, who was then the pilot of an air observation post Auster. He describes the battle to free the northern bank of the River Scheldt:

> On the extreme left edge of this northern flank of the conflict the Germans resisted even more desperately, throwing in the Battle Group Chill, one of their toughest formations that had originally formed to stem the British advance beyond Brussels. The key position here was the village of Woensdrecht that commanded the mainland approach to the South Beveland Isthmus. Although the 2nd Canadian Division soon obtained a foothold on the base of the isthmus it was held up there from 7–16 October, losing very heavily in a series of unsuccessful frontal attacks, there being no possible way here of outflanking the German defences. The stalemate was ended only when the 4th Canadian Armoured and the 49th British Division pressed forward farther inland to capture Bergen op Zoom and Roosendaal, thus sealing off the South Beveland isthmus.

The story of the 9th in October 1944 is told in two parts. The first describes how it helped to protect and push out the north-western flank of the Nijmegen salient. The second deals with the approach to and the capture of Roosendaal as part of the freeing of the Scheldt waterway.

ENLARGING THE NIJMEGEN SALIENT

The War Diary, 8–16 October 1944

8 October: Arriving in Holland, the battalion came under command 51st (Highland) Division and were given the task of preparing to meet any counter-attack from the north-west against Eindhoven and also to worry the enemy by carrying out repeated raids. B Squadron and Recce Troop were still awaiting transporters in France; meanwhile, C Squadron established themselves at Zonsche and A Squadron at Acht.

9 October: The first two raids by C Sqn were carried out in support of 152 Brigade, operating in the area of Best. Captain Link and 11 Troop supporting 5th Camerons advanced in north-west direction east of road Eindhoven – Boxtel and combed woods in that area. Major Holden with two tanks supported 2nd Seaforths in an advance west, crossing the road/rail junction and shooting up a suspected Company HQ.

10 October: A Squadron was now given the role of supporting 153 Brigade and moved to St. Oedenrode where HQ also established itself.

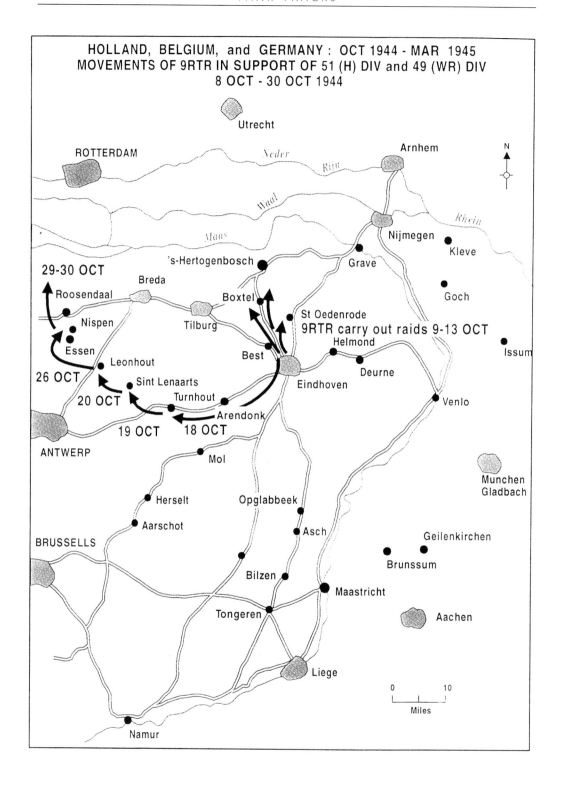

HOLLAND, BELGIUM, and GERMANY : OCT 1944 - MAR 1945
MOVEMENTS OF 9RTR IN SUPPORT OF 51 (H) DIV and 49 (WR) DIV
8 OCT - 30 OCT 1944

Utrecht

ROTTERDAM

Neder   *Rijn*   Arnhem   N

Waal   *Rhein*

Maas   Nijmegen   Kleve

's-Hertogenbosch   Grave

29-30 OCT   Breda   Boxtel   Goch

Roosendaal   St Oedenrode

Nispen   Tilburg   9RTR carry out raids 9-13 OCT

Essen   Best   Helmond   Issum

Leonhout   Deurne

26 OCT   Sint Lenaarts   Eindhoven

20 OCT   Turnhout   Venlo

19 OCT   18 OCT   Arendonk

ANTWERP   Mol

Munchen
Gladbach

Herselt   Opglabbeek

Aarschot   Asch   Geilenkirchen

BRUSSELS   Brunssum

Bilzen   Maastricht

Tongeren   Aachen

Liege

0   10

Miles

Namur

1330: 13 and 15 Troops under OC C Squadron supporting an assault troop of Derby Yeo (51st Recce Regiment) carried out a very successful raid on wood west of Donderdonk. Fire support was given by artillery, 4.2 in mortars, and medium machine-guns. Three Spandaus were silenced before the beating of the wood began and finally one Sgt. and thirty-three ORs from 6 Company 1034 Grenadier Regiment were taken prisoner. The ground was exceedingly soft and intersected by ditches and considerable skill was shown by tank commanders in completing the operation without any vehicles being bogged. It is said some tanks came out like speedboats with noses well up in the air. There were no casualties among our troops.

11 October: Was a complete day of maintenance and rest, but 12 October found C Squadron busy again.

12 October: OC C Squadron with 14 Troop carried out a raid on houses in the same area and generally shot up line of railway tracks. During the afternoon B Squadron and Recce Troop arrived and were allotted a reserve role. During the evening St. Oedenrode was shelled, resulting in Troopers Snowy Fisher and Ellis and Corporal Moore, who were relaxing in a pub, being wounded. Shelling continued throughout the night and though a number of houses were destroyed there were no further casualties.

13 October: C Squadron still busy. Another raid with 5th Camerons. Enemy withdrew hurriedly but eight of them were killed and one prisoner-of-war taken, whose identity proved to be 5 Coy 1036 Grenadier Regiment. A day of rest followed and then A Squadron did their first raid which had as an object the collecting of prisoners for identification. The area chosen was enemy

Sgt. Jim Proctor, sergeant in the Recce Troop, HQ Squadron. This photo was taken at Mehle, Germany, 24 November 1945.

positions west of Donderdonk. The first phase was concentrations by Brigade artillery and heavy mortars and also medium machine-gun fire. This was followed by about thirty minutes of tank movement and then a broadcast was made to say that the enemy faced a considerable force and would thus show discretion by deserting, and a smoke screen was laid to give cover to our lines. Fifteen to twenty Germans were seen to move towards the lines of 5/7 Gordons. Two prisoners were brought back on the tanks and three Spandaus were destroyed.

16 October: Information was now received that the battalion role was to be handed over to 33 Armoured Brigade and the necessary arrangements were made. This week of harassing raids had proved quite enjoyable, for every night the troops returned to the comfort of billets and were spared the discomfort of living in open fields. It is perhaps worthwhile noting that at no time during these raids did the enemy infantry make use of any anti-tank weapon.

Personal recollections

Beside recollections of the actions in which they took part, many people commented in this period on the different attitudes found in Belgium and Holland on the one hand, and in France on the other. Also it was now October, and it was cold and often wet. Billets of any kind – and they were of many kinds – were certainly preferable to tank bivvies. For these few days there was also the RAF-like situation, where you went out and fought during the day and came back to comfortable and reasonably safe billets at night.

When Dickie Hall arrived in Eindhoven he also found billets with a Dutch family:

The father worked at the Phillips factory. He was most impressed that the RAF had managed to 'post' a bomb right into a vital area, and not into other parts where there would have been many casualties. It was becoming extremely cold now. Near the village of Best we made a few sallies up the road and over the canal to harry the Germans, who were still quite near. We held south of the railway line, the Germans north. Our squadron leader, Ronnie Holden, told me he wanted to attack a German dining hut just over the railway line, and I was to go along. We drove up the village street abreast, and while Ronnie blasted the Germans (I think it was their dinner time) my gunner Johnnie Oakley put down a lot of fire to our left. We had surprised them, and we came away without drawing any fire.

One night in this period we slept in a long covered way which contained a row of beehives. In my efforts to obtain some honey, I dropped the frame. Thinking I had put all the sleepy bees back in the hive, we had our 'honey' tea. Later, as we slept in our blankets, the air began to be full of much swearing as the bees became active with the warmth!

Jack Woods remembers – and doesn't remember – these ten days: 'We travelled through the night (the one and only time I saw Brussels) finally arriving in Eindhoven where we stayed for ten days in civvy billets, the Dutch population not allowing us to sleep with our tanks. The story of that ten days is a bit of a blur, and on returning to Eindhoven in 1990 I was taken to the area – but I couldn't remember the family I stayed with or the house, only the area.'

Fred Glasspool of C Squadron remembers the family he stayed with, as well as the other tank crews staying in the house, from a photo taken at the time. 'The photo was taken by the Cornelius family in Eindhoven. Our tank (15 Troop Leader Seymour Francis') had broken down and Sgt. Trevor Greenwood had been left with us. Along with me in the photo are John "Smudger" Smith, who was killed at Vinkenbroek, "Titch" Mead, who was wounded in the same action, and John Davis who died when our billets caught fire in Roosendaal. We rejoined the squadron at Best, and took part in "heavy reconnaissance" with infantrymen riding on top of the tanks.'

The first battalion newsletter contains two items about this period, the first from the A Squadron scribe: 'On 8 October we were in Holland, and found ourselves in St. Oedenrode. Here we were with the 51st Division and did one little party with them when our 2 i/c Ken Kidd and Roy Clarkson, commanding 4 Troop, with four tanks shot up a couple of spandau positions and brought in two very dejected looking prisoners. Again, no casualties.' The second item was from C Squadron and was rather longer:

Then Eindhoven. Here a big halt by the complete battalion, tanks, cars, trucks, bicycles, everything, but what now? Still we were in the dark. We were near the Boche once again and yet no sound of gunfire.

C Squadron were wanted immediately for a job. We are off again, passing over the Wilhelmina canal, and we find ourselves once more among the wreckage of battle.

Settling ourselves into a tiny modern hamlet on the outskirts of Best, we were allotted the RAC cum RAF task of daily raids into enemy territory. These were partly for hate, partly for testing their defences, and partly for the amusement of the troops in the line at that point.

Our raids were most successful. Each day found us on another part of the front, and we carried out some pretty harrowing expeditions into the dark forests. We always expected unknown quantities, but in fact never met any except the day we collected thirty-four prisoners and found we had no escort party for them.

OPERATIONS 'REBOUND' AND 'THRUSTER': THE CAPTURE OF ROOSENDAAL

Extracts from the history of 34 Tank Brigade

At the beginning of October 1944 34 Tank Brigade consisted of 7 RTR, 9 RTR, 107 Regt RAC (Kings Own Royal Regt) and 147 Regt RAC (Hampshire Regt). On 1 October 7 RTR was detached to help in the siege of Dunkirk, where it eventually remained for some four months. The remainder of the brigade took part in the actions north and north-east of Eindhoven described in the previous section, and on 14 October passed from the command of 51st Highland Division to that of 49th West Riding Division (the Butcher Bears). 49th Division's task was to push the Germans north to the River Maas, and by doing so to assist the Canadian Army in their push up the Beveland isthmus to free the Scheldt waterway.

The commander of 49th Division requested 34 Brigade commander, Brigadier W.S. (Wahoo) Clarke to form a mobile task force (Clarkeforce) with the following role: to launch through a gap made by 49th Division (supported by 9 RTR) north of St. Leonard, advance northward to protect the right flank of 4th Canadian Armoured Division, and to gain ground as a spearhead to 49th Division whose main bulk would follow up and take over as opportunity occurred. In the operations that took place Clarkeforce performed as envisaged, launching through a hole made by 9 RTR supporting 56 Infantry Brigade, who speeded the force with all possible help. Thereafter the somewhat tenuous lines of communication connecting Clarkeforce with the rest of 49th Division were subjected to fierce counter-attack from the east by enemy infantry and armour. In Operation 'Rebound' (19–24 October) all the brigade were heavily involved.

In Operation 'Thruster' (26–30 October) the Hallams with 9 RTR came up on the right flank of Clarkeforce, and then 9 RTR were used fully in capturing Roosendaal. During this time 147

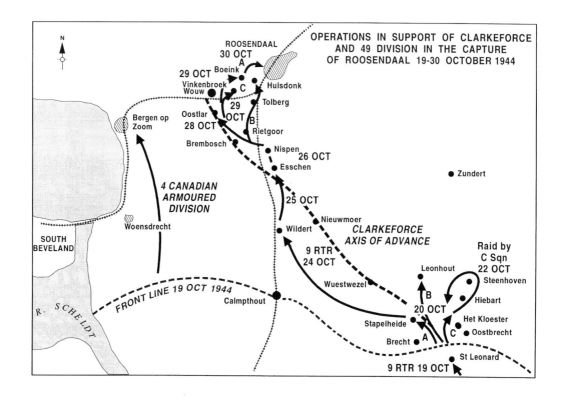

Regt RAC operated even further east to cover their flank under command 104th (Timberwolf) US Infantry Division, who had come under command I British Corps for about a month and were having their initial blooding.

9 RTR War Diary, 19–30 October 1944

Note: there are no entries in the War Diary for 17 and 18 October, on which days the battalion was moving from Eindhoven to just west of Turnhout and getting established in the new area.

19 October: Move to Forward Assembly Area for Operation 'Rebound' in area of St. Leonard.
Tasks:
  (a) 9 RTR in support of 56 Brigade to clear the enemy from an area between the road through Ostbrecht on the left and a line from Beekhoven to Konings Ven on the right.
  (b) To relieve Clarkeforce in Leonhout.
Plan:
        On the right C Squadron with 2 Glos
        On the left A Squadron with 2 SWB (South Wales Borderers)
        B Squadron in reserve with 2 Essex
        In support C Squadron Fife & Forfar Yeomanry (flame-throwers)
        C Squadron 22 Dragoons (flails)
        D Oct 20: H 0730 hrs

20 October: No rain; dull; ground soft after heavy rain.
  0730 Crossed start line. Attacks began well – within twenty minutes C Squadron had advanced 800 yards. Prisoners coming in – no serious opposition. By 0830 C Squadron

outpaced infantry and found a number of Germans in wood and there had to wait for infantry. A Squadron advance slower. By 0805 two troops were busily engaged in Stapelhoede where an anti-tank gun and numerous infantry were causing trouble. One tank out of action. Prisoners had, however, been taken. [Note: 'Stapelhoede' is alternatively spelt 'Stapelheide'.]

By 0845, C Squadron had reached a wood close to their objective, having captured 88 mm and crew. At 0910 were joined by infantry and clearing up began – more prisoners taken and position clear by 0945.

Meanwhile, Stapelhoede was still being cleared but the rear of A Squadron had got to area woods.

1100 C Squadron with infantry established on final objective – more prisoners had been taken and suspected enemy position to the north engaged – enemy artillery located and dealt with.

1116 A Squadron established area Stapelhoede where 75 mm and dummy anti-tank guns were captured with ten prisoners. Fighting Stapelhoede finished but other enemy posts to south still to be cleared. By 1330 only occasional opposition was found in the area, which was systematically cleared. 276 prisoners taken during the whole operation.

1445 C Squadron for rally, leaving one troop for eyes on final objective. To this point A Squadron had lost one tank, and Lt. Terry Smythe and his wireless operator, Cpl. Macdonald, had been wounded; C Squadron had had no casualties.

1430 B Squadron move forward to follow up Clarkeforce. It was however nearly dark before B Squadron and Essex were able to move into Leonhout and as Clarkeforce had not entered the village, B Squadron and Essex sat south of the village during the night.

C Squadron laagered with the 2 Glos while A and HQ leaguered area Het Kloester, supplying own patrols from personnel of A Echelon. Recce Troop was posted at Chateau de Yeuse. The night was generally quiet with occasional shelling of heavy calibre.

21 October: B Squadron and Essex moved into Leonhout and found little opposition – one anti-tank gun was encountered east of village. A couple of abandoned 88 mms were discovered by C Squadron in area north-west of Kloester and there was sufficient evidence to presume that they were the guns firing during the night. No further orders. Meanwhile squadrons to form defensive positions.

1400 A report of five armoured vehicles moving direction Stone bridge. B Squadron warned; later report that two tanks destroyed by infantry holding position. During afternoon occasional shelling by guns of heavy calibre – suspected firing from area north-west. Shelldrake informed.

22 October: Raid by two troops, C Squadron and Recce Troop, to harass enemy positions on right flank. C move east, shoot wood and shoot up houses in Steinhoven and Hiebart, retiring south to original area. Twenty-one enemies killed; two prisoners taken; one half-track; 1/75 mm; 1/50 mm; 1/20 mm destroyed. Recce Troop carrying out patrol on road St. Leonard–Hoogstraeten lost two tanks – as the tanks approached the mines were pulled across road by infantry hiding in ditch, one German killed – own casualties were Capt. Frank Haydon, Sgt. Butch Robinson and Tpr Jameson, all wounded. Report of fifteen armoured vehicles and infantry forming up area Kruisweig – no serious developments.

23 October: Battalion concentrated for purpose of moving north to support 56 Brigade in taking over Esschen from 6 Canadian Brigade.

24 October: Battalion arrive Wildert and are dispersed as follows in support of 56 Brigade: A Squadron in support of South Wales Borderers (SWB); B Squadron in support of 2nd Essex; C Squadron in reserve with HQ.

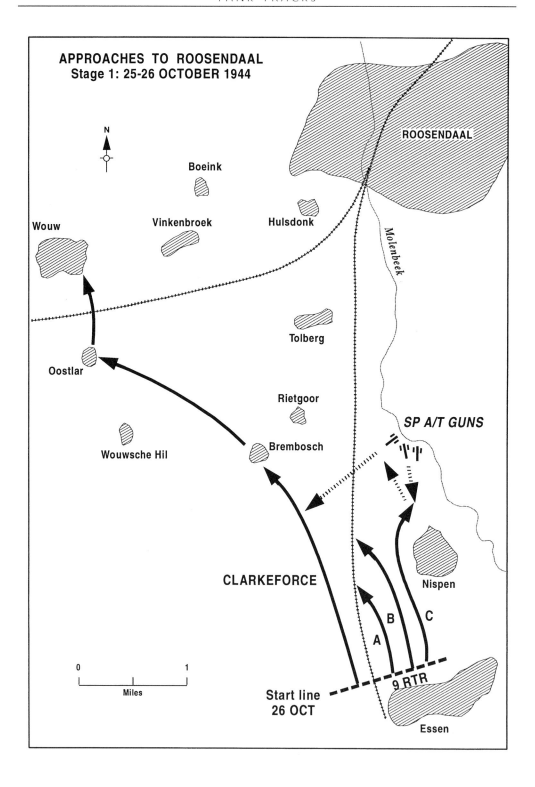

APPROACHES TO ROOSENDAAL
Stage 1: 25-26 OCTOBER 1944

N

ROOSENDAAL

Boeink

Wouw

Vinkenbroek

Hulsdonk

Molenbeek

Tolberg

Oostlar

Rietgoor

SP A/T GUNS

Wouwsche Hil

Brembosch

CLARKEFORCE

Nispen

B

C

A

0   1

Miles

9 RTR

Start line
26 OCT

Essen

25 October: C Squadron and HQ move forward in preparation for Operation 'Thruster', the capture of Nispen

Plan:

Phase 1: capture of wood to west of Nispen by SWB to take place during night 25/26 October. A Squadron 9 RTR to stand by and be prepared to support at first light.

Phase 2: B Squadron to support 2nd Essex in capture of woods south-west of Nispen with one troop of Fife and Forfar Yeomanry (FF Yeo, flame-throwers) in support.

Phase 3: C Squadron to support 2nd Glos in capture of Nispen, attacking from west to east; one troop of FF Yeo under command.

During Phase 1 two troops of A Squadron will support 1/4 KOYLI (146 Brigade) in capture of wood to south-east of Nispen.

Attack is to have artillery support and at the conclusion of Phase 2 Clarkeforce will pass through having as its objective Wouw.

26 October: By first light, 2 South Wales Borderers had gained objective and there was no call for A Squadron to support. The two troops with KOYLIs on the right, under command Capt. Kidd, experienced 88 HE fire and Capt. Kidd was wounded in the head when his cupola was blown off. KOYLIs had little difficulty in reaching objective, but the two troops remained in support throughout the day.

0730 B Squadron crossed start line and a quarter of an hour later had passed through positions previously captured by South Wales Borderers. Visibility bad owing to mist and maximum shooting range 500 yards.

0800 Supported by tank fire and Crocodiles, infantry had secured left flank of objective. On right the infantry were consolidating. Resistance had only been spasmodic and about forty prisoners taken – identification 857 GR.

As soon as objective had been taken, the area was continually mortared and shelled. Sgt. Ken Virgo of 10 Troop was wounded. One 88 mm SP and 75 mm anti-tank gun worrying the right flank were knocked out. Infantry and tanks cleared area north of road to allow Clarkeforce to pass through. C Squadron suffered two officers casualties (Capt. A.J. Morgan; Lt. A.P. Boden) in the forming up point as a result of mortaring and shelling; both remained at duty.

1120 C Squadron cross start line and very shortly had the outskirts of Nispen under fire. The enemy appeared to have evacuated the village but securing it was delayed as infantry had some difficulty in getting up. Shelling still continued and three spandaus were reported north-east of village on far side of Moolenbeek.

1225 Infantry clear houses supported by tanks from east – a few prisoners and considerable defensive mortaring.

1330 Firmly established in village – targets to east and north-east stonked by Shelldrake.

1550 Half of B and C Squadrons withdraw for replenishment.

1615 Shelling more intense and spandaus engaged tanks from well-concealed positions. Two tanks damaged and Sgt. Tom Tomney and Tpr Ginger Kirk of 13 Troop C Squadron were wounded. This skirmish was no doubt a diversion to cover engineer party who blew bridge on road Nispen–Roosendaal at 1630. One spandau and 75 mm anti-tank gun abandoned by enemy under fire.

1635 Essex and Glos defence positions complete. B & C Squadrons released and join HQ, where the night was spent in laager.

27 October: From first light two troops of each squadron move forward in support of infantry – remainder of battalion stand down.

1530 Following orders from 34 Tank Brigade, B Squadron with one Company The Duke of

Wellington's Regiment, previously established in area Brembosch with Clarkeforce, move forward and take over Rietgoor. No opposition encountered. 7th Battalion the Duke of Wellington's Regiment establish themselves in village, B Squadron and Royal Regiment (RR) Brembosch. C Squadron now responsible for giving support to Essex and Glosters.

28 October: A Squadron move forward to be on call by 2 South Wales Borderers who had overnight established themselves area east of railway and west of Moolenbeek.

1700 Two troops B Squadron with Company Duke of Wellington's Regiment clearing area north-east of railway/road junction. Shot at by two SPs firing down line of road; one tank hit; no casualties. Bad light prevented pin-pointing its position – not destroyed but later put out of action by Med. Regt RA.

1730 Battalion less B Squadron who remain with Duke of Wellington's Regiment move to area Wouwsche Hill 6827 with intention of supporting 146 Brigade. Plan made for occupation of Boeink and Vinkenbroek, preparatory to an attack on Roosendaal. Attack to be supported by 2 Med. Regiment and 4 Fd. Regiment RA.

Phase I: C Squadron with A Company Hallams to capture Vinkenbroek.
Phase II: A Squadron with B Company Hallams to capture Boeink.
H – 1200 hrs, 29 October.

29 October: C Squadron cross start line and have little difficulty in overcoming obstacle of railway. By 1225 forward infantry in village but four tanks were already bogged. AP fire from SP in area Boeink knocked out two tanks. Infantry had no trouble at all and collected about forty prisoners.

1248 A Squadron began to move up and anti-tank fire was fairly heavy from area Boeink. SP very active but infantry again met with little resistance, and soon reached the village and the SPs withdrew north under cover of a gentle slope.

1355 While infantry mopping up village, A Squadron steadily losing tanks – one SP and 75 mm anti-tank gun knocked out in area Boeink. Tanks had to push on to Boeink despite losses to ensure infantry took over their objective.

1410 Fairly quiet – third company established itself in area but A Squadron had now only three tanks left from the eleven that started. More prisoners had been taken and total count by infantry was over a hundred.

1520 Squadron rear rally.

In the action to take Boeink A Squadron had the following casualties: Killed: Lt. Roy Clarkson, commanding 4 Troop, his driver Cpl. John Tucker; Sergeant John Snowden, troop sergeant of 3 Troop, his driver L/Cpl. John Hamill, his gunner Tpr Stan Lawson, and his wireless operator Tpr Geoff Taylor; Tpr Alf Cowton of 3 Troop and Tpr Ray Hughes of 5 Troop; wounded were Tpr Abbott, Tpr Jack Coolin, Tpr Cope, Tpr Davies, Tpr Honan, Tpr Humphreys, Cpl. McConnell, Tpr Moulson, Tpr Oram, and L/Cpl. Powell.

In the action around Vinkenbroek C Squadron had the following casualties: Killed: Tpr John ('Smudger') Smith, co-driver of 15 Troop Leader's tank; wounded: Major Ronnie Holden, squadron leader, his gunner Sgt. Taylor, Tpr Board and Tpr Macdonald; and Tpr Titch Mead, driver of 15 Troop Leader's tank.

This was purely a tank versus anti-tank and SP battle and it was obvious that the Germans were using their SPs in force as a last defence to cover a general withdrawal north and to prevent any armoured thrust from disorganizing their retreat.

As a result of the battle, it must be emphasized that the infantry must release the supporting tanks far quicker in open flat country; otherwise unnecessary and expensive casualties are suffered.

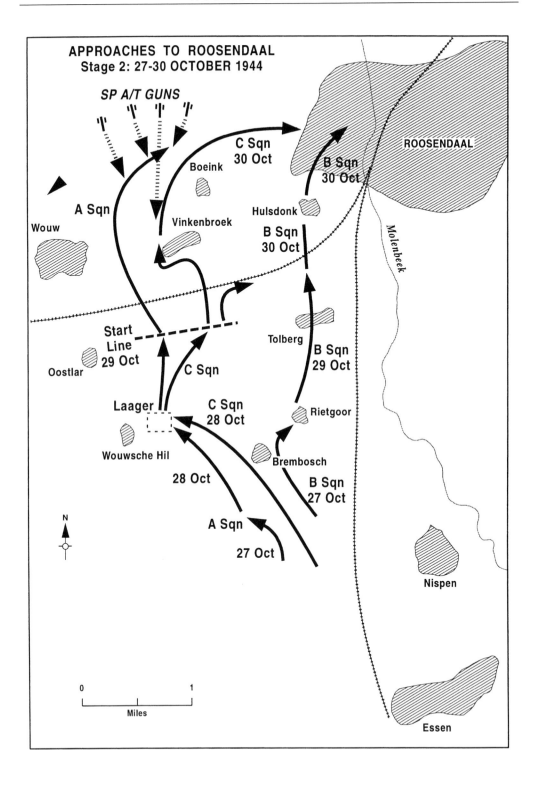

APPROACHES TO ROOSENDAAL
Stage 2: 27-30 OCTOBER 1944

SP A/T GUNS

C Sqn
30 Oct

ROOSENDAAL

B Sqn
30 Oct

Boeink

A Sqn

Hulsdonk

Vinkenbroek

B Sqn
30 Oct

Wouw

Molenbeek

Start
Line

29 Oct

Tolberg

Oostlar

C Sqn

B Sqn
29 Oct

Laager

C Sqn
28 Oct

Rietgoor

Wouwsche Hil

Brembosch

28 Oct

B Sqn
27 Oct

N

A Sqn

27 Oct

0   1

Miles

Nispen

Essen

A Churchill bridgelayer lays a bridge capable of carrying 60 tons over the Roosendaal Creek on 30 October 1944. The bridgelaying arm was operated hydraulically, and this type of bridge was particularly suitable for a waterway with solid banks. (IWM B11485)

Troop sergeant Reg Mead of 11 Troop, C Squadron (on right in turret) commands his tank Intensive *over the bridge just laid in Roosendaal; this bridge was called by Roosendaal inhabitants 'London Bridge'. Reg's wireless operator (on left in turret) is Vic Jewell. The wireless operator in the troop corporal's tank* Impassive *following behind is Bill Thompson. Reg Mead was killed in the Reichswald in February 1945. (IWM B11490)*

1545 B Squadron support Leics in area north of Tolberg having as a task the enlarging of the small bridgehead made by Duke of Wellington's Regiment across anti-tank ditch. Operation completely successful despite soft ground – no casualties and some prisoners taken.

30 October: B Squadron cross anti-tank ditch which had been made passable by bulldozing and establishing themselves during darkness in area Hulsdonk.

The tanks were heavily camouflaged in defensive positions placed to break up any counter-attack that may have been made against the bridgehead. One troop Armoured Vehicles RE and one troop Flails were under command. To ensure perfect liaison, 2 i/c B Squadron was in W/T communication with 147 Brigade and radio operator was with the Leics, the most forward battalion. The further task of B Squadron was to support 147 Brigade in clearing Roosendaal south of Bredaschebaan but recce reported that that part of the town was clear.

0930 C Squadron supporting KOYLI (146 Brigade) passed through but the Churchill bridge had to be used to cross the canal. Tanks and infantry moved down the streets but no enemy was found. The battle for Roosendaal had obviously been fought the previous day. Various orders followed which included the change of command to 56 Brigade and the movement to a

The burghers of Roosendaal are pleased to see Infernal, *8 Troop Leader's tank, on 30 October 1944. The crew members from left to right are Reg Terrington (wireless-op), Cpl. Norman Fraser (gunner), Lt. Fred Critchley (troop leader), Bert Sutcliffe (driver), and 'Jeep' Greet (co-driver). (IWM B11482)*

battalion area in Oudgastel for which recces were carried out but later instructions followed that batallion was to remain in Roosendaal, which was to be concentration area for 34 Tank Brigade. Since 20 October 9 RTR tanks with 49th Division had advanced 12½ miles against many obstacles and a determined enemy.

31 October: 9 RTR tanks remain in Roosendaal under orders of 34 Tank Brigade.

Personal recollections, 19–30 October 1944

The actions of these few days are remembered particularly for the bad weather and heavy going, the determined opposition and the casualties, and the fluidity of the front line.

On 22 October C Squadron were ordered to carry out a 'mystery tour' into enemy territory to find out if they were still there, if so how many, and so on. This reconnaissance in force was led by Ronnie Holden, and he took with him 13, 14 and 15 troops. After a while they had difficulty in getting the ground to agree with the map – they were lost! All that this meant, however, was that the recce was longer and proportionately more successful. Trevor Greenwood took part in this operation.

Sunday 22 October 1944, D + 138

11.00 a.m: Major called for troop leaders: Something in the wind? – Yes: Mr Francis soon returned with orders to stow everything: be ready to move into attack at twelve o'clock. This time, the plan was to make a quick raid into enemy territory, going further in than yesterday, and make a circling move north and then back west: two troops to remain behind on the defensive role, the rest to carry out the raid, i.e. 13, 14, 15 and HQ.

It is difficult to give a description of an operation of this kind – everything happens so quickly and the enormous concentration upon one's own particular problems leaves little opportunity for observing the whole picture.

However, we crossed the start line at 12 noon, and tore past the three 88s immobilized yesterday in a few minutes. And then our firing commenced. It was like hell let loose. There were twelve vehicles, all going flat out, and firing their guns in all directions except to the rear. Hedgerows, ditches, trees, houses – any mortal thing that could provide cover for Jerries was saturated with MG fire and HE. Terrified horses were running wildly around the fields; cows scampering about, careering through ditches and barbed-wire fences; our own vehicles lumbered over ditches, through hedges, across ploughed fields, turnip fields, crashed through plantations – uprooted trees; it was sheer destruction, but rather thrilling – and how terrifying for the enemy! At one point, my troop leader's vehicle became ditched: it looked rather bad – but somehow the vehicle extricated itself, whilst Dicky and I provided some protection with our guns. This was quite open country, with houses and farm buildings lying fairly well scattered. The nearest were almost 2,000 yds; we plastered them pretty well.

My gunners put two belts of Besa into one house at 3,000 yds – and set it on fire – adding one more blazing pile to the wreckage we were creating.

After half an hour or so, the Major admitted over the air that he had lost his bearings – and wasn't sure of his position. This was not surprising. The speed of our advance, plus the type of country made map-reading practically impossible. However, we carried on and now bore to the north, thus approaching some of the area we had been shooting up.

As we neared some of the farms and houses, I was amazed to see civilians standing outside frantically waving white 'flags'. They must have been crazy to have remained in the area, knowing that it was a battle area. Possibly we killed some of them; we certainly destroyed much of their property. Somehow, I couldn't feel sorry for them. We were fighting for our lives, and we knew that the enemy often concealed his troops and anti-tank guns in houses and farm buildings; the civilians must have known it too. We simply *had* to prevail with dealing with the Hun.

At one point of our journey, the Major had a narrow escape. A carefully concealed 75 AT gun opened up at 50 yards – and hit the rim of his 95 gun muzzle. Luckily, the Major saw the gun, and his own gun was suitably traversed. Before the enemy could fire a second shot, the Major had fired a 95 HE – a direct hit . . . And the Jerry gun went up in bits; two more 95s were pumped in – just to make sure! By this time, we seemed to be in an area of scattered houses – and they all had their groups of people, including children, waving white clothes. They seemed to regard these as ample protection!

Dicky discovered another gun – this time a 50 mm, and shot it up – using HE also on the fleeing crew! No prisoners!!!

Eventually, the Major gave the order to return to harbour – and so we reached the end of the most hectic two hours I have known for some time. Our 'terror raid' had involved a run of over 7 miles, instead of the 4 miles previously planned. No wonder the Colonel seemed anxious about our whereabouts, over the air. But he congratulated all of us later, and took all details of gun positions, enemy troop locations etc. I think we did a useful job of reconnaissance, and no doubt killed many Jerries. And we must have terrified many more. Two of them were so anxious to surrender that they ran after one of our tanks and more or less compelled the commander to have them! This was Frank Hodgson; he was certainly amused by the incident.

Later: Today's two prisoners seemed very happy to be with us; they said that most of their comrades were anxious to surrender, but were unable to do so because of their officer's threats to shoot all intending deserters and defeatists. They were waiting for our tanks to advance, they said, to provide an excuse for surrendering. These prisoners disclosed too that there is much friction between the Reichwehr and the SS and that they are expected to be in open conflict before long.

The next day of significant action was 26 October, when all three squadrons took part. A Squadron's objective was easily taken, but Capt. Ken Kidd was wounded by 88 mm HE – the squadron's only casualty on that day. Both B and C Squadrons took part in the capture of Nispen, and both had triumphs and tragedies.

B Squadron took their objective, but were then subjected to continuous mortaring and shelling. Their two casualties were Cpl. Ficker and Sgt. Ken Virgo. Ken had won the MM at Grainville in June, and had been 10 Troop Sergeant since then. He was badly wounded by mortar fire, and died of his wounds on 31 October. During this action 8 Troop under Freddie Critchley knocked out an 88 mm SP and a 75 mm anti-tank gun. For this he was subsequently awarded the MC.

As related in the war diary Sgt. Tom Tomney of 13 Troop and his gunner Ginger Kirk were wounded on this day. Tom recalls what he remembers of that day, and shows how the whole of 34 Armoured Brigade co-operated in the operations of Clarkeforce. This force was commanded in person by Brigadier 'Wahoo' Clarke, and its strike formations were 107 RAC and 49 Div Recce Regiment, supported by flame-throwers, engineers, SP anti-tank guns and artillery.

Clarkeforce passed through A and B Squadrons of 9 RTR at about the same time as C Squadron started its attack on Nispen. Tom Tomney recalls:

We had just moved through Nispen when Brigadier Clarke came on the air asking if anyone could see the SP up on the hill some 1,000 yards away. I was the only one who said I saw it, and the Brigadier replied: 'I don't care what you do but empty your entire tank stock of ammo if you must and put it out of action; its blowing our battalion to blazes'. We did just that and set it on fire. Meanwhile another SP was sitting in a ditch a few hundred yards away from our tank. The last thing I remembered was seeing orange balls floating towards us. These were of course the shells from the SP which hit us.

Tom's sacrifice relieved the pressure on Clarkeforce, and for this action he was awarded the MM. Cyril Rees was Tom's driver, and the other members of the crew were Norman Hopkins (wireless operator), Ginger Kirk (gunner) and Don Foster (co-driver). The troop leader was Des Lilley and the troop corporal Frank Hodgson. Cyril writes:

The circumstances and conditions under which we had existed during the last five or six months made trying to remember the day or date a rather fruitless exercise. However, I believe it was 26 October 1944 since I always tried to remember birthdays in my own family, and I was sure it was my brother's who was serving with the Pacific Fleet. [It was 26 October.]

I wasn't in Nispen very long so I wasn't able to form much of a picture of it, but I vaguely see a long village street with houses on each side and not much depth. It was a gloomy October afternoon as we moved out from the village into the fields behind. The soil was dark and very heavy and seemed to be wholly covered with some sort of root crop.

We were in a one-up position as we came to a halt about 200 yards from the village, the houses forming a backdrop. We crossed easily a small drainage ditch, of which there were many. I left the engine on a fast tick-over and tried to take in what I could see. There was the occasional view of infantry men advancing slowly, keeping low, otherwise I had that usual feeling that many tank crews experience of being isolated and on your own. Ahead, I could see the flat country, receding into the gloom, with a few trees and here and there a hedge or two. It reminded me of the fens in so many ways, and I would not have been too surprised to see that dim and magnificent bulk of Ely Cathedral rising above the distant trees. The troop leader was about 30 yards ahead in his Mk VII and about the same distance to my right. My visor was shut and I couldn't see Frank Hodgson who was even further away on my right.

Two flashes in fairly quick succession from the hedge 800 yards or so away, followed at once by two loud metallic bangs to my right, indicated that some tank was on the receiving end of some AP shot. I heard our breech block close as Hoppy banged in a round and heard Tom give Ginger the order to fire. I kept my foot on the brake pedal as Ginger got off a couple of rounds fairly smartly. Seven or eight more flashes from ahead plus the impact noises from my right suggested someone in our troop was getting a pasting.

Twice more I heard the empty cases crash on to the turret floor. Then it was our turn to be hit. I felt rather than heard the first hit (on the left-hand side of the turret, near the top and near the edge), which then ricocheted away harmlessly. The next one gave the whole tank a jolt. Small debris rained down into the turret, and as I turned in my seat to look through to the fighting compartment I could see Ginger Kirk, on to whom Tom Tomney had collapsed. I have to be honest. I felt no panic and I wasn't all that scared, but I switched off the engine and pushed open the top hatches. Don Foster did the same.

Clambering out on to the mudguards on my side, I saw that Hoppy was already on the engine hatches looking down at Tom and Ginger below. The shot that got us had lifted off the commander's cupola and deposited it about 50 yards behind. Tom had been looking through the periscopes, observing. Ginger was all right, it seemed, and he started to push Tom up towards us, and Hoppy and I leaned over as far as possible till we could grab some part, any part of Tom, that was nearest.

It was a desperate few minutes. We eventually got Tom's arms, then held him under his shoulders. I noticed his hair was matted with blood and his head was slightly squashy – like a boiled egg that has been tapped with a spoon before peeling off the shell. We did not know, of course, if there were other injuries, though I thought his hands or wrists might have been broken when the cupola was blasted away. Speed was essential. We had to get him out and hope we did not aggravate any other injuries. At last, with a superhuman effort from Ginger, below in the turret, and with Norman's and my help, we were able to drag Tom from the gaping hole in the roof and lay him on the engine hatches. In this position we were protected from any frontal attack.

As this rescue got under way Frank Hodgson was able to lay down some smoke from his tank, which seemed to have been unscathed. In the meantime, Don Foster had managed to get hold of what looked like a wooden door. We placed Tom on this and lowered him to the ground behind our tanks where one or two other troop members were waiting. We all jumped to the ground and Ginger, Norman and I, using our tank as cover, carried our improvised stretcher back to the cover of the village, now and then tripping and stumbling over the uneven ground and ditches. At last we came to the Field Dressing Station. Tom was quickly sent back to a Field Hospital.

The rest of us were beginning to feel shocked but had no visible injuries. A mug of hot sweet tea soon put us right. A bloodstain on Ginger's shirt revealed a large flake of white enamel had broken off on impact and had embedded itself quite deeply. He had to stay and have it removed. Although in some pain, Ginger was able to use his great strength to raise Tom high enough for Hoppy and I to reach. Without his help, we would have had a long tough job on our hands. [Tom Tomney sent a photo of Ginger Kirk from Canada; on the back it reads: Ginger Kirk – I owe him my life.]

I decided to go back to the place we had left our tank. *No heroics, just a snap decision on my part.* After all, the tank was perfectly operational, at least the running gear was when I switched off the engine. Although getting dark, I was surprised to find a great deal of machine-gunfire and some mortars were still raining down. Bent double, and moving as fast as I could over the heavy ground, I soon covered the few hundred yards to the 13 Troop position. Of *Independent*, our reliable and faithful Mk III, there was no trace. Someone had recovered her.

The lonely hulk of our troop leader's MkVII stood empty, with hatches open nearby. I walked right round it and counted seven direct hits on the front, none of which had penetrated. One shot was jammed almost dead centre of the driver's visor. I thought of trying to drive it back. A quick examination of the driver's compartment was enough to tell me it was undriveable. Amongst other things, the shock waves from several hits on the glacis plate had caused the bolts holding the hydraulic reservoir to sheer off, spilling most of the fluid. *So – no throttle control, no brakes, no clutch.* This must have been the result of the impact noises I had counted earlier.

It was almost dark and fairly peaceful as I made my way back to Nispen, to our troop, and to C Squadron. *A memorable day – 26 October.*

Postscript

Tom Tomney was flown back to England that night. He had brain surgery and a titanium plate was inserted under his scalp at the Radcliffe Infirmary, Oxford. Like most of us he is now retired, and lives with his wife in Canada. He was at our 1991 reunion, a picture of rude

Jock Pearson, Bernie Kirkpatrick and (front) Ginger Kirk. This photograph was supplied by Sgt. Tom Tomney MM of 13 Troop, and of Ginger Kirk Tom says 'I owe him my life'. The story of this is related in the battle for Nispen, October 1944.

health. The brass name-plate and log-book of *Independent* VM31023B, Mk III are now with the Tank Museum at Bovington.

For his action in going back under fire to attempt to recover his tank and the troop leader's tank Cyril was subsequently awarded the MM.

The next day of significant action – and the last, in this particular segment of the campaign – was 29 October. This was a three-part attack on the outskirts of Roosendaal. On the left C Squadron were to take Vinkenbroek, A Squadron were to pass through and take Boeink, and B Squadron were to attack on the right, advancing to Hulsdonk.

The first newsletter describes a well-remembered situation relating to maps. This time it happened to C Squadron. 'The officers of the squadron indulged until well after midnight in making indecipherable chinagraph inscriptions by the light of a Helleson lamp on the talc covering no fewer than four neatly folded large-scale maps. The unpronounceable objective, Vinkenbroek, lay at the junction of all four.'

The casualties on this day were recorded in the War Diary. Trevor Greenwood was closely involved in the C Squadron action, saw A Squadron coming through to the further objective of Boeink, and saw and heard some of the aftermath of A Squadron's action.

Sunday 29 October 1944, D + 145
Two days have elapsed since I wrote the foregoing – rather bad days – and my mind is a bit confused, but I want to try and record events in sequence. We moved out last evening from

Nispen at about 5.00 p.m. – and headed westwards; we had no orders, but were aware of several rumours concerning 107 RAC who were reported to have had a hammering during the day; it seemed fairly obvious that we were taking over from them on the left flank of the salient.

We eventually harboured close to the village of Wouwsche Hil – a 3 mile journey through the usual scenes of destruction and death – dead cows littered the fields; dead Germans lay by the roadsides; derelict houses and farms; smashed up telegraph poles; scarred and torn trees.

Our harbour was an open field; to our front, about a mile away to the north, several buildings were blazing; the whole forward horizon was, in fact, a mass of blazing buildings; and that was where the enemy were. The Major was obviously uneasy about the situation. We harboured in the darkness, and the absence of orders, or 'information' left him in an unenviable position. The enemy may have been nearer than presumed – and it was doubtful whether there was a screen of our infantry ahead of us. And so, we had to be on the alert all night – one man in each vehicle constantly acting as observer.

107 RAC had been taken by surprise the morning before – some SPs having drawn up close during the night, and they were shot up in harbour the following morning. We had to avoid a repetition of that. We went to bed beneath the vehicle, not knowing what the morrow held in store, but expecting the worst.

There were too many signs of heavy fighting for our presence there to be merely defensive. Until late in the evening, we had witnessed signs of a battle about a mile to the west – a bitter battle, it sounded.

Reveille this morning was 5.30 a.m. with all kit stowed and vehicle ready for action by 6.00 a.m. – just in case some SPs tried to catch us as they had caught 107. But nothing happened, and we were able to stand down and have breakfast at 7.30 a.m. Meanwhile, we learned of the orders which had been issued during the night. We were going into battle that morning – the whole battalion, each squadron having an individual role to play. C's objective the village of Vinkenbroek – about 2,000 yards due north, and 400 yards beyond the railway running across our front. A's objective the village of Boeink – about 600 yards further north. B were 'going in' to our right – one of the suburbs of Roosendaal.

The surrounding country was very flat – and quite open, but fairly well infested with ditches and drainage channels, as is most of the country in this area.

We know little about the enemy, other than that he had some SPs in the area. Our infantry were the Hallams (Crevecoeur!). At about 12 noon, C went in. 11 and 12 took up hull-down positions behind the railway embankment to protect the R. flank. 13, 14, 15 and HQ then crossed the railway and turned left – running across the southern front of the village. This move was made at speed, with all guns trained on the village 400 yards away. We poured shot and shell into every building, shed, bush and ditch which could possibly harbour the enemy.

We ran diagonally towards the western edge of the village – about 1,000 yard run, and reached this point without trouble, although two or three vehicles had difficulty in the heavy ground and were ditched for a time. 15 Troop were on the extreme left of our advance; we took up positions behind some burning buildings on the main road through the village. And at about this time, our infantry approached from the railway embankment. I was glad to see them. We received orders to move a little further forward – to protect the infantry from possible enemy fire from Boeink – and then the fun started.

My troop leader, Mr Francis, moved out to cross the road, and I followed. Through my periscope, I saw Mr Francis' vehicle make a quick dash back to the protection of the house. Had he been fired at? I wasn't left long in doubt. There came a heavy bang, and bits of debris fell into the turret. My vehicle shook a bit, and the crew swore we had been hit. I ordered the driver to reverse, and the vehicle responded immediately – the hit had apparently left us undamaged. We went back painfully slowly, our right and rear being meanwhile completely exposed to the north and north-east – from where the shots appeared to come.

Each second of that journey back seemed an age. Each moment I expected to be hit again; and how damnably provoking that we couldn't fire back – I had no idea of the precise location of whatever was firing – either an AT gun or a SP. The enemy was, as usual, using flashless ammo, and was exceedingly well camouflaged. I scanned the presumed location of the gun, using binoculars, but could see nothing – only houses and haystacks and innocent looking bushes.

Our journey in reverse was only about 40 yards, but it was one of the longest runs I have ever known. I cannot describe my relief when eventually we got round to the rear side of that house – snuggling as near to it as possible, even though it was blazing. My troop officer was already there, apparently unharmed.

Soon he moved forward a little and ordered me further back – to observe around the western side of the house . . . And then I noticed the Major clambering from his vehicle about 30 yards ahead. He had been hit – presumably by the same gun. His crew seemed to 'bale out' all right, although the Major had to assist one man from the track cover. Three of his crew lay down in a nearby ditch, and the Major chased off to the rear – and I soon had his voice on the air again requesting medical help for his wounded crew. He had boarded another vehicle, and taken command again almost immediately. It was good to hear him over the air assuring the Colonel that he was absolutely all right and unharmed.

A little later, only a minute or two, I heard the characteristic swish of an AP, followed by a terrible bang, immediately to my right . . . I looked and saw Mr Francis and some of his crew clambering from their vehicle; he had been hit and was wisely baling out instantly. Mr Francis didn't look so good. Meanwhile, Dicky Hall's vehicle, further to the right, had become ditched – and his crew had baled out and were sheltering behind their vehicle; I believe Mr Francis joined them. The next few moments were sickening. The enemy must have known my vehicle was hiding, but apparently he couldn't see me. Nevertheless, he kept firing and hit Mr Francis' vehicle a second time and followed this by a few random shots in my direction. I cannot imagine a more terrifying sound than the vicious hiss of those rounds as they whizzed by, so close to my vehicle. We seemed to have been literally condemned to death – with no chance of retaliating.

Thinking became difficult: every single fibre and nerve being too occupied in trying to see from where the shots were fired. There were anxious mutterings from my crew over the intercom – I could do nothing but try to reassure them: we *couldn't* bale out from an apparently undamaged vehicle. But the temptation can perhaps be imagined. During my terror-stricken searching for the enemy, I looked to the rear – back to the railway line – and my heart gave a leap as I beheld a number of tanks followed by infantry approaching rapidly. It was A Squadron. They had commenced their attack, and were going to pass beyond us, and so on to Boeink beyond. How grateful I was to see those tanks – and how my heart warmed towards A – I didn't then know what lay in store for them.

About this time, Mr Francis signalled for me to lay a smoke-screen to enable him to rescue the wounded from his vehicle; this was soon done. A little later, Mr Francis himself appeared on top of my vehicle – I knew instinctively that he was taking my place, and I 'baled out' at once – sorry to be leaving my crew. In a few seconds I had crawled to comparative safety behind Dicky Hall's tank – stopping en route by the side door of Mr Francis' vehicle to try and drag out his co-driver, Jimmy Smith. Mr Francis had asked me to do this as I left him; I doubt whether I would have thought of it, even had I known Smith was still in the vehicle. But one glance convinced me that he was beyond earthly aid. Already his eyes were glazing and staring horribly; his mouth was open, and skin already turning that ghastly grey-yellow of death. He was on the exposed side of the vehicle, and so I wasted no time seeking cover.

Dicky's crew were all quite OK, but Mr Francis' driver, Titch Mead, was lying on the ground in a pool of blood. His left leg had been almost amputated; and his left hand badly injured – but he was conscious, and making no complaint. Dicky was fixing a tourniquet to his leg and others were improvising a rough stretcher from two gun-cleaning poles and an overcoat.

How on earth Mead was removed from his vehicle I don't know, but Dicky told me later that they had to give him two ampoules of chloroform before he 'went out'. And a little later, Dicky injected a dose of morphia. How grand to have a chap like Dicky around in such an emergency. How I admired him; and what gallantry on the part of all of them in dragging Mead from that vehicle under heavy fire. It was a bit of a job to place Mead on that crude stretcher, but we managed it – and the rough splint on his leg remained in position.

And now Wilde and Thomas crawled away in search of an ambulance or stretcher-bearers. Mead accepted a cigarette – !

Meanwhile, Mr Francis had drawn away in my vehicle – leaving the shelter of the house in the protection of a smoke-screen. I heard nothing more of him until much later. Dicky and I crawled back to have a final glimpse of Smith – but he was now dead: we left him and crawled back to our refuge beside Dicky's tank.

Wilde and Thomas soon returned with information that there was a first-aid post in the brickworks about half a mile to our rear. It seemed a hopeless business trying to carry Mead so far on the crazy stretcher – but something had to be done – and Dicky said let's go – and that was the beginning of a horrible journey. There were six of us, beside Mead, and we learned that a human body is a heavy load, especially when the route includes ditches and ploughed fields torn by tank tracks.

It must have taken us almost an hour to reach that brickworks: an hour of very unpleasant recollections, including enemy fire and fatigue. Dicky worked like a horse – and Mead made little complaint, even when we stumbled and heaved him across the ditches.

At the brickworks, the ambulance was waiting, and we parted with our colleague, thankful to have got him away from that hell on earth . . . And now we returned to the tanks – the battle having moved a little further north. On this return journey, I saw a little of the price paid by A in making their advance beyond our original objective. There were at least half a dozen disabled tanks lying out in the open, and at least one blazing furiously. The crews who had 'baled out' were returning southwards, some of them supporting wounded colleagues. God knows what had happened, but it seemed obvious that the enemy had been well prepared to deal with a tank attack.

It was some consolation to see batches of prisoners being marched back by our infantry – the latter grinning cheerfully – the former dirty and dishevelled, but seemingly quite happy.

We reached Dicky's vehicle without mishap and the crew started unloading their personal kit. Eddie Wilde, stout fella!, started to make a brew. Dicky and I and one or two others returned to Mr Francis' vehicle – and dragged out Smith. He was by now a ghastly sight. It was difficult to drag his body from the vehicle and eventually Dicky had to lever his limbs while two of us dragged from the outside. His body then came out – leaving most of his legs in the vehicle; he had been cut in two by an AP, and must have died from loss of blood very quickly.

We lay the body on the ground and covered it with a tarpaulin. I felt rather sick. Back again to Dicky's tank – and a cup of tea. What a grand drink that was! By now, the battle had passed its peak, and the entire neighbourhood was a mass of blazing buildings, and damaged tanks.

Major Mockford (A) appeared from somewhere on foot. He looked pretty bad and told us that he only had three tanks left! He passed on looking for HQ. I couldn't help wondering what had happened to the rest of C – and those lads in my vehicle. . . .

After our cup of tea, during which several AP shots whistled overhead uncomfortably low, all personal kit was collected and the two tanks closed up. We then returned to the brickworks. Someone there had kindly made tea, and we had another drink.

It was there that I overheard the Colonel of the infantry inform our second in command that he had only had four casualties all day, all wounded, 'thanks to the assistance of the tanks'. He added 'I hope you haven't many casualties'. I was glad to hear the tribute; it is something to know that our efforts are of some use to those grand infantry lads. But I knew that our casualties would far exceed those for the infantry.

Our HQ squadron tanks had by now taken up a position behind the railway, about half a mile from the brickworks – and they were our next objective. Once again we had tea, provided by HQ crews from their own rations – and we answered a few questions from the Colonel. And then C squadron tanks appeared – and I was darned thankful to see almost a full squadron of tanks, including my own. The Major too was with them.

I joined my crew – and a hot dinner was soon being prepared – and yarns swapped. But everyone looked pretty ghastly. The day had left its mark all right. The Major had been hit in the head with shrapnel from an HE, but he seemed cheerful enough, and dismissed the wound very lightly. A very brave man, and a great leader. Our meal in this location was interrupted by a few rounds of HE and one or two air bursts. It was not a healthy spot, so we had to move to a harbour near our original start point. And there we dug in and slept.

Unfortunately, before bedding down, it became known that another infantry Colonel (the KOYLIs) had been requesting our assistance for an assault the following day on Roosendaal. This was dreadful news. We were all exhausted – and had had enough to last us for a long time. And an attack on a large town like Roosendaal! Well, no wonder we were worried; personally, I felt terrified of going in again so soon – especially with so many SPs in the neighbourhood.

But we slept – and did our guard during the night.

B's action had proceeded very well. They met little opposition, and suffered no casualties.

Monday 30 October 1944, D + 146

This morning, I learned a few results of yesterday's action. C had one killed and four wounded – three of the latter in the Major's tank, and one in Mr Francis's. A had eight killed and six wounded. Vehicles I am not sure of – C had the Major's and Mr Francis's disabled by AP – both recoverable. Dicky Hall's vehicle was OK, but still badly ditched. At least one of A's burned out – a 'write off' – five or six others were hit by AP – and two or three badly ditched. . . . The infantry took eighty prisoners – probably most of the enemy infantry in the villages. I don't think any of the SP crews were captured, but believe a couple of 75 ATs were knocked out.

In yesterday's action, the 'hit' on my vehicle caused a bit of amusement later. The shot had dislodged a tin box from the rear, and gone clean through the enormous bedding roll strapped to the rear of the tank; no other damage. There were four sleeping kits in that roll of bedding – and we debated upon whose blankets had been ruined. When we opened the bundle, it was found that my bedding had been hit – and what a mess it was! The blankets were a mass of large holes; my denims in shreds; and gas-cape torn to pieces. Pedder remarked philosophically that I ought to be thankful not to have been sleeping in them at the time – so 'stop ticking'. I slept in the torn blankets last night, but have had them replaced today.

We learned this morning that Roosendaal was definitely being attacked today, and some of our vehicles were 'going in' with the infantry, the KOYLIs. In view of our battered state, the tanks were 'pooled' and about nine of them detailed for the job. The reactions of the crews can be imagined. It looked like being a hell of a battle.

I was thankful to have my vehicle left out of the first phase of the attack, but I had to stand by to go in as reserve, if necessary. The next four hours were a nightmare. We seemed to get little news over the air from the attacking force, and their fate was a mystery. Meanwhile I waited for the worst – hoping and hoping. . . .

After lunch, rumours started spreading that our tanks had entered the town without opposition – a state of affairs which seemed too good to be true. But it was true, Thank Heaven.

Bill Thompson was the wireless operator in Corporal Freddie Horner's tank *Impassive*, corporal's tank of 11 Troop commanded by Eb Wood. On 29 October:

We were fighting our way over bogs and dykes in pouring rain, and came to open country. Our tank moved alongside a farm outbuilding with the other two tanks of our troop to the rear. We had been there only a matter of minutes when through the periscope I saw a flash about a mile away and was sure it was a German '88. There was a second shot which hit the ground next to the tank; it became obvious that it was an '88 and he was finding the range.

Without hesitation our tank commander Freddie Horner instructed our driver to reverse out as quickly as possible, which he did. Over the B set came our troop leader Mr Wood telling us to get back into position. When we didn't move he moved his tank into exactly the position we had been alongside the outbuilding. Within seconds there was one almighty bang and he had taken a direct hit on the front of his turret. When the dust had settled and he had made a dazed but hurried retreat it was discovered that an AP shot had penetrated 7½ inches into the turret, just as though it had been drilled by a huge drill.

At the point of impact the thickness of the turret armour was 9 inches, Mr Wood's tank being a new Mark VII. Ours was a Mark IV, and the thickness of our turret at the same point was only 6 inches. Had we not moved quickly from our position the AP shot would surely have holed our turret and killed the turret crew, and possibly blown the tank up completely had the ammunition been struck. Needless to say we were forgiven for moving from our original position. Mr Wood's tank went back to the REME workshop for repair and was soon returned ready for action again.

The C Squadron newsletter scribe wrote of the final stages of the Vinkenbroek action: 'Our job done we withdrew to a more comfortable position called Forward Rally, leaving one troop up. This doubtful honour was bestowed on Eb Wood and his 11 Troop, who on their return calmly informed us that all was well except for a hole 6 inches deep in the turret.' Taffy Leyshon was the driver of Eb's tank: 'Our troop acted as rear guard, and our tank took a hit in the turret; it went in 8 inches but did not penetrate.' Whether it was 6, 7½, or 8 inches, it certainly made an impression! But the Churchill could take a lot of punishment. The *34 Armoured Brigade History* recorded: 'One notable tank casualty was a Mark VII of 9 RTR which sustained nine direct hits in front from 75 mm AP shot at short range without being completely penetrated by any!' Cyril Rees is convinced that 'this was 13 Troop Leader's tank which I tried to recover from the Nispen battle, and on which I counted seven hits in spite of the gloom. This tank was for some time at the Armoured Vehicle Proving Establishment (AVPE) at Chobham, an exhibit for military technicians and students studying and researching armour plate technology.'

CHAPTER 9

Waiting for Hitler

AFTER ARNHEM AND ANTWERP

The broad picture

The capture of Roosendaal was part of the process by which the banks of the Scheldt and its estuary were cleared of German troops, and allied shipping could reach the docks of Antwerp. While this operation had a very clear and important objective, there seemed to be some uncertainty in the allied high command as to what its overall strategy should be. This was resolved just before Christmas by Hitler in his Ardennes push, but the reasons for the indecision up to that point appear to have been:

1. Eisenhower's general policy of action all along the line, rather than concentration of forces on one or two main objectives;
2. the deteriorating weather and the nature of the terrain, resulting in a marked decline in mobility;
3. the very long supply lines until (and to a considerable degree after) the opening of the port of Antwerp on 28 November;
4. a shortage of artillery ammunition, especially for the Americans;
5. the great skill with which the Germans re-armed and positioned their armies after the retreat from Normandy.

The result of these factors was a stalemate all along the front – indeed, there were some of the older and more senior soldiers who saw with consternation the possibility of a return to First World War fighting.

Until the stalemate was broken by Hitler's Ardennes push one of the operations that was undertaken was the capture of Geilenkirchen by 43 Wessex Div and 84 US Div. This was to have been followed by a push further eastward to the River Roer, Operation 'Shears', and in this the 9th were to have taken part.

The effect of these conditions, decisions, and plans on the movements of the 9th was that we remained in Roosendaal for nearly a month to refit and relax – although <u>rest</u> was not something that happened to most people; we then moved to Geilenkirchen in early December to prepare for Operation 'Shears'; finally we moved to form part of a counter-attack force on the northern flank of the Ardennes 'bulge'.

ROOSENDAAL

The War Diary, 31 October–29 November

November in Roosendaal
Following the entry into Roosendaal, it was uncertain what the future would bring, and the first few days were spent in very active maintenance and reorganization; new tanks and fresh crews

'Snuffy' Lewis, Jack Richardson and John Wright, all of HQ Squadron.

were wanted from the Forward Delivery Squadron, and the welders were busy again filling in unpleasant looking holes in both C and A Squadron's tanks; Major Holden being especially delighted that *Incredible* was battle-worthy again and Eb Wood, troop leader of 11 Troop, was seen proudly watching the 6-inch hole in his turret gradually decreasing.

The days passed with general routine, broken only by the excitement of an outbreak of fire in the school used by HQ and C Squadrons. It turned out that there was more smoke than fire, but before this was discovered, unfortunately, four ORs of C Squadron were injured jumping from the roof into an improvised sheet held by a rescue party organized by RSM Palmer. The local fire brigade got the fire under control and though one of the lower rooms was gutted, no kit was lost except for the odd articles that disappeared.

News finally came that the stay in Roosendaal, where the 9th were still considered as liberators, was likely to be prolonged and, consequently, organized trips were made into Antwerp where for the first time it was possible for the troops to spend money.

On a more operational note, a series of trade-tests were started following a brigade order to test in an orthodox manner those who had been mustered in the field as tradesmen. Later, D&M Wireless and Gunnery courses were started to improve the technical training of those recently absorbed from the Forward Delivery Squadron, and a range was made in the area of Willemstadt where all gunners were to fire a series of practices to ensure that their efficiency did not decrease.

Cambrai Day (20 November) was celebrated not only on the day itself but also on every day of the previous week; the purported excuse for this extravaganza was that the local hall could hold only one squadron at a time.

During the morning of Cambrai Day the forty-a-side football match occupied everyone's attention. Officers and men were seen grovelling in the mud; at times chasing the ball, at others pursuing personal vendettas, while smoke screens were laid and goals barricaded. A Squadron have to be congratulated as victors and they carried away their barrel of beer chanting some hoodoo that is believed to have been a ritualistic thanksgiving to the mystic goddesses of Wine and Women.

The afternoon passed with entertainment provided by 'Four Smart Girls' and though the show was pleasant enough 'Smart' was an exaggeration and girls an understatement. Nevertheless, the tradition of the day was kept – the meals were abundant and served in Cambrai style and there is no doubt that everyone enjoyed themselves.

To overcome whatever effects those gaieties might have there was a certain amount of sporting activity. The football field was occupied most afternoons, and each troop produced a seven-a-side team, and after a lot of excitement and many struggles C Squadron HQ (F) were hailed the victors. An exhibition rugby match was held in aid of the Red Cross, and hockey matches were arranged against local teams, but no amount of physical exercise could repair the damage caused by C Squadron's notorious 'spigot support' which was given to unsuspecting visitors with the result that they departed in rather too hilarious a mood. Lt. Seymour Francis was the reputed creator and architect of this remarkable homage to Bacchus.

As the month drew to an end, it became clear that the battalion would definitely not be the guests of Roosendaal for Xmas. On 26 November all courses were cancelled and by the 29th the squadrons were lined up in the Wildert area ready for transporters which were to take the battalion to XXX Corps area, established on the left flank of the Ninth US Army.

Personal recollections

Roosendaal, the valley of the roses (where were they?), was the major place in Holland liberated by the 9th, who were supporting the Hallamshire Regiment (49 Div).

Because the campaign had slowed down somewhat, the 9th remained in Roosendaal for a month. Sentimental attachments grew both in general terms – the town to the division and its units – and in personal terms. The general terms are still very strongly continued, especially through people such as Henk Bredevolt who runs a military museum in the town. This museum does much to commemorate the exploits of the Dutch Resistance, 49 Div, and the 9 RTR. In the town itself there is a column surmounted by a polar bear, the divisional emblem of the 49th.

There were undoubtedly many attachments made between the local inhabitants and the British soldiers, some of friendship and some of romance; these were hinted at in the War Diary, and in some of the personal recollections.

Apart from social activities, the most vividly remembered features of the month at Roosendaal were the fire in one of the billets, formal training in tank crew skills (especially gunnery at Willemstadt), a lot of sport (probably to counteract the effects of the demon drink), and Cambrai Day, on which sport and the demon both prevailed.

Some of the inhabitants of Roosendaal had collaborated in various ways with the Germans. Taffy Leyshon: 'I watched two women having their hair shaved off by a barber for being very friendly with Germans'. And Jack Woods:

We stayed in Roosendaal for a month to refit and relax, during which time we took part in football matches, dances, and general social activities, and others got leave in Brussels. We were all billeted with civilian families. Charlie Merry, Sergeant Jakeman's co-driver, and I were with German collaborators. They had their heads shaved and we had no communication with them all the time we were there. There were two of them, mother and daughter. The mother had been a washerwoman for the Germans and the daughter was six months pregnant from a German boyfriend. I wonder whether he returned after the war?

But Taffy Leyshon had happier memories of Roosendaal: 'In Roosendaal we slept in the café by the canal and every night we had a party; four girls, friends of the owner, used to come, and the owner, who had hidden special drinks in a wall, opened a bottle every night.' For every person, surely.

As mentioned in the War Diary, one of the major activities at Roosendaal was to train, re-train and trade-test tank crews who had joined the squadron since the first battles. This training covered all the trades. All training was done at Roosendaal except firing the tank armament, which was done at Willemstadt, an old town on the southern bank of the Maas estuary. John Hodges found it a beautiful old town, but not so Trevor Greenwood:

Friday 24 November 1944, D + 171
Raining again – and misty. On parade at 8.15 with 15 troop and HQ gunners, commanders, loaders ready for journey to Willemstadt. Left the course in Jim Bevan's hands. About 15 miles to Willemstadt. We had hardly left Roosendaal when the appalling amount of water in this area became apparent. Every field is surrounded with ditches; every road has ditches on each side – the whole damn landscape is a maze of ditches; a most depressing place. As we got nearer west, the fields gradually became more waterlogged – until finally they disappeared, and we found ourselves riding along elevated roadways with water all around. This was the result of the bursting of the dykes by the enemy. The countryside had become a shallow inland sea, with waves lapping against the road banking – leaving a tide mark of foam – presumably salt water. Houses stood gaunt and desolate in this mass of water – literally a waste land. Occasionally, we passed through inhabited villages, most of them badly damaged. They appear to have been built alongside the elevated roadway purposely to avoid flooding. There were several civilians about – mostly sorting out wreckage from ruined homes. There must have been fairly heavy fighting in this almost treeless and dead flat country. . . . The high roads must have been blown too – judging by the number of Bailey bridges we passed over.

Eventually reached the range – to the left of Willemstadt. Did our 'shoot' – in the rain – and departed for Roosendaal at noon – arriving in time for lunch.

Just before this shoot the unit, along with all other battalions of the Royal Tank Regiment, celebrated Cambrai Day. This commemorates the first major successful use of tanks in the First World War when an attack was made towards Cambrai on 20 November 1917. There are certain traditions to be observed, as the first newsletter records:

A Squadron: By this time (mid-November) we had begun to think that the 9th had been forgotten so we began to plan for the celebration of Cambrai Day. The do extended over a whole week and a lot of wood-alcohol (commonly called cognac for brevity's sake) was consumed. To add to our good fortune in drawing Cambrai Day itself for our squadron dance we managed to win a barrel of beer by licking all comers in a forty-a-side soccer match.

B Squadron: Cambrai Day was celebrated in traditional style. As a prelude the squadron gave a very successful dance organized by Capt. Roger Long and an able band of helpers on the 18th. Sunday the 19th was spent in recuperating.

B Squadron farewell concert, Mettingen, 16 June 1945. Jim Lewis signs a souvenir programme; at the back is Sgt. Bill Minton, and in the front SQMS George Rathke, Sgt. Taffy Jones, Jim Lewis, Sgt. Ron Maddick, and Sgt. Gordon Dobinson.

Cambrai Day itself opened with cups of tea in bed, brought round by the officers; this was much to the consternation of Sgt. Jock Riddell who had just joined the squadron. Then followed a forty-a-side football match against A Squadron, which was a simple straightforward mud-bath.

After this the squadron enjoyed a dinner of roast beef and roast pork beautifully cooked by Sgt. Busty Nuttall and his staff, followed by plums, ice cream, grapes, cigars and plenty of weak beer. The dinner was held in a warm café with plates, glasses and cutlery all arranged by SQMS Jim Lewis. Major Michael Reynell made a speech of sorts ably assisted by Troopers Adrian Dibben, Hoppy Hopkins and Norman Hughes.

C Squadron: The morning of Cambrai Day was spent in a forty-a-side all-in rugby which thoroughly convinced the Dutch populace of our mental instability. A very excellent meal was laid on which could certainly hold its own with Cambrai dinners of other years. ENSA and band concerts filled in the afternoon and evening.

One or two people have recorded their personal memories of this day:

Jock Cordiner: 'How could an ordinary bod like me describe Cambrai Day? Magic! I loved being served by officers. It did my inferiority complex a lot of good.' Ginger Gadd remembers the football match: 'It was decided that we should have a forty-a-side football match, the prize for the winners a barrel of beer. The pitch was well underwater – but then it was Holland. To cut a long battle short, A Squadron carried off the "Cup" or I should say "Barrel".' It appears from the accounts of the Cambrai Day game that no one was sure whether they were playing soccer, rugby, or some other type of football – or just having a good fight. But in spite of the weather and all other circumstances such as training, women, and drink, there was a lot of sport played.

Peter Beale had been wounded in Normandy and after a few months in hospital in England he rejoined the 9th at Roosendaal on 25 November.

Eventually I caught up with the 9th at Roosendaal, and found quite a few changes. Mike Reynell was still OC and Roger Long 2 i/c. Johnnie Brecknell was now RO, Peter Bracewell 6 Troop, Johnnie Stone 7 Troop, the only surviving troop leader from when we landed, Freddie Critchley 8 Troop, David Scott 9 and Mike gave me 10. Not knowing the battle situation, I had expected that the squadron would either be in action or preparing for it. Instead the greeting was: good to see you back, you're just in time to play hockey against the locals!

DECEMBER NOMADS: GEILENKIRCHEN

As described at the beginning of this chapter, there was some indecision – or as Monty would say, lack of grip – in the higher command of the allied forces at this time. The result for many units was to intensify the well-known military complaint of 'order, counter-order, disorder'. By this time, however, the great majority of Canadian, American, and British units had become very capable and philosophical about dealing with changes in plan. The War Diary for this period gives chapter and verse for the changes and the capability to deal with them. To establish continuity the last paragraph of the War Diary quoted in the previous section is here included.

The War Diary, 29 November–16 December 1944

As the month of November drew to a close it became clear that the battalion would not be the guests of Roosendaal for Christmas. On 26 November all training courses were cancelled. By the 29th the squadrons were lined up in the Wildert area ready for the transporters which were to take the battalion to XXX Corps area, established on the left flank of the Ninth US Army in the vicinity of Geilenkirchen.

The 9th moved slowly through Belgium and Holland and reached the Dutch mining town of Brunssum on 3 December. After a few days there the battalion moved forward into Germany, passing through the town of Geilenkirchen to take up positions in the villages of Hockheide, Bauchem, Rischden, Niedenheide and Gillrath in support of 43 Div.

On 10 December the CO attended an O group at 214 Brigade at which 43rd Division Operation 'Shears' was outlined, whereby the enemy divisions disposed west of the River Roer between Roermond and Geilenkirchen were to be destroyed. 34 Tank Brigade with 43rd Division were to do the break-out and 52nd Division with 8 Armoured Brigade and Guards Armoured Division the mopping-up. 9 RTR tanks in support 214 Brigade were to complete the first phase of the break-out.

Following heavy and continual rain the ground provided poor tank going and frequent reports showed no improvement. Nevertheless, thousands of air photos and maps were issued and every plan was complete when the news came that the operation was cancelled.

The battalion remained in its position with its role unchanged.

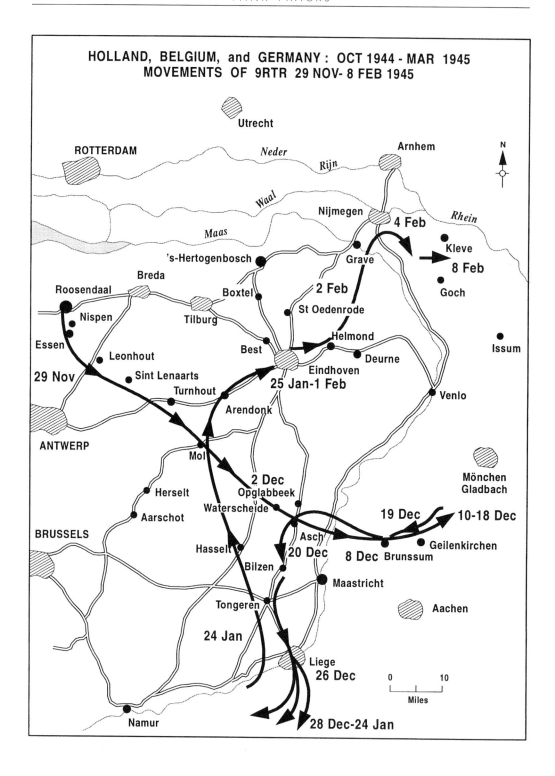

HOLLAND, BELGIUM, and GERMANY : OCT 1944 - MAR 1945
MOVEMENTS OF 9RTR 29 NOV- 8 FEB 1945

Utrecht

ROTTERDAM

Arnhem

N

Neder

Rijn

Waal

Nijmegen

4 Feb

Rhein

Kleve

8 Feb

Maas

's-Hertogenbosch

Grave

Breda

Boxtel

2 Feb

Goch

Roosendaal

St Oedenrode

Nispen

Tilburg

Helmond

Issum

Essen

Leonhout

Best

Deurne

29 Nov

Sint Lenaarts

Eindhoven

Turnhout

25 Jan-1 Feb

Venlo

Arendonk

ANTWERP

Mol

2 Dec

Mönchen
Gladbach

Herselt

Opglabbeek

Aarschot

Waterscheide

19 Dec

10-18 Dec

BRUSSELS

Asch

Geilenkirchen

Hasselt

20 Dec

8 Dec Brunssum

Bilzen

Maastricht

Tongeren

Aachen

24 Jan

Liege

26 Dec

0   10

Miles

Namur

28 Dec-24 Jan

GEILENKIRCHEN AREA

Tripsrath

Hatterath

Wurm

Wurm

Hochheid

Bruggerhof

GILLRATH
Niederheide

Rischden

Bauchem

Prummern

GEILENKIRCHEN

TEVEREN

Immendorf

Frelenberg

0   1
Miles

On 16 December news was received of the German counter-offensive against the American First Army front, attacking with the 5th and 6th Panzer Armies.

Personal recollections

Most people remembered one thing about Geilenkirchen – mud. The second most common memory was of ominous, almost Teutonic, eerieness. Was it perhaps because it was the first time we had set foot on German soil and the spirits, if not the Wehrmacht, were there to harry us? Associated with Geilenkirchen in our memories will always be Brunssum, a Dutch coal-mining town which boasted at least three main attractions; comfortable billets, pit-head baths, and a photographer's studio. Jack Woods:

We left Roosendaal en route to Geilenkirchen via Brunssum. I mention Brunssum because there for some reason most of B Squadron had their photographs taken at the local studio and

Jack Woods, 9 Troop, B Squadron, at Brunssum, Holland, December 1944. Jack is wearing one of the tank suits (zoot suits) specially designed to keep crews warm in the winter.

Cyril Handley of 13 Troop (I trained with him) eventually married a girl from there; one day I'll find out what we did there. In Geilenkirchen we were line holding; we crept into our positions in first gear in order not to alert the enemy of our coming. *Inspire* IV was parked under a brick arch adjoining a house in whose cellar we installed ourselves. The cellar came up into the doorway of the house; there was no longer a front door, just a gap, and it was there we mounted guard at night. The form was that a piece of string was attached to David Scott's wrist and led up to the guard post. If something happened and David was required, whoever was on guard could pull the string and David would come up. My turn on guard, my personal weapon was a green Sten gun with a shaped butt which I acquired during the Le Havre battle and I didn't even know whether it worked. When I heard a patrol coming up the road, I didn't know whether to pull the string, fire the gun, or keep my head down. I chose the latter; fortunately it was a British patrol so I breathed again. When we left the area we were well and truly stonked, the Guards who replaced us made more noise than Larry coming in.

Jock Cordiner:

The Brunssum/Geilenkirchen area I certainly did not like. We were parked much too close to the enemy in mud, mud, mud, and existence, when not on lookout in the cold, damp, dark cellar of a ruined house, was awful. The pile of mouldy potatoes in the cellar came in handy, but with restrictions on sound and choked by cooking smoke in our underground cell the days and nights were never-ending. I never heard a satisfactory explanation for the muffled footsteps heard one night outside our tiny ground-level window as we crouched silently waiting for the grenade which never came. It was an eerie, creepy place.

Ginger Gadd remembers a very similar incident. Ginger was then wireless-op to Lt. Gerry Wells, commanding 5 Troop of A Squadron.

We had reached a little place in Germany called Geilenkirchen. It was late evening, and my commander was Lt. Wells, known to us as 'Gaffer'. We were posted one crew on guard at a time, with one man on each tank and two men at the door of the house. The Gaffer patrolled round the house, and I was at the door. We weren't to make any noise, for we could hear the Jerry patrols going through. Suddenly I heard a step behind me. I thought my last moment had come, waiting any moment for a bayonet in the back – I was absolutely transfixed.

When the Gaffer came to the house again I just made signs behind me. The top of the house was blown off at the back, and a brick had been dislodged. Until the Gaffer spoke I didn't get my voice back; believe you me, when you are in that frame of mind you just pray and hope.

Some people, however, viewed Geilenkirchen and the surrounding villages of Niederheide, Hochheid, Bauchem, Rischden and Gillrath in a much more positive way. The B Squadron newsletter:

Our stay in Brunssum was uneventful but comfortable and hot baths at the pit-head were a great attraction. Some astonishment was caused by two notices on the one house. The first read: 'Allied soldiers avoid this house; German sympathizers'; and the second 'Officer Commanding B Squadron'. It was a very comfortable house.

After a week in Brunssum we moved into the line north of Geilenkirchen where we lived in the cellars of ruined houses entirely surrounded by a sea of mud. We ate German cow and German vegetables and reaped the benefit of German agriculture.

Tpr Jimmy Roberts proved himself to be a first-class butcher and he and Sgt. Brierley ran a well-stocked butcher's shop which kept us all well supplied with steaks and roasts.

7 Troop, commanded by Lt. John Stone, were also positive about the area: 'In due course 7 Troop arrived at Niederheide where a good time was had by all and everyone declared "It's the best bit of line we've struck." The housewives soon got cracking and roast joints and baked apples with honey were the order of the day. The honey was provided courtesy of the bee-keeping skills of L/Cpl. Boyce Dunsford and Tpr Eric Bunce.'

From all the previous accounts it looks as though an abundance of local produce was turned into delicious meals by the tankmen's culinary skills. Not all tankmen were good cooks, however. Peter Bracewell, commanding 6 Troop, promised his crew that he would cook an apple pie for them according to his mother's recipe. The apple was very tasty, but the crust was cooked simply of flour and water. The result was a revolutionary armour-plate, and determined attempts to cut or bludgeon it into edible pieces resulted only in shattering the plates on which it lay – without having any noticeable effect on the pastry at all.

The 9th had been in the Geilenkirchen area for some eight days, and planning for Operation 'Shears' was going ahead, when on 16 December Hitler launched his Ardennes offensive. We will consider the effect of the Ardennes campaign on the 9th very shortly, but first we must turn the spotlight on Capt. Neville Lord, of whom HQ Squadron newsletter reports: 'On

Officers of B Squadron at Brunssum, Holland, December 1944, about half-way through the campaign. Top: Lt. Peter Bracewell (6 Troop); Centre: Lts. Gerry McMahon (reserve), Fred Critchley (8 Troop), John Stone (7 Troop), David Scott (9 Troop). Front: Capt. John Brecknell (Reconnaissance Officer), Major Michael Reynell (squadron leader), Capt. Roger Long (2 i/c), Lt. Peter Beale (10 Troop). Michael Reynell was killed in the Reichswald on 12 February 1945.

16 December Capt. Lord, in a state of nervous collapse, was led off to Brussels and there married Miss Mary Anderson Bellaby. Profiting by our pre-occupation with this notable event, Hitler treacherously launched his counter-offensive.'

Neville was a delightful charming character – although perhaps slightly accident-prone, as a broken nose and broken wrist in six months of campaigning would testify. Comments in the various newsletters show something of the affection in which he was held.

A Squadron: At this time we had Neville Lord with us. His motives in rescuing a young collaboratress from the hands of the Orange Brigade are beyond question. Neville bears a selfless devotion to the British way of life, and any references to the young lady's undoubted physical charms are to be discouraged. From this time on we heard a number of Dutchmen refer to us as the Royal Amour Corps. (Note: this was <u>before</u> Neville's marriage.)

C Squadron: Capt. Neville Lord took the opportunity of a lull to ride off in a jeep and get married in Brussels. We offer to him as an old member of the squadron our heartiest congratulations, and to his wife our deepest sympathy!

Hitler's attack, initially camouflaged by Neville's wedding, certainly took the allied high command by surprise. For a few days there was some very confused sorting-out, as well as some very gallant fighting by the American soldiers on whom the blow had fallen. But at least two senior commanders, after thinking about it carefully, realized there could be great benefits for the Allies. Lt.-Gen. Brian Horrocks:

> Then, as I studied the map, I realized that it was really an act of madness, probably inspired by Hitler. The Germans were doing us a favour by saving us the trouble of a winter offensive across flooded rivers like the Roer, on the other side of which we would be vulnerable to counter-attacks by panzer divisions. Instead it was they who would now be vulnerable, and I concluded that the further they came the fewer would get back, and that we had a good chance of eliminating much of their remaining armoured forces.

And Gen. George Patton, commanding Third US Army, is reported to have said: 'Fine! We should open up and let them get all the way to Paris. Then we'll saw 'em off at the base!'

To the Ardennes and Back, 17 December 1944 –25 January 1945

On realizing the seriousness of the German thrust the allied high command took several steps: it divided the front into two commands, the northern under Monty and the southern under Bradley; it halted Patton's eastward advance and turned it north to make a firm southern shoulder to hold the German advance; and it committed some of the theatre reserves to the battle.

On the northern flank of the German salient Monty moved immediately to defend Brussels and to establish a strong Recce line along the River Meuse from Charleroi in the west to Vise in the east. The formation charged with this task was XXX Corps, which comprised 43rd, 51st, 53rd Infantry Divisions and the Guards Armoured Division, supported by 29 and 34 Armoured Brigades. This defensive position was established on 20 December. By 23 December it was clear that due to determined fighting by the Americans, the clearing of the weather which at last allowed allied air forces to strike, and supply difficulties for Germans, the push had been contained. It was now possible for the counter-attack formations to move south of the River Meuse and thus allow the American formations on the north and south of the salient, and the XXX British Corps at the western end, to push the Germans back harder.

The process continued steadily until by 16 January 1945 the First and Third US Armies made contact at Houffalize. By this time it was possible for XXX Corps to disengage and return to the north to plan for the next operation, code-named 'Veritable'.

For the 9th these large-scale movements had the following consequences:

1. after withdrawal from the Geilenkirchen area it became part of the defensive screen of Brussels and the River Meuse;
2. when that danger had subsided, the battalion moved south of Liege to act in a counter-attack role;
3. as the German forces slowed down and finally retreated the battalion remained in that counter-attack position;
4. when XXX Corps moved north to prepare for Operation 'Veritable', the 9th did the same.

It should also be said that in the first few days there was some uncertainty as to where we would go next. Since this period included Christmas Day, the odds seemed against tradition being observed. But ingenuity and organization triumphed against adversity, and everybody had an excellent Christmas dinner – some people more than one.

The War Diary, 16 December 1944–25 January 1945

On 16 December news was received of the German counter-offensive against First US Army front, attacking with the 5th and 6th Panzer Armies.

Owing to the dropping of parachutists the guards were far more alert and even those supplied by A Echelon were known to be aggressive. Enemy air activity increased both during the day and night and shelling became more frequent. Finally, orders were received that 34 Tank Brigade with 43rd Division were to be withdrawn and go to the area of Tilburg to undergo special training for future operations. On 19 December the battalion's role was handed over to No. 2 Squadron Grenadier Guards and the tanks set off on a road march to Waterscheide where they were to be picked up by transporters. BHQ moved back to Brunssum, complete with new furniture, to join the wheels column which was to leave at 0630 hours the following morning.

The road march was made in thick fog and a number of wheels of the leading regiments were passed ditched by the side of the road.

After a few miles, the column was stopped and informed that the brigade would now concentrate in the area Asch and there await further orders. It was appreciated that the German counter-offensive might develop unpleasantly. XXX Corps moved south and established itself on the west of the River Meuse in mobile reserve. The task given to 34 Tank Brigade and 43rd

B Squadron, 8 Troop: troop leader's crew taken in Holland, February 1945. 'Jeep' Greet (co-driver), Bert Sutcliffe (driver), Lt. Freddie Critchley MC (troop leader), Reg Terrington (wireless operator); the gunner, Cpl. Norman Fraser, was elsewhere when this photograph was taken.

Division was to destroy any bridgeheads made by the enemy between Huy and Liege. The battalion was to support 214 Brigade in these possible operations.

By the night of 20 December the battalion had established itself in Bilsen and it was there, a day later, that confirmation was received that the award of the MC had been granted to Lt. Tom Fawcett and Lt. Freddie Critchley for personal bravery and devotion to duty during operations around Boeink and Nispen. 13 Troop were proud to claim MMs awarded to Sgt. Tomney and Tpr Rees, and C Sqn HQ Troop the MM awarded to Tpr Lowe during the same series of operations.

On 23 December, the German offensive looked less dangerous and the battalion was placed at three hours' notice – there were also rumours that Xmas would be celebrated and these were proved true the following day. In consequence the battalion decided to move to more comfortable billets but owing to unforeseen difficulties and a number of false starts, the move was not completed until mid-day of Xmas Day. Nevertheless, there was time to lay on the traditional meal by the evening.

On Boxing Day the battalion was detached from 34 Tank Brigade and came under command 51st (H) Division in reserve to the First US Army and, after another difficult road march in thick fog, concentrated in Ougree, south of Liege. It was here that the battalion had its first experience of flying bombs. They were heard chugging in the skies at frequent intervals and though some fell unpleasantly close, destroying billets, there were no casualties.

Here the Division Commander visited the battalion and suggested an alternative concentration area be found.

On 28 December the battalion moved again and established in the small village of Villers-aux-Tours and there saw out the last day of 1944 surrounded by ice-frozen roads and snow-

C Squadron tanks at Limont in the Ardennes just south of Liege, January 1945.

white fields. The inhabitants were glad to see British troops again and were generous in their welcome, while the battalion waited to strike against any enemy penetrations that might be made from the east or south.

After a few days it became clear that the German counter-offensive had lost the initiative. On 7 January 1945 the 9th came under command 53 Div and remained in a counter-attack role. On 19 January 53 Div moved and the 9th reverted to the control of 34 Armoured Brigade. On 24 January the 9th moved with considerable difficulty along the snow and ice-bound roads to Liege, and thence by transporter to Eindhoven where concentration was complete by 25 January.

Personal recollections

The first few days after moving back from Geilenkirchen are remembered mainly for the stop-start confusion and the hope that Christmas could be celebrated in traditional style. Liege and flying bombs were synonymous, and the three small villages of Villers-aux-Tours, Limont, and Hestreux Tavier were remembered for snow, comfortable billets, and some quiet drinking. Trevor Greenwood had some excitement before Christmas:

Sunday 24 December 1944, D + 201
A little excitement this evening. A young lady burst into the men's billet in a semi-exhausted state: she gasped 'Germans' – and waved her arms wildly. She only spoke 'Flams', but we learned that three Jerries had broken into her next-door neighbour's house and demanded food. The neighbour had somehow signalled to her through the wall – and she immediately mounted her bike and rode the half mile to our billet. There were only about half a dozen of us in the place – the rest of the lads being out celebrating Xmas Eve. We grabbed our arms and followed the girl. The night was bitterly cold, with bright moonlight, and already the ground was white with frost.

After quarter of an hour's walking, we found ourselves in a lonely country area – with a few scattered cottages straggling along the narrow country lane. One of them, 150 yards ahead, had lighted windows, and this was pointed out as our objective.

We went forward quietly, with weapons cocked, not knowing what was in store for us – whether fanatical Nazis dropped by parachute in the present offensive, or the more docile Jerry, willing to surrender on sight. When quite close to the house, I noticed a dark object moving in the shadow of a barn adjoining the house. I decided to investigate, fearing an ambush. But the 'object' soon moved forward into the moonlight, and I beheld a woman. I had withheld my fire, fortunately. Almost simultaneously, I heard a thump and the house door flew open, revealing Ginger Young and two others standing in the beam of light from the house. They started a hell of a hullabaloo, inviting the 'bastards' to give themselves up. There was a rush inside by four of us, and I noticed three terrified looking Jerries raising their hands as they rose from the table at which they were having supper! No doubt we looked pretty desperate, and all had arms. We quickly searched the prisoners, removing all papers etc. They had no arms. They were unshaven and looked very dirty. Their clothing too was in rags and totally inadequate for the cold weather. None of them wore an overcoat.

I have dim recollection of two other people in the room – probably the husband and wife – but was too busy searching the prisoners, and on the qui vive for treachery to pay any attention to them. We soon had the prisoners outside, and marched them back to our billet. We detained them while transport and an escort was organized, and then despatched them to the POW camp at Hasselt. I was glad to see them go. Had they been in the billet when any of our semi-drunk lads returned, there may have been trouble.

The second battalion newsletter records what happened to the squadrons in the period around Christmas.

HQ Squadron: We got rid of the CO on leave and set off in high spirits and a thick fog to go from Geilenkirchen to Belgium. In spite of the thick mist the rear of the column, ably led by SSM Ossie Joyce, only succeeded in getting ten lorries past Capt. George Eaton at the head of the column. Poor show, chaps, poor show!

   Elaborate preparations had been made for Christmas Day but Hitler's little effort came close to upsetting the whole show, and even brought the CO back. A series of depressing night marches followed: We marched on Christmas morning, we marched on Boxing Day. But from mid-day on Christmas Day we were static. Everybody got cracking with tables and forms in the village hall and the locals helped us out with the cooking – so the dinner was a great success. Even the cigars, brown paper wrapped, soldiers' Christmas free issue, were enjoyed.

A Squadron: On a dark and filthy night we moved off and crossed the border into Belgium. What now? Christmas was right on our heels and we were at an hour's notice to move. Dreams of Holland misted and the voice of rumour rose – and nothing he had to say was pleasant. And so we sat for a day or two in a very large and hellishly cold furniture warehouse. Here we found beds for all which would have been a good thing if we had been allowed to use them. Luckily we were undisturbed on Christmas Eve, and although we moved again on Christmas Day we had time to get in some pretty solid eating and drinking.

B Squadron: Christmas Eve was spent in putting all the cognac in the town out of bottles into much better receptacles. George Bone and Willie Kembery used half-pint tumblers as intermediaries; Sammy Linton was not so pansy. On Christmas Day we found ourselves on the move again, but fortunately we had to move only 3 miles. There we settled down to a first-class Christmas dinner, which Busty Nuttall and his crew produced miraculously in record time.

Freddie Critchley, commanding 8 Troop of B Squadron, remembers the tribulations of the B Squadron officers on that memorable Christmas Day.

First we had to move. As soon as we had harboured, the cooks got cracking on the Christmas dinner. In traditional style the sergeants and the officers served the dinner to the rest of the squadron, encouraged by such remarks as: 'Come on waiter, we haven't got all day' and 'If you can't give better service than this, you certainly won't get a tip from me.' Sergeants and officers then sampled the meal to see that it was alright: Christmas dinner number one. This was of course washed down with copious draughts of lubrication.

   Then Tommo (SSM Tomlinson) invited all the officers to partake of Christmas dinner number two at the sergeants' mess, again washed down with copious draughts.

   And finally we returned to our own mess and found Christmas dinner number three waiting for us. Encouraged by further draughts of stronger fluid, we had no trouble at all in putting this away as well.

   Some years after the war I recounted this story to a Dutch friend who had been in Holland north of the Rhine at that time, and very short of food. Why couldn't you have shared all of those dinners with us he said, quite horrified. Bit difficult to get over to you, I told him.

A tank of A Squadron at Hestreux Tavier in the Ardennes just south of Liege, January 1945.

C Squadron: At Bilsen we had a carol service on Christmas Eve, but our actual Christmas dinner had to be held in a village outside wedged in between two moves. Corporal Blackman and the cooks worked wonders and a convent school provided two classrooms as dining halls. The nuns hurried about lighting fires and moving up desks and chairs for us to sit at. Tank sheets were used for black-outs and the village people lent us plates so that by nine at night we were all happy and well fed. Peter Boden returned clean and well from hospital and 14 Troop had got as far as wandering around singing carols when their ardour was considerably dampened by the news of another move to be made before daylight on Boxing Day.

The move on Boxing Day of 1944 took the battalion from the area of Bilsen to the south, and ended in the suburbs of Liege on the southern side of the River Meuse. Peter Beale remembers it vividly:

We received orders during Christmas Day that we were to move south at 0700 hrs on Boxing Day. Due to the alcoholic and gastronomic rigours of the day I omitted to find out exactly where all my troop were billeted. The officers were woken the next morning – with some difficulty – and proceeded to look for the crews. Every other troop except 10 was ready to move by 0730. Mike Reynell, our squadron leader, wasn't very impressed. 'You should have known where they were, Peter; anyway, follow us as soon as you can.'

It took nearly two hours to round up everyone, and I remember my co-driver, Ray Webb, looked absolutely green when he got into the tank. It was a beautiful day as we crossed the plain leading toward Liege and the River Meuse, but the sun didn't do much to keep out the perishing cold. Our new tank suits (goon skins, zoot suits etc., a garment with approximately 100 ft of zipper) were at least partially effective, however, and we arrived at the outskirts of Liege in good spirits – the resilience of youth!

The valley of the Meuse is quite deep at Liege, and in those sort of weather conditions can produce a real pea-soup fog. And this it had certainly done on Boxing Day 1944. But we found that the Military Police had prepared excellent signs, and we were able to follow the tortuous route down through the northern suburbs, across the river and the railway to our rendezvous point with very little trouble. When we got to the RV Johnnie Breck (Capt. John Brecknell, B Squadron Recce Officer) was there to meet us. 'Good to see you, Peter, the rest of the squadron behind you?' 'Good God no,' I said, 'they left two hours before us.' 'Well,' said John, 'I'll show you your billets and you can settle in.'

Which we did, and about twenty minutes later the rest of the squadron arrived – to be greeted with some derision by 10 Troop. 'What kept you so long?'

The problem, of course, was the fog, and the fact that the MPs hadn't done any signing when the first tanks of the squadron arrived. So they had the miserable business of trying to find their way through the tortuous streets of a fog-bound unknown town without suitable maps or any other guides. Not bad to have made it at all!

The things we noticed about Liege at once were: the friendliness of the inhabitants, the comfort of our billets, and the flying bombs – the pilotless planes loaded with explosive, technically

Indomitable *(13 Troop Leader Peter Boden's tank) in the Ardennes, January 1945. The crew members are Geoff Bound (gunner), Bob Tyler (wireless-op) and Arthur 'Zeik' Vardy (co-driver).*

called V1s, alternatively called robots, bombes-volants, doodle-bugs, buzz-bombs, or flying farts. We had not experienced them before at close hand, with their rather nasty habits. Their engines were timed to switch off when they were over the target area – which had to be large. Then they would glide to the earth and explode on impact. If you heard an explosion you were all right; if you heard the swishing of wind through their wings as they glided down, you were almost certainly all right, although the explosion might be quite close. But if you heard the engine shut off – watch out! It might go anywhere. Jock Cordiner, along with everybody else, didn't like the flying bombs:

> Liege (Seraing) was the place of V1s. I arrived at our billet a little later than my mates – can't remember why. I joined them and the Belgian family around the large kitchen table in a game of cards. A screaming noise sent me diving under the table fearing the explosion that never came. I was alone, looking at legs and hearing general laughter. Someone eventually was good enough to tell me that the loud explosion which I had just ignored was the screaming thing which seconds later had set me diving. That took a long time to live down.

There was no particular need to stay in Liege itself, because the role allocated to the 9th could just as well be carried out a few miles further south, nearer the front line. On 28 December the battalion moved to villages south of Liege: A Squadron to Hestreux Tavier, C Squadron to Limont, and HQ and B Squadrons to Villers-aux-Tours.

Jack Woods remembers the food and drink at the billet he shared with Charlie Merry, as well as one of the more curious begging positions:

> Rumour had it that it was Mol in Belgium for Xmas and civvy billets, in the end it was the Ardennes and Xmas on the way; we skated into a village south of Liege and settled down in reserve supporting 51st Highland Division. I was billeted with an old lady and her son and daughter-in-law, once again I was with Charlie Merry. The son and daughter-in-law were newlyweds and we had to go through their bedroom to reach ours. I still smile occasionally when I recall the son in the midst of his honeymoon activities with one hand out of bed begging for a cigarette. His mother made the largest and fluffiest omelettes I have ever eaten, even now, but the obligatory 'Tasse de malt' [hot malted milk drink] which went with them, Ugh!

CHAPTER 10

Fighting in the Forests

The broad picture

Before Hitler pushed into the Ardennes there had been some indecision at Allied HQ as to the best strategy to adopt to defeat Germany. However, it was clear even at the end of November 1944 that the Allies would have to close up to the Rhine prior to crossing it and advancing on the Ruhr. This operation had been code-named 'Veritable', and was re-activated as soon as it was clear that the Battle of the Ardennes was over. This time it formed part of a broader strategy, which was spelled out in the plan prepared by Eisenhower on 30 January 1945. He stated:

My plan is:

1. To carry out a series of operations north of the Moselle with a view to destroying the enemy and closing to the Rhine north of Düsseldorf.
2. To direct our efforts to eliminating other enemy forces west of the Rhine which still constitute an obstacle or potential threat to our subsequent Rhine crossing operations.
3. To seize bridgeheads over the Rhine in the north and the south.
4. To deploy east of the Rhine and north of the Ruhr the maximum number of divisions that can be maintained (estimated at thirty-five). The initial task of this force will be to deny to the enemy the industries of the Ruhr.
5. To deploy east of the Rhine, on the axis Frankfurt–Kassel, such forces as may be available after providing thirty-five divisions for the north and essential security elsewhere. The task of this force will be to draw enemy forces away from the north by capturing Frankfurt and advancing on Kassel.

The task outlined in paragraph (1) was to be carried out by 21st Army Group, using appropriate formations of the First Canadian, Second British, and Ninth US Armies. The plan for this task was for a two-pronged attack: the northern prong would consist of XXX Corps under command First Canadian Army, and the southern prong would consist of formations of Ninth US Army, attacking across the River Roer slightly later than the XXX Corps attack. The Second British Army was to hold the line of the River Maas from Cuyk to Roermond.

In the initial stages of its attack XXX Corps comprised the following formations:

Guards Armoured Division
15, 43, 51, 53, 2 Canadian and 3 Canadian Infantry Divisions
6 Guards, 8, and 34 Armoured Brigades
3, 4, 5, 9 and 2 Canadian AGRAs (Army Groups Royal Artillery)
Support formations including: two searchlight batteries, eleven regiments of 79th Armoured Division (specialized armour), two Assault Regiments Royal Engineers. The total strength of the Corps was just over 200,000 all ranks.

The XXX Corps plan of attack was to have five divisions up and two in reserve. The line-up of the assault divisions, and their initial objectives, were:

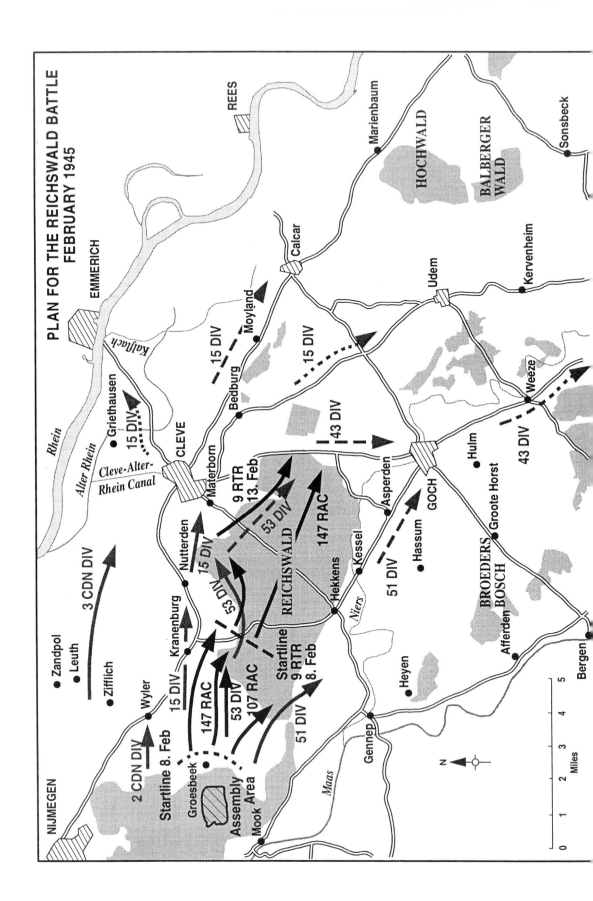

PLAN FOR THE REICHSWALD BATTLE
FEBRUARY 1945

North

3rd Can : Capture Zifflich and Leuth and drive east to
Cleve–Alter Rhein canal

2nd Can : Capture Wyler

15th Scottish : Capture Kranenburg and the high ground
overlooking Cleve

Direction of advance

53rd Welsh : Seize high ground at NW corner of Reichswald
and then move east through the northern half of
the forest

51st Highland : Capture SW corner of Reichswald and prevent
any enemy movement from the south

South

Various plans were made for exploitation after the capture of the initial objectives, both for the assault and for the follow-up formations. The execution of these plans would be dependent on enemy reaction, weather, and casualties to the allied units. The units of 34 Armoured Brigade were allocated as follows: 9 RTR and 147 RAC to 53rd Division; 107 RAC to 51st Highland Division.

THE REICHSWALD: TRAINING WITH 53RD DIVISION

The 9th fought with 53rd Division throughout the Reichswald Battle, and trained with it beforehand. This section describes some of the training and other preparations that were made, but before starting it is helpful to know the order of battle of 53rd Division and its tank support. The General Officer commanding the division was Major-General Ross and it consisted of three brigades. The list below shows those brigades, their constituent units, and the initial attachment of tank units.

		Supporting Tanks
71 Infantry Brigade		147 RAC
4 Bn Royal Welch Fusiliers	4 RWF	
1 Bn Ox and Bucks Light Infantry	1 OBLI	
1 Bn Highland Light Infantry	1 HLI	
158 (Royal Welch) Infantry Brigade		
7 Bn The Royal Welch Fusiliers	7 RWF	
1 Bn The East Lancashire Regiment	1 E LAN R	
1/5 Bn The Welch Regiment	1/5 WELCH	

		9 RTR
160 (South Wales) Infantry Brigade		
6 Bn The Royal Welch Fusiliers	6 RWF	C Sqn
4 Bn The Welch Regiment	4 WELCH	A Sqn
2 Bn The Monmouthshire Regiment	2 MONS	B Sqn

Machine-Gun Battalion
  1 Bn the Manchester Regiment   1 MANCH

General Ross decided that to fulfil the corps plan, which was to traverse the whole length of the northern edge of the Reichswald in the first 24 hours, he had to have close tank support for the infantry inside the forest both day and night.

In the Ardennes 53rd Division had formed a high regard for the capacity of tanks to demoralize the enemy by crashing through trees at night. It was realized that little or no observed fire would be possible, but it was felt that the tanks would be amply justified merely by their presence and speculative fire.

The 9th, whose task lay solely in the forest, did intensive training with 160 Infantry Brigade in the area of Helmond. This training was to check the ability of the Churchill tank to knock over various sorts of trees, and to develop skills in maintaining contact with the infantry when advancing through forests both day and night. As a result of this training Lt.-Col. Berry Veale was full of confidence in his ability to remain with the infantry throughout the advance.

Maintenance of direction by night was the problem that caused Lt.-Col. Veale most deliberation. Eventually the CRA (Commander, Royal Artillery) agreed to shine two vertical pilot lights. These were to be set approximately 3,000 yards apart, and to make it easier to recognize them one was to flash the letter O and the other the letter H throughout the night. It was hoped that tank commanders would be able to check their position by taking readings on the lights with hand compasses. It was ensured that spotlights were fitted to tanks for these night operations.

Expected opposition: enemy formations and defensive works

In early February 1945 the enemy strength and dispositions were estimated to be as follows:

1. *Order of Battle*
    The sector between the Rhine and the Maas is known to be under the control of 84th Division, with under command Battle Group Katzmann and III Battalion 2 Para Regiment, and is divided into eight battalion localities. The only immediate tactical reserves available to 84th Division are two or three battalions. The enemy is unlikely to leave that vital sector so weakly defended and the presence of a reserve infantry division in the Cleve – Goch area must be accepted.

    In spite of the allied move eastwards, the enemy, by virtue of his withdrawal to the Siegfried Line in the Ardennes and his abandoning of the offensive and subsequent withdrawals in Alsace, has some fifteen divisions out of contact on the allied front, in the proportion of two panzer type to one infantry. Some of these could be made available to reinforce his troops in the 'Reichswald Plug'.

2. *Defences*
    The enemy has constructed three main lines of defence on the Reichswald front – a forward line, the Siegfried Line and the Hochwald 'lay-back' Line.

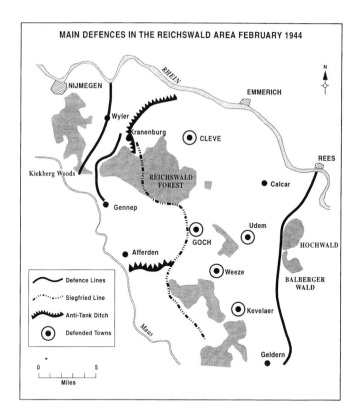

MAIN DEFENCES IN THE REICHSWALD AREA FEBRUARY 1944

The present enemy positions are in the nature of strong outposts to the main Siegfried defences and are being manned in strength. These outposts are organized in two lines. In the first, depth from outposts to rear companies is about 2,000 yards and an average battalion front is 1,500 yards. Behind this is a second line running north from the River Maas along the western edge of the Reichswald and then to Kranenburg.

Further west is an elaborate trench system and an anti-tank ditch forming an advance position in front of the Nutterden area which is the Siegfried Line. This trench system continues through the forest to Hekkens and then in a south east direction.

The Hochwald 'lay-back' Line is a recently constructed defence line which runs from Rees south past the Hochwald Forest towards Geldern.

Concrete defences appear on the Nutterden feature. West of this none are visible except for some possible concrete shelters around anti-aircraft sites.

53rd Division plans, operational and administrative

The plan for the initial assault by 53rd Division was for 71 Infantry Brigade, supported by 147 RAC, to reach the north-western corner of the Reichswald and in particular to capture the Branden Berg feature.

160 Infantry Brigade, supported by 9 RTR, would then pass through 71 Brigade and advance to capture the Stoppelberg feature (height 300 ft). 158 Infantry Brigade were also to pass through 71 Brigade's position and mop up within divisional boundaries.

From there on the division and its supporting armour were to advance in a south-easterly direction parallel with the edge of the forest; 160 Brigade and 9 RTR were on the left, closest to the edge of the forest, and 71 Brigade and 147 RAC on the right; at various stages 71 Brigade was replaced by 158 Brigade.

Provision of supplies

The divisional front, at the start line little more than 1,000 yards wide, contained only one road running parallel to the attack. Even this road was only 14 feet wide with very little metalling and, as the whole impetus of the advance was to depend on it, all rearward movement was forbidden. Refilling had therefore to be done forward, but it was felt that wheeled columns could not be relied on to reach the tanks. To overcome those maintenance problems brigade applied for twenty gutted carriers and ten sledges. The carriers were not forthcoming in time but ten sledges were obtained on D–1. Those were loaded with petrol and ammunition and to avoid embarrassment to 147 RAC during the first phase of the attack, 9 RTR tanks was detailed to tow all sledges forward. A percentage were to be jettisoned in the Plak area west of the forest for 147 RAC. Stuart tanks were to be filled with petrol, each tank capable of carrying approximately 160 gallons. 147 RAC also had two turretless Churchills which Lt.-Col. Blain stocked with ammunition.

The War Diary

This account of the Reichswald battle is taken from 34 Armoured Brigade sources, rather than the 9 RTR War Diary. This makes it possible to see the interaction between 147 RAC and 9 RTR on D-Day and D + 1. From there on the account follows 9 RTR only, although some general comments about the battle are included on many days.

Final Preparations

A general thaw set in at the end of January and the hard snow quickly disappeared to reveal extensive damage done to minor roads by the frost. When the brigade moved to its assembly area south of Nijmegen on the night 3/4 February the tank column was routed on the main road via Nijmegen to avoid further damage to partially metalled roads. The move went exactly to time and by first light all vehicles were as well camouflaged as netting and natural cover permitted. A total distance of 53 miles was covered by the column (120 tanks) in nine hours.

The next few days were occupied in tieing-up finally for the attack. Opportunity was taken to study the ground from the Windmill at Groesbeek, from which vantage point an excellent view of the enemy forward offensive area and the western edge of the Reichswald could be obtained when visibility was good enough.

The fears for the effect of a thaw on the 'going', entertained in the earlier planning days, proved to be only too well founded. The weather had definitely broken and periodic rain made unmetalled roads almost impassable. The tank routes from Malden to the battle assembly, previously improved by Canadian Engineers, worsened rapidly and on D–1 the CRE (Commander, Royal Engineers) of 53rd Division, in response to an urgent request from brigade, produced engineers and bulldozers to work on the worst places. Also on D–1, 147 RAC sent three RHQ Churchills and one flail forward to prove the route and these did valuable work in forcing fresh tracks through the forest. The route chosen by 9 RTR tanks was in better state and a Churchill tank commander, sent with his tank to prove the route, reported it passable.

A brigade coordinating conference, attended by CO's 9 RTR, 147 RAC and Westminster Dragoons (flails) was held at 1730 hours, 7 February. The Brigade Commander expressed his opinion that flails would be unable to operate over the ground conditions then obtaining, and repeated to 147 RAC that he was determined, if necessary, to expend a complete squadron

A tank of 2 Troop, A Squadron, on the outskirts of Groesbeek on 5 February 1945 just before the Reichswald battle. (IWM BU1770)

before giving up the attempt to lead the infantry to the edge of the Reichswald. All preparations had been made.

D-Day, 8 February 1945
More than 1,000 guns, taking part in the artillery preparation programme, opened fire at 0500 hours 8 February. At 0630 hours 147 RAC Group moved out of Malden and advanced to the forward assembly area in the woods west of Groesbeek where squadrons married up with their infantry. By 0800 hours Tactical HQ (Tac) 34 Armoured Brigade established near Tac 71 Infantry Brigade on the high ground immediately west of Groesbeek. 9 RTR Tanks Group moved from Malden at 0815 hours and concentrated in the forward assembly area in the woods between Malden and Groesbeek by 1030 hours.

H-Hour: A Squadron 147 RAC and 4 RWF
The advance began at 1030 hours but the ground was in a parlous state and 'flails' and 'Crocs' could make no headway, and the area of the start line was soon jammed with bogged vehicles. Ordinary Churchills, however, made steady if slow progress across the heavy fields. No opposition was met in the first 1,000 yards but speculative Besa fire was freely used to the front and flanks. The first enemy were encountered but they were quickly mopped up and thirty prisoners of war were taken.

All the flails were still bogged down near the start line but happily the defence overprints had grossly exaggerated the extent of the minefield and the tanks continued to advance. By 1155 hours, tanks and infantry, keeping well up to the barrage, were on the objective and another thirty to forty prisoners of war had been taken.

Breaching the anti-tank ditch: B Squadron 147 RAC and 1 HLI, C Squadron 147 RAC and 1 OBLI

As A Squadron and 4 RWF advanced to the first objective, B and C Squadrons followed as closely as possible in order to make maximum use of the timed barrage. On the right B Squadron, cooperating with 1 HLI, succeeded in getting all their tanks including the two Churchill bridgelayers, to the start line. On the left C Squadron, cooperating with 1 OBLI moved up via the railway track but had considerable difficulty with wire.

The angle of the barrage across the obstacle permitted B Squadron to attack first and, noticing no mines, they quickly got a Churchill bridgelayer forward and established a crossing. Two troops of tanks went over at once and took up fire positions, but the approach to the bridge worsened so quickly that the third troop was unable to cross. Some shelling and small arms fire were experienced but the second bridge was also laid; unfortunately the ground at this point was too bad to permit of its use. The ditch proved to be much narrower than it appeared on the air photos and certain places were found where it was possible for tanks to get across unaided, provided they did not attempt to move in the tracks of a previous tank. The remainder of the squadron got across in this manner.

On the left C Squadron had to attack without flail support, relatively unimportant in view of the apparent absence of mines; much more seriously without their fascine AVsRE, all four having failed to get through to the start line. The squadron commander's only hope therefore was to seize intact the bridge on the axis, and this was accomplished by one company of infantry supported by one troop of tanks.

1 HLI and 1 OBLI having formed up east of the ditch were supported into the forest by B and C Squadrons. Opposition was slight and objectives were taken by the infantry without great difficulty.

147 RAC less A Squadron, no longer required by 71 Infantry Brigade, rallied in area Plak west of the Reichswald and restocked from Stuarts and the turretless Churchills, and subsequently from sledges pulled up by tanks of 9 RTR.

Capture of the Siegfried Line in the Reichswald

By 1540 hours 71 Infantry Brigade had reported the consolidation of their final objectives, the Branden Berg features. During the morning and afternoon 9 RTR Tanks Group had remained in the forward assembly area but at 1645 hours C Squadron, followed by the remainder of the group, moved forward to marry-up with 160 Infantry Brigade for the next phase of the operations. Occasional rain during the day had further worsened the ground and Lt.-Col. Veale had to walk ahead of his party to pick out the best 'going'. Two tanks were put out of action by mines and all the Stuart tanks were hopelessly bogged, as tank movement was stringently forbidden on the only road, and no flails could operate even if any could have been unbogged.

By 1815 hours C Squadron had entered the forest and were moving up to their start line. Heavy shelling was encountered on two occasions but no casualties were sustained. The tanks avoided the tracks and broke their way through the trees, troops in line ahead and each troop leader preceding his tanks on foot. The move took a long time as it was now very dark, raining again, and frequent detours had to be made to avoid infantry who were digging in, but eventually the squadron reached the start line and tied up with 6 RWF.

A Squadron 147 RAC, due to support 1 E LAN Regiment were less successful – moving over the anti-tank ditch six tanks were bogged and had to be left. Owing to the tremendous traffic congestion on the one axis the infantry and tanks did not link up until 1915 hours. The group then moved forward and the infantry passed into the wood.

Meanwhile I E LAN Regiment had reached the start line, with 6 RWF and C Squadron 9 RTR tanks ready on their left. It was apparent that A Squadron 147 RAC would be unable to get through to the start line to support the operation. So the attack went in at 2300 hours with only 6 RWF supported by armour. C Squadron advanced with all four troops in line, meeting little opposition on the right but mopping up some Spandau teams on the left. Opposition was not great and the objectives were secured by 0005 hours. The remainder of 9 RTR moved forward into the forest to join C Squadron.

'Veritable' D-Day : 8 February 1945, general comments
The divisional plan was behind schedule but this could not have been otherwise in view of the appalling conditions – in the circumstances the advance had progressed at a remarkable rate. Previous to the attack it was feared that the enemy may have divined our intentions and false-fronted us by pulling back to his second defence line, but his dispositions showed that this was not the case – 84th Infantry Division had been hit squarely in the localities anticipated. The enemy, stunned by the weight of the artillery bombardment to which he had been subjected, gave in quite easily when tanks and infantry appeared on the tail of the barrage. This day's operations put 53rd (W) Division across the open defended zone of 4,000 yards and into the Reichswald.

9 February 1945: 'Veritable' D + 1, through the Siegfried forest belt to Stoppelberg and beyond

RHQ, A and B Squadrons 9 RTR tanks, having entered the forest just after midnight, moved forward throughout the night. Progress was slow by reason of difficult conditions and traffic

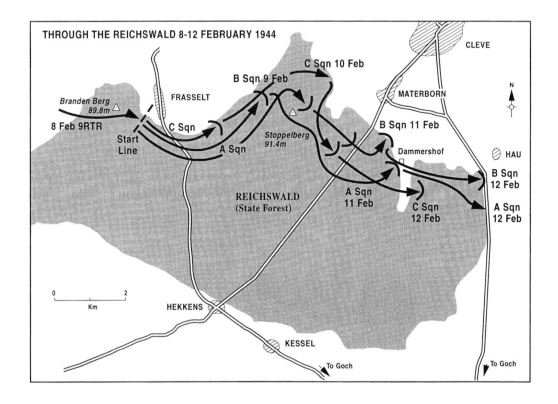

congestion but at first light A Squadron and 4 WELCH passed through C Squadron. The group kept to the northern edge of the forest and met slight opposition only – by 0915 hours the objective on the north-western edge of the forest had been secured, an advance of some 2,000 yards.

B Squadron, moving up with 2 MON to continue the attack, came under fire from two field-guns firing from just outside the northern boundary of the forest. These were engaged with 95 mm at a range of 2,200 yards, hits were observed and the guns silenced.

B Squadron and their infantry passed through A Squadron at 1015 hours, and, meeting no opposition, had secured the Stoppelberg feature by 1100 hours.

C Squadron had remained in their overnight position astride the Siegfried defensives until 1200 hours when, with 6 RWF, they were relieved by 158 Infantry Brigade. They then moved forward along the routes forced through the trees by the preceding squadrons and crossed the start line at 1200 hours. Opposition was slight and two hours later the objective, at the edge of the forest to the east of Stoppelberg, had been captured and secured. Sorties were made into the thick plantation in front of the position and a total of fifty-two prisoners of war taken. Enemy transport and personnel in the area of Materborn were engaged with good effect; this harassing of the enemy continued intermittently all day and four machine-guns which were holding up elements of 15th (S) Division were knocked out by an artillery concentration directed by C Squadron Commander.

General comments, Veritable D + 1

By evening a total of 2,580 prisoners of war had been taken on the 'Veritable' front and the ground conditions were still handicapping the advance more than the enemy. Movement on the divisional axis was strictly controlled and it was necessary to close it completely from time to time in an effort to improve it. By evening 9 February, brigade succeeded in establishing an ammunition point and a petrol point at Frasselt by running a column up the axis.

10 February 1945: 'Veritable' D + 2, Moving on

During the afternoon 160 Infantry Brigade was ordered to advance southward along the edge of the forest in order to assist 43rd Wessex Division in their advance south-east of Materborn. Accordingly at 1800 hours A Squadron and 4 WELCH moved through the Stoppelberg position and by 2200 hours had secured a locality astride the main road Cleve–Hekkens.

The day was generally spent in expansion and consolidation within the divisional bdys against light opposition, though 6 RWF were involved in fierce fighting which resulted in twenty enemy dead and two prisoners of war. A Brigade RASC column had succeeded in getting through to regimental areas and 9 RTR tanks ferried the much-needed petrol and ammunition round squadrons on RHQ tanks. 147 RAC were in a slightly better supply situation as they had been able to get some Stuart tanks forward and these had been kept busy ferrying supplies.

The advance had continued on the corps front throughout the day despite the enemy's desperate efforts to stabilize his line by rushing up reinforcements. By evening 7th Para Division, a second regiment of 180th Division and elements of 6th Para, 15th Panzer Grenadier and 116th Panzer Divisions had been identified.

11 February 1945: 'Veritable' D + 3

Owing to adjustments in the corps plan 53rd (W) Division now had the task of advancing south eastwards to clean up the Reichswald. The day saw impressive advances through the forest,

Logging track through the Reichswald, photographed by Berry Veale in 1978. He identified this as the place where he held an O Group in February 1945 with his squadron leaders and officers of the 53rd (Welsh) Division.

despite the stiffer resistance. One squadron of 147 RAC fought forward more than $6\frac{1}{2}$ miles. Almost every cross-track in the forest had its bazooka pits, although relatively few of the very large number of Panzerfaust found had been fired, for in most cases crews had not tarried long enough for even one shot.

While 147 RAC pushed through the heart of the Reichswald, 9 RTR and 160 Infantry Brigade advanced down the north-eastern edge of the forest.

As B Squadron and 2 MON passed their start line at 0900 hours they came under heavy mortar fire and soon afterwards machine-guns and bazookas were encountered. There were several skirmishes during the advance and some prisoners of war were taken, but by 1000 hours the objective, just to the west of the farm Dammershof, had been captured. A Jagdpanther, which opened fire and advanced towards the positions, was engaged by M10s and forced to retire.

At 1100 hours C Squadron and 6 RWF crossed the Cleve–Hekkens road and destroyed some enemy machine-guns; by 1350 hours the tanks and infantry were firmly established on their objective level with B Squadron.

At 1500 hours A Squadron and 4 WELCH passed between B and C Squadrons and occupied the farm at Dammershof by 1640 hours. A Jagdpanther creeping about in the farmyard was KO'd by 75 mm AP from 3 Troop at a range of approximately 400 yards, two shots breaking the track and damaging the suspension. The crew baled out and sought refuge in the farm but were subsequently rounded up there by Lt. Tom Fawcett.

During the night enemy patrols were active in C Squadron (9 RTR) area. Sgt. Michael Mead was shot through the head while on guard duty and his tank bazooka'd from a range of five yards, but the bomb struck the front plate and did no more than gouge it. This incident is typical of the general stiffening of opposition and from now on the enemy tried to infiltrate whenever possible by day and night.

The Germans had blown several Rhine dykes, causing floods over a wide area. The Kranenburg road was by this time under water and it was no longer possible to get supplies forward to the ammunition point and petrol point established at Frasselt. The divisional axis was still kept in a useable state only by continual and enormous engineer and prisoner-of-war labour. Tanks were still forbidden the use of all roads so that the Stuarts of 9 RTR, endeavouring to get forward with the urgently required replenishments, were frozen in Groesbeek where they had to remain until their unit was withdrawn from the forest.

9 RTR were having considerable difficulty in maintaining communications and were in urgent need of an instrument mechanic. That it was necessary to obtain a written permit from Divisional HQ to get him forward in a jeep illustrates the stringency of the road discipline.

Permission was obtained, however, to take essential supplies forward and at 2100 hours the DAA and QMG left Malden with a supply column with which he established a new ammunition point and petrol point on the main road Cleve–Hekkens. This time he had to go on 51st (H) Division's route south of the forest as the 15th (S) Division axis, hitherto used to replenish the ammunition point at Frasselt, had been flooded.

12 February 1945: 'Veritable' D + 4

During the day the enemy counter-attacked all forward tanks and infantry, but all these attacks were repulsed with heavy losses in killed to the enemy. Further rain caused tracks in the Reichswald to deteriorate even more and in many places a Weasel was the only vehicle capable of movement.

B Squadron and 2 MON resumed the advance at 0730 hours. Heavy opposition was overcome and a further thirty prisoners of war were captured before the objective was secured at 1130 hours. Major Michael Reynell, the squadron commander, was fatally wounded by mortar fire during this advance. 8 Troop was later sent to the eastern edge of the forest just south of Hau, cleaning up some machine-guns and taking seven prisoners of war en route. On reaching the objective a fierce action was fought in complete darkness and pouring rain, ending in the capture of another forty prisoners of war. This was only a raid, and after remaining on the edge of the forest for an hour 8 Troop returned to the squadron laager at 2100 hours.

In the meantime A Squadron and 4 WELCH had advanced at 1130 hours and by 1415 hours were established on the eastern edge of the forest south from B Squadron. At 1500 hours there were signs of a counter-attack from the south-east and a party of fifteen enemy, who stumbled onto a troop, promptly surrendered. By 1515 hours the situation was well in hand and the squadron remained in the area. By night 12 February both regiments were very weak in tanks. Figures were:

> 9 R Tanks: 14 battleworthy with a further 8 capable of support to the infantry in the Forest
>
> 147 RAC 24 battleworthy – of which several were capable of support to infantry in the forest only

The majority of tank casualties were caused by bogging and by conditions peculiar to forest fighting. So far it had not been possible to get the fitters' half-tracks forward and a number of tanks off the road needed minor repairs only. Lack of spare batteries and almost constant usage of wireless had thrown a heavy strain on the electrical systems.

Denys Graddon, A Squadron, wounded in the Reichswald, 12 February 1945.

C Squadron Armoured Recovery Vehicle (ARV) being repaired during the campaign (date and place unknown). The crew of an ARV consisted of a Sergeant vehicle mechanic (REME), two vehicle mechanics and a driver; thus even though this ARV looks a mess, the crew were quite capable of putting it in order.

During the day the enemy opposition had increased sharply, particularly to the south of Cleve. The enemy encountered on the divisional front fought fiercely to retain their hold on the edge of the forest, doubtless to keep open the road Cleve–Goch.

The weather showed no sign of improving and the full weight of the divisional traffic, plus considerable traffic of other formations, afforded no opportunity to improve the tracks.

13 February 1945: 'Veritable' D + 5

By noon 71 Infantry Brigade had drawn up level on the right of 160 Infantry Brigade, and the area was solidly held.

9 RTR RHQ moved to a clearing just west of Dammershof where it was joined at 1800 hours by B and C Squadrons. No squadron actions took place and opportunity to maintain the tanks was eagerly taken; many people were able to shave for the first time in several days.

During the first few days shortage of washing water had been a problem for the tank crews – this, however, had been remedied when the ammunition point and petrol point was established on the Cleve–Hekkens road, and since then all types of supplies had been readily available to regiments. To establish this waterpoint it was necessary to scour the rear areas for water jerricans as two-wheel drive watertrucks were unable to get forward.

Owing to the state of tanks in the units special permission was obtained to move unit fitters and LADs forward during the night 13/14 February.

With the exception of one or two tracks, today saw the final clearance, after six days, of the Reichswald.

Nothing happened during the day to change the general enemy situation on the 'Veritable' front. Taking advantage of the Roer valley flooding, which secured him against a serious American thrust for at least a week, the enemy launched his two reserve armoured formations into a counter-attack for which they appeared unprepared, and which availed him no success.

14 February 1945: 'Veritable' D + 6

A Squadron rallied with the remainder of the battalion and at 1730 hours 9 RTR moved back to Groesbeek for rest and maintenance, leaving 147 RAC to support 53rd Division.

In seven days' fighting 9 RTR and 147 RAC co-operated with 53rd Division in clearing some seven-eighths of the Reichswald. Some significant observations on this battle were made in a 34 Armoured Brigade summary:

1. The numerous brigade conferences held in the planning stage at Eindhoven were amply justified in the event. For instance if routes to the assembly area had not been prepared as insurance against a thaw, it is likely that the majority of tanks would have failed even to reach the start line. In particular, had not provision for maintenance been made by using sledges, Stuarts and turretless Churchills, it is certain that regiments could not have been replenished in the first 36 hours of the battle. These are only two examples of the way in which the time and facilities available for planning were of benefit in practice.
2. The ability of the Churchill tank to give close up support to infantry through forests of the Reichswald type, both by day and night, was proven. It is believed that no other allied tank now in service could have done as well, or even have reached the forest over the same country.
3. Personnel casualties were low but it was found that this type of fighting, with necessity for constant vigilance by every man, imposed a severe strain on tank crews. This was

especially the case with squadron and regiment commanders whose nights were normally spent in visiting their commands or attending O groups.

4. Although few tank casualties were caused by enemy action regiments were, at times, sadly reduced in tank strength. In view of the severe weather and ground conditions it was inevitable that many tanks should become, at least temporarily, unbattleworthy. While tank casualties were undoubtedly considerable, they were expected, and the success obtained was worth the cost in loss of, and damage to equipment. Many tanks backloaded for complete overhaul and rebuilding were already old and due for backloading in the near future in any case.

Forest fighting facts

Mr A.D. Bolland has written a book called *Team Spirit*, the story of the administration of 53rd Division in North West Europe. The Reichswald battle was one in which supply was of particular importance, and some of the facts recorded in Mr Bolland's book relate to supplies of various sorts.

During this battle the division received 78 officer and 2,103 other rank reinforcements. These were to replace casualties as shown below (9 RTR casualties are shown for comparison):

	Killed	Wounded	Missing	Missing Rejoined	Total
53 Div					
Officers	12	46	–	–	58
ORs	206	861	104	48	1219
Total	**218**	**907**	**104**	**48**	**1277**
9 RTR					
Officers	1	–	–	–	1
ORs	1	6	–	–	7
Total	**2**	**6**	**–**	**–**	**8**

Another item of particular interest during this battle was the issue of rum. During the complete campaign in North West Europe 53rd Division issued 2,894 gallons of rum; in the seven days of the Reichswald 1,228 gallons were consumed!

Personal recollections

The common themes of people's recollections are mud, exhaustion, snow, and the strain of being vulnerable to stalking parties in the forest. However, there was the satisfaction of achievement and of a difficult job well done. There was also some particularly good co-operation between the infantry and their supporting tank crews

As the account of the Reichswald battle described, A Squadron fought for almost all the time with the 4th Battalion of the Welch Regiment (4 WELCH). The third newsletter describes liaison with 4 WELCH before the battle:

When 1 Troop moved out to Helmond to train with the 4th Welch speculation ran high. But SECURITY had clamped down and no rumour proved to contain even a grain of truth.

On 31 January we ran a dance which was large, noisy, and very, very wet. As a result it was extremely successful. 1 Troop had returned in a 3-tonner bringing a selection of platoon and section commanders from the 4th Welch. These chaps appeared to be having quite a lot of fun one way and the other. Late in the evening they gave vociferous expression to their pent-up emotions by singing many savage chansons in a remote and ancient tongue. They were led by one Cpl. White who beamed on our L/Cpl. Jackie Hughes when the latter, casting off the thin veneer of civilization which his service in the 9th had bestowed upon him, burst forth into the songs of his childhood. This sort of liaison was indeed to justify itself before many days had passed.

Jack Woods was a member of 9 Troop Leader's tank crew, and he had drawn one of the early numbers for leave.

I went on leave from Villers-aux-Tours having drawn No. 12 in the battalion draw and when I returned the battalion was back in Eindhoven prior to moving forward to take part in Operation 'Veritable'. We moved up through Nijmegen to our assembly area early in February 1945 and were billeted in the barn of a farmhouse, which was filled with straw so it was quite cosy. In the mornings we had to wash under the pump in the yard (in February?) the only consolation being that the farmer had six daughters and we had to queue up with them. On the day of the battle, 8 February, we had to wait among the guns all day for our turn to enter the forest which we did in the evening, advancing steadily through the trees until we reached the other side five or six days later. *Inspire IV* opened fire on a target and the 75 barrel split like a Xmas lantern so we became troop corporal's tank under Corporal MacDonald. We didn't mind that because we still had two Besas and a Bren gun and could do a fair bit of damage with them if required. When we reached the edge of the forest we pulled back and parked in a clearing for a night and then next day moved back to Groesbeek. We were billeted in a house that had no furniture, so we laid the tank sheet on the floors, put all our bedding on that, pulled the engine sheet over us and slept, we were clapped out. Next day we were transported into Nijmegen to a mobile bath unit for a shower and clean clothes and away to pick up a replacement tank. *Inspire IV* had come all the way from the bridgehead and now she was done for, sad moment, but to our delight we collected a brand new Mk. VII, much better, *Inspire V*.

Peter Beale started to keep a diary on 1 January 1945. Most of the time it simply recorded the place where he had slept that night, but several of the entries have been expanded. At that time Peter was commanding 10 Troop, Jock Riddell was his troop sergeant and Len Holloway his troop corporal.

2 Feb. Helmond. Stayed with Freddie Herbert and Bill Perkins of 2 Mons. Tomorrow we will be training with them in some woods nearby.

3 Feb. Malden: In morning training in woods near Helmond with Freddie Herbert's company. We worked at various ways of communication between tanks and infantry and vice versa. The best way for infantry to talk to a tank commander was to use the handset in the box at the back of the tank. And the best way for a tank commander to talk to the infantry seemed to be getting out and finding them on the ground. One really good thing was getting to know Freddie and Bill and the platoon commanders.

We left there late afternoon and did a night march to our assembly area at Malden. It was a bit over 50 miles and took nine hours. Really tough going for the commanders and drivers – everyone else could go to sleep.

Sometimes the column came to a halt for good reason, other times because a driver and commander had gone to sleep. Went forward a few times and banged on the commander's hatch when the tank was stopped and nothing in front of it; the only worry then was whether the up route was sufficiently well signed for that commander not to lose his way.

4 Feb.–7 Feb. Malden: troop living in a barn. The barn is warm and dry which is good because it is bloody cold. On the 5th we went to a windmill in Groesbeek to have a look at the ground for the first part of the advance. We have had to remove all cap badges and other identification such as flashes, *Qui s'y frotte* etc.; security is very tight. Couldn't see too much from the windmill except that the ground up to the forest looks pretty waterlogged and the forest looks dark and unfriendly.

8 Feb. Reichswald Forest. Immense barrage starting at 0400 hours; met Bill Clement of RWF on the edge of the forest. Attack began at 1030 hours, but we didn't move until some time after 1700 hours. Once we had started we moved on and off all night. Immense amount of noise, searchlights in the sky, shots seemed to be going in all directions. Once again drivers and commanders kept falling asleep and had to be thumped back into activity. We got into the forest just after midnight and went forward slowly.

9 Feb. Reichswald Forest. At first light we managed to get some breakfast. Finally at 1015 hours we went through A Squadron and advanced to Stoppelberg, our objective, without any opposition. Going wasn't too bad and we went through the forest knocking down trees without too much difficulty at all. Went back a little way to laager and found they had decided to make a rum issue. Found a trench and some straw to make it comfortable. Sammy Joule and Titch Caldwell don't like rum so I had three servings! The trench was really comfortable and I got into it at 1800 hours and woke up at 0700 next morning, thirteen hours much-needed sleep!

10 Feb. Reichswald Forest. Sat in clearing and watched 43rd Division pass through. They are evidently to go north out of the forest towards Materborn.

11 Feb. Reichswald Forest. Advanced with A Company; SPs and bazookas. On the start line we looked down a ride going south-east and there was one of the Germans' horse-drawn supply carts. The cart must have just got up to the front line as our attack started and the people in charge of it had disappeared. The poor wretched horse was standing between the shafts shaking and quivering in absolute terror. I don't know what happened to the horse because we took to the forest and drove steadily through the trees. My driver Sammy Joule drove really well. We got to our objective and could see Dammershof farmhouse across some open ground. I could see what looked to be a tank or an SP among the buildings. Our 75 mm was out of action temporarily, but over to my left I could see a troop of M10 tank destroyers. So I went over and told the Canadian troop commander what was going on. He said he would do what he could from the left flank. When I asked him how he was going he said he had buried two and evacuated four of his crew that morning. Getting it tougher than us.

A few moments later A Squadron passed through us. Tommy Fawcett came to ask me what the situation was, so I explained and suggested he should do a fairly wide right flanking movement and I would support him from where I was in whatever way I could. It turned out to be a Jagdpanther, and Tommy and his 3 Troop knocked it out and captured the crew. Slept that night with Freddie Herbert and Bill Perkins of 2 Mons in a trench. It was snowing some of the time, but it wasn't too bad in the trench.

12 Feb. Reichswald Forest. Advancing again. Mike seriously wounded by mortar landing on turret, hear later that he died in hospital. Roger (Long, the squadron 2 i/c) takes over for the moment.

13 Feb. Reichswald Forest. Moved back about a mile into a clearing. Able to do some maintenance on the tanks and get a bit cleaned up ourselves.

14 Feb. Groesbeek. Moved back here out of the Reichswald for rest and maintenance, but it looks as though it may not be for very long. Had a bath in Nijmegen.

As the War Diary relates, Sgt. Michael Mead of C Squadron was killed on 11 February. Many people were sad at Sgt. Mead's death – he was, incidentally, always known as Reg, even though this was neither of his two names. Bill Thompson was in the same troop: 'From 8–13 February the squadron fought through the Reichswald Forest and 11 Troop suffered the loss of Reg Mead our well-loved troop sergeant, one of the nicest guys that ever walked this earth.' Dickie Hall also remembered Reg Mead's death, as well as many other things about the Reichswald:

Before we had our expedition down to the Ardennes, we should have gone into the Reichswald Forest to attack the enemy there. So, on our return north from the Ardennes the advance was set in motion. Our line of advance was to be from Groesbeek, through the northern half of the forest with 53rd Division. Troops to the north of the forest were also to advance, and both lines would converge on the town of Goch. First of all we were told that we could expect no supplies of rations and water till Goch. Petrol would come up if possible. We soon evolved a system of cooking inside the tank, which generally meant the driver or co-driver having the pressure stove between his knees to boil or heat water, everyone else putting jam on biscuits, or opening the different tins from the '5 man pack'. If things were quiet we could use the 'tin, sand and petrol' method for heating, or, if we were moving, putting an empty biscuit tin tied to the exhaust pipe with water in it, and the tin of food to be heated in the water. I said that we should not receive petrol supplies – but we did. A 3-tonner driver, Jock White from Glasgow, got up to us on several occasions through 'rides' which were not suitable for trucks really, but he managed it. We were instructed to keep off the 'rides' in the forest, as enemy anti-tank guns were sighted along them. So we were to move through the forest, demolishing trees, and with the turret and 75 mm barrel fixed over the front idler-wheel – otherwise our turret ring would almost certainly get stripped by the trees. When we halted overnight we had to keep as quiet as possible, as several times we could hear SPs moving about quite close; and there was dear Ronnie Holden walking about saying, 'We can't sit here, lets have a party!' – which of course meant having a go at these wretched SPs.

One night we halted in a thinly wooded part of the forest. Everyone was on the alert for roaming tank-hunting squads. Poor Reg Mead was killed in his tank by a burst of fire from one of these squads (we all heard the shots). He had challenged but had not fired quickly enough. He was a charming chap and a great loss to his troop and to the squadron.

So our advance proceeded. We had a lot of rain, and being February it was very cold, so we were glad of the rum ration that someone from each tank had to collect in a mug. In the dark one night I tripped and lost the lot, and on going back for more was told I was a 'lying so-and-so'. But I got a refill! We were in many ways protected from the weather. But we felt very sorry for the infantry nearby in the slit trenches; and in the cold wet mornings the poor chaps looked so dejected, but they kept going. They were very tough!

One night, just as it was getting dark, we caught a small pine-tree in the track which immediately shed. We were separated from the other two tanks of the troop – not difficult! The question was, what to do? I knew where HQ was, so told the crew to shut down and keep dark and quiet, while I went to report. I had no password and we were in front of the infantry. I crept back, and every time I was challenged I used all the language that troops are familiar with, and as it happened it worked. I told HQ that at first light I would repair the track and rejoin, and this we did without any further trouble.

I can remember spending what seemed hours, shut down, waiting for the next move. One of the times, we had a whole platoon of German infantry burst out of the forest and charge us; we had no infantry support so we had a clear field of fire. I think this was one of the very few occasions when we actually saw the Hun face to face – who we repulsed.

THE BROEDERSBOSCH AND BEYOND

The Broedersbosch was a plantation of young pine-trees varying in height from 12 to 20 feet. They were close together, and were probably due for an early thinning. This resulted in visibility being very poor once a tank was in the trees. There were many rides criss-crossing the plantation, but there was every likelihood that they would be covered by anti-tank weapons of some sort. The 9th withdrew from the Reichswald on 14 February, on which day they salvaged bogged tanks, maintained tanks generally, and as many people as possible had a bath at Nijmegen. The unit had been hoping for 48 hours rest, but it turned out to be 24 hours instead. On 15 February the 9th was attached to 52nd (Lowland) Division, and began preparations for an attack south and east parallel with the River Maas. The War Diary takes up the story.

The War Diary, 15 February–12 March 1945

On 15 February 9 RTR was briefed for operations south of Gennep with 52nd (Lowland) Division. Information about the enemy was as follows.

It was known that 2nd Para Regiment originally holding line of the River Maas had to swing right to meet the threat from the north flank and were holding line running approximately south-west to north-east from just north of Afferden with 2nd Battalion right – 1st Battalion left. Between 2nd/2nd Para Regiment and 20th Para Regiment, who were holding the area south of Hassum, is Battalion Reigels, a rather nondescript GAF Battle Group. All these battalions had suffered heavily in the last week. Six Jagdpanthers had been encountered south of Heyen, probably elements of 683 Anti-tank Battalion and a few SP guns.

The 51st Highland Division were holding this part of the front line. 52nd Division were to pass through 51st Division and seize the Broedersbosch, the high ground about Grootehorst, and the village of Weeze.

The intention of 9 RTR, less A Squadron, was to support 157 Brigade in the capture of the Broedersbosch, and then to exploit to the line Afferden, Rempeld, Kasteel Blijenbeek. The first phase was the capture of the Broedersbosch, and the order of battle was:

Left	*Right*
5 HLI	5 KOSB
C Squadron 9 RTR	B Squadron 9 RTR
1 platoon 7 MANCH	2 platoons 7 MANCH
Troop (SP) 214 A/Tk Bty	Troop (SP) 214 A/Tk Bty
Objective	*Objective*
NE corner of main body of the Broedersbosch	SE corner of main body of the Broedersbosch

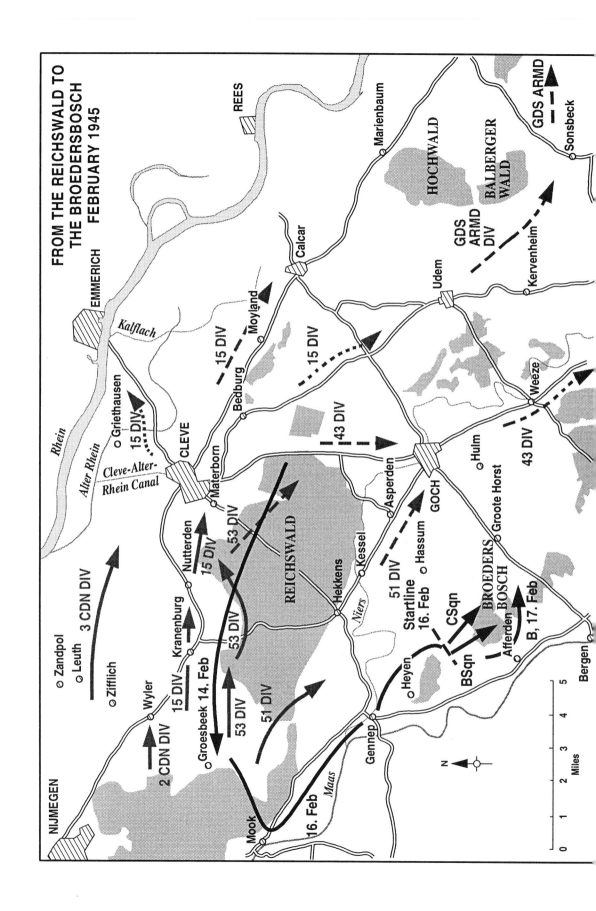

FROM THE REICHSWALD TO
THE BROEDERSBOSCH
FEBRUARY 1945

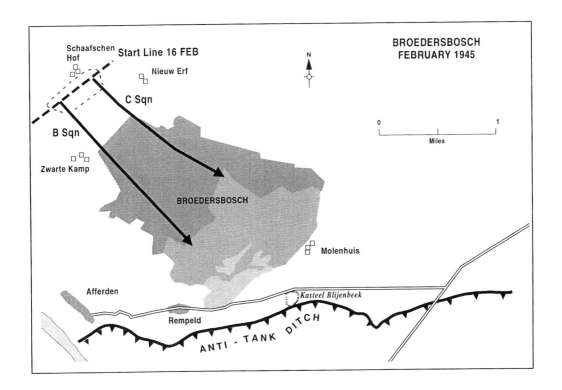

16 February. 0600 hours. 9 RTR tanks less A Squadron left Groesbeek, and passing through Mook and Gennep arrived in the assembly area at 1000 hours, each squadron having eleven battleworthy tanks.

1500 hours. Squadrons crossed start line in support of infantry. On the right there was only slight opposition. One strongpoint, however, at Zwarte Kamp had to be reduced with a combined assault with close artillery support; thirty prisoners of 2nd Para Regiment were taken and many killed. From the left heavy HE fire was reported from the direction of Nieuw Erf and OC C Squadron lost his tank on a mine. Resistance was stiffer on this flank and a pocket of enemy which had been left by the infantry fought strongly using a considerable number of Panzerfaust which, fortunately, fell short or wide of the two troops who had become involved in this little battle. Short range HE and machine-gun fire eventually broke resistance and by 1615 hours the tanks had joined up again with the infantry who, though fighting well in the open, appeared to lack confidence in wood clearing and tank co-operation. By 1700 hours, two troops on the right and one on the left had reached their objectives and fifteen minutes later another troop on the left reported in position. In centre of the left sector infantry were held up 30 yards short of objective by heavy Spandau fire and the troop in support was threatened by frequent Panzerfaust. This enemy position took some time to destroy because concentrated and accurate fire from the tanks was not possible owing to damaged traverse systems. One tank was hit by a Panzerfaust and brewed up. The crew were badly burnt and Trooper Norman Hopkins had his leg crushed as he fainted in front of a neighbouring tank [see Cyril Rees' account for correct facts]. By 1830 hours all objectives had been secured, but between 1900 and 1940 the artillery had to be called twice to break up the enemy forming up for a counter-attack.

At 2300 hours SPs and anti-tank guns had been moved up into position and the squadrons were released and joined RHQ at Schaafschen Hof, where it had been established for the battle.

During the day's fighting two officers and 73 ORs had been taken prisoner all belonging to 2nd Para Regiment.

17 February. 9 RTR tanks continued to support 52nd (Lowland) Division in carrying out their original intention, which resulted in a series of local and somewhat abortive actions. The plan of Phase 1, the capture of Afferden, had been changed. It had been intended that B Squadron should support 1st Glasgow Highlanders in this task, but as B Squadron had not been released till late the previous evening, the Glasgow Highlanders were given the support of the Crocs which were not used. Afferden fell quickly after an early attack.

At 0700 B Squadron with eleven tanks reported to 52nd Division Recce, and remained at thirty minutes' notice for a combined attack in clearing (i) down to anti-tank obstacle between Afferden and Grootehorst; (ii) triangle Afferden – Grootehorst – Bergen.

At 0900 C Squadron were sent to rest and refit, but at 1100 hours, following an O group held at 155 Infantry Brigade HQ, it was decided that A Squadron, still resting and refitting at Groesbeek, would support 7th/9th Royal Scots in (i) attacking farm Molenhuis and pt 22.7, (ii) support infantry by fire from high ground to anti-tank ditch, and in placing fascines in ditch at three places. The first phase was to be carried out with two companies and two troops up – H-hour 1600 hours.

At 1530 B Squadron move in support Recce Regiment to clear road Afferden–Grootehorst. Opposition light – enemy in houses engaged with HE. However, large craters and very soft ground delayed a further advance, though 52nd Recce succeeded in clearing wood to the west of Rempeld. B Squadron later pushed on to Rempeld and there formed a firm base.

Meanwhile, A Squadron had been summoned from Groesbeek but owing to the roads being blocked with traffic their attack did not start according to plan.

Reinforced by two tanks from RHQ, the squadron had mustered two troops and a command tank, and though troop leaders were only given hasty orders, they did not succeed in crossing the start line until H + twenty minutes. 7th/9th Royal Scots had already moved forward and B Company was contacted south of the start line, but no contact was made with the other company, visibility being poor among the 3–4 ft high trees in thick young fir wood. The tanks got to within 300 yards of farm but no infantry could be seen. Enemy were now using Panzerfaust in large numbers, most of which, however, exploded against the trees. One commander was injured. Eventually, one infantry platoon was found in a small clearing digging-in under heavy mortar fire. One mortar position was destroyed by 95 mm HE. At 1800 hours the infantry command was at last contacted and A Squadron, being released half-an-hour later, moved to join RHQ.

At 1830 B Squadron was contacted by a patrol from 5 KOSB and then withdrew to Afferden for the night. RHQ and A Squadron moved to harbour area on the southern edge of the Broedersbosch at 2040 hours.

18 February. During the night 17/18 February the 7th/9th Battalion The Royal Scots (7/9 RS) occupied objectives that had not been captured the previous day. At 0600 hours an O Group was held at which A Squadron was ordered to support the 4th Battalion The Kings Own Scottish Borderers (4 KOSB) in the following operations:

Phase 1: crossing anti-tank ditch south of Rempeld
          assist Assault Engineers in placing fascines at crossing
          silence strongpoint at Kasteel Blijenbeek
Phase 2: support two companies in attack on woods south of Kasteel Blijenbeek
          silence enemy position 400m south of the anti-tank ditch

A Squadron had only six tanks available, two of which had only recently been delivered and these not thoroughly checked. Organized in two troops of two tanks each, supported by a Close Support 95 mm tank, A Squadron left their harbour at 0730 hours and crossed the start line one hour later. One troop was to support the crossing of the anti-tank ditch and the other to attack the strongpoint. Both troops, however, were soon engaged by SPs situated to the south of the ditch, and as the infantry came under heavy fire success looked doubtful from the first. One of the tanks, attacking the strongpoint, had three bogies shot away and the main armament was jammed. The other tank advanced firing eighty-six 6-pounder rounds at the concrete defences at 50 yard range and then was hit, becoming immovable. On the right the situation was no better. Anti-tank fire had brewed one Churchill and the other was pinned. The AVRE was also hit and the CO 4 KOSB reported the operation not possible. At 0910 tanks and infantry rallied north of Rempeld and at 1220 A Squadron was released and returned to RHQ area.

B Squadron operating with 52nd Recce Regiment had moved back to Rempeld at first light and with eight tanks straffed known enemy positions south of River Beek. It was soon appreciated, however, that no further advance could be made under existing conditions and the squadron returned to Afferden in a counter-attack role. In these actions, clearing difficult wooded country stubbornly defended, the regiment lost three tanks by enemy action and suffered six casualties among tank crews.

The poor nature of the ground with so many obstacles did not allow constant use of tanks, and 19 February was a quiet day though there was heavy mortaring during the night. Tank replacements had begun to arrive and refitting was begun on the next day when the regiment concentrated at Heyen. The main task had been achieved and a congratulatory message was received from the Corps Commander.

Six days in tents and bivouacs passed with the regiment either leisurely doing maintenance or resting, and then on 27 February the regiment moved to take up a counter-attack role with 156 Brigade, 52nd (Lowland) Division, who were relieving 51st (Highland) Division, on the night 27/28 February.

C Squadron were to support either 7 CAM or 4 RSF in the area of Hulm and Boyenhoff, while A Squadron were to be prepared to move south in support of 7/9 RS or 6 CAM.

B Squadron were to remain in reserve.

On 1 March the regiment moved forward to support infantry of 156 Brigade who had now extended positions to include Grootehorst, a bridgehead over anti-tank ditch south of Grootehorst, and Neider Helsun.

Enemy resistance on the right was believed to be slackening but 53rd Division were fighting hard in Weeze, which was believed to be a hinge for the enemy withdrawal to a bridgehead round Wesel.

C Squadron in direct support to 156 Brigade were situated at Hulm with A Squadron in reserve. B Squadron moved to the east of Grootehorst in support 155 Brigade. RHQ established itself in a broken-down farmhouse west of Goch.

C and B Squadrons experienced some shelling, resulting in damage to two vehicles and Lt. Peter Beale was wounded slightly below the right eye.

On 2 March snow made life less comfortable and the day looked as if it would be quiet but now the divisional front was gradually moving forward; ground being taken over as it was vacated by the enemy.

As a result of a division conference, C Squadron were given the task of supporting 156 Brigade in clearing Hees wood 9034 in order to open road Hees – Wemb.

The regiment less C Squadron was to support 157 Brigade now concentrated south of Goch and be prepared to pass through 53rd (W) Division and 8 Armoured Brigade if necessary on axis Kevelaer – Geldern. The regiment was placed at two hours' notice and at 1000 hours on

3 March A Squadron moved across country to area of 1st Glasgow Highlanders who had already concentrated. The roads, however, were frozen by corps to allow the Guards Armoured Division to move south. B Squadron did not move.

C Squadron had been unable to move south as there was no way across anti-tank ditch owing to demolitions – one Stuart was lost on a mine in an endeavour to find a route. 156 Brigade, however, carried out its task and took fifteen stragglers, one of whom was drunk.

53rd Division and 8 Armoured Brigade had meanwhile contacted the Americans and the bridgehead was slowly being squeezed. It was still possible, however, that 52nd Division and 34 Armoured Brigade would be needed and orders were issued to concentrate at Walbeck.

On 4 March the regiment began to move but having reached the area of Langstraat were then ordered to move no further.

It was thought that 53rd (W) Division and the 8 Armoured Brigade would be punched out by the Americans and Guards Armoured Division but on 6 March they were still in the line regretting, it is reported, that they did not have the support of 9 RTR tanks.

Again it was possible that 52nd Division and 34 Armoured Brigade would pass through and the brigade groups – 147 RAC in support 155 Brigade and 9 RTR tanks in support 156 Brigade – were warned to stand by. The following day, however, 34 Armoured Brigade ceased to be under command 52nd (Lowland) Division and the regiment remained in the area of Langstraat, having baths and doing washing, awaiting its next orders.

The regiment was warned of a possible short rest but suddenly, at 7 o'clock on the evening of 8 March, a warning order was received whereby the regiment would be moving at 6 o'clock the next morning. During the last 24 hours enemy resistance around the Wesel bridgehead was as determined as ever; reports indicated the para regiments holding the line were being reinforced and the appreciation was that there would be some tough fighting before the German positions were destroyed.

II (Canadian) Corps took over the whole front and the plan was 52nd (Lowland) Division with 34 Armoured Brigade in support would relieve 53rd (W) Division and the 8 Armoured Brigade who had not yet been pinched out by the 35th US Infantry Division of Ninth US Army.

At 2300 hours on 8 March the CO was still trying to get definite orders which had already been changed twice. Eventually, however, it was decided that the regiment would move at 0700 hours on 9 March and take over that day from 13/18 Hussars, 9 RTR tanks were to support 155 and 156 Brigades, while 147 RAC supported 157 Brigade, whereupon A Squadron were allotted to 7th/9th Royal Scots (155 Brigade) and C Squadron to 4/5 RSF (156 Brigade).

The enemy bridgehead was still thought to consist of 2,000 fighting troops, elements of 6th, 7th and 8th Para Divisions, and 180th and 190th Infantry Divisions. 24th Para Regiment was believed to be facing 52nd (Lowland) Division.

Small local attacks gradually nibbling away the enemy positions were considered a waste of time and the intentions for 10 March were to carry out a set-piece attack on the Wesel bridgehead. 52nd Division supported by 34 Armoured Brigade were to be on the left and 35th US Division (part of the Ninth US Army) on the right.

In the early morning, with heavy artillery fire, the attacks began, but there was no resistance and only enemy stragglers were picked up; one, a GAF NCO, stated that all possible equipment had been evacuated across the Wesel railway bridge by 0500 hours and the bridge itself had been blown two hours later.

Word came that there might be the inevitable gallop, but as there was now no further need for tank support the infantry gradually took over the ground up to the Rhine. The Wesel bridgehead petered out without even a whimper, though the BBC reported that same night that enemy resistance was slackening.

B Squadron, 8 Troop: troop sergeant's tank Inferno. *Charlie Mansell, Sgt. Bob Mann, George Bone in Holland, February 1945.*

The 9th spent 24 hours in the woods, where the CO and Major Holden, using Very lights from an abandoned ammunition dump, amused themselves and others with a firework display.

The regiment journeyed back on 12 March over the Maas and, with the brigade, prepared to relax in the area of Deurne, some 15 miles east of Eindhoven.

Personal recollections, 15 February–12 March 1945

John Hodges' diary has entries for the days up to 20 February. The 9th was then static for a few days, and John went on leave to England from 27 February to 11 March.

15 February. Day of so-called rest. Orders for a fresh attack – so busy after all. Had a shower at Nijmegen – first since 19 December!! Heard that Mike Reynell died and is buried at cemetery near Nijmegen. Blast the war – all the nicest people get killed.

16 February. B and C Squadrons attack woods north of Afferden on the Maas. Very tired before we started. The Boche, from 2nd Para, fought well and as our infantry didn't seem too good the party didn't go with a swing. However we reached our objectives at a cost. Ronnie Holden's tank went up on a minefield where a lot of infantry were injured. Later C had a tank fired up by bazooka and three of crew were badly burnt and one run over. Eventually we managed to get what was left of both squadrons back but it was not a happy party.

17 February. Another party laid on today – A Squadron with 155 Brigade, B Squadron with Recce Regiment – tank chaps are on their knees, so am I! We didn't get awfully far and spent an uncomfortable night with periodical stonks falling about. Woke up wet and miserable!

Peter Beale's diary resumes on 15 February:

15 February, Groesbeek. Spent the day maintaining tanks and getting ready for action with 5 KOSB of 52nd Division. Company Commander is Arthur Jardine-Paterson. We have to attack through a wood called Broedersbosch and apparently it is held by some para troops.

16 February, Schaafschen Hof. This was our start line this morning and it was good to get back here. Started early and went through Mook and Gennep and got to assembly area at 1000 hours. Hung around till mid-afternoon. Army photographer – only one I've ever seen – took pictures of all the crews in their tanks lined up along the edge of the wood. Hoppy (Eric Hopwood, my wireless-op) didn't seem too impressed with this performance because I asked the photographer to get a picture of us!

Going through the wood wasn't too bad, and the map was amazingly accurate; you could tell which cross-track you had got to by the angle at which you reached it.

Got to our objective as it was getting dark, and the tanks were on either side of the ride in the trees. Had a nasty shock when I heard a tank coming along the ride from the enemy direction. I was out of the tank talking to Arthur – who had lost nearly two platoons during the day – and didn't have time to get back to it. So just waited for it to arrive, and it turned out to be – a Valentine! Didn't think they were still used, but this was a FOO (Forward Observation Officer) tank, and I suppose the commander hadn't much idea of where he was. Eventually got back to Schaafschen Hof, and slept very comfortably on top of the engine hatches. Bloody cold when you wake up in the morning, though.

17 February, Afferden. We were working with 52nd Recce Regiment and in the end we took Rempeld, a bit south of yesterday's wood. Then we laagered in Afferden, which had been captured this morning and was badly knocked about.

18–20 February, Afferden. The ground was bad for tanks to the south and evidently the infantry CO didn't think there was much point in pushing too hard when the Jerries would probably get pinched out anyway and have to move back to the east. Squadron HQ in a cellar and we played bridge most evenings with two of the troop leaders from the Recce Regiment. One evening (20 February) I got the feeling the Germans had my range and were pursuing me with mortars – certainly improved the acceleration!

21–6 February, Heyen. We moved back from Afferden to Heyen and Roger said we were likely to have a few days there. He decided to set up an officers' mess-tent, but most evenings we have been in Nijmegen to the club. It has meant that I've been able to have breakfast, lunch, tea and dinner with the crew and in the mess – eight meals a day! But it is cold, and we're outside 24 hours a day, so it burns itself off no trouble.

27–8 February, north of Hassum. Moved to support 52nd Division in another advance to the south. Went into Nijmegen to look for a bath, but couldn't find one; met Geoff Shepherd, now Adjutant of 147 RAC; finally had a shower at Mook.

1 March, Nijmegen. Moved south via Goch in support of 155 Brigade. We were just to the east of Groote Horst and I was siting the tanks when a shell or mortar or something landed close by and I was hit on the right cheek by a shrapnel fragment. It didn't seem much but reckoned it was best to check with Doc Paddy Knox (our Medical Officer). So off to RHQ and Paddy reckons it is OK but should be checked out at hospital. Next stop 3 CCS (Casualty Clearing Station) at Nijmegen. They said it was OK, nothing left in, so stay overnight and back to the unit tomorrow.

2 March, Asperheide. Left hospital in morning. Went to look at Mike's grave (Mike Reynell, killed in the Reichswald on 12 February). Went back to squadron echelon and spent night with Tommo (SSM Tomlinson) and Sgt. Butch Robinson.

3 March, Malden. Went back to Battalion HQ and stayed there till 1500 hours. Returned to squadron in Adjutant's jeep. Saw Crerar (General Harry Crerar, GOC First Canadian Army).

4 March, Langstraat. To Nijmegen in morning. Travelled down through Gennep and Afferden to Langstraat by tank. Saw Churchill and Monty in Gennep.

[Note: this is confirmed by Arthur Bryant's *Triumph in the West*, where Lord Alanbrooke records for 4 March: 'We (Winston Churchill, Montgomery and Alanbrooke) then proceeded to Gennep to see the Bailey bridges which had been put up on the Maas; they were even longer than the one I saw over the Sangro River last year.']

Cyril Rees describes the action in which four of his crew (himself, Norman Hopkins, Graham Gordon and Syd Hazel) were wounded:

The general line of advance toward Goch and beyond involved negotiating a large wooded area, and the area in which C Squadron was involved reminded me very much of similar tracts of Forestry Commission woodland in England. Those who exercised around Thetford will remember the large stands of fairly mature conifers bisected here and there with wide sandy rides and firebreaks; and there were similar types of forestry in Sussex and Surrey.

Mark VII Churchill Indomitable, *commanded by Peter Boden, 14 Troop, C Squadron, near the Broedersbosch, February 1945.*

13 Troop were to move up the left side of this particular ride, and our infantry would be further in the wood and move with us. I have no idea of the disposition of the rest of the squadron; perhaps there were other troops on the right side of the ride, but I don't know. Since the rides would almost certainly be covered by 88s, either as field guns or mounted on SPs or tanks, the 9th senior commanders and OCs and commanders of supporting units decided other strategies were needed. As a result, I found myself waiting for the off, with the engine running and my visor open, hard up against rows of conifers (Scots Pine, I think), with row upon row ahead of me, as far as I could see.

Our tank was about a yard inside the wood, parallel with the ride. Our troop leader, Lt. Des Lilley, was about 25 feet ahead of me, and off to my left, so that our left-hand track would roughly follow the right-hand track of his tank. The pine-trees immediately ahead of me were not very old, varying between 4 to 6 inches in diameter (though there were older trees as we went deeper into the forest). The plan seemed to be that by ploughing a swathe two tank widths through the trees, we would create some surprise to the enemy and lessen our chance of being hit by the 88s.

Independent now had 'Tosh' Brooks as commander since Tom Tomney was wounded at Nispen. Norman Hopkins was still our Op. Ginger Kirk had had his arm knocked by a 3-tonner a day or so previously, so we had a spare crew gunner and a spare crew co-driver. So, of our original troop sergeant's crew from Charing, Norman and I were the sole survivors. Unseen behind us was Frank Hodgson's tank.

Some weeks earlier many tanks had been getting spare track plates tack-welded on to any flat exposed surface as additional protection against bazookas fired at close range. So this was a slight comfort to us. 'Driver advance,' said Tosh over the intercom.

The troop leader, Desmond Lilley, was also moving off. I slipped into first and closed the top hatches. A small amount of throttle and I let in the clutch. *Independent* leaned gently on the trees immediately in front of us and they slowly fell away and were snapped off at belly height as we edged forward in first gear quite effortlessly at little more than tick-over speed. I kept my front visor open so we could maintain station and observe what was happening ahead.

The first 25 yards or so was a piece of cake. Then the problems started. I could see the tank ahead as it smashed down the trees and the thicker parts of the trunks as they were picked up by the tracks and carried up to the top return run. The mud shields were being ripped off on each side and after a short distance both top tracks were totally without any cover. Of course, this was happening to us also, though I could see nothing except when a battered piece of sheet metal was carried round by our tracks and dropped on to the fallen trees in front.

But I could now see a far more serious thing happening. Both our tanks now had no mudguards and I could watch as the splintered trunks were jammed in the tracks and carried forward to the point where they were forced under the overhanging turret. With the tremendous leverages involved something had to give, and this happened to be the teeth of the turret ring. It was happening to us, too. I could hear and feel the teeth ripping off, with a sound like a football rattle. I watched helplessly as the turrets swung first one way and then the other, quite out of control. Thus, both our tanks would have been unable to use, or have any control over, the main armament.

I had little idea what distance we had travelled, though probably we had been moving slowly ahead for about ten minutes. Then, for some reason unknown to me, the troop leader's tank stopped. I slipped into neutral but didn't bother using the handbrake, just waiting to see what happened next. The tank ahead began to reverse, and I expected to hear Tosh say 'driver reverse' to me. I was on the point of dipping the clutch and selecting reverse when

Independent was rocked by a violent explosion. The compartment was filled with vicious searing flames and nothing was visible to me except the red ignition warning light on my dashboard.

I was wearing a chunky knit khaki pullover which my mother had knitted and sent a few weeks before. My lanyard was round my neck and although quite irregular, my Smith and Wesson was tucked into my trouser pocket and not into my holster. Self-preservation being uppermost in my mind, I had to escape from this inferno. I pushed open the top hatches and tried to stand up on my seat, but the lanyard must have caught on some obstruction, perhaps the gear lever. Straining against this the lanyard must have burned through and parted. Heaving myself on to the bare track, I lay gasping and smouldering for a split second before launching myself head first into the shrubbery and grass below, alongside the bogies. *Then, merciful oblivion.*

How long it was before coming to, I've no idea, but it was dusk when I became aware that I was lying on a stretcher on top of a Bren carrier. Alongside was another stretcher, occupied by someone in field grey, but I could find no hate or enmity in me at that time. I was fairly drowsy; looking at my hands I could see they were quite black and had large blisters. The pullover I was wearing had begun, as far as I could see, to melt and turn black and glossy. I was aware of voices but was unable to pick up much. Someone nearby produced a tube of morphine and jabbed it into my lower arm, I think it was. I think this chap was Frank Risbridger.

It wasn't long before I began to feel drowsy. I was vaguely aware of figures approaching the carrier and looking down on the occupants of the stretchers. Before lapsing once more into unconsciousness I heard the familiar voice of our much-respected squadron leader, Major Ronnie Holden. 'My God, it's Rees,' were the last words I heard before leaving C Squadron and the 9 RTR in Germany.

In the event this was the finish of the original troop sergeant's crew of 13 Troop from the Charing days. Norman lost his sight as a result of this last action and I was slightly burnt on my hands and face. My clothes, particularly the woollen jumper, seemed to have prevented more serious burns, though most clothes had to be cut off with scissors. The 9th was disbanded a few months later, so Major Holden's words really were my last remembrances of C Squadron.

While I was lying recumbent alongside the bogies, and unknown to me, the rest of our crew were rapidly abandoning our stricken Mk III. Whether Norman had already been blinded by the internal blast or whether this occurred shortly afterwards is unclear. He was soon feeling his way round the back of the tank, stumbling over the piles of crushed and splintered pines. One account from one member of the shocked and shaken crew said that he fell between two of the trunks. The troop leader was still reversing at this time and in the partial dimness could not see what was behind, particularly the frenzied attempts to attract the crew to Norman's plight, with the result that this tank reversed over Norman.

It seems that the fallen trees took most of the weight with Norman wedged between them. Even so, he suffered pelvic fractures and other severe abdominal injuries as well as bone breakages. After this severe shock and exposure he got pneumonia. This account is largely borne out by Norman's own recollections which were aural rather than visual. We can at least be grateful that during all this, the troop leader's tank does not seem to have made any major change of direction. This most horrendous event is one that few of us were ever called upon to endure.

CHAPTER 11

Wind Down

The broad picture, 23 March–5 May 1945

On the night of 23 March 1945 the Second British Army and the Ninth US Army forced the crossing of the Rhine on the northern sector of the allied line. Lodgements had already been made by the Americans at Remagen and Mainz, but the northern attack was the one that was to constitute a major threat to the Ruhr and the Germans' ability to continue the conflict.

The crossing was most successful, and the CIGS, Lord Alanbrooke, who was at Monty's HQ that night, said on 24 March: 'Looking at the day as a whole and the successes of the American forces in recent weeks south of the Moselle I am quite certain that the end of the Germans is very near. In a few days we will be in a position to let Monty's eight armoured divisions operate boldly through North Germany, maintained if necessary by air supply.'

In fact it was not necessary to use air supply, and the troops of 21st Army Group pressed forward at great speed, and on 5 May 1945 the German Armies in the north surrendered.

9 RTR was held with the rest of 34 Armoured Brigade as a reserve striking force that could be used if opposition stiffened. In fact it didn't, and we remained on the western side of the Rhine until 6 April. This final chapter gives the history of the 9th over the months April to June 1945, a few personal recollections, and an account of the celebrations on VE Day.

THE ANTI-CLIMAX ACROSS THE RHINE

The War Diary, 13 March–30 June 1945

On arriving at Deurne, the regiment immediately began overhauling the tanks – changing engines, tracks, sprockets and doing less strenuous maintenance, while the Battalion Technical Adjutant (BTA) sorted out the more war-weary tanks and began to backload those that had travelled well over 1,000 miles. These battered old warriors disappeared and replacements arrived to refit the regiment for what was believed to be its last battles across the Rhine. On 14 March General Sir Miles Dempsey, KCB, DSO, visited the regiment and on leaving was heard to say that he had been most favourably impressed by what he had seen. The same day, the Brigadier passed more bouquets declaring that during the period which the regiment had served under XXX Corps, the Corps and Divisional Commanders had nothing but praise to offer for the regiment's efficiency and fighting spirit. Major R.E. Holden was awarded the DSO for his outstanding ability as a squadron leader and the morale of the regiment began to mount to such an extent that it accepted without protest the demands of 'Bullshit'.

Soon the regiment was ready once more for action, but the speed of the advance of other formations made it progressively less likely that 9 RTR would again take part in the fighting. Finally, on 1 April, a move was made to Sevenum, preparatory to crossing the Rhine, but now everyone was bored and impatient and a little irritated by the publicity given to other formations.

The brigade now came under the control of I British Corps and on 6 April the regiment crossed the Rhine to take over military control of Gelderland and a small area of Germany

9 RTR tanks (11 Troop of C Squadron in the foreground) waiting to cross the Rhine, April 1945.

12 Troop C Squadron start to cross the Rhine via 'Westminster Bridge' as seen from the leading tank of 11 Troop.

surrounding Bocholt. Here the regiment was given the unattractive job of acquiring information about German war materials left behind in their retreat; of recceing routes and ensuring that no subversive activities were carried out by the populace. Each squadron was given an area to clear up and the regiment was dispersed with RHQ at Aalten, A Squadron at Groenlo, B Squadron at Lichtenvoorde, and C Squadron at Winterswijk.

Recce parties reported the states of road, blown bridges and minefields, while salvage parties collected into dumps the miscellaneous ammunition lying about the area. Nothing really interesting was found and everyone was glad to hand over the area to the 3rd Heavy Regiment RA of 9 AGRA.

On 14 April the whole brigade moved into Germany and 9 RTR became responsible for part of Kreis Bentheim and Ahaus with the same responsibilities of battlefield clearance, route reconnaissance and security.

RHQ established itself in the fifty-year-old castle at Bentheim, with A Squadron at Emsburen, B Squadron at Gronau, and C Squadron at Schuttorf.

As the days passed the squadron ammunition dumps became larger and the maps heavily marked with chinagraph; patrols roamed the area in an attempt to control the numerous Displaced Persons who had now become the vagabonds of Germany, eating, sleeping and taking revenge as they wished. In an effort to control this gypsy life, the Ems River was made a stop line where all Displaced Persons attempting to cross were diverted to proper reception camps and preparations were made to seal off Germany by closing the Dutch/German frontier.

B Squadron were made responsible for the 25 miles of frontier in the regiment area and work

Bob Young, Desmond Lilly and Peter Boden with a 12-cylinder Maybach saloon 'rescued' on the German-Dutch border. The car is identified as belonging to C Squadron by the circle on the rear door.

was begun on marking the frontier and carrying out recces preparatory to setting up an evacuated frontier zone. Meanwhile, by house searches and enquiries, the area was cleared of all firearms and German deserters. Houses were searched for food hoarding, wireless transmitters and Nazi documents, and the list of Nazi officials who were to be arrested, grew longer. All ideas of fighting another battle had been abandoned but those of the past were recalled when the Brigadier decorated the Colonel with the DSO and confirmation of other awards was received as follows:

Military Cross to Lt. W.J. Waters (A Squadron)
Croix de Guerre with Silver Star to Lt. A.P. Boden (C Squadron)
Military Medal to L/Cpl. A.J. Towlson (C Squadron)
Croix de Guerre with Bronze Star to Cpl. F.D. Horner (C Squadron)

On 28 April, as their area was now clear, it was decided to move A Squadron to Lingen where they were to help control the Displaced Persons camp which was now responsible for some thousands of Russians and other nationalities. But before leaving, an ammunition clearance party of RASC and Pioneers exploded an R mine which resulted in the whole dump at Emsburen blowing up. As a result, vehicles were destroyed and houses collapsed, and though the clearing party suffered casualties, no member of A Squadron was injured.

By 8 May, despite the difficulty of liaison with Forward Security and Military Gov, the frontier zone had been evacuated and marked with warning notices, roads had been closed and frontier control posts established at three points (i) on the Oldenzaal/Bentheim Road; (ii) Enschede/Gronau Road and (iii) Enschede/Ahaus Road. B Squadron were now the busiest of all squadrons, coping with hundreds of Dutch returning to Holland and preventing the use of unauthorized vehicles. The impounded vehicle park harboured all types of civilian cars and many unfortunate people were faced with a long hitch-hike back to their units. On 18 May C Squadron took over the northern part of the frontier and, in consequence, moved to Bentheim where, since the regiment's arrival, numbers of the population had sought out RHQ in order to tell of their troubles and the I office added to its list of miscellaneous jobs that of a Civil Affairs Department.

With the war in North West Europe now over and the celebrations of VE Day but a memory, news of the regiment's future began to be disclosed. The regiment was to become an Armoured Regiment of Occupation, with the establishment of a few soft vehicles and other odds and ends.

All but six Churchills and six Stuarts were handed over to 267 Forward Delivery Squadron for disposal, and on 30 May the regiment moved, being given Kreis Tecklenburg as the area of responsibility.

RHQ established itself at Ibbenburen, A Squadron at Westerkeppeln, B Squadron at Mettingen, C Squadron at Lengerich.

There the regiment, occupied by guarding a few VPs, mainly hospitals, awaited the arrival of the 4 RTR who were to be made up to strength by an exchange of Age and Service Groups and then train with Churchills preparatory to embarkation for SEAC. The 9 RTR were to be partly responsible for the training, but before the end of June the regiment would not be recognizable as the one that had fought for ten months in North West Europe.

The interchange between 4 RTR and 9 RTR took place during the last week of June 1945, and 9 RTR moved to Luthe. In September 1945 a further move eastward took the 9th to Wunstorf, just west of Hanover.

The unit's last job, under 5th Infantry Division, was to protect the Germans in the isolated villages of the Harz Mountains from the murdering, pillaging and raping Displaced Persons (DPs) who were in DP camps or hiding in the forests.

C Squadron officers after the campaign, taken at Lengerich, Germany, June 1945. Back: Lts. Jack Southall, Desmond Lilly, Bob Young. Front: Capt. Sidney Link, Major Ronnie Holden, DSO, MC; Capt. Alan Morgan, Lt. Keith Lloyd. Lt. Peter Boden, the only troop leader who survived the campaign without injury or promotion, was away when this photo was taken.

The final act was the disbanding of 9 RTR, which was authorized to commence on 30 November 1945 and which was complete by 13 December 1945.

Personal recollections

Trevor Greenwood remembers the parade when Ronnie Holden was awarded the DSO for his inspired leadership of C Squadron.

Thursday 15.3.45
Best BD parade this a.m. for clothing exchange – preparatory to a round of 'bullshit' parades and inspections, presumably. This parade was followed by a battalion parade for an address by the colonel. He repeated some of the compliments mentioned by Captain Link – viz. 53rd Division had had to be relieved before completing their offensive towards Wesel. We had been detached from them a few days previously. One of the divisional officers stated that they would easily have reached the Rhine in three days had the 9th Battalion RTR been with them!

Other compliments about the brigade came also from General Dempsey and General Horrocks, and the former spoke of the 9th as a fine regiment on his visit yesterday. But the most interesting part of today's little ceremony was the colonel's announcement that the king has confirmed the award of the DSO to Major Holden – a high honour for the unit, but particularly for C Squadron. The colonel pinned the medal on Ronnie's breast alongside his earlier MC. If any man has earned it, he has.

14 Troop Leader's crew on 'holiday camp' near the River Elbe. L/Cpl. Johnnie Towlson MM, Arthur 'Zeik' Vardy, Geoff Bound, Bob Tyler.

Crombie Cordiner remembers one of the chores that the 9th was required to do, and the actions of some of the Russians who were stationed nearby:

On 28 April, as their area was now clear, it was decided to move A Squadron to Lingen where they were to help to control the DP camp which was now responsible for some thousands of Russians and other nationalities; but before leaving, an ammunition clearance party of Royal Army Service Corps and Pioneers exploded an R mine, which caused the whole dump at Emsburen to blow up. As a result, vehicles were destroyed and houses collapsed, but though the clearing party suffered casualties, no member of A Squadron was injured.

The barracks at Lingen was on four sides of a barrack square. Memory has the number of occupants as Russians 8,000, others 6,000. The Russians, comprising men, women and children of all ages were under the brutal control of a self-appointed Commissar who had his own staff, bodyguard, and executioners. He had his own guard at the only gate, alongside the A Squadron guard. The language problem created very great difficulty and the arrogance and insolence of the Russian command brooked no interference. For the small A Squadron party control was superficial and only a brave or foolish man entered Russian-controlled buildings.

No member of A could forget the daily disciplinary court which was held by the Russians on the parade ground opposite A Squadron quarters. In view of all the Russians, who were commanded to be there, wretched people guilty of some offence were tried before the Commissar and dealt with. The platform at the edge of the square had a crude gallows permanently mounted on which regularly someone was put to death. Gunshots were often heard – it was seldom possible to tell if someone had been shot, though this was likely. As the Russian guards were so heavily armed nothing could be done, though protests were made.

Lt.-Col. Berry Veale has two recollections of this period. The first is of a problem with a victory salute, the second of snapping up a good opportunity.

Castle Bentheim

Does anyone remember VE Day at Castle Bentheim? We had arrived at Castle Bentheim, just across the Dutch border near Enschede on or about 5 May 1945. The castle, a magnificent medieval pile, was indeed a lavish home with all its trappings, built on a hogs-back ridge overlooking a flat farm vista. Regimental HQ was allocated the castle (why not) and the squadrons were spread out on a 15-mile radius from HQ.

We knew that 8 May would be VE day and it was not possible for us to be involved in further war with the Germans. In fact we were informed that our daily rations would be drastically reduced so that all available food could be diverted to northern Holland. We were encouraged to go hunting for game birds, deer, mouflon and wild pigs to supplement our diet.

We were also instructed to engage some local person – bilingual English/German as an interpreter and liaison with local authorities, and we found a Feldwebel (Sergeant) who must have been educated in the Hitler Youth. I'll call him Heinz.

Tank gun salute for VE day at Schüttorf. This was more successful than the salute at Bentheim, as Berry Veale's story tells.

So what about VE Day?

I said in Part I orders on 7 May 1945 that 9 RTR would celebrate VE Day with all due pomp and ceremony; to this end I said we'd fire a 21-gun salute from the hogs-back ridge at 1100 hours 8 May.

Upon talking it over with the Intelligence Officer who was in charge of the HQ tanks, I said that each tank crew should set to work dismantling twenty-one rounds of ammunition, discarding the shot and stuffing paper into the casing, then stacking them in the turrets ready to fire.

All four tanks should be lined up on the ridge ready to fire the salute at 1100 hours the following day.

The interpreter Heinz was ordered to see that the available populace of Bentheim would turn out to witness this historic occasion.

'*Jawohl*' he said.

Next day at 1050 hours 8 May 1945 four HQ tanks were lined up on the ridge, including *Ironside*, guns elevated 15° and pointed north ready to fire.

Fifty to seventy-five local elderly Germans were scattered around, pushed and shouted at by Heinz.

The CO arrived, climbed into his tank, put on his earphones and established that 'All Stations' are on 'Net'.

He checks his watch and starts the countdown:

3 – 2 – 1 – Zero – Fire!

Bang! Bang! Pl??? – Plop.

CO begins the countdown again:

3 – 2 – 1 – Zero – Fire!

Bang! Pl??? Pl??? – Zero

CO looks a bit puzzled but begins the countdown again:

3 – 2 – 1 – Zero – Fire!

Bang —— Silence ——

CO notes crews of three HQ tanks are dismounting and one is belching smoke. He starts to count again:

3 . . .

but then he feels strong arms grasp him round the ankles and eject him from the cupola. The rest of the crew tumble out of the tank, coughing and gagging, and then smoke starts pouring out of the hatch.

The CO, who hadn't swallowed any smoke, grasped the situation and turned to Heinz, ordered him to rally the spectators to climb up and shut all the tank hatches, then pile dirt on to restrict air flow thus douse the fires.

The spectators ran to help, some fetched shovels, buckets for water and with tremendous enthusiasm doused all the fires.

The CO then instructed Heinz to have all four tanks' interiors stripped of wiring and any damaged equipment, and the tanks repainted and refitted with new wiring and equipment under the guidance of our QM and REME Officer.

The orders were carried out seriously, diligently and without complaint. The RQMS was able to replace all damaged parts and the incident closed without any further ado.

Later we learned that genuine 'Blank' ammunition is loaded with black powder which goes 'BANG' even when not restricted.

Gun ammunition, however, has cordite as the propellent. Cordite looks like spaghetti and burns, rather than explodes, when not restricted. Hence after calling 'Fire' by the CO, the cordite starts to burn and is still burning when the gun breech is opened. The burning cordite sticks spill out of the gun and on top of the stacked rounds waiting to be loaded; then 'away we go'.

– 21-gun salute it was not –

Oddly enough it seemed to us that the spectating Germans were as distraught by the sight of four British tanks burning as we were, and very anxious to put things right with all possible speed.

I wonder if the Burgermeister of Bentheim recorded this incident in his municipal minutes? Good enough for Gilbert and Sullivan, wouldn't you say?

Flying with Fido

The war with Germany was over and we were more or less in limbo, moving around running a German demob camp but mostly waiting to find out if we were going to be sent to the Far East or to England for the Golden Handshake.

On one of my 'Recces' I came across an airstrip, very active it was with a stream of all kinds of American and British fighters and light bombers landing and others taking off.

Intrigued, I turned my jeep in through the gate and up to what looked like a Nissen hut. Inside were two or three desks with radios and a couple of operators and a counter behind which was a tall American with Sergeant's stripes and a long cigar. He wore the inevitable leather bomber jacket festooned with all kinds of badges and ribbons. There was also a patch on which was the one word COX. As I came over to the counter he said 'You're a Lootenant Colonel ain't you – Sir. See I've studied you limey officers ranking marking and there's not many I don't know.' Then he said, 'I'm Flight Sergeant Cox – Sir. What can I do for you?' From Flight Sergeant Cox I learned that this was a temporary stop for all sorts of aircraft refuelling, before taking off for home stations in England and Scotland. 'Is that your home – England, I mean,' Cox said. 'D'you like a short quiet weekend at home eh? Where you from?' I said a weekend at home would be very acceptable and that my current home was in North London. 'North London,' he mused. 'Is Northolt North London?' I said it was and only about a ten-minute taxi drive from my house. 'Great,' he said. 'If you get your ass back here next Friday, I might be able to find you transportation to Northolt.'

Well that was an offer I couldn't refuse. So Friday 0900 I was back with my haversack and toothbrush. Who needs anything else on a weekend? I waited and saw many pilots come in, sign for his refuelling and leave. I began to have some doubts but then, in came a pilot in a battered blue RAF cap and the other standard equipment, flight boots and bomber jacket. No insignia. He signed for his refill and turned to go when Cox said, 'Say Joe, ain't that crate you're flying a Mitchell?' Joe said yes it was. Then Cox said, 'Your flight sheet says you're terminating at Northolt. You'd have room there for my friend the Colonel here. Wouldn't you?' 'Sure,' Joe said, then turned to me and said, 'You wouldn't mind travelling in the bomb bay would you?' I said I wouldn't mind so long as he didn't ditch me into the channel.

The bomb bay was designed to house 500 lb bombs, so lying prone on some odd kit and greatcoats it was quite comfortable.

Time to wonder at the gear stacked in that confined space, drink my coffee and eat a chocolate bar from the NAAFI and pretty soon we were over Deal and then I noted some anxiety from Joe in his chit-chat over the radio.

Then he turned and called down to me, 'Sorry chum – Northolt is socked in so we can't get down there. Traffic is trying to find us an open window.'

A bit later he called down again, 'We're going into Blackbushe they have FIDO there.' I wondered what wonder dog was this that could assist an aircraft land in fog?

Joe again, 'This landing is going to be rough because they can only turn FIDO on for two and a half minutes and we've got to rush in there before the fog closes in again. Hang on.' I could feel the Mitchell making steep banks, then the engines cut and with a hard solid bump we were down.

Further instructions from Joe, 'We'll taxi to the end of the runway and stop. We'll then open the bomb doors and you must get out quickly and clear the aircraft. Turn right and walk or run to the boundary of the field. The A30 is the main road right there and you'll have no difficulty hitching a ride to London. Good luck and go to Croydon for your return trip.'

We continued taxiing and then I felt the brakes being applied and then the hiss of the bomb doors opening. Some wispy fog streaming in – I shouted 'Thanks' and let go and dropped about four feet on to the runway, got up turned right and made off into the fog. After twenty paces I could no longer see the Mitchell but did catch the lights of the tow truck which would take the Mitchell back to its report centre.

I reached the perimeter fence without problem and there sure enough was the A30 – I knew which way to go but made sure by asking the first lorry which was crawling along. This was an RASC 3-ton and its driver, a corporal, was glad to have some company.

We reached London in about two hours where I got out and hopped into the Underground, made a phone call and arrived at my house at about supper time. I had time to wonder about FIDO but still don't know what the letters stand for – Fog Dispersing something something. Essentially air flares set round the perimeter of our airfield. Light them all together and it burns off the fog – very expensive but did save a lot of lives and aircraft.

What's that you say? What happened then? Well if you must know, on Sunday the fog had dispersed and I got a regular flight back to Brussels; from there I hitch-hiked my way back to Germany. No sweat.

Envoi

To make a final comment on the 9th's history in the Second World War, what better person could there be than our Commanding Officer for most of the campaign in North West Europe. Lt.-Col. Peter Norman (Berry) Veale had won the MC with 8 RTR in the Western Desert, and came to 9 RTR as Battalion Second in Command in late 1943. He became CO in mid-July 1944, and commanded the 9th for the remainder of the campaign.

His leadership was courageous, intelligent and compassionate, and for his leadership he was awarded the DSO in April 1945. After the war he emigrated to Canada, and in 1978 he was in Germany on business. He records how he revisited the Reichswald.

The Reichswald Forest

In the autumn of 1978 I was in Dusseldorf in connection with a trade show in which some Canadian manufacturers were exhibiting their machinery sponsored by the Canadian government.

I had very little to do between opening and closing the show and spent some time on short day trips. One of these trips took me to Cleve, which is on the northern edge of the

Field Marshall Montgomery decorates Lt.-Col. Berry Veale, MC, with the DSO, Berlin, June 1945.

Reichswald Forest. I intended to walk south-west through the forest to Hekkens and Gennep on the Dutch border. I had a sandwich lunch and camera with me intent on finding and photographing some, at least, of the reference points that we picked out during that memorable action we shared with the 53rd (Welsh) Division and 52nd (Lowland) Division between 8 and 18 February 1945.

From Cleve I took a taxi through 3 miles of Cleve suburbs and paid it off just where the road enters the forest. This was the point I had chosen for my HQ and it was established as planned on or about 10 February 1945.

Over the past five to six weeks in 1945 we had had lots of snow then lots of rain so that the ground conditions were as bad as I have ever experienced. It took our tank drivers all the skill at their command to slowly move their vehicles through the quagmire until they got into the forest where the traction improved.

We had caught the Germans by surprise apparently, for during that first 24 hours we encountered only light resistance. Personnel casualties were light but the tanks had suffered much damage; not from enemy fire but from the trees and underbrush jamming the turret traversing mechanisms.

By the time we were due to commence the final thrust through to the objective, which was the main Cleve–Goch road on the eastern edge of the forest, we had to meet with the Infantry Commanders to tell them of our difficulties and could only promise to render moral support and fixed-turret fire from our machine-guns. I therefore called an O group meeting at a cross-track reference which was half-way between Cleve and Hekkens in the middle of the forest.

Now in late September 1978 I marched into the forest to find that spot. It was a fine autumn day and the 'track' I had remembered was now a four-lane highway with Mercedes and BMWs racing along it at 100 mph.

About 3½ miles in, I found my 'spot'. The cross-ride was exactly as I remembered it, with several large logs to sit on, a carpet of fallen leaves and gentle autumn temperature. I ate my lunch and opened a can of beer; sat on the same log I had sat on thirty-three years earlier and savoured the moment remembering February 1945 – Ronnie Holden, Mike Reynell and Peter Massy were with me and with the 53rd (W) Infantry we thrashed out a plan.

Time to move on out, I thought, at least 3½ miles to Hekkens.

About half a mile along the road the forest on the east side suddenly cleared and I was looking on a cultivated area where there were tall 60 ft trees thirty-three years ago. Now I slowly realized it was a large cemetery and then I saw the gatehouse and read the inscription: The Reichswald Forest War Cemetery.

I walked into this most impressive place, in ideal surroundings of tall majestic trees. Quiet, with well-tended grass and ornamental trees and then thousands upon thousands of identical plots, each with a headstone precisely lined up north to south and east to west.

I walked up and read on a stone 'Private Smith J.G. Somerset Light Infantry, Died Feb. 17th 1945 aged 19 years' then on the other side 'A/C Kowalski C.T. 215 Sqn RCAF. Died in action Dec. 14th 1944 age 20 years', and so on and on. Rows on rows on rows. So many young men.

I turned round and walked into the gatehouse where there is a roster of every occupant with a reference indicating where to find his grave.

I started to leaf through the pages to find Reynell M. and Mead M. and then I stopped – I couldn't go on – I knew that if I found a grave of someone I knew, I would be helpless and unable to continue. As it was I was emotionally very distraught. So I took some photographs, said my sad farewells – and left.

I had a long way to go and now cannot remember anything but the anger and frustration and the criminal waste of the flower of the youth of both ours and Germany.

The Reichswald Forest War Cemetery, photographed by Berry Veale in 1978.

It was well I was alone for I could not have spoken a civil word to anyone.

Eventually fatigue, hunger and the lowering skies urged me on to Hekkens and Gennep where I climbed into a taxi for the ride to Goch to catch the train back to Dusseldorf.

Now it's etched there forever.

I shall not forget.

It's good to remember.

It's good to march to the cenotaph on 11 November each year.

It's good to meet your comrades over a beer now and then.

It's good to reminisce.

It's good to tell your offspring 'Don't do as I did, but do as I say.' They won't listen anyway. But, hopefully, one day when we have repeated the message one million times, it will get through and all this stupidity will be outlawed.

Casualties

This casualty list has been compiled from the following sources: the casualty list kept by the 9 RTR Orderly Room; references in contemporary newsletters, letters, and diaries; personal memories, relating both to the individual and to others.

The information presented is as accurate as possible using the sources mentioned and the occasional inconsistencies between those records.

The entries are in date order of occurrence, and within each date in alphabetical order.

The summary of casualties includes killed in action (KIA) and died of wounds (DOW) under the same heading 'Killed'. Some of the casualties that have been included could more correctly be listed as died on active service, for example,

> Lt. Les Wintle, ran over by a tank transporter at St Omer
> Sgt. Ernie Bottoms, killed by a V2 in Antwerp
> Cpl. John Davis, died as a result of injuries sustained after jumping out of a burning building in Roosendaal.

Another small number of injuries were caused by malfunction of armament, for example Besa blowback. All of these incidents have been included in the main casualty list.

Squadron	Killed in Action or Died of Wounds				Prisoners of War			Wounded				Total Casualties
	Off	WO & Sgt.	OR	Total	Wo & Sgt.	OR	Total	Off	WO & Sgt.	OR	Total	
HQ	1	1	3	5	–	1	1	3	1	23	27	33
A	4	3	28	35	1	7	8	8	4	38	50	93
B	4	2	8	14	–	–	–	6	7	35	48	62
C	–	4	10	14	–	–	–	7	6	29	42	56
Total	9	10	49	68	1	8	9	24	18	125	167	244

Serial No. of Entry	Army Number	Rank	Surname	Initials, Given Names, Nicknames	Squadron & Troop	Trade	Function	Date of Occurrence	Nature of Occurrence	Place of Occurrence	Details of Wounds and other Comments
1	14330228	Tpr	AKASS	D.	HQ			26 June 1944	Wounded	Cheux	Shrapnel wound to leg from mine
2	552601	TPR	BARKER	H.	C	GM		26 June 1944	Wounded	Cheux	Blast
3	14418000	TPR	BARNATT	R.	A.2			26 June 1944	Wounded	St. Manvieu	Shrapnel wound
4	7939481	CPL	CHAPMAN	Sydney James (Jim)	C, 11	GM	Troop Corporal	26 June 1944	KIA	Cheux	
5	4972596	CPL	ELLIS	R.	C.	DO		26 June 1944	Wounded	Cheux	Shrapnel wound right hand
6	7934375	TPR	GOTOBED	David Anger	C,12	DM	Troop Sergeant's driver	26 June 1944 / 26 June 1944	Wounded / Died of wounds	Cheux	Leg severed above knee
7	7931181	CPL	KILLICK	Harold Godfrey (Nobby)	A.2	DM		26 June 1944	KIA	St. Manvieu	
8	14236106	TPR	MADDOX	Reginald (Reg)	C.15	DM		26 June 1944	Wounded	Cheux	Gun shot wound to back
9	14402419	TPR	MOORE	G.	C			26 June 1944	Wounded	Cheux	Gun shot wound right hand
10	14241457	TPR	PAINTER	Royston Ivor (Roy)	C.12	GM	Troop Leader's driver	26 June 1944 / 28 June 1944	Wounded / Died of wounds	Cheux	Shrapnel wound right hand
11	14521458	TPR	RAWSON	W.	C			26 June 1944	Wounded	Cheux	Shrapnel wound to back
12	5836773	TPR	WEBB	J.	A.2	GM		26 June 1944	Wounded	St. Manvieu	Shrapnel wound
13	7939190	TPR	WHOLEY	J.	HQ	DO		26 June 1944	Wounded	Norrey En Bessin	Shrapnel wound right leg
14	7932452	TPR	ANDERSON	James (Wally)	B.9	DM	Troop Leader's driver	27 June 1944	KIA	Grainville sur Odon	Tank destroyed by tank gunfire
15	7955391	TPR	CRAWLEY	Michael	B.10	GO		27 June 1944	KIA	Grainville sur Odon	Tank destroyed by tank gunfire
16	7925860	L/CPL	DEEM	James "Jimmie"	B.9	DO	Troop Leader's Wireless operator	27 June 1944	Wounded	Colleville	Seven lacerations to right leg, and burns to hands & feet
17	14422203	TPR	JEBB	J.H (Johnnie)	B.10	GM		27 June 1944	Wounded	Colleville	Wounded in chest by machine gunfire
18	7952295	TPR	KEEBLE	Edward Joseph	C.11	GO		27 June 1944	KIA	Cheux	Direct hit on head by sniper
19	247485	LT	MOTT	Edward K. (Teddie)	B.9		Troop Leader, 9 Troop	27 June 1944	Wounded	Grainville	Both legs amputated below knee
20	7948183	L/CPL	MYCROFT	Edward	B.10	DO		27 June 1944	KIA	Grainville	
21	14269981	TPR	MYRING	Alleyn Robert "Bob"	B.9	GO	Troop Leader's Gunner	27 June 1944	KIA	Grainville	
22	7926096	TPR	ROBERTSON	J. (Jock)	B.9	GM	Troop	27 June 1944	Wounded	Colleville	Wounded in chest, and burns to arm
23	3716484	TPR	SHIMMIN	G.	HQ	DM		27 June 1944	Wounded	Grainville	Shrapnel wound buttocks and leg;remains at duty
24	7918108	SGT	SIMMONS	Harry (Cushy)	B.10		Troop Sergeant, 10 Troop	27 June 1944	Wounded	Colleville	Shrapnel wounds both legs
25	14420479	TPR	ARNOLD	Leslie John (Les)	HQ, OP	GO	OP tank gunner	28 June 1944	Wounded	Colleville	Shrapnel wounds right arm and thigh
26	14375370	TPR	BENNELL	Arthur James (Jimmy)	A.1	GO	Tp Leader's W/Op	28 June 1944	KIA	Colleville	Tank destroyed. no remains
27		TPR	BUTTERFIELD	Daniel (Danny)	A.1		Tp Leader's W-op	28 June 1944	Wounded	Grainville	Shrapnel wounds to face
28	6352994	TPR	COSTIN	Edward Alfred (Ted)	A.3	DM	Tpr Cpl's driver	28 June 1944	KIA	Colleville	
29	14366734	TPR	EDGAR	R.	HQ		Tp Leader's driver	28 June 1944	Wounded	Colleville	Shrapnel wound to fingers
30	5723432	TPR	HARLOW	K. (Kit)	A.1	GM	Tp Ldr's gunner	28 June 1944	Wounded	Grainville	Burns face and hands, wound to left knee

Serial No. of Entry	Army Number	Rank	Surname	Initials, Given Names, Nicknames	Squadron & Troop	Trade	Function	Date of Occurrence	Nature of Occurrence	Place of Occurrence	Details of Wounds and other Comments
31	7295875	CPL	HUDSON	J. (Jack)	A. 3	DM	Tp. Cpl.	28 June 1944	Wounded	Grainville	Blast: remains at duty
32	7909613	TPR	KILLEEN	Edward (Eddie)	A	VM		28 June 1944	Wounded	Grainville	Gunshot wound right foot
33	2589917	CPL	PALMER	Albert	A. 2	DM		28 June 1944	Wounded	Grainville	Shrapnel wound stomach
34	7948576	TPR	PETTIGREW	Charles Francis (Jock)	A. 3	DO	W/op. Tp Cpl's tank	28 June 1944 / 11 July 1944	Wounded / Died of wounds	Colleville	
35	14270035	TPR	SAMUELS	John	A. 3	GM	Co-driver, Tp Cpl's tank	28 June 1944	KIA	Colleville	
36	3317554	SGT	ANDERSON	Robert (Bob)	C. 12		Troop Sergeant	28 June 1944	KIA	Grainville	Blast (mortar)
37	7901689	SGT	HALL	Richard (Dicky)	C. 15		Troop Sergeant	29 June 1944	Wounded	Grainville	Gunshot wound right hand from Besa blow back
38	14401474	L/CPL	SAXTON	Len	B. 7	DM		29 June 1944	Wounded	Colleville	Shrapnel wound groin
39	14236710	TPR	THOMPSON	F.	C.	GO		29 June 1944	Wounded	Grainville	Mortar blast right eye
40	4868019	TPR	RADLEY	L. (Les)	B. 7	GM		29 June 1944	Wounded	Grainville	Shrapnel wound to finger of left hand
41	7925922	L/CPL	ALDCROFT	James (Jimmie)	B. 8	DO	Tp Sergeant's wireless operator	8 July 1944	Wounded	Verson	Burns
42	7895962	SGT	ARLETT	Robert Charles (Bob)	C			10 July 1944	Wounded	Eterville	Wounded in right arm
43	7926012	CPL	ARMSTRONG	Fred	A. 5	DO	Troop Corporal	10 July 1944	Wounded	Maltot	Phosphorus burns face and hands
44	14552768	TPR	BALL	Charles Abbott (Charlie)	B. 8			10 July 1944	KIA	Hill 112-Chateau de Fontaine	
45	52578	MAJOR	BALLANTINE	James Douglas Haddow (Duggie)	A. SHQ		Squadron Leader A Squadron	10 July 1944 / 10 July 1944	Wounded / Died of wounds	Maltot	Wounded by mortar head and chest, both legs broken
46	14234489	TPR	BARBER	Roy (Ali)	B. 8	GM		10 July 1944	Wounded	Hill 112-Chateau de Fontaine	Shrapnel wounds face and legs, burns
47	7925894	TPR	BATES	E.	A. 1	DO		10 July 1944	Taken prisoner	Maltot	
48	14425253	TPR	BLANCHARD	Alan	A. 1			10 July 1944	KIA	Maltot	
49	7877365	SSM	BRADLEY	C. (Monty)	A. SHQ		Squadron Sergeant-Major, A Squadron	10 July 1944	Wounded	Fontaine-Etoupfour	Shrapnel wound face and leg
50	14425343	TPR	BUNCH	N.	A			10 July 1944	Taken prisoner	Fontaine-Etoupfour	
51	7934584	TPR.	CARTER	William Mark	HQ			10 July 1944	Wounded	Maltot	Shrapnel wound right buttock: remains at duty
52	273364	LT	CHAPMAN	Alan H.	C. 11		Troop Leader	10 July 1944	Wounded	Eterville	Grenade wound face and eye
53	7943360	TPR	CLARK	C. (Nobby)	A. 5	DO		10 July 1944	Wounded	Maltot	
54	7955928	TPR	CROUCH	Edward (Ted)	B	GM		10 July 1944	Wounded	Chateau de Fontaine	Mortar wound face and jaw
55	14308386	TPR	CUTLER	Herbert	A. 4	GM		10 July 1944	KIA	Maltot	Confirmed KIA 8 Aug 1944
56	4362386	TPR	DANGERFIELD	Samuel (Sammie)	B. 8	GO		10 July 1944	Wounded	Hill 112-Chateau de Fontaine	Burns face and hands
57	5827267	L/CPL	DARGUE	R.	A. 2	GM		10 July 1944	Wounded	Maltot	Burns to face
58	14401355	L/CPL	DAWKINS	M. (Bill)	A. 4	GM		10 July 1944	Taken prisoner	Maltot	
59	7886713	SGT	DOBINSON	G.	B			10 July 1944	Wounded	Chateau de Fontaine	Shrapnel wound neck: remains at duty

Serial No. of Entry	Army Number	Rank	Surname	Initials, Given Names, Nicknames	Squadron & Troop	Trade	Function	Date of Occurrence	Nature of Occurrence	Place of Occurrence	Details of Wounds and other Comments
60	245379	LT	DOUGLAS	Michael Shepherd (Shep)	A2		Troop Leader	10 July 1944	Wounded	Maltot	Injury to eye
61	249320	LT	DREW	Frank	C. 12		Troop Leader	10 July 1944	Wounded	Maltot	Gunshot wound to face
62	7925871	CPL	EVANS	Robert (Bob)	A	DM		10 July 1944	Wounded	Maltot	Gunshot wound to face
63	7948759	L/CPL	FARRELL	J.	A	DM		10 July 1944	Wounded	Maltot	Shrapnel wound face
64	14269871	L/CPL	FODEN	John Charles (Johnnie)	B. 7		Troop Sergeant's gunner	10 July 1944	KIA	Chateau de Fontaine	
65	7909605	SGT	GALLAGHER	John (Jackie)	B. 7		Troop Sergeant	10 July 1944	Wounded	Chateau de Fontaine	Shrapnel wound back
66	14291460	TPR	GORDON	Raymond (Ray)	A. 2	GO		10 July 1944	Wounded	Maltot	Burns face and hands
67	7878300	SGT	GRAY	A. (Paddy)	A			10 July 1944	Wounded	Maltot	Shrapnel wound
68	307770	2/LT	HENDRIE	George Watt	A. 1		Troop Leader	10 July 1944	KIA	Maltot	Decapitated by AP shot
69	6354488	TPR	HILL	N.	HQ			10 July 1944	Wounded	Fontaine Etoupfour	Shrapnel wound shoulder and leg
70	7925909	TPR	HINSON	Edward (Ted)	A	DM		10 July 1944	Wounded	Maltot	
71	7954383	L/CPL	HOWELLS	Thomas James	C. 11	GO	Tp Sgt's W/op	10 July 1944 / 11 July 1944	Wounded / Died of wounds	Maltot	
72	4868886	TPR	HUTCHINSON	Jack	A. 2	DM		10 July 1944	KIA	Maltot	Confirmed KIA 8 Aug 1944
73	7925876	CPL	JACKSON	Frederick (Fred)	A. 1	GO		10 July 1944	Wounded	Maltot	Serious shrapnel wounds both legs
74	7926055	TPR	KEAY	J.	A	GM		10 July 1944	Wounded	Maltot	Shrapnel wound to forehead from HE
75	69340	CAPT	KIRBY	E. (Ronnie)	A. HQ		Squadron Recce Officer	10 July 1944	Wounded	Maltot	Shrapnel wound to leg
76	14216966	TPR	KNIGHT	Richard Geoffrey (Dick)	A. 2	GO		10 July 1944	KIA	Maltot	
77	14280849	TPR	LARNER	Ronald (Ronnie)	B. 8	DM		10 July 1944	Wounded	Hill 112 - Chateau de Fontaine	Burns to face
78	4868366	TPR	LINDLEY	R.	C. 11			10 July 1944	Wounded	Eterville	Lacerations to scalp
79	14415017	TPR	LIVINGSTONE	John Douglas	A			10 July 1944	KIA	Maltot	
80	14280853	TPR	MACINTOSH	E. (Dave)	A	GM		10 July	Taken prisoner	Maltot	
81	5574799	TPR	MANSELL	Charles	B. 8	GO	Troop Sergeant's gunner. 8 Troop	10 July	Wounded	Hill 112-Chateau de Fontaine	Burns
82	14407925	TPR	MASLEN	Stanley	C. 11	GM	Tp Sgt's gunner	10 July 1944	KIA	Maltot	Confirmed KIA 8 Aug 1944
83	4279282	TRP	MENNIM	Thomas Rippon (Tommy)	A. 3	GM		10 July 1944	KIA	Maltot	Confirmed KIA 8 Aug 1944
84	14219698	TPR	MILLS	Victor Leonard (Vic)	A 5	GO	Tp Corporal's Wireless Op	10 July 1944	KIA	Maltot	
85	7020992	TPR	MORRIS	William Ernest (Bill)	A. 2	GM		10 July 1944	KIA	Maltot	Confirmed KIA 8 Aug 1944
86	7957814	CPL	MOSS	M. (Maxie)	C. 14	GO		10 July 1944	Wounded	Eterville	Shrapnel wound to back
87	14328335	TPR	MUNNS	R. (Bert)	A. 4	GO		10 July 1944	Taken prisoner	Chateau de Fontaine	
88	5782897	SGT	NORMAN	J. (Nobby)	A. 4			10 July 1944	Taken prisoner	Maltot	

Serial No. of Entry	Army Number	Rank	Surname	Initials, Given Names, Nicknames	Squadron & Troop	Trade	Function	Date of Occurrence	Nature of Occurrence	Place of Occurrence	Details of Wounds and other Comments
89	7893731	TPR	NORRIS	L.	A.			10 July 1944	Taken prisoner	Maltot	
90	5575597	TPR	O'BOURN	Percy	B. 8	GM	Troop Cpl's gunner, 8 Troop	10 July 1944	Wounded	Hill 112-Chateau de Fontaine	Burns to face and hands; traumatic amputation of left foot
91	7933999	CPL	OSWIN	R.	A.	GM		10 July 1944	Wounded	Maltot	Left arm severely fractured by shell
92	7927311	TPR	PEARSON	George	A.	GO		10 July 1944	Wounded	Maltot	Shrapnel wound to leg, captured, then liberated by US forces and evacuated to UK
93	14219450	TPR	POWELL	John Henry	B. 7	DO	Tp Sergeant's Wireless Operator	10 July 1944	Wounded	Chateau de Fontaine	Shrapnel wound to back, penetrating wound left thorax
94	3317545	SGT	PURDY	John	C. 11		Troop Sergeant	10 July 1944	KIA	Maltot	Confirmed KIA 8 Aug 1944
95	7901786	SGT	QUINN	Frank	A.			10 July 1944	Wounded and taken prisoner	Maltot	Released from captivity in Paris and evacuated to the UK
96	14310591	TPR	SALISBURY	Norman William	A. 4	GO		10 July 1944	KIA	Maltot	
97	7926066	SGT	SMITH	James David (Jock)	A. 2		Troop Sergeant, 2 Troop	10 July 1944	KIA	Maltot	
98	7951722	L/CPL	SMITHERS	Douglas Arthur (Doug)	A. 2	GO		10 July 1944	KIA	Maltot	
99	7956323	TPR	SNELGROVE	J.	A.	DM		10 July 1944	Taken prisoner	Maltot	
100	14276116	TPR	SPIGHT	Edward (Ted)	A.	GO		10 July 1944	KIA	Maltot	Confirmed KIA 8 Aug 1944
101	5835845	TPR	SUFFOLK	Percy Edward	A. 4	DO		10 July 1944	KIA	Maltot	Confirmed KIA 8 Aug 1944
102	5835436	TPR	TAYLOR	Robert (Bob)	A. 5	GM	Tp Cpl's gunner	10 July 1944	Wounded	Maltot	2nd degree burns to face
103	7958946	L/CPL	TURTON	William	A.	DO		10 July 1944	KIA	Maltot	Confirmed KIA 8 Aug 1944
104	5575459	TPR	WAKEFORD	Clifford Jack (Jack)	B. 8	DM	Troop Corporal's driver, 8 Troop	10 July 1944	KIA	Hill 112-Chateau de Fontaine	Confirmed KIA 8 Aug 1944
105	7934439	CPL	WALKER	T. (Johnnie)	B. 8		Troop Corporal's driver, 8 Troop	10 July 1944	Wounded	Hill 112-Chateau de Fontaine	Burns to face and limbs
106	7955909	TPR	BUTTON	E. (Ken)	HQ	DO		11 July 1944	Wounded	Fontaine Etoupfour	Phosphorous burns
107	5837258	TPR	JONES	E.	B.			15 July 1944	Wounded	Hill 112	Gunshot wound left forearm
108	14553999	TPR	AGAR	Stanley Masters	HQ	DO		16 July 1944	KIA	Hill 112	
109	14324412	TPR	BELL	M	HQ			16 July 1944	Wounded	Hill 112	
110	7916194	CPL	COVE	D.	HQ	DM		16 July 1944	Wounded	Hill 112	Shrapnel wound to face
111	7907538	L/CPL	CUNNINGHAM	J.	HQ	DO		16 July 1944	Wounded	Hill 112	Shrapnel wound to feet
112	14215279	TPR	EDMUNDS	A.	HQ	GM		16 July 1944	Wounded	Hill 112	Head and shoulder injuries
113	33681	LT. COL	EVERARD	Sir Nugent H, Bart	HQ		Commanding Officer	16 July 1944	Wounded	Gourny-Hill 112	Shrapnel wounds ear and back
114	7926004	TPR	SHARPE	A.	HQ			16 July 1944	Wounded	Hill 112	Shrapnel wound left shoulder, remains at duty
115	6028798	TPR	WRIGHT	J.	HQ			16 July 1944	Wounded	Hill 112	Head injuries
116	14403257	L/CPL	BLATT	J.	B			18 July 1944	Wounded	Hill 112	Flesh wound right side
117	3453020	TPR	GARFORTH	A.	B	DO		18 July 1944	Wounded	Hill 112	Flesh wound right shoulder, remains at duty
118	7958072	CPL	PEAKALL	Eric	B. 10	DO		18 July 1944	Wounded	Hill 112	Wound to hand

Serial No. of Entry	Army Number	Rank	Surname	Initials, Given Names, Nicknames	Squadron & Troop	Trade	Function	Date of Occurrence	Nature of Occurrence	Place of Occurrence	Details of Wounds and other Comments
119		SGMN	TUMBRIDGE	Ernest	C			18 July 1944	KIA	Eterville	Shrapnel wound left shoulder
120	14231996	TPR	MASON	R.	C	GM		19 July 1944	Wounded	Hill 112	Shrapnel wounds to head, chest and back
121	7891859	TPR	MORGAN	Victor	HQ			21 July 1944 / 22 July 1944	Wounded / Died of wounds	Hill 112	
122	263479	LT (QM)	PATRICK	R.A.	HQ		Regimental Quartermaster	21 July 1944	Wounded	Cagny	Shrapnel wound to left shoulder: remains at duty
123	7907329	CPL	SOUTHERN	Reginald (Reg)	B	DO		21 July 1944	Wounded	Hill 112	Shrapnel wound
124	7907834	SGT	TITO	Michael (Mick)	B, HQ		Squadron Ldr's Wireless Operator	21 July 1944	Wounded	Hill 112	Right hand blown off, extensive shrapnel wounds to chest and head
125	170589	MAJOR	WARREN	Percy Herbert (Bob)	B		Squadron Leader, B Squadron	21 July 1944	Wounded	Gournay-Hill 112	Shrapnel wounds right hand and side
126	6028870	TPR	WILCOX	H.	B	GO		21 July 1944	Wounded	Hill 112	Shrapnel wound right arm
127	8593953	L/CPL	HUTTON	James (Jim)	A, 1	DM	Troop Leader's driver	22 July 1944	Wounded	Fontaine Etoupfour	Gunshot wounds to right calf and foot from German aircraft. Also perforated left eardrum from blast. Colleville 28 June 1944
128	269609	LT	BEALE	Anthony Peter (Peter)	B, 8		Troop Leader, 8 Troop	26 July 1944	Wounded	Bretteville	Shrapnel wound lower back (S-mine)
129	228181	LT	CARGILL	James (Jimmie)	B			26 July 1944 / 3 Aug 1944	Wounded / Died of wounds	Bretteville	Penetrating shrapnel wound of abdomen and broken left femur (S-mine)
130	7925880	SGT	NICHOLLS	William Risdon (Nicky)	B	VM	Fitter Sergeant	26 July 1944	KIA	Bretteville	S-mine
131	308080	2/LT	SMART	Frederick Richard (Freddie)	B, 6		Troop Leader, 6 Troop	26 July 1944	KIA	Bretteville	Both legs blown off, died in 10 minutes (S-mine)
132	249324	LT	WOLSKEL	Richard Hawthorne (Dickie)	B			26 July 1944	KIA	Bretteville	S-mine
133		TPR	PICKERILL	R.	HQ			2 Aug 1944	Taken prisoner		
134	307737	2/LT	WELLS	Gerald D. (Gerry)	A, 5		Troop Leader	4 Aug 1944	Wounded	Etregy	Gunshot wound to head; remains at duty
135	162122	CAPT	PATERSON	J.	A.			5 Aug 1944	Wounded	Epinay-sur-Odon	Facial wounds (mine)
136	7919239	SGT	SMALE	Clifford Henry	A			5 Aug 1944 / 5 Aug 1944	Wounded / Died of wounds	Epinay-sur-Odon	Right leg amputated, right arm severely wounded (mine)
137	7928618	TPR	STUBBS	G.	HQ			5 Aug 1944	Wounded	Epinay-sur-Odon	Wounds to face and left leg (mine)
138	7925893	SGT	BASHAM	William (Bill)	B	DM	Troop Sergeant	10 Aug 1944	Wounded	La Hogue	Shrapnel wound head and hand: remains at duty
139	6105455	TPR	BOWEN	W.	HQ	DO		10 Aug 1944	Wounded	La Hogue	Shrapnel wound (mortar)
140	7926074	L/CPL	BROWN	L.G.	HQ	DO		10 Aug 1944	Wounded	La Hogue	Shrapnel wound (mortar)
141	7926103	SGT	HOLDING	Frank	A			10 Aug 1944	KIA	La Hogue	Mortar
142	7926145	TPR	HUNN	N.	B	GO		10 Aug 1944	Wounded	La Hogue	Shrapnel wound (mortar)
143	7925947	TPR	PARK	Thomas	A	GO		10 Aug 1944	KIA	La Hogue	Mortar
144	7926066	SGT	PHILLIPS	Thomas Arthur	C			10 Aug 1944	KIA	La Hogue	Mortar
145	14217776	TPR	REYNOLDS	S.	C	GO		10 Aug 1944	Wounded	Chicheboville	Wounded in arm
146	7963140	L/CPL	TELFORD	D.B	HQ	DM		10 Aug 1944	Wounded	La Hogue	Shrapnel wound penetrating chest
147	7881719	SGT	TURNER	William (Bill)	HQ		HQ Fitters	10 Aug 1944	KIA	Cagny	Mortar

Serial No. of Entry	Army Number	Rank	Surname	Initials, Given Names, Nicknames	Squadron & Troop	Trade	Function	Date of Occurrence	Nature of Occurrence	Place of Occurrence	Details of Wounds and other Comments
148	7961354	L/CPL	MILLER	D. (Dusty)	C	GM		12 Aug 1944	Wounded	La Hogue	Gunshot wound left shoulder
149	4621549	TPR	EAMES	Claude Ernest	HQ		Padre's driver	14 Aug 1944	KIA	Quesnay	
150	7963012	TPR	HALL	A.	HQ	GM		14 Aug 1944	Wounded	Quesnay	Head wound from HE shell
151		REV. CAPT	MC MAHON	Patrick	HQ		Padre	14 Aug 1944	KIA	Quesnay	Killed while attempting to rescue Canadian soldiers from knocked-out tank
152	240859	CAPT	BREWER	Geoffrey W.	B		B Squadron Recce Officer	19 Aug 1944	Wounded	Crevecoeur	Bullet wound to stomach
153	14377522	TPR	BARKER	Frederick (Fred)	C	GO		20 Aug 1944	Wounded	St. Laurent du Mont	Shrapnel wound left leg (HE)
154	3449160	TPR	BOLAND	John (Johnny "Tiger")	C	DM		20 Aug 1944	Wounded	St. Laurent du Mont	Shrapnel wound left scapula (mortar)
155	14222620	TPR	BRIDGEMAN	Roger (Taffy)	C	DM		20 Aug 1944	KIA	St. Laurent du Mont	
156	7925993	CPL	GEARY	William (Bill)	C	DO		20 Aug 1944	Wounded	St. Laurent du Mont	Shrapnel wound left forearm (HE)
157	7926088	TPR	LATHAM	Thomas (Tommy)	C	DO		20 Aug 1944	Wounded	St. Laurent du Mont	Shrapnel wound fingers of left hand
158	264485	LT	MOORE	Arthur C. W. (Dinty)	C			20 Aug 1944	Wounded	St. Laurent du Mont	Gunshot wound
159	7922871	TPR	RAEBURN	T.	C	DM		20 Aug 1944	Wounded	St. Laurent du Mont	Chest wounds
160	4420812	TPR	CROUCHER	E.	A	DO		22 Aug 1944	Wounded	Coquanvilliers	Shrapnel wound (mortar) left hand and face
161	249320	CAPT	DREW	Frank	A		Squadron Recce Officer	22 Aug 1944	Wounded	Coquanvilliers	Shrapnel wound to head; loses eye
162	14219581	TPR	FITZGERALD	Dennis	B	DM		22 Aug 1944	Wounded	Coquanvilliers	Shrapnel wound right arm and neck
163	7918134	CPL	FRASER	A.	B	VM		22 Aug 1944	Wounded	Coquanvilliers	Shrapnel would left leg; remains at duty
164	2755424	TPR	GAULD	H	B	GM		22 Aug 1944	Wounded	Coquanvilliers	Shrapnel wound back
165	14221054	TPR	GILMORE	C	GO			22 Aug 1944	Wounded	St. Laurent du Mont	Gunshot wound left hand
166	7932447	CPL	GRAY	L.	B	DM		22 Aug 1944	Wounded	Coquanvilliers	Shrapnel wound right side and head
167	2022212	SGT	JONES	A. (Taffy)	B		Troop Sergeant	22 Aug 1944	Wounded	Coquanvilliers	Shrapnel wound right hand; remains at duty
168	14343805	TPR	LAMB	W.	B	DM		22 Aug 1944	Wounded	Coquanvilliers	Shrapnel wound back and left arm
169	4868366	TPR	LINDLEY	A.	B			22 Aug 1944	Wounded	Coquanvilliers	Shrapnel wound (mortar) left side of head
170	228898	CAPT	LONG	Roger Ernest	B		2 i/c Squadron	22 Aug 1944	Wounded	Ouilly-Le-Vicomte	Shrapnel wound right let, remains at duty 8 days
171	14408178	TPR	POLLINGTON	E.	B	GO		22 Aug 1944	Wounded	Coquanvilliers	Shrapnel wound (HE) head, shoulder and chest
172	7952958	TPR	RAWE	George	B	GO		22 Aug 1944	Wounded	Coquanvilliers	Shrapnel wound right foot
173	7911873	SGT	SHUTTLEWORTH	H	B	VM		22 Aug 1944	Wounded	Coquanvilliers	Shrapnel would left side
174	14416289	TPR	WATERTON	A.	B			22 Aug 1944	Wounded	Coquanvilliers	Shrapnel wound right foot and resticles
175	7933479	CPL	WATSON	Albert (Bert)	B	DO		22 Aug 1944	Wounded	Coquanvilliers	Shrapnel wound back and left thigh
176	7926161	TPR	WOODFINE	Wilfred	B	DO		22 Aug 1944	KIA	Coquanvilliers	HE Shell
177	7958886	TPR	BUTTON	Kenneth James (Ken)	C. 14	GO		25 Aug 1944 / 25 Aug 1944	Wounded / Died of wounds	Epaignes	Shrapnel wound back

Serial No. of Entry	Army Number	Rank	Surname	Initials, Given Names, Nicknames	Squadron & Troop	Trade	Function	Date of Occurrence	Nature of Occurrence	Place of Occurrence	Details of Wounds and other Comments
178	14409241	TPR	HAZEL	Sydney	C. 13	GO		10 Sept 1994	Wounded	Le Havre	Blast to eye from Besa blowback; remains at duty
179	7902628	SGT	HEWITT	Victor (Vic)	C			10 Sept 1944	Wounded	Le Havre	Injuries right arm; Besa blowback
180	7955833	TPR	HOWARD	Patrick (Pat)	C. 14		Wireless op. Tp Sgt's tank	11 Sept 1944	Wounded	Le Havre	Compound fracture of four fingers of right hand; 75mm blowback
181	5835965	TPR	HUMPHREY		A	GM		11 Sept 1944	Wounded	Le Havre	Blast to eye; Besa blowback
182	273392	LT	PICKIN	James	A			11 Sept 1944	Wounded	Le Havre	Mortar fragment right eye; remains at duty
183	5835136	TPR	TAYLOR	Robert (Bob)	A, 5	GM		11 Sept 1944	Wounded	Le Havre	Fragment right eye; Besa blowback
184	7957878	TPR	THOMAS	A.	A	DO		11 Sept 1944	Wounded	Le Havre	Injury right elbow; gun recoil
185		LT	WINTLE	Leslie Hubert	A		Troop Leader	5 Oct 1944	Accidentally killed	St. Omer	Run over by tank transporter
186	6850051	TPR	ELLIS	E.	HQ	GM		12 Oct 1944	Wounded	St. Oedenrode	Glass & shrapnel wounds to head (Shelled while relaxing in a pub) - War Diary
187	7925933	TPR	FISHER	J. (Snowy)	B	DM		12 Oct 1944	Wounded	St. Oedenrode	Glass & shrapnel wounds to head (Shelled while relaxing in a pub) - War Diary
188	7947226	CPL	MOORE	C.	B	DO		12 Oct 1944	Wounded	St. Oedenrode	Glass & shrapnel wounds to leg (Shelled while relaxing in a pub) - War Diary
189	7961470	TPR	HUDSON	E	A	DM/GO		20 Oct 1944	Wounded	Stapelheide	Blowback from Besa
190	7926029	CPL	MACDONALD	A.	A	GO		20 Oct 1944	Wounded	Stapelheide	Shrapnel wound (HE) head
191	193295	LT	SMYTH	T.J.F. (Terry)	A		Troop Leader	20 Oct 1944	Wounded	Stapelheide	Shrapnel wound (HE) right shoulder
192	7961360	LT.CPL	FERRIER	K.	HQ	DO		20 Oct 1944	Wounded	St. Leonard	Sprained ankle
193	243526	CAPT	HAYDEN	Frank O.	HQ			22 Oct 1944	Wounded	St. Leonard	Cut and bruised face; tank blown up by teller mine
194	7931407	TPR	JAMESON	A.	HQ	DO		22 Oct 1944	Wounded	St. Leonard	Damage to feet and legs
195	7908827	SGT	ROBINSON	W.J. (Butch)	HQ	DO		22 Oct 1944	Wounded	St. Leonard	Cuts left eye and nose. and bruises
196	281944	LT	BODEN	Arthur Peter (Peter)	C. 14			26 Oct 1944	Wounded	Nispen	Head wound from shell; remains at duty
197	7913142	CPL	FICKEN	R.E.	B	DM		26 Oct 1944	Wounded	Nispen	Partial amputation middle finger
198	190564	CAPT	KIDD	Kenneth Aurius (Ken)	A		2 i/c A Squadron	26 Oct 1944	Wounded	Nispen	Head wound, shell
199	7938282	TPR	KIRK	J.W. (Ginger)	C. 13	GM		22 Oct 1944	Wounded	Nispen	Wounded in back, shell
200	247501	CAPT	MORGAN	Alan John	C		Recce Officer, C Squadron	22 Oct 1944	Wounded	Nispen	Wound back of neck; remains at duty
201	3317551	SGT	TOMNEY	Thomas	C. 13		Troop Sergeant	22 Oct 1944	Wounded	Nispen	Severe wounds to head. shell
202	7925951	SGT	VIRGO	Kenneth George (Ken)	B. 10		Troop Sergeant	22 Oct 1944	Wounded	Nispen	Severe wounds head (mortar)
203	14562053	TPR	ABBOTT	R.	A	DO		22 Oct 1944 / 31 Oct 1944	Wounded / Died of wounds	Boenk	Slight burn finger, remains at duty
204	14288232	TPR	BOARD	J.	C. HQ	GM		29 Oct 1944	Wounded	Vinkenbrook	Serious shrapnel wound right shoulder blade and arm (AP)
205	240852	LT	CLARKSON	Ernest Roy	A. 4		Troop Leader	29 Oct 1944	KIA	Boenk	Burns to both hands
206	7951021	TPR	COOLIN	J. (Jack)	A	GM		29 Oct 1944	Wounded	Boenk	Burns to both hands
207	7963403	TPR	COPE	P.	A	DM		29 Oct 1944	Wounded	Boenk	Burns face and hands (serious)

Serial No. of Entry	Army Number	Rank	Surname	Initials, Given Names, Nicknames	Squadron & Troop	Trade	Function	Date of Occurrence	Nature of Occurrence	Place of Occurrence	Details of Wounds and other Comments
208	14221917	TPR	COWTON	Alfred Samuel	A. 3	DM		29 Oct 1944	KIA	Boeink	
209	14424459	TPR	DAVIES	A.	A	GO		29 Oct 1944	Wounded	Boeink	Wounds left arm and leg
210	553840	L/CPL	HAMILL	John Redman	A. 3	DM	Troop Sergeant's driver	29 Oct 1944	KIA	Boeink	
211	123895	MAJOR	HOLDEN	Ronald Edwin	C		Squadron Leader, C Squadron	29 Oct 1944	Wounded	Vinkenbroek	Head wound from shrapnel (HE); remains at duty
212	7925936	TPR	HONAN	M.	A	GM		29 Oct 1944	Wounded	Boeink	Burns to face; remains at duty
213	7896866	TPR	HUGHES	Roy Stafford	A. 5	DM		29 Oct 1944	KIA	Boeink	
214	5835965	TPR	HUMPHREYS	A.	A	GM		29 Oct 1944	Wounded	Boeink	Slight cut to face; remains at duty
215	14369506	TPR	LAWSON	Stanley	A. 3	GM	Troop Sergeant's gunner	29 Oct 1944	KIA	Boeink	
216	7961299	TPR	MACDONALD	A.	C. HQ	DM		29 Oct 1944	Wounded	Vinkenbroek	Shrapnel wounds (serious) arm, right shoulder and right chest
217	7938986	CLP	MCCONNELL	B.	A	GO		29 Oct 1944	Wounded	Boeink	Compound fracture right leg, burns to hands (serious)
218	6028276	TPR	MEAD	A.J (Titch)	C. 15	DM	Troop Leader's driver	29 Oct 1944	Wounded	Vinkenbroek	Compound fracture left femur (serious)
219	7962516	TPR	MOULSON	J.	A	DO		29 Oct 1944	Wounded	Boeink	Shrapnel wound right leg and arm; burns to face (serious)
220	4620939	TPR	ORAM	E.	A.	GM		29 Oct 1944	Wounded	Boeink	Cuts to left hand
221	14301169	L/CPL	POWELL	W.	A	GM		29 Oct 1944	Wounded	Boeink	Shrapnel wound to left arm (AP)
222	7908782	TPR	SMITH	John (Smudger)	C. 15	DM	Troop Leader's co-driver	29 Oct 1944	KIA	Vinkenbroek	
223	7883373	SGT	SNOWDEN	John	A. 3	DM	Troop Sergeant	29 Oct 1944	KIA	Boeink	
224	7948815	TPR	TAYLOR	Geoffrey	A. 3	DO	Troop Sergeant's Wireless Operator	29 Oct 1944	KIA	Boeink	
225	318808	SGT	TAYLOR	E.	C. HQ		Sqn Ldr's gunner	29 Oct 1944	Wounded	Vinkenbroek	Wounded in both legs (AP)
226	7926127	CPL	TUCKER	John Vernon	A. 4	DM	Troop leader's driver	29 Oct 1944	KIA	Boeink	
227	14424459	TRP	DAVIES	A.	A	GO		29 Oct 1944	Wounded	Boeink	Burns to hands and face and injury to knee. (Second entry: see 209)
228	7933415	SGT	BOTTOMS	Ernest Lionel	C. 14		Troop Sergeant	27 Nov 1944	KIA	Antwerp	Killed by V2
229	7958192	TPR	BURDEN	B.	HQ		Adjutant's driver	9 Feb 1945	Wounded	Reichswald	Shrapnel wound left knee
230	7952015	TPR	ASHWORTH	W.	C			11 Feb 1945	Wounded	Reichswald	Shrapnel wound right chest
231	6028277	SGT	MEAD	Michael Lawrence (Reg)	C. 11		Troop Sergeant	11 Feb 1945	KIA	Reichswald	
232	4272001	SGT	RITSON	W.	A. 3		Troop Sergeant	11 Feb 1945	Wounded	Reichswald	Gunshot wound abdomen
233	7942563	TPR	HANDS	W.	B. 7			12 Feb 1945	Wounded	Reichswald	Gunshot wound to face with fractured jaw
234	6300251	TPR	GRADDON	Denys	A			12 Feb 1945	Wounded	Reichswald	Shrapnel wound left eye
235	170281	MAJOR	REYNELL	Michael John (Mike)	B. HQ		Squadron Leader, B Squadron	12 Feb 1945 / 12 Feb 1945	Wounded / Died of wounds	Reichswald	Head wounds (mortar)
236	14556250	TPR	SPELMAN	R.	A.			12 Feb 1945	Wounded	Reichswald	Fractured right ankle
237	3907792	TPR	GORDON	G.	C. 13			16 Feb 1945	Wounded	Reichswald	Burns to face and hands

Serial No. of Entry	Army Number	Rank	Surname	Initials, Given Names, Nicknames	Squadron & Troop	Trade	Function	Date of Occurrence	Nature of Occurrence	Place of Occurrence	Details of Wounds and other Comments
238	14409241	TPR	HAZEL	Sydney	C. 13			16 Feb 1945	Wounded	Broedersbosch	Burns to face and hands
239	14308397	TPR	HOPKINS	Norman	C. 13			16 Feb 1945	Wounded	Broedersbosch	Burns to face and hands; crush injury knee to buttocks
240	14241463	TPR	REES	Cyril Anthony	C. 13			16 Feb 1945	Wounded	Broedersbosch	Burns to face and hands
241	240870	LT	LLOYD	Keith B	C. 15		Troop Leader	17 Feb 1945	Wounded	Reichswald	Stellate fracture of left patella
242	269609	LT.	BEALE	Anthony Peter	B. 10		Troop Leader	1 Mar 1945	Wounded	Groote Horst	Shrapnel wound right cheek
243		L/CPL	HUBBARD	George Ellis	A			9 Mar 1945	KIA	Alpen	
244		CPL	DAVIS	John William George	C			4 Nov 1944	Accidental death	Roosendaal	Jumped from window during fire; leg broken but complications led to death

APPENDIX II
Honours and Awards

DISTINGUISHED SERVICE ORDER

Number	Rank	Name	Date of Award and Authority
123895	T/Major	Holden, Ronald Edwin	Suppl. to LG 29/3/45; Appx B 21 GRO 80 (1097) 30/3/45
69755	T/Lt.-Col.	Veale, Peter Norman	C9/6/69 21/4/45 21 AG List 141 14/4/45 Bde A901 (Approved by King)

MILITARY CROSS

Number	Rank	Name	Date of Award and Authority
123895	T/Major	Holden, Ronald Edwin	Appx B 21 GRO 60 10 Nov 1944; date of award 19 Oct 1944
190465	T/Capt.	Kidd, Kenneth Aurius	Appx B 21 GRO 60 10 Nov 1944; date of award 19 Oct 1944
276084	Lt.	Critchley, Frederick Aloysius	Appx B to 21 GRO 81 (1117)
295841	Lt.	Fawcett, Thomas Cyril	Appx B to 21 GRO 81 (1117)
311938	Lt.	Waters, William John	21 AG List 141 dated 14.4.45 (9/9/69 dated 21 Apr 1945). Bde A901 (approved by King)
264938	Lt.	Stone, John Alan Castleman	In final list of Periodical Awards published after 14 November 1945

MILITARY MEDAL

Number	Rank	Name	Date of Award and Authority
7925957	A P/Sgt.	Virgo, Kenneth George	Date of award 19 Oct 1944 21 GRO 60 dated 10 Oct 1944
3317551	W/Sgt.	Tomney, Thomas	LG Supplement dated 1 Mar 1945; Appx B to 21 GRO 81 (1117) dated 6 Apr 1945
14241463	Tpr	Rees, Cyril Anthony	LG Supplement dated 1 Mar 1945; Appx B to 21 GRO 81 (1117) dated 6 Apr 1945
14413698	Tpr	Lowe, John Christopher Cecil	LG Supplement dated 1 Mar 1945; Appx B to 21 GRO 81 (1117) dated 6 Apr 1945
7917835	W/Sgt.	Atkinson, Thomas	

Number	*Rank*	*Name*	*Date of Award and Authority*
7932461	W/Sgt.	Stalley, James William	In final list of periodical awards published after 14 Nov 1945
7940511	W/Sgt.	Brook, Henry	In final list of periodical awards published after 14 Nov 1945
7955829	APL/Cpl.	Towlson, Albert John	LG Supplement dated 24 May 1945; 21 AG List 141 dated 14 Apr 1945 C9/9/69 dated 21 Apr 1945 Bde A901

MENTIONED IN DESPATCHES

170589	T/Major	Warren, Percy Herbert	Supplement to LG dated 20 Mar 1945
52518	T/Major	Ballantine, James Douglas	Supplement to LG dated 20 Mar 1945
7926006	W/Sgt.	Smith, James David	Supplement to LG dated 20 Mar 1945
218709	Revd Capt.	McMahon, Patrick J.	Supplement to LG dated 20 Mar 1945
7934589	Tpr	Carter, W.	Supplement to LG dated 20 Mar 1945
7578978	W/Sgt.	Lyall, Anthony	Supplement to LG dated 20 Mar 1945
262393	Lt.	Wintle, Leslie Herbert	Supplement to LG dated 20 Mar 1945
7926109	L/Cpl.	Stubbs, Samuel	Supplement to LG dated 20 Mar 1945
14280840	Tpr	Horner, Frederick	Supplement to LG dated 20 Mar 1945
7925922	L/Cpl.	Aldcroft, James	Supplement to LG dated 20 Mar 1945
7895962	W/Sgt.	Arlett, Robert	Supplement to LG dated 20 Mar 1945
7907151	W/Sgt.	Rathke, George	Supplement to LG dated 20 Mar 1945
228898	T/Capt.	Long, Roger Ernest	Supplement to LG dated 20 Mar 1945
7957814	AP/Cpl.	Moss, Max	
7926074	L/Cpl.	Brown, L.	
307737	2nd Lt.	Wells, Gerald D.	
7925972	W/Cpl.	Minton, William H.	
7901689	W/Sgt.	Hall, Richard S.	
166685	Capt.	Link, F. Sidney	
256504	Lt.	Francis, Seymour W.	LG Supplement dated 10 May 1945
7961140	Tpr	Patchett, R.C.	Supplement 37072 dated 10 May 1945 to LG dated 8 May 1945
7925987	AP/Sgt.	Berry, Frederick	Supplement 37072 dated 10 May 1945 to LG dated 8 May 1945
170281	T/Major	Reynell, Michael John	
16214	T/Major	Mockford, Herbert G.	
249290	T/Capt.	Lister, Thomas C.	
228898	T/Capt.	Long, Roger Ernest	
256504	AP/Capt.	Francis, Seymour W.	
78833645	W/Sgt.	Findlay, Ernest Gordon	
7932461	W/Sgt.	Stalley, James William	
3781272	W/Cpl.	McLeish, N.	
7942563	Tpr	Hands, W.E.	

222648	T/Major	Hodges, A.E.W.
63641	T/Major	Massy, H. Peter
7932456	W/Sgt.	Dyson, Arthur
7909610	L/Cpl.	Ray, George
228895	T/Capt.	Brecknell, John G.

COMMANDER-IN-CHIEF'S CERTIFICATE

Gallantry

793145	AP/L/Sgt.	Bottoms, Ernest Lionel	Appx B to 21 AG GRO No. 67 (875) dated 29 Dec 1944
14236715	Tpr	Vardy, Arthur	Appx B to 21 AG GRO No. 67 (875) dated 29 Dec 1944
14403869	Tpr	Pearson, B.	Appx B to 21 AG GRO No. 67 (875) dated 29 Dec 1944
14308397	Tpr	Hopkins, Norman	Appx B to 21 AG GRO No. 67 (875) dated 29 Dec 1944
281944	Lt.	Boden, Arthur Peter	Appx B to 21 AG GRO No. 89 (1280) 1 June 1945
7938282	Tpr	Kirk, J.W.	

Good Service

7876990	WOII (QMS)	Williams, J.	Appx B 21 AG GRO 76/45
7592696	WOII (QMS)	Wilding, Granville Richard	Appx B 21 AG GRO 93/45 (1356)
456011	WOII (RQMS)	Armstrong, R.A.	Appx B 21 AG GRO 78/45 (1059)
7910706	Cpl.	Leatham, Ernest	Appx B 21 AG GRO 85/45 (1194)
7908206	SSM	David, Douglas	Appx B 21 AG GRO 85/45 (1194)
162639	Capt.	Brook, R.C.	
14311768	Sgmn	Searle, G.N.P.	
7926064	AP/L/Cpl.	Nunn, H.	Appx B 21 AG GRO 93/45 (1356)
4612264	AP/Cpl.	Reynolds, W.	
7885969	SSM	Joyce, Oswald D.	
7995342	SSM	Edwards, P.T.	
7926000	AP/L/Cpl.	Moulding, E.J.	
405413	SQMS	Lewis, James H.	
7947791	Tpr	Gresham, R.L.	
7906818	W/Sgt.	Maston, Victor B.	

CROIX DE GUERRE

| 281944 | Lt. | Boden, Arthur Peter | Silver Star | Appx B 21 AG1282/#/MS dated 9 Apr 1945; Appx B21 AG RO 1176 dated 27 Apr 1945 |

14280840   Tpr   Horner, Frederick D.   Bronze Star   Appx B 21 AG1282/#/MS dated 9 Apr
                                                        1945;
                                                        Appx B21 AG RO 1176 dated 27 Apr
                                                        1945

BRITISH EMPIRE MEDAL

3781272   WS/Cpl.   McLeish, N.   (R. Sigs)
4612264   AP/L/Cpl.   Reynolds, W.   (REME)

Abbreviations:

LG	London Gazette
21AG	21st Army Group
AP/	Acting Paid
W/ or WS/	War Substantive
T/	Temporary

CITATIONS FOR DECORATIONS

Decorations awarded to members of 9 RTR are shown earlier in this Appendix. Citations for those decorations are recorded below. In two cases (MC for Major R.E. Holden and MM for Sgt. T. Atkinson) it has not yet been possible to locate the citations. It should also be noted that there are some inconsistencies between the citations and the same events as related by participants or observers.

1.   WS/Major T/Lt.-Col. 69755 Peter Norman VEALE MC
      Recommended for Immediate DSO

      Lt.-Col. VEALE MC commanded his regiment with conspicuous success in support of 53 (W) Division which fought through the Reichswald Forest from end to end, from 8–11 February.
      During four arduous days and four nights of almost continuous fighting which, with extremely difficult going, reduced the effective strength of his regiment from fifty odd to less than twenty battleworthy tanks, this CO never failed to support his infantry under the most trying and exhausting conditions of atrocious weather and morass of mud.
      In particular on night 8/9 February his regiment supported the infantry in a night attack of 6,000 yds through the forest, an unorthodox and extremely difficult and dangerous operation for tanks, which nevertheless was entirely successful.
      Had it not been for his enthusiasm, drive and complete disregard for his personal safety during these four days and nights of almost continuous fighting, the tank support afforded to the infantry, to which they give the most generous praise, could never have been achieved. His judgement and inspiring grip of all ranks down to individual fighting crews in his regiment contributed enormously to the success of a very difficult operation. Throughout the whole period under review this officer has displayed the same qualities of leadership and outstanding personal example and I have no hesitation whatever in strongly advocating the immediate award of the DSO to this very gallant officer.

Recommended by:

Brigadier W.S. Clarke	34 Armoured Brigade	1 Mar. 1945
Maj.-Gen. Ross	53rd Infantry Division	4 Mar. 1945
General H.D.G. Crerar	First Canadian Army	9 April 1945

Authorized by:

| Field Marshal B.L. Montgomery | 21st Army group | 24 May 1945 |

2. WS/Capt. T/Major 123895 Ronald Edwin HOLDEN MC
Recommended for Periodical DSO

This officer has commanded C Squadron during every single action in this theatre of war.

He has shown the very highest qualities of leadership and is cool and sound in all his decisions. Always in the forefront of the battle, he is continually to be found leading his squadron into fire positions.

On numerous occasions he has distinguished himself as a Squadron Commander in battle, only some of which are quoted:

> At Epaignes on 25 August he pressed home his attack with such determination and skill that, in spite of the fact that the village was strongly held, it surrendered without inflicting many casualties on our own infantry.
> At Le Havre on 12 September he and one troop of tanks pressed home their attack with such determination that they broke through the defences and caused much confusion in the rear areas, thus making the enemy surrender quickly.
> At Best, between 9 October and 13 October, he carried out five raids on the enemy positions with great dash and determination, inflicting heavy casualties and capturing many prisoners, without suffering any loss to his own troops.
> At St. Lennards on 20 October his squadron suffered no loss yet it inflicted heavy casualties on the enemy, breached a strong position, and secured the infantry on their objective on schedule.
> At Vinkenbroek on 29 October his tank was knocked out but he continued to control the action on foot until his 2 i/c took over. Later on, despite his wounds, he refused to leave the position. In fact he continued in action until relieved at dusk.

By his courage and leadership his coolness in and out of action, he has made C Squadron into a very fine fighting unit. The officers and men have every confidence in him and would follow him into any action. He has been given difficult and dangerous tasks to carry out and he has never shown anything but eagerness and enthusiasm for the task.

Every Infantry Commander with whom he has worked has commended him after the action.

Major HOLDEN is a very gallant and courageous officer and his fearless and daring leadership commands the respect of the whole regiment.

Recommended by:

| Lt.-Col. P.N. Veale | 9 RTR | 8 Nov. 1944 |
| Brigadier W.S. Clarke | 34 Tank Brigade | 9 Nov. 1944 |

Authorized by:

| Lt. Gen. H.D.G. Crerar | First Canadian Army | 27 Nov. 1944 |

3.   T/Capt. 190465 Kenneth Aurius KIDD
    Recommended for Immediate MC

The action took place on the evening of 29 June 1944 at the sector between Mondrainville and Grainville.

    C Squadron was ordered by the Comd 46 Bde to counter an attack by enemy infantry and tanks in the area of x rds north-east of Le Valtru.

    Capt. Kidd in his capacity as Sqn. RO immediately went forward to this area, contacting the infantry FDLs in his scout car; he gained information which was passed back and then went further forward in an endeavour to locate the enemy.

    Locating enemy position, he ran back, climbing on to his squadron leader's tank to pass the information verbally, which enabled the squadron to be deployed to positions which could dominate the enemy advance, and countering the attack which failed in consequence.

    During the whole action, which lasted some two hours, Capt. Kidd displayed time and time again determination of purpose to carry out his duty with a complete disregard for his personal safety and gaining the admiration of the whole squadron and inspiring them to greater effort.

    During this time one Panther was knocked out. Capt. Kidd dismounted and ran forward to capture the crew who baled out fully armed. He did this act single-handed, armed only with his pistol.

    On arrival back with the squadron, as the enemy approached, Capt. Kidd reported verbally information to the squadron commander, and then worked forward alone and on foot at great personal danger, as by now the area of the tanks was being very heavily mortared and machine-gunned by the enemy, quite apart from a number of snipers endeavouring to pick off the tank comds, encouraging the infantry to hang on and have confidence in their tanks' support.

    In my opinion it was the skill and daring of Capt. Kidd which influenced the battle in our favour by bringing invaluable information (which included the location of Panther tanks) thereby providing the squadron commander with an up to the moment picture of the situation.

Recommended by:

Lt.-Col. N.H. Everard	9 RTR	
Brigadier G.S. Knight	31 Tank Brigade	9 July 1944
Lt.-Gen. R. O'Connor	VIII Corps	3 Aug. 1944

Authorized by:

Field Marshal B.L. Montgomery	21st Army group	11 Aug. 1944

4.   W/Lt. 276084 Frederick Aloysius CRITCHLEY
    Recommended for Immediate MC

On 26 October 1944, during an attack on Nispen, Lieut. CRITCHLEY's troop, together with a platoon of infantry, was detailed as cut-off force to capture and hold the road bridge north of Nispen.

    The tanks came under heavy SP fire and all tanks were hit, while at the same time infantry sustained casualties due to mortar and machine-gun fire.

    Lt. CRITCHLEY continued to manoeuvre his troop by hand signals owing to damaged wireless, and with daring leadership knocked out an SP gun and an 75 mm anti-tank gun.

The force was now not strong enough to continue so he manoeuvred his tank to engage enemy machine-guns, silencing two, while the other two tanks shielded infantry. He then loaded wounded infantry on to these two tanks and covered their withdrawal with his own tank.

Lt. CRITCHLEY remained in that position for the next two hours, without support or communication, until relieved by another squadron.

This officer, in his first action, displayed the highest qualities of leadership and courage and was an inspiration to all those who took part in the action.

Recommended by:

Lt.-Col. P.N. Veale	9 RTR	2 Nov. 1944
Brigadier W.S. Clarke	34 Armoured Brigade	4 Nov. 1944
Maj.-Gen. E. Barker	49th Infantry Division	7 Nov. 1944
General H.D.G. Crerar	First Canadian Army	5 Dec. 1944

Authorized by:

Field Marshal B.L. Montgomery	21st Army group	1 Mar. 1945

5. W/Lt. 295841 Thomas Cyril FAWCETT
    Recommended for Immediate MC

On 29 October 1944 at Boeink Lt. FAWCETT was in command of a troop of Churchill tanks supporting a company of infantry. His troop came under heavy fire from enemy SP and 75 mm guns and all tanks were hit. The troop pushed on until the infantry took cover to avoid heavy mortar and small arms fire. His tank again sustained a serious direct hit but he continued amid a hail of shell fire to seek and destroy two enemy machine-guns, thus dominating the position and enabling the infantry to continue their advance. He then engaged and destroyed an anti-tank gun. His crew was then put out of action and he saw his crew to safety. The other two tanks of his troop were also knocked out so he went to them on foot, under heavy fire, evacuated the wounded to shelter and dressed their wounds. He then reported back to his squadron leader, gave an accurate account of the situation on the objective and the location of two SP guns.

Due to this officer's courage and determination the infantry gained their objective with only two casualties, and furthermore, regardless of his personal safety, he persisted in recovering and tending to the survivors of his troop.

Lt. FAWCETT displayed the highest qualities of leadership, and his gallantry is an inspiration to the regiment.

Recommended by:

Lt.-Col. P.N. Veale	9 RTR	2 Nov. 1944
Brigadier W.S. Clarke	34 Armoured Brigade	4 Nov. 1944
Maj.-Gen. E. Barker	49th Infantry Division	7 Nov. 1944
General H.D.G. Crerar	First Canadian Army	5 Dec. 1944

Authorized by:

Field Marshal B.L. Montgomery	21st Army group	1 Mar.1945

6. W/Lt. 311938 William John WATERS
    Recommended for Immediate MC

On 10 February 1945 Lt. WATERS was in command of a Churchill troop, in support of an infantry company, during the advance through the Reichswald Forest. On approaching the objective our troops were subjected to heavy spandau and bazooka fire. Lt. WATERS' tank was ditched when manoeuvring into position so he immediately baled out in spite of heavy fire and took over his sergeant's tank. He then manoeuvred this tank to drive off the enemy bazooka teams to a safe distance and went on to destroy the enemy machine-guns, thus stabilizing the situation. In spite of heavy artillery and mortar fire he then proceeded to recover his own tank by personally attaching the two ropes and supervising the unditching although his person was in full view of the enemy. The Commanding Officer of the infantry battalion writes of him: 'Over a period of days he commanded his troop so skilfully and with such dash that the company was saved numerous casualties. His aggressiveness, in country both difficult and dangerous for tanks, was such that the men in the company were imbued with the utmost confidence in their supporting tanks from the outset. His determination under the most adverse conditions to maintain himself and his tanks in the forefront of the battle and in support of infantry could not have been greater. He kept going with one tank, and when that eventually broke down, he tried every means to obtain yet another to enable himself to advance with the company. His example was an inspiration to all around him.'

This officer showed great courage, dash and inspiring leadership under intense fire in the face of the enemy. His devotion to duty under the most difficult conditions was beyond praise.

His gallantry was an inspiration to all troops taking part in the action.

Recommended by:

Lt.-Col. P.N. Veale	9 RTR	24 Feb. 1945
Brigadier W.S. Clarke	34 Armoured Brigade	27 Feb. 1945
General H.D.G. Crerar	First Canadian Army	9 April 1945

Authorized by:

Field Marshal B.L. Montgomery	21st Army group	24 May 1945

7.   W/Lt. 264523 John Alan Castleman STONE
         Recommended for Periodical MC

Lt. Stone has commanded a troop in B Squadron in every action in which the squadron has taken part since June 1944.

On 27 June 1944, at Grainville-sur-Odon, Lt. Stone's troop was the right-hand troop of the squadron supporting an attack by the Cameronians. The infantry were held up 500 yds short of the objective and a strong enemy counter-attack supported by tanks developed towards Haut de Bosq. The right flank of this attack was directed against the Cameronians' position. Lt. Stone took his troop forward into the open to entice the enemy from their cover. His tactics were so successful that he was able to destroy a Tiger tank and force the counter-attack to a standstill. The Cameronians then advanced to their objective.

On 12 February 1945, during an attack in the Reichswald Forest, Lt. Stone's troop, consisting of only two tanks, supported by C Coy of the 2nd Mons in an attack. The attack took the enemy by surprise and penetrated their main position. The enemy then put in a series of heavy counter-attacks firing over fifty Panzerfausts at Lt. Stone's two tanks. Despite the fact that his gunner was seriously wounded, Lt. Stone refused to give ground and repelled all attacks for 45 minutes until flank attacks had eased the pressure and the objective consolidated.

This officer thoroughly deserves recognition for his courage, devotion to duty and the consistency with which he has carried out every task entrusted to him.

Recommended by:

Lt.-Col. P.N. Veale	9 RTR	27 June 1945
Brigadier W.S. Clarke	34 Armoured Brigade	9 July 1945
Lt.-Gen. S.C. Kirkham	I Corps District	31 July 1945
Authorized:		9 Nov. 1945

8.   WS/Corporal 7925951 Kenneth George VIRGO
    Recommended for Immediate MM

On Tuesday 27 June 1944, 10 Troop were ordered to make a right flank attack on the village of Grainville-sur-Odon.

After a short while the infantry with whom they were co-operating reported the centre of the village to be held by Panther tanks, and withdrew. The tanks were ordered to advance through a plantation to the church in the centre of the town. When 100 yards away they met with heavy anti-tank fire and the troop sergeant's tank was knocked out, Corporal Virgo, knowing that his tank was jamming in reverse gear whenever he engaged it, advanced with his troop leader.

From very close range, one of his bogey wheels was shot out. The tanks met with heavy anti-tank and machine-gun fire from less than 100 yards range. It was necessary to change positions constantly to secure alternate covering fire positions in the plantation.

On at least two occasions, under intense fire, Corporal Virgo got on to the back of his tank and, with a crowbar, manhandled the gear rods out of reverse. The crowbar was, on one occasion, knocked out of his hand by a bullet, but he picked it up and carried on. There were several snipers in the trees at the time and Corporal Virgo, seeing one firing from close range while on the back of the tank, shot him with his pistol before getting back into the tank to continue firing on the centre of the town.

Later, in the same plantation, he went back to the troop sergeant's tank which was by this time burning fiercely. Again he dismounted, and with ammunition from the burning tank bursting near him, and heavy enemy fire, he fearlessly did his best to protect Sgt. Simmons who was seriously wounded from the burning ammunition and enemy fire. He then mounted his tank again and brought it up to his troop leader and remained there firing less than 100 yards from the church, until ordered to withdraw.

During the whole of the 30 minutes during which Corporal Virgo was in the plantation, he showed great courage, initiative and powers of leadership. This coolness in the face of enemy fire was magnificent.

Recommended by:

Lt.-Col. N.H. Everard	9 RTR	7 July 1944
Brigadier G.S. Knight	31 Tank Brigade	9 July 1944
Lt.-Gen. R. O'Connor	VIII Corps	2 Aug. 1944
Authorized by:		
Field Marshal B.L. Montgomery	21st Army group	24 May 1944

9.   W/Sgt. 3317551 Thomas TOMNEY
       Recommended for Immediate MM

On 26 October 1944, at the attack on Nispen, Sergeant TOMNEY's troop was eastern protection troop. When his troop leader's tank was hit he took control of the remaining two tanks, engaged enemy SP guns, and covered the withdrawal of his troop leader's crew. He continued to hold the enemy SP guns for 45 minutes until further troops could be manoeuvred into position. His action forced the enemy SP guns to withdraw. During this period his tank was hit repeatedly wounding him seriously, but he continued the engagement to its conclusion, and only then lapsed into unconsciousness.

     This NCO fought a very gallant action with superb discipline under very heavy fire.

Recommended by:

Lt.-Col. P.N. Veale	9 RTR	2 Nov. 1944
Brigadier W.S. Clarke	34 Tank Brigade	4 Nov. 1944
Maj.-Gen. E. Barker	49th Infantry Division	7 Nov. 1944
Gen. H.D.G. Crerar	First Canadian Army	5 Dec. 1944
Authorized by:		
Field Marshal B.L. Montgomery	21st Army group	1 Mar. 1945

10.   Trooper 14241463 Cyril Anthony REES
       Recommended for Immediate MM

On 26 October 1944 during the attack on Nispen Trooper REES was driving his troop sergeant's tank. This tank received a direct hit wounding the sergeant, and the crew were evacuated to a village some 400 yards away. Trooper REES suffered shell shock, was treated, and then sallied forth single-handed back to the tank under heavy small arm, mortar, and shell fire to try and recover his tank. The tank had been recovered so he proceeded to recover another tank some 200 yards further on but found it to be undriveable.

     This single-handed, determined and gallant act, under heavy fire, shows a spirit of self-sacrifice to save tanks from further damage.

Recommended by:

Lt.-Col. P.N. Veale	9 RTR	2 Nov. 1944
Brigadier W.S. Clarke	34 Tank Brigade	4 Nov. 1944
Maj.-Gen. E. Barker	49th Infantry Division	7 Nov. 1944
Gen. H.D.G. Crerar	First Canadian Army	5 Dec. 1944
Authorized by:		
Field Marshal B.L. Montgomery	21st Army group	1 Mar. 1945

11.   Trooper 14413698 John Christopher Cecil LOWE
       Recommended for Immediate MM

On 29 October 1944 during the attack on Vinkenbroek Trooper LOWE was gunner in a Churchill tank. During the battle his squadron leader's tank received a direct hit, wounding three of the crew. He jumped out of his own tank, under heavy fire, and assisted in dressing the wounded. He then obtained permission to try and recover the tank. He made two attempts but was driven back by enemy fire. Finally he reached the tank and drove it back amid a hail of fire from SP guns.

Trooper LOWE displayed gallantry in face of heavy enemy fire and by his courage saved the tank from complete destruction.

Recommended by:

Lt.-Col. P.N. Veale	9 RTR	2 Nov. 1944
Brigadier W.S. Clarke	34 Tank Brigade	4 Nov. 1944
Maj.-Gen. E. Barker	49th Infantry Division	7 Nov. 1944
Gen. H.D.G. Crerar	First Canadian Army	5 Dec. 1944

Authorized by:

Field Marshal B.L. Montgomery	21st Army group	1 Mar. 1945

12.   Lance-Corporal 7955829 Albert John TOWLSON
Recommended for Immediate MM

During the battle for the Reichswald Forest a Churchill squadron attacked the Siegfried Line extension through the forest at 2230 hrs on the night of 8/9 February 1945. The night was dark except for artificial moonlight, and unfortunately the troop commander's tank, of which Lance-Corporal TOWLSON was the driver, fell into a large, well-camouflaged dug-out. All efforts failed to extricate the tank from the dug-out with the result that it had to be left and the troop leader mounted another tank.

The advance continued and the crew were left alone in the middle of this part of the forest with no protection apart from their own personal weapons. There were many enemy left round the position including bazooka teams who repeatedly attacked. A spandau team worked their way towards the tank and engaged the crew who replied with bren and sten. Later they came under enemy artillery fire. Despite all this Lance-Corporal TOWLSON rallied the crew together and worked unceasingly throughout the night to free the tank.

By this display of courage and devotion to duty in the face of the enemy, a valuable piece of equipment was saved from destruction, and furthermore was brought back into action at the earliest opportunity when it was badly needed.

Lance-Corporal TOWLSON has earned a reputation with his colleagues who have applauded his example, and inspired them at a time when the hazards of war were at their worst, all with a complete disregard for his own personal safety.

Recommended by:

Lt.-Col. P.N. Veale	9 RTR	24 Feb. 1945
Brigadier W.S. Clarke	34 Tank Brigade	1 Mar. 1945
Gen. H.D.G. Crerar	First Canadian Army	9 April 1945

Authorized by:

Field Marshal B.L. Montgomery	21st Army group	24 May 1945

13.   WS/Sgt. 7932461 James William STALLEY
Recommended for Periodical MM

This NCO has been a troop sergeant throughout the campaign in Europe. He has on four occasions taken over control of his troop in the middle of an action and never failed to command it with skill and determination.

At Maltot on 10 July 1944 his troop officer was killed and troop corporal's tank knocked out. Alone for 25 minutes, Sgt. Stalley provided left-flank protection and when his own tank was hit and immobilized he stayed in position firing the guns. His tank was hit again and set on fire but Sgt. Stalley refused to leave the battlefield, helping to evacuate the wounded and reporting the situation to his squadron leader.

At St. Leonarts on 20 October 1944 he was again left in command of his troop when the troop officer was wounded. He continued in action, knocking out a 75 mm anti-tank gun and causing the surrender of a German strongpoint which was bypassed by the leading troops. This without support of any sort.

On 18 February 1945, at Castel Biljenbeck, Sgt. Stalley again took over control of the troop when the troop officer's tank had to go out of action. On this occasion he remained with his tank in an exposed position completely dominating the enemy position until all his ammunition had run out.

Sgt. Stalley has always displayed great courage and determination. He has always provided a fine example of coolness and fighting spirit worthy of the highest merit. His squadron leader would entrust him with a troop in the most difficult of actions, confident that Sgt. Stalley would command the troop with the same skill as an experienced troop officer.

Recommended by:

Lt.-Col. P.N. Veale	9 RTR	27 June 1945
Brigadier W.S. Clarke	34 Tank Brigade	8 July 1945
Lt.-Gen. S.C. Kirkham	I Corps District	31 July 1945
Authorized:		20 Oct. 1945

14.   W/Cpl. A/Sgt. 7940511 Harold BROOK
Recommended for Periodical MM

On 24 August 1944, during the attack on Epaignes, Sgt. Brook's tank developed a mechanical fault preventing him crossing the start line with his troop.

He quickly corrected the fault and carried out a reconnaissance on foot to determine the whereabouts of his troop. He saw that the enemy were about to launch a flank attack upon his troop position. He ran back to his tank and reported the situation to his troop officer and then moved his tank forward where he could ambush the enemy. As the enemy moved forward across his field of fire he caught them in enfilade, inflicting heavy casualties. The counter-attack failed and the position was easily consolidated.

On 27 October 1944, C Squadron was in support of The Gloucester Regiment in an attack on Nispen. During the consolidation, Sgt. Brook's troop officer's tank was knocked out and the troop sergeant severely wounded. Sgt. Brook took over command and with his own tank and the troop sergeant's tank, now without a commander, held the position against several enemy counter-attacks supported by SP guns.

During the Broedersbosch action on 16 February 1945, Sgt. Brook's troop were actively engaged in clearing the NE corner of the wood. Having swept the wood clear and reached the objective Sgt. Brook's tank was hit and set on fire. He immediately pulled the other members of the crew out of the tank, all of them badly wounded – all this while under constant Spandau fire. Having evacuated his crew to the RAP, Sgt. Brook, who was burned about the face and hands, refused medical attention and returned to his troop position and with a Sten gun beat off enemy infiltration parties who were endeavouring to fire Panzerfausts at the other two tanks of the troop.

This NCO has displayed a determination and coolness in action which has been a fine example to all ranks.

Recommended by:
Lt.-Col. P.N. Veale   9 RTR   27 June 1945
Brigadier W.S. Clarke   34 Tank Brigade   8 July 1945
Lt.-Gen. S.C. Kirkham   I Corps District   31 July 1945
Authorized: 24 Oct. 1945

9 RTR Tank Names

RHQ

CO	2 I/C	I.O	ADJUTANT	OP TANK 1	OP TANK 2
IRON DUKE	IRONSIDE	IRON RATION	IRONCLAD	INVINCIBLE	

A SQUADRON		B SQUADRON		C SQUADRON	
O.C.	INVERNESS	O.C	IROQUOIS	O.C.	INCREDIBLE
2 I/C	INVERGORDON	2 I/C	IMPERATOR	2 I/C	ICH DIEN
R.O.	INVERARY	R.O.		R.O.	
ARV	IRON LUNG	ARV		ARV	
1	IMPUDENT	6	INTACT	11	INCISIVE
1A	IMP	6A		11A	INTENSIVE
1B		6B		11B	IMPASSIVE
2		7		12	IBN EL KELB
2A	ICENI	7A		12A	INFAMOUS
2B		7B		12B	IBN SAUD
3		8	INFERNAL	13	
3A	IRATE	8A	INFERNO	13A	INDEPENDENT
3B	IMPETUOUS	8B	INFIDEL	13B	
4		9	INSPIRE	14	INDOMITABLE
4A	ILLUSIVE	9A	IMMUNE	14A	INDEFATIGABLE
4B	IBEX	9B	IMPULSE	14B	
5	IRAQ	10	INTERCEPT	15	ILFORD
5A	ISMAILIA	10A	IMMORTAL	15A	ILKLEY
5B	INDIA	10B	IMPRINT	15B	IRLAM

Other names identified in histories and photographs, but not as yet attributable to a particular appointment, are:

INDUS: possibly B Squadron
INFIGHTER: 13 Troop
INCISOR
INJECTOR

Glossary

AA	Anti-Aircraft (guns, shells, or tanks)
AFV	Armoured Fighting Vehicle
AP	Armour Piercing shot
AMGOT	Allied Military Government of Occupied Territory
ARV	Armoured Recovery Vehicle
A/T	Anti-Tank gun
AVRE	Armoured Vehicle Royal Engineers (modified Churchill tank)
BESA	7.92 mm machine-gun
BTA	Battalion Technical Adjutant}
BTO	Battalion Technical Officer } alternative names for the same function
CMP	Corps of Military Police
CPL	Corporal
DM	Driver Mechanic
D & M	Driving & Maintenance
DO	Driver operator
DR	Despatch Rider
EME	Electrical & Mechanical Engineers
FDS	Field (or Forward) Dressing Station
FDS	Forward Deliver Squadron (vehicle and crew replacement)
FFI	Free From Infection
FFI	French Forces of Interior (resistance groups), *Forces Françaises de L'Interieur*
FUP	Forming Up Point
GM	Gunner Mechanic
GO	Gunner Operator
HE	High Explosive
HONEY	Small light reconnaissance tank
HQ	Headquarters
I/C	In command (e.g. 2i/c)
LAAGER	Tank harbour, all round defensive position
LAD	Light Aid Detachment (under REME control)
LOB	Left Out of Battle (official rest period)
LCT	Landing Craft Tank
LST	Landing Ship Tank
ME	German Messerschmitt Me109 fighter aircraft
MG	Machine Gun
MINNIES	German Nebelwerfer mortars ('Moaning Minnies')
MITCHELL	American B-25 twin-engine medium bomber
MO	Medical Officer
MT	Motor Transport
NEBELWERFER	German multi-barrelled mortar – also known as 'Moaning Minnies'

PANTHER	German tank with long barrel 75 mm gun
PETARD	25 lb AVRE-mounted mortar to penetrate concrete
PIAT	Projector Infantry Anti-Tank
POW	Prisoner of War
RAC	Royal Armoured Corps
RASC	Royal Army Service Corps
RE	Royal Engineers
REME	Royal Electrical & Mechanical Engineers. Same as EME
RO	Reconnaissance Officer
RSM	Regimental Sergeant Major
RTR	Royal Tank Regiment
SGT	Sergeant
SHELLDRAKE	A concentration of allied artillery fire
SHERMAN	American tank
SP	Self-propelled (but often used to denote a self-propelled anti-tank gun)
SPANDAU	German rapid-fire machine-gun
SQMS	Squadron Quarter Master Sergeant
SQN	Squadron
SSM	Squadron Sergeant Major
STONK	Heavy barrage of mortar or shell fire
TDU	Tank Delivery Unit
TIGER	German tank with 88 mm main armament
TPR	Trooper
TYPHOON	British (Hawker) low level fighter-bomber

Bibliography

Blake, George, *Mountain and Flood: the History of the 52nd (Lowland) Division 1939–1946.* Jackson Son & Co. (Glasgow, 1950)

Blizard, Derek, *The Normandy Landings.* Hamlyn (London, 1993)

Bolland, A.D., *Team Spirit: the Administration of an Infantry Division (53 Welsh) 1944–45.* Gale and Polden (Aldershot, 1948)

Bryant, Arthur, *Triumph in the West.* Collins (London, 1959)

Chappell, Mike, *British Battle Insignia (2) 1939–45.* Osprey (London, 1987)

De Guingand, Francis, *Operation Victory.* Hodder and Stoughton (London, 1947)

D'Este, Carlo, *Decision in Normandy.* E.P. Dutton (New York, 1983)

Ellis, Chris, *Tanks of World War 2.* Octopus Books (London, 1981)

Essame, Hubert, *The 43rd Wessex Division at War 1944–1945.* William Clowes (London, 1952)

Forty, George, *A Pictorial History of the Royal Tank Regiment.* Spellmount (Tunbridge Wells, 1988)

Gilbert, Martin, *Second World War.* Weidenfeld and Nicolson (London, 1989)

Goodsall, Robert H., *The Ancient Road to Canterbury.* Constable (London, 1959)

Greenwood, Richard Trevor (ed. Barry Greenwood), *One Day at a Time: a Diary of the Second World War.* Privately published, 1988

Horrocks, Brian, *A Full Life.* Collins (London, 1960)

—— *Corps Commander.* Magnum Books (London, 1977, 1979)

How, J.J., *Hill 112.* William Kimber (London, 1984)

Liddell Hart, Basil Henry, *The Tanks: the History of the Royal Tank Regiment 1914–1945.* Cassell (London, 1959)

—— *History of the Second World War.* Pan Books (London, 1970, 1973)

Macksey, Kenneth, *Tank Facts and Feats.* Guinness Superlatives (London, 1976)

—— *Tank Versus Tank.* Guild Publishing (London, 1988)

Martin, H.G., *The History of the 15th Scottish Division 1939–1945.* Blackwood (Edinburgh, 1948)

McKee, Alexander, *Caen: Anvil of Victory.* Papermac (London, 1964, 1985)

Montgomery, The Viscount, *Normandy to the Baltic.* Houghton Mifflin (Boston, 1948)

—— *Memoirs.* Collins (London, 1958)

Perrett, Bryan, *The Churchill.* Ian Allan (London, 1974)

—— *The Churchill Tank.* Osprey (London, 1980)

Randel, P.B., *A Short History of 30 Corps in the European Campaign.* Privately published, 1945

Rosignoli, Guido, *Army Badges and Insignia of World War 2.* Blandford Press (Dorset, 1983)

Ryan, Cornelius, *A Bridge Too Far.* Simon and Schuster (New York, 1974)

Shulman, Milton, *Defeat in the West.* Secker and Warburg (London, 1951)

The Tank Museum, *Churchill Tank.* HMSO (London, 1983)

Taylor, George, *Infantry Colonel.* Self Publishing Association (Upton-on-Severn, 1990)

34 Armoured Brigade, *The Story of 34 Armoured Brigade.* Privately published (Germany, 1945)

Vauxhall Motors, *Driver's Handbook for the Churchill Tank* (1944)

Whitaker, W. Denis and Whitaker, Shelagh, *The Battle of the Scheldt*. Souvenir Press (London, 1985)

—— *Rhineland: the Battle to End the War*. Leo Cooper (London, 1989)

White, B.T., *Tanks of World War II*. Peerage Books (London, 1972)

—— *British Tank Markings and Names*. Arms and Armour Press (1978)

Whitehead, William, *Dieppe 1942*. Richard Drew Publishing (Glasgow, 1982)

Williams-Ellis, Clough and Williams-Ellis, A., *The Tank Corps* (1919)

Wilson, Andrew, *Flame Thrower*. William Kimber & Co. Ltd (London, 1956)

Woollcombe, Robert, *Lion Rampant: the 15th Scottish Division, Normandy to the Elbe*. Leo Cooper (London, 1970)

Index

The great majority of the entries in this Index are for names and places. Details of casualties and honours and awards are not included, but can be found in Appendices I and II. Where individual tanks are mentioned in the text or shown in illustrations they are included in this Index; as many tank names as can be remembered are listed and assigned in Appendix III. Where ranks are indicated against names they are for the most part the ranks held at the time of the occurrence or during the campaign generally; many people subsequently achieved higher ranks than those shown in this Index.